THE
ANAHEIM
ANGELS

D0879614

• A COMPLETE HISTORY •

THE

ANAHEIM ANGELS

ROSS NEWHAN

HYPERION

NEW YORK

Designed by Ruth Lee

Library of Congress Cataloging-in-Publication Data

ISBN: 0-7868-8450-9

FIRST EDITION

10 9 8 7 6 5 4 3 2 1

For Connie, Sara and David,
with all my love

ACKNOWLEDGMENTS

Compiling a 38-year history of the Angels, with all of the highs and lows, the twists and turns, the misfortune and, at times, mismanagement would not have been possible without the help and support of many people.

The work of several reporters helped provide a road map, and I leaned heavily on their excellent coverage. They included Mike Penner, Helene Elliott, Mike DiGiovanna, John Weyler, Bill Shaikin and Elliott Teaford of the *Los Angeles Times*, and Steve Bisheff and Mark Whicker of the *Orange County Register.*

I am indebted to the cooperation of the Angels' public relations department, headed by Tim Mead. His staff of Larry Babcock, Nancy Mazmanian, Eric Kay, Aaron Tom and Lisa Parris never seemed to tire of my frequent calls and questions.

It is impossible to list all of the people who consented to interviews, but I owe special thanks and gratitude to Jackie Autry for her time and hospitality during the difficult period following her husband's death.

I would be remiss not to thank Gretchen Young and Jennifer Morgan, my editors at Hyperion, for their patience and advice, and above all, the members of my family—Connie, Sara and David—for their encouragement, support and inspiration. Not to mention occasional typing skills and computer insights.

CONTENTS

THE

ANAHEIM

ANGELS

1

THE PARADE OF AGONY

The Singing Cowboy died on October 2, 1998. Gene Autry was 91, an entertainment legend, the only performer with five stars on the Hollywood Walk of Fame—one each for recordings, movies, radio, television and live appearances. He had risen from the dust and poverty of Tioga, Texas, to become a piece of Americana, an improbable success in all areas of show business and big business, a white hat hero in a more innocent time and a man with a seemingly Midas touch on the corporate stage.

He owned radio and TV stations, hotels, real estate and music publishing companies. He displayed an extraordinary ability to put the right people in the right places, established his handshake as a code of honor, and became—for several years—one of the 400 richest Americans as tallied by *Forbes* magazine, the only entertainer on that celebrated list in 1990 and a "near miss" in 1995, when his net worth was reported to be $320 million.

Autry, undoubtedly, would have been more than that "near miss" if he hadn't made an estimated $180 million in charitable donations during his career, according to *American Benefactor* magazine, which ranked him 17th among the country's 100 most generous citizens. The Autry Tower at the Eisenhower Medical Center near Palm Springs is one measure of that generosity. The Gene Autry Western Heritage Museum in Griffith Park near downtown

Los Angeles is another, an acclaimed example of his preservationist instinct and love of the West.

In addition, there are dozens of current and former major league baseball players who can speak of Autry's generosity, bestowed with millions of dollars on behalf of the futile attempt to "win one for the Cowboy" during his 36 years as owner of the Los Angeles turned California turned Anaheim Angels of the American League, the one enterprise eluding that Midas touch and the one that Autry, the lifetime fan who was buried with an Angel schedule and league pass in his suit pocket, wanted golden more than any of his 24-karat successes.

"For sure," Autry said late in his ownership, "baseball has been the most exciting and frustrating experience of my life. In the movies, I never lost a fight. In baseball, I hardly ever won one."

He won only three division titles in those 36 years, never reaching the promised land that is the World Series. The tantalizing Angels, so close in so many Septembers, were one strike away from an Autry World Series in 1986 and one last ninth inning hit in 1982, but the only Champion in the Cowboy's corral would be the celebrated horse he had ridden in movies and rodeos.

The frustrations hurt, of course, but what cowboy isn't hardened to adversity?

The resilient Autry, a fan's fan, a man who kept score of every game in his private box, a former sandlot player who loved to sit with his managers on the dugout bench before games and who frequently visited players in the clubhouse before and after games, kept coming back for more, opening his wallet and soul as the frustrations mounted and the people who were charged with running the Angels searched for ways to "win one for the Cowboy"— often at the expense of stability, continuity and judgment.

Committed to the farm system and building from within one year, the Angels would be trading the best products of that farm system the next or out signing free agents and trying to buy that elusive championship—if not in an attempt to get Autry to the World Series, then preoccupied with the marquee and the attendance battle with the popular Dodgers some 35 miles to the north.

Nolan Ryan, Frank Robinson, Reggie Jackson, Rod Carew and Don Sutton all stopped in Anaheim on their way to the Hall of Fame, lighting up the billboard and playing field, but unable to put a ring on Autry's finger. The ever changing philosophy, former club president Richard Brown said, was "eclectic at best. There was a different approach every year. There was seldom any consistency."

Jackie Autry, who became a force in the club's operation after her 1981 marriage to the Cowboy, doesn't dispute that perception. She acknowledged that a sense of urgency developed within the organization, but that it didn't come from her husband.

"To my knowledge," she said, "Gene never once said, 'Look, guys, I'm not going to be around much longer, we've got to get it done this year.' Gene wanted to win for the fans and the people who worked for him in the organization, but as he aged and his health began to fail, there were times I got a sense of urgency and even panic from our baseball people that if we don't do it this year, he may not be around next year, and that wasn't beneficial to the organization. We started skewing in wrong directions. We simply mortgaged the future at times. We probably could staff two major league teams with the kids we lost from our farm system."

Mismanagement at times compounded a numbing history of misfortune—a star-crossed siege that left Richard Brown wondering at one point if Anaheim Stadium, as it was then named, hadn't been built on the site of an Indian burial ground.

Buzzie Bavasi, who had reached the World Series eight times as general manager of the Dodgers and who served as Autry's general manager from late 1977 to late 1984, was so frustrated by the disheartening and, at times, bizarre pattern of injury, illness and even death that he considered having a priest perform an exorcism at Anaheim Stadium before the 1982 playoff with the Milwaukee Brewers. He decided against it when his wife convinced him that he would be portrayed as a fool by the media and public.

Gary Gaetti, an All-Star third baseman with the Minnesota Twins who signed a four-year, $11.4 million contract with the Angels as a free agent in 1991, encountered such a prolonged slump in two years with the team that he often wondered aloud if the stadium was haunted by witches. The Angels traded him to Kansas City in 1993, and he promptly shook off the demons and regained his batting stroke.

Los Angeles Times columnist John Hall labeled it a "parade of agony," but it wasn't just Anaheim that bedeviled the Angels. The litany has spanned their existence. Call it the Curse of the Angels:

- 1961: Johnny James, a promising pitcher acquired from the New York Yankees earlier in that first season, broke a bone in his right arm while throwing a curve ball and never pitched again.
- 1962: Outfielder Ken Hunt, who hit 25 home runs the year before, flexed a bat behind his back while in the on-deck circle waiting to hit, broke his collarbone and never played a full season again.
- 1962: With the second-year Angels making an improbable pennant run, top relief pitcher Art Fowler was lost for the final six weeks and was never the same pitcher after losing the sight in his left eye when hit by a line drive during batting practice.
- 1964: Ken McBride, ace of the early pitching staffs and a winner of 10 straight games at one point, suffered neck and back injuries in a car accident and won only four more games in his career.
- 1964: Autry gave University of Wisconsin outfielder Rick Reichardt a then record $200,000 signing bonus and Southern California high school catcher Tom Egan a $100,000 bonus only to have both encounter misfortune. A blood disorder forced Reichardt to have a kidney removed, and he never displayed the power and aggressiveness that had attracted the Angels. Egan became the No. 1 catcher but was beaned by Detroit's Earl Wilson in 1969 and lost partial sight in his left eye.
- 1965: Rookie pitcher Dick Wantz, having earned an unexpected spot on the Angel staff with a strong spring, died four months later of a brain tumor at 25.
- 1968: First baseman Don Mincher, 25 homers the year before, was beaned by Cleveland's Sudden Sam McDowell and never regained a groove. Third baseman Paul Schaal suffered a broken jaw when beaned by Boston's Jose Santiago later that year, was soon traded and never fulfilled his earlier promise.

- 1968: Minnie Rojas, a brilliant and tireless relief pitcher for three straight seasons, was permanently paralyzed in an off-season car accident in which his wife and two of three children were killed.
- 1972: Utility infielder Chico Ruiz, 33, was killed in an off-season car accident.
- 1973: Infielder-outfielder Bobby Valentine, a charismatic and talented young player who now manages the New York Mets, broke a leg so severely when his spikes caught in the outfield fence that he never played on a regular basis again.
- 1974: Rookie Bruce Heinbechner, 23, expected to be the left-handed relief specialist, was killed in a spring car accident.
- 1977: Shortstop Mike Miley, 23, expected to be a rookie of the year candidate, was killed in a pre-season car accident.
- 1977: Outfielder Joe Rudi and second baseman Bobby Grich, two veteran players for whom Autry paid $2 million and $1.5 million in the first winter of free agency, were lost for the majority of the season—Rudi with a broken hand and Grich with a herniated disc suffered when lifting an air-conditioning unit.
- 1978: Outfielder Lyman Bostock, a $2.2 million free agent, was shot and killed while riding in a car with family and friends in Gary, Indiana.
- 1979: Pitcher Jim Barr broke his hand in an altercation during a party in which the Angels were celebrating their division title and was unavailable for the playoffs.
- 1980: Pitcher Bruce Kison, a $2.4 million free agent, won only three games before requiring wrist and elbow surgery.
- 1981: Center fielder Fred Lynn, a former winner of the Most Valuable Player Award who was acquired from Boston in a major off-season trade and signed to a four-year, $5.3 million contract, injured his left knee, hit only .219 and had season-ending surgery. Pitcher Bill Travers, given a five-year contract as a free agent, pitched only 9⅔ innings after developing shoulder tendinitis in the spring.
- 1982: Shortstop Rick Burleson, acquired in 1981 in another major trade with Boston, tore his rotator cuff in spring training—virtually ending his career.

- 1986: First baseman Wally Joyner, after a sensational rookie year, developed a staph infection in his leg and was unable to play the final two games of the league championship series with Boston, both of which the Angels lost.

- 1989: Former Angel Donnie Moore, who threw the celebrated pitch that Dave Henderson hit for a ninth-inning homer in the fifth game of the 1986 playoff with Boston, turning that series around when the Angels were one strike from winning it, shot and seriously injured his wife, then fatally shot himself.

- 1992: Third baseman Kelly Gruber, obtained as damaged goods in a December trade with Toronto, never played a game with the Angels after reporting with a neck injury—only one of the setbacks during a year in which coach Deron Johnson died of lung cancer, pitcher Matt Keough required emergency surgery after being hit in the head by a line drive during a spring training game, and manager Buck Rodgers suffered serious injuries when the team bus went off the New Jersey Turnpike, an incident that seemed to take the heart out of the season.

- 1995: All-Star shortstop Gary DiSarcina broke his thumb on August 3, did not return until late September, and the Angels blew an 11-game lead, ultimately losing a one-game playoff with Seattle for the division title.

- 1997: Chuck Finley, the staff ace, opened the season on the disabled list after suffering a broken orbital bone when hit in the face by an errantly flung bat during spring training and went on the disabled list again in August after he slipped and injured his left wrist while backing up the plate—the two unlikely injuries depriving the Angels of their No. 1 pitcher during a year in which they finished only six games behind Seattle in the division race, a year in which they also suffered the crippling loss of their catalytic leadoff man, Tony Phillips, when he was arrested on a cocaine charge in August.

- 1998: Pitcher Ken Hill, obtained from Texas in midseason of 1997 and signed to a three-year, $16.5 million contract prior to the 1998 season, had elbow surgery on June 15 and returned only a 9–6 record in the first year of the investment, a year in which the Angels used the disabled list 23 times.

- 1999: Perhaps the most frustrating siege yet, given the expectations that followed the off-season signing of former Boston Red Sox slugger Mo Vaughn to a six-year, $80 million contract as a free agent, the biggest contract in club history.

    First, shortstop DiSarcina, who represents much of the team's heart and soul, was lost for half the year when he broke a forearm bone in a freak spring training accident that occurred when he left the batting cage and walked smack into a bat being swung by coach George Hendrick. Then Vaughn, in the first inning of his first regular season game with the Angels, toppled down the dugout steps in pursuit of a foul pop-up, sprained an ankle, missed two weeks, and was never 100%. Then, even before the return of Vaughn, center fielder Jim Edmonds, a Gold Glove outfielder and one of the American League's most productive power hitters, was found to have a tear behind his right shoulder and was lost for a minimum of four months because of surgery. With all of that, right fielder Tim Salmon, off to the strongest start of his career, strained ligaments in his left wrist attempting a diving catch in early May and did not return until July.

DiSarcina. Vaughn. Edmonds. Salmon. Virtually half of a lineup expected to be among baseball's best. The optimistic season deteriorated into bickering among players and the eventual resignation of the manager and general manager. Is it any wonder that a former Angel shortstop, Leo Cardenas, convinced that he had encountered evil spirits in Anaheim, considered piling his slump-ridden bats in the back of his car and driving through a cemetery in an attempt to exorcise that evil?

"I tell you, it's been like a black cloud hanging over that franchise," said Richard Brown, shaking his head.

How often had Autry searched for the rainbow? The oft-frustrated Cowboy had thrown money and effort at the numbing pattern of misfortune, but his Midas touch, the ability to have the right people in the right place at the right time, often eluded him when it came to the business he loved most. Some of the most successful managers and general managers in baseball were unable to get it done for the Cowboy—often leading to managerial and front office changes that defied logic.

Prior to 1996, when the Walt Disney Company took control of the organization in a purchase agreement with the Autrys, the Angels had 15 managers (counting Gene Mauch twice but not counting interim managers), eight general managers and four presidents in 36 years.

Sometimes the changes came faster than Autry's cinematic draws:

- They had six managers in a seven-year span in the 70s, including one who moved almost directly from college coaching and four others who had also never managed in the majors.
- They brought back two of the original players and two Autry favorites, Jim Fregosi and Buck Rodgers, as managers and both went out firing when fired, critical of the club's leadership and direction.
- They won two division titles during Mauch's two managerial stints in the 80s, but each ended in his resignation.
- They had two general managers—Whitey Herzog and Dan O'Brien— at the same time in the 90s, "an experiment in hell," said a reflective Richard Brown, who had been the club president at the time.
- They hired three of baseball's most esteemed executives in the mid-70s—first Harry Dalton, then Red Patterson, then Buzzie Bavasi— with each move undercutting the previous and creating a dog fight over areas of responsibility and control.
- They brought in a young executive named Mike Port as assistant to Bavasi in 1977 and changed his job title so often in a 13-year ascension up the ladder that he never knew what he would find stenciled on his office door. This much he did know: At one point he was promoted from general manager to a breath-defying "executive vice president, general manager and chief operating officer" only to be demoted back to general manager.
- They also talked a reluctant Marcel Lachemann, the respected pitching coach, into becoming manager in 1994 only to have Lachemann resign in 1996 because he hated managing.

All of this transpired a long way from the Bronx, where the New York Yankees thrived despite an often chaotic enviroment, but there were times when the Autrys seemed to be custodians of their own zoo. Autry himself held the title of club president for 13 years, coinciding with the arrival of Bavasi and Port in 1977, but he never occupied a stadium office. He and his wife were frequently on the phone to their chief executives and had the final say on major expenditures and player moves, but they basically entrusted daily decisions to the people they had hired.

"Absentee ownership is not a good idea," Jackie Autry said as she relaxed at her exquisite Palm Springs home several months after her husband's death. "But Gene's philosophy, and it had worked so well in the other businesses, was hire the best people and stay out of their way unless there was a problem. He laid out certain parameters. . . . 'Don't ever lie to me, surprise me or embarrass me. Do a good job and I'll take care of you.'

"He could not have dealt with other aspects of his life if he had been at the stadium all the time. Only one other club owner [Peter O'Malley of the Dodgers] did that anyway, and baseball was Peter's only business. Would the franchise have been more successful [if he had been on site every day]? I'm not sure. If Gene hired a general manager and told him, 'I'm relying on you to do certain things in coordination with your people,' Gene had to believe that's what they were going to do. Whether the media or anyone else believed it was immaterial. Gene believed he was hiring good people."

Ultimately, the years took a toll. On his health. On his wealth. The industry changed, and the people in it. Autry had been awarded the American League's expansion franchise in Los Angeles in 1961. He paid $2.1 million and got 28 players. By the early 1990s, when the Autrys began to seriously contemplate selling the team, Autry was paying individual players $2.1 million and more.

The club payroll was more than $20 million, and operating losses, Jackie Autry said in reflection, had forced the owners to borrow heavily. They were $40 million in debt to Wells Fargo Bank, she said, and at one point thought that the Angels might have to declare bankruptcy—a traumatic step that Major League Baseball would probably not have allowed, using money from the industry's central fund to bail out the club, as the Detroit Tigers, at about the same time, had been similarly bailed out, Autry said.

Escalating salaries and payrolls had created a volatile shift in baseball ownership. The cost had become prohibitive for longtime family operations such as the Carpenters in Philadelphia and the Griffiths in Minnesota. The Autrys and O'Malleys were last of a breed. Corporate ownership took root, the potential baseball losses only a blip on the ledger of a Time-Warner in Atlanta, a Disney now in Anaheim, a Rupert Murdoch's News Corporation now in Los Angeles.

Having become, in Jackie Autry's words, disillusioned about the future of the game, weary of the long and disconsolate drives back to their Studio City home after losses in Anaheim and forced to sell several properties to control and reduce the Wells Fargo debt (basically "disenfranchised" by the industry's economics), she and her husband ultimately pursued a solution that would allow the increasingly frail Cowboy to retain ownership without the decision-making aggravation or economic responsibility.

Several groups responded, but it ultimately came down to a choice between a group headed by former baseball commissioner Peter Ueberroth, a member of the Angels' board of directors, and the Walt Disney Company, which already had deep roots in Orange County and a long association with Gene Autry.

Autry and the late Walt Disney had long been neighbors in the San Fernando Valley and members at Lakeside Country Club, where they often shared lunch and Disney's visionary view of burgeoning Orange County. Disney had already built his Magic Kingdom in little-known Anaheim, a city then of 150,000, and he encouraged Autry to move his relatively new team there when the Cowboy was looking to get out from under the Dodgers' yoke as a tenant at Dodger Stadium in the mid-60s. Autry heeded the advice. He moved the Angels into the new Anaheim Stadium in 1966, the same year Disney died of lung cancer, foreclosing the possibility that he would join Autry as a minority owner and member of the club's board of directors.

Almost 30 years later, the purchase of the Angels seemed to be a natural. Disney was building a new theme park as a complement to an expanding Disneyland in Anaheim and had become owner of the Mighty Ducks of the National Hockey League, a 1993 expansion team operating out of the new Arrowhead Pond of Anaheim, within a ground-rule double of the outfield fences at Anaheim Stadium.

In a complex transaction that was on, off and on again, and hinged on the city agreeing to provide economic help to Disney in the renovation of the stadium, the entertainment giant agreed on May 18, 1995, to buy 25 percent of the Angels for $30 million. The 25 percent was an arbitrary figure that did not reflect the total sales price of $130 million. The Ueberroth group matched that figure but would not agree to pick up $10 million of the Autrys' 1996 operating losses, as Disney did, making it a $140 million transaction. Disney, with the $30 million down, would take control of the Angels and be responsible for all management decisions, while the Autrys would remain as limited partners until the Cowboy's death, when Disney would have 180 days to exercise the $100 million option on the remaining 75 percent.

Autry would not get his World Series ring, but amid failing eyesight and deteriorating health, his final two years of ownership were eased by the knowledge that his wife would not be burdened by a debilitating baseball debt and that his franchise would remain in Anaheim under ownership of an entertainment giant with resources to cope with industry inflation. Amid that inflation, however, it took only three years before Disney was weighing the wisdom of its purchase.

2

RUDOLPH TO RIGNEY

Pat Buttram, Gene Autry's comic sidekick on radio and television, liked to say of Autry that "he used to ride off into the sunset and now he owns it." Buttram would also say of the Corporate Cowboy, "He can't sing and he can't act, but he sure can count."

When Buttram wasn't repeating those lines, a laughing Autry was, adding: "I know I can't act, but what the hell is my judgment against that of 50 million fans?"

Gene Autry always considered himself more a personality than actor, more a storyteller than singer. He made 635 records, nine of which sold more than one million copies, including the first, "That Silver-Haired Daddy of Mine," which he co-wrote with Jimmy Long, and which established the gold standard that honors million sellers. His "Rudolph the Red-Nosed Reindeer" sold more than 25 million copies and remains the third biggest-selling single in history. Autry had initially rejected it as being silly. His late wife, Ina Mae, insisted he record it, saying it reminded her of the story of the Ugly Duckling. "Kids will love it," she said.

She was right. Kids from 8 to 80 still love it. Rudolph's success moved Autry out of the country class and to the top of the pop charts for the first time. It was his single biggest success in a career that wasn't really that improbable, Autry would insist.

"Whatever I own, whatever I have accomplished," he often said, "didn't happen by chance. Even as a boy I planned ahead. When I was a baggage handler at 15 for the Frisco Railroad, and later a telegrapher, I still took correspondence courses and became an accountant. There has always been this kind of linkage in my life."

Along with an innate sense of when and how to move on.

"Johnny Bond, who toured and worked with me on radio, once told me about an Old West tradition," Autry said. "Whenever an Indian or lone cowboy had to take a long trip, he would generally ride one saddled horse and lead another bareback. When his horse began to tire, he didn't have to stop for a rest. He simply slipped the saddle onto the spare horse and continued on. I kind of went from performer to businessman in the same way. I kind of just changed horses."

The cornerstone of Autry's business empire was Golden West Broadcasting, whose umbrella at one point sheltered AM radio stations in Los Angeles and San Francisco, AM-FM affiliates in Portland, Seattle and Detroit, a UHF station in Oklahoma City, subscription and cable TV outlets in Memphis, Omaha, Dallas, Providence, Chicago and Atlanta, a Los Angeles TV station, a ten-acre movie and TV production center, a national agency for selling radio time, and a baseball team known as the Angels, which operated as Golden West Baseball Company.

At various times he also owned hotels in Chicago and Palm Springs, another on Sunset Boulevard and the Mark Hopkins in San Francisco. He also owned a 20,000-acre cattle ranch in Winslow, Arizona, four recording and music publishing companies and the 100-acre Melody Ranch in Newhall, California, where Autry made his first starring movies, propelled from obscurity by his records and the 1935 serial "The Phantom Empire."

In a career that spanned two spheres—entertainment and business—renowned for their often cutthroat methods, Autry was never known as the kind of person who reached the summit by climbing over the bodies of those who failed.

They told the story in Hollywood about the time Autry was staging a salary strike at Republic Studio, which, while conducting a publicity campaign designed to promote Roy Rogers, was ready to sweep Rogers out when Autry returned. Autry reportedly refused to let the studio do that, demanding it continue the buildup for the young cowboy who would soon become his chief competitor—and longtime friend.

The late Herb Green, Autry's personal pilot for 30 years, remembered Autry taking his show to a theater in Milwaukee for a week. It was during a polio epidemic and the house was empty, creating panic for the theater owner, who had a contract with Autry and could see himself going broke.

"At the end of the week," Green said, "Gene tore up the contract and took the loss out of his own pocket. He's that kind of guy. He's a giver. But try to cheat him out of a dollar and he'll fight you like a grizzly."

Shrewd, determined, self-educated and gifted with unique instincts, Autry changed horses and prospered, making only one illogical investment, he frequently said, suppressing a smile. That, of course, was his purchase of a baseball team, a step that might not have been taken if the late Walter O'Malley, who moved his Dodgers from Brooklyn to Los Angeles in 1958, had kept the game broadcasts on Autry's radio station (KMPC) rather than moving them to another (KFI).

It was a step that also might not have been taken if Autry had not once done a favor for the then American League president, Joe Cronin, and if the Japanese had not bombed Pearl Harbor on December 7, 1941.

All of that, of course, was a long way off when Orvon Gene Autry was born on September 19, 1907, in Tioga, Texas, the place where he first swung a bat and strummed a guitar.

The guitar was purchased for $8 through a Sears Roebuck catalogue. The 12-year-old Autry had earned the money by baling and stacking hay on his Uncle Calvin's farm. Autry was always cognizant of the value of money because there was so little of it then. His mother, who played the guitar and organ at church and family functions and put her son in the church choir at five, died when she was 45 because she was unable to afford the proper medical care. His father drifted off soon after, a self-styled merchant and trader who on most days found business more difficult to cultivate than that arid land.

Autry was 15 when he went to work as a baggage handler on the Frisco Line. He was 19 and earning $35 a month as a railroad telegrapher when, while picking at his guitar to kill time during a four-to-midnight shift in Chelsea, Oklahoma, a visitor to the office asked him to keep at it while he prepared some copy for Autry to send.

The enthusiastic young telegrapher began to sing, finishing at about the time the visitor finished his copy. The man said, "You know, with some hard work, young man, you might have something. You ought to think about going to New York and get yourself a job on radio." The visitor's name was Will Rogers, who never met a man he didn't like and was among the first to express an appreciation for Autry's musical ability.

Autry went to New York, had an unsuccessful audition, then took a job with a Tulsa radio station, ultimately becoming known as Oklahoma's Yodelin' Cowboy, which led to a 1929 record contract and the 1931 release of "That Silver-Haired Daddy of Mine."

The remarkable events that followed—much like the series of ironies that found him coming away with the American League's Los Angeles franchise in 1960—might never have occurred had Rogers not been visiting his sister in Chelsea that summer, and had the St. Louis Cardinals offered more than $100 a month to Autry when he tried out with their Tulsa farm club as a 19-year-old shortstop who had gained experience playing with Tioga's American Legion team.

The scouting report on the guitar player was that he was a banjo hitter who could make all the fielding plays. There were no big bonuses then, no multiyear contracts of the type that an owner named Autry would eventually give out, and he decided to reject the St. Louis offer in favor of the Frisco Line's security.

The dream of playing, however, didn't die easily. Baseball was truly the national pastime then, a national avenue of escape, particularly for white youths born to poverty. The game remained Autry's passion, nurtured by the success of boyhood friend Dizzy Dean, during his own success in other entertainment arenas. He attended games whenever he could. He became friends with owners and players, the athletes as anxious to meet him as he was to meet them.

He scheduled the World's Championship Rodeo in Madison Square Garden each October in the hope that one of the New York teams would be in the World Series—never envisioning, all the while, that he would some day own a team.

People pursue sports franchises for varied and complicated reasons. Tax shelter. Lifetime dream. Ego trip. Autry would make his move after Dodger owner Walter O'Malley had made one of his own, purchasing a summer home in the San Gabriel Mountains above Los Angeles.

It was the summer of 1960, and O'Malley would later inform Autry that on nights when the Dodgers were on the road he was unable to pick up KMPC's signal at his mountain retreat. O'Malley offered the explanation only after Autry had read about the Dodgers' decision to switch stations in *Variety*, the show business newspaper.

"I was shocked," Autry said. "Bob Reynolds, my partner, and Stan Spero, my general manager at KMPC, had personally negotiated with O'Malley and believed they had his word on a contract renewal. We had spent all kinds of money in supporting his fight to build in Chavez Ravine. It was hard to believe. The ironic thing is that the Dodgers ultimately ended up on a station whose nighttime power is so weak you have trouble picking up the games even in Orange County. I guess those things have a way of evening up."

O'Malley, at that point, had been in Los Angeles for three years, his team generating a popularity and success that even a visionary such as himself could not have predicted. The West Coast became the Gold Coast, and the American League became keenly interested in doing its own mining.

On October 26, 1960, at a New York meeting, the league voted owner Calvin Griffith permission to move his Washington Senators to Minneapolis-St. Paul and also voted to expand to 10 teams in 1961, creating franchises in Los Angeles and Washington, D.C.

Hank Greenberg, a Hall of Fame hitter who was a part owner of the Chicago White Sox, was asked by the league to take over the Los Angeles club, and Greenberg indicated he hoped to form a syndicate that would include San Diego banker C. Arnholt Smith, ex-major leaguer Ralph Kiner and the flamboyant Bill Veeck, then a Greenberg partner in the White Sox.

Autry, at the time having lost the Dodgers to KFI, was more interested in acquiring a client than a franchise. He wanted to retain KMPC's reputation as Southern California's sports station, and he knew it would be difficult if both the Dodgers and the new American League team were on other channels. Autry quickly made arrangements to meet with Greenberg and Veeck on one of their trips to Los Angeles, and they agreed to have KMPC broadcast the games if their deal with the league went through.

It did not. The obstacle was O'Malley, who argued that existing rules did not permit the American League to move into his territory, and he was supported by then Commissioner Ford Frick. The problem really seemed to be one of personality and money. Greenberg and Veeck were not interested in meeting O'Malley's demand for $450,000 in indemnification, and O'Malley, not anxious to share his chunk of the Gold Coast with anyone, was particularly not anxious to do it with a magnetic showman such as Veeck.

Amid the threat of a war between the two leagues, the American League met in New York again on November 17 and awarded the Washington franchise to a syndicate headed by Lieutenant General Elwood R. (Pete) Quesada, a World War II hero and chairman of the Federal Aviation Agency. The league agreed on a course of action for amending the expansion rules O'Malley had cited and accepted Greenberg's withdrawal from the Los Angeles picture.

The new bidder became a Gary, Indiana, insurance man named Charles Finley, who would eventually become the colorful and eccentric owner of the Kansas City A's, a team he would move to Oakland as a powerhouse in the late 60s and early 70s.

Meanwhile, back at Melody Ranch, Autry and partner Robert Reynolds, with the urging of a friend, construction magnate and Yankee co-owner Del Webb, were now considering the possibility of bidding themselves. Reynolds, a strapping 6-foot-4 piece of steel who was an All-American tackle at Stanford and the only man ever to play three 60-minute games in the Rose Bowl, had first met Autry as a youth in Oklahoma, where Reynolds' father was a driller in the oil fields, the same fields in which his son spent the summers. Reynolds ultimately went on to play professional football with the Detroit Lions, owned by George A. Richards, Autry's predecessor as owner of KMPC, where Reynolds, having been given a job by Richards, worked his way up from salesman to general manager. When Richards died and his family needed to sell KMPC to cover the estate taxes, Reynolds evidenced interest while also expressing need for a backer. Horace Lohnes, a partner in the law firm that represented both Autry and Reynolds, suggested the union.

KMPC was purchased for $800,000, with the lawyers creating the package in which Autry owned 56 percent of the station and Reynolds 30 percent, the other shares being made available to key employees. Reynolds became president of Golden West and Autry chairman of the board, the same positions they would assume with the Angels. They were friends and business partners, and when Autry said, "You know, Bob, I don't know why we shouldn't do it, why we shouldn't bid for the franchise ourselves, if only to protect the broadcast rights," Reynolds quickly agreed.

Autry's next step was to call Joe Cronin at the American League office. He had known the league president since the days when Cronin was the shortstop and boy manager of the Washington Senators. Cronin was later managing the Boston Red Sox when Autry took the Gene Autry Rodeo into Boston Garden. It was before a Saturday matinee there that Cronin knocked at the stage door, his three sons at his side.

"Think we could get in to see Gene?" he asked Pat Buttram.

"Sure," replied Buttram. "Don't know whether the boys will be more excited seeing Gene or he'll be more excited seeing you."

The Cronins visited with Autry while Buttram raced off to find three cowboy hats that Autry later autographed for the youngsters.

That memory may have been with Cronin when Autry called.

"I hear Greenberg and Veeck have pulled out of the running for the team here," Autry said, getting right to the point. "I'd be interested in taking it, Joe. We have a group of radio stations out here. We used to carry the Dodger games. I once had stock in the Hollywood Stars team in the Pacific Coast League. I've been a baseball fan all my life. Would there be any objection if we applied?"

"None that I know of," Cronin said. "The question is one of time. There's another group. We'd need O'Malley's permission, your financial statement, information on what stadium you'd play in and a letter of credit. We'd need the letter by Monday."

It was Friday.

"How big a letter?" Autry asked.

"Million and a half," Cronin said.

The letter was there on time, and Autry soon followed it, traveling to a joint American and National League meeting that began December 5 at the Park Plaza Hotel in St. Louis. He was accompanied by Reynolds, longtime baseball man Fred Haney (serving in an advisory capacity) and Paul A. O'Bryan, a Washington, D.C., attorney who had met Autry through his role as counsel to the Federal Communications Commission and who would later become a minority investor in the Angels.

An agreement in which the American League would accept the National League's expansion into New York in 1962 paved the way for O'Malley's acceptance of an American League franchise in Los Angeles in 1961, and Cronin's memory of a long-ago favor paved the way for the American League's acceptance of Autry.

"Anybody who loves kids that much," Cronin told the owners, "has to be good for baseball."

Autry was approved on December 7, a date that will live in infamy and confirmation that the calendar had taken a curious turn.

Exactly 19 years before, Donald Barnes, then owner of the financially and artistically beleaguered St. Louis Browns, had gone to the baseball meetings in St. Louis carrying documentation that he believed would justify his desire to move to Los Angeles. The meetings began December 8, 24 hours after the Japanese had bombed Pearl Harbor. There was speculation that California would be attacked next. Barnes' papers went into a trash can. The Gold Coast would remain untapped until 1958, discovered first by the National League.

O'Malley was now among the first to congratulate Autry. The

St. Louis meeting had no sooner ended than O'Malley extended an invitation to his suite. It was hardly a social affair. There, until three in the morning, over room-service dinner and repeated calls for coffee, the new owners received a proper introduction to the power and persuasiveness of the man who was frequently credited with being baseball's real commissioner. O'Malley's was the final word as they hammered out an arrangement in which the Los Angeles Angels of the American League would play the 1961 season in 20,500-seat Wrigley Field, former home of the Los Angeles Angels of the Pacific Coast League, and then move into the stadium O'Malley was building in Chavez Ravine. Autry agreed to a four-year lease in the new Dodger Stadium with the option to renew for three.

When he emerged from the meeting, he confided to Reynolds and O'Bryan that he believed the club would be unhappy with some of the provisions, that joint tenancy wouldn't work and that he would never take advantage of the option. But this was a time of elation and exhilaration. He was thrilled to be in, to be part of that private society of club owners. The problems, if any, could wait. His euphoria was such that he could laugh along with those who noted that he had received help in assembling the needed capital from a four-legged associate named Champion.

"For the first time in baseball history," Pulitzer Prize–winning columnist Red Smith wrote, "a franchise has been awarded to an entire horse."

Autry agreed to pay $2.1 million for the 28 players he would select in the expansion draft and $350,000 indemnification to O'Malley for what Autry called "grazing rights" in Los Angeles. This was major league baseball's first expansion, and the entry fee would increase dramatically over the years. Owners of the Arizona Diamondbacks and Tampa Bay Devil Rays paid $135 million each when baseball expanded to 30 teams in 1998, a figure that did not include many millions more in start-up costs.

Autry now had everything except for a bat, ball, players and organization. The next morning, after four hours' sleep, he acquired his first player.

Autry and Haney had breakfast with second baseman Red Schoendienst and catcher Del Rice. Both had played for the Milwaukee Braves when Haney managed the Braves to back-to-back National League pennants in 1957 and 1958. Both lived in St. Louis, had played for Autry's favorite Cardinals, and both were now free agents, this being 15 years before that categorization was thought of in terms of multiyear contracts and millions of dollars.

Rice and Schoendienst were simply out of work and of the opinion they could still play. Autry offered the opportunity to both. Schoendienst said he wanted to remain in St. Louis. Rice accepted. The Angels had a 38-year-old catcher and Autry was on his way.

He was also on his way back to Los Angeles. It was December 8, just 24 hours after he had received the franchise, a little more than three months since O'Malley switched stations. Autry, Reynolds and Haney drove right from the airport to a press conference at the Sheraton Town House on Wilshire Boulevard. They walked into the lobby and Reynolds pulled Autry aside.

"Gene," he said, "we can't walk in there without a general manager. What about Fred? He's got the qualifications. Let's offer him the job."

Haney *had* a job. He was under contract to NBC as an analyst on their *Game of the Week* telecasts, after having served in just about every baseball capacity. He had been a scrappy, no-quarter-given-or-asked Detroit teammate of Ty Cobb. He had been a manager, general manager and broadcaster in the minors. He had been manager of a world championship team. Haney had done it all and seen it all. He was a resident of Los Angeles, respected and well liked throughout the game, and he was happy with NBC.

"It's going to be five to ten years before these people see daylight," Haney told his wife, Florence, after accepting Autry's and Reynolds' offer to accompany them to St. Louis as adviser. "If anything were to come from this, the only thing I wouldn't mind doing is broadcasting their games."

Now, in the lobby of the Sheraton Town House, still under contract to NBC, Haney thought about the proposition just offered by Autry and Reynolds, thought about the immense job of building an organization from dust, of the five to ten years before daylight, and said, "Yes. If you have that kind of faith in me. I have that kind of belief in myself. It's a challenge, but we can do it."

It was only moments later that Haney was introduced to the media as the club's general manager, and only moments later that the former NBC analyst was asked if he had decided yet on his choice of managers. Haney said no, but in actuality the answer was yes. He had discussed the obvious choice with Autry and Reynolds on the flight from St. Louis. All three thought it was a natural. All three wanted Casey Stengel as their manager.

The irrepressible Stengel had managed the Yankees from 1949 through 1960. He won ten pennants, talked in a language few could understand and seemed totally out of place in a uniform, a bent and wrinkled man who had been unpopularly fired by the Yankees at age 70. Autry and Haney knew what kind of a team they would have and felt that Stengel's flair and wit would provide entertainment while the team struggled to attain respectability. Stengel was hot dogs, apple pie and Chevrolet. The Angels, competing in the shadow of the Dodgers, faced a struggle for survival—on and off the field.

Autry invited Stengel, who lived in suburban Glendale, to lunch at his Studio City home. They sat on the patio by the pool and talked for two hours. Stengel discoursed on everything from economy to ecology. Finally, growing impatient, Autry said, "Yes, Casey, but what about the job? Will you take it?"

Stengel shook his head. He told Autry that he would like to, but that he had two problems. The first was that he had signed a lucrative contract to serialize his story in *The Saturday Evening Post*, and part of the agreement was that he had to stay out of baseball until the story appeared. The second was that he had just become a director and stockholder of a Glendale bank, and he needed to spend some time there. Stengel said his situation would be different in a year, but he knew the Angels couldn't wait even a week.

A year later, of course, Stengel was hired to manage the New York Mets, a marriage deemed to be made in heaven, although the same might have been said if Stengel had accepted the Angels' offer, since there were times the Angels were every bit as Amazin', as Stengel put it, as the mediocre Mets of those early years.

But with Stengel out and the expansion draft scheduled for Boston on December 14, the Angels quickly turned to their list of managerial applicants and narrowed the choice to two: the controversial Leo Durocher and a Durocher disciple, Bill Rigney, who had succeeded Durocher as manager of the New York Giants in 1956 and had been fired by the San Francisco Giants in June 1960 with his team in second place.

Durocher, a colorful umpire baiter known as The Lip, a man who once said, "Nice guys finish last," represented some of the same qualities as Stengel, an instant opportunity to battle the Dodgers for the top half of the sports page. Yet Haney was concerned that Durocher would be unable to retain his patience with a team that figured to finish near the bottom in 1961 and for several summers after that.

"If we were going to have a winner right away, a really good club," Haney told Autry, "I wouldn't hesitate to hire Leo. But this is going to be the type of team that will test a manager's patience and temper. I'm not sure Leo can handle it. Rig's a fine manager and I think he'd be better suited for what we're going to go through."

A few weeks earlier, Rigney had been one of two finalists to succeed Joe Gordon as the Detroit Tigers manager. The Tigers chose Bob Scheffing. Rigney, believing he had been unjustly fired in San Francisco, was keenly disappointed again. He restlessly spent the days playing golf and making phone calls, hoping to find a job. Then he heard Autry and Reynolds had been awarded the Los Angeles franchise. He quickly sent off a letter of application, and was soon en route to Los Angeles, flying in from his San Francisco area home to have dinner with the owners. The date: December 11. The next day Rigney became the first manager of the Angels, a position he would hold for more than eight years, with the next eight years producing seven successors.

Rigney, believing that with an expansion team he required a measure of security, the assurance that he'd get more than a year to construct his building blocks, asked for and received a three-year contract.

The contract was an antacid of sorts, since the performance of the Angels would constantly eat at the ulcer of an animated man whose intensity was on a par with Durocher's and whose temper could occasionally match that of The Lion, another Durocher sobriquet.

This, however, was four months before the Angels would play their first game and about six months before a doctor would recommend to Rigney that he keep a piece of sponge cake and a glass of milk near the dugout as a midgame retardant for the inflamed stomach. It was also about seven months before the cake and milk began to mysteriously disappear before Rigney could get to it. He ultimately discovered that catcher Earl Averill was pilfering the snack. When finally apprehended, Averill said, "Hell, Rig, I thought it was there as a treat for the players."

This was now December 12. Rigney huddled briefly with Haney and then flew home to pack for the trip to Boston. He was met at the San Francisco airport by his close friend, Giants general manager and future National League president Charles (Chub) Feeney, who six months earlier had had the unfortunate assignment of informing Rigney that owner Horace Stoneham had decided on a managerial change. This time Feeney did Rigney a favor. He handed him an envelope containing the Giants' scouting reports on the American League teams.

Rigney had spent his entire career in the National League, and now he had 48 hours to prepare for the selection of a team to compete in the American League. The Giants' reports were one source of information. Another was Casey Stengel, who briefed Haney, a National League veteran like Rigney, on the players Stengel suspected would be on the draft list, particularly the Yankee players. The Angels also got a helping hand from an unexpected source. E. J. (Buzzie) Bavasi, then general manager of the Dodgers, agreed to provide close friend Haney with the Dodgers' American League reports. Bavasi might have refused, believing it was to the Dodgers' advantage to see the Angels stutter and stumble, leaving the Los

Angeles market to O'Malley, but a long and warm relationship with Haney prompted the favor.

Walter O'Malley, sounding a bit facetious, told reporters, "We want them to be a happy tenant when they move into the new stadium in 1962."

Now Rigney and Haney had their paperwork for the flight to Boston, where the Angels and Senators would select 28 players at $75,000 each. Del Rice would soon have teammates. Gene Autry would soon have a team for his franchise. Autry knew he would get the dregs, the players their current teams didn't want, but he couldn't have been more confident, more filled with anticipation.

Pat Buttram told him that the purchase of the club was the wisest move he had ever made. "Hell, Gene," he said, "on the sports pages a man can live forever. Look at Dempsey. They still call him Champ. Look at DiMaggio. He's been retired for years and he's now bigger than ever. If he was an actor out of work, he'd be looked on as a has-been. I mean it, Gene. On the sports pages you never die."

3

ANGELS FOR THE OUTFIELD

At the press conference where it was announced that he had agreed to become general manager of the Angels, Fred Haney told the media that it felt strange to be in charge of a team that had everything except players and equipment. The next day Haney received a special-delivery package from Chub Feeney of the Giants. In it was a bat, accompanied by a message that read, "Now you're on your way."

And now Haney and Bill Rigney were on their way to Boston to select the players who would swing the bat. They were armed with the Dodgers' and Giants' scouting reports and a differing philosophy as to which players they should select. Haney believed that the Angels had to make an immediate impact on the Los Angeles market, cutting into the Dodgers' popularity. He believed that the club had to acquire as many veteran or "name" players as possible, providing the Angels with instant identity.

Rigney understood, but he also believed the Angels needed to build a base for the future, that since it would be several years before the club's farm system was producing major league players, they had to focus on the best of a slim number of young players that the established eight teams had exposed to the draft.

"Don't forget," Feeney had told him, "you're going to be playing for many years, not just 1961."

The scouting reports were invaluable. They provided the Angels with clues to the ability of that largely anonymous group of prospects, clues the Washington Senators, represented in the draft meeting by manager Mickey Vernon and general manager Ed Doherty, lacked.

A year later, in fact, Senators owner Elwood (Pete) Quesada, whose team would quickly strangle on the age and ineptitude of the players it had selected, invited Rigney to play golf on an off day in the capital and asked plaintively, "What led you to draft those kids? How did you know about them?"

He referred to a group that included: Buck Rodgers, who would be the Angels' catcher for almost seven years and a future manager; shortstop Jim Fregosi, who would become a six-time All-Star and future manager; and pitchers Fred Newman and Dean Chance, the latter a future winner of the Cy Young Award. It was a group that helped the Angels maintain a modest respectability through the early years, establishing a foundation that the early farm system, generally underfunded, failed to sustain.

The league's expansion plan called for the eight established teams to submit a list of 15 players from their 40-man rosters. A price of $75,000 was set for each player to be picked, and each of the new clubs was required to select 28, at least three but no more than four from each of the older clubs.

Haney and Rigney flew to New York and took a train to Boston, a severe snowstorm having closed airports and delayed the draft by a day, giving the two California officials a window in which to conduct mock drafts, their only opportunity to speculate on who the Senators might take and who might be left. Arizona and Tampa Bay, the two most recent expansion teams, had three years in which to scout players and several days in which to conduct simulated drafts after receiving the lists of protected players from other clubs.

The 1961 selections began with a coin flip. Haney won it and made pitcher Eli Grba, a 26-year-old right-hander from the New York Yankees, the historic first pick of the first expansion draft.

The selection was based on the recommendation of Grba's former manager, Casey Stengel, under whom Grba won six of 10 decisions in 1960. Some four months later, the Angels won their first ever regular season game, beating Baltimore, 7–2, with Grba pitching a six-hitter and Stengel, the man the Angels wanted as their manager, getting an assist.

Grba, whose name seemed to be missing a vowel, consistently provided headline writers with material such as "Grba Ptchs 4-Httr." He always maintained that being the first pick was a greater thrill than winning that first game. Ultimately, the Angels emerged with 30 players, including two selected at $25,000 each from a minor league pool. They were first baseman Steve Bilko, one of the most popular athletes ever to perform in Los Angeles, having led the Pacific Coast League in homers with 37, 55 and 56 as a member of the minor league Angels in 1955–57, and outfielder Albie Pearson, the littlest Angel at 5-feet-5 and 140 pounds. Pearson was selected from the Baltimore system while Bilko had been the property of Detroit. The Angels benefited from both acquisitions, particularly that of Pearson, who shared Bilko's popularity. Pearson ultimately became the club's first .300 hitter and participated in one of Rigney's most interesting maneuvers.

The manager elected to room the diminutive Pearson with 6-foot-2, 240-pound first baseman Ted Kluszewski, who promptly set down the rules. "I get the bed and you get the dresser drawer," Klu informed Pearson. A few months later, Klu came in late one night, lifted Albie out of bed, and attempted to prove to him that he would indeed fit in the drawer.

Kluszewski, a power hitter out of the Bilko mold, was one of those 30 players selected in the draft, his name submitted by the Chicago White Sox after he had concluded a distinguished career with the Cincinnati Reds. He was 37 at the time and, to some measure, characteristic of the type of player the Angels and Senators encountered on the big board in the American League office. They were players whose skills seemed eroded by time, or fringe players whose skills never reached a point where erosion would have been noticed. There was also that small group of promising young players who were exposed by clubs hoping their anonymity would escape the attention of drafting executives, particularly those with National League experience.

Rigney would later say that he had no illusions about the abilities of the organization's selections but that he was exhilarated to have at least emerged with a small nucleus for the future. Attempting to merge Haney's desire for a few veterans with familiar names as potential gate attractions and Rigney's desire for younger players around whom the Angels would build, the team leaders selected:

Pitchers: Dean Chance and Ron Moeller, Baltimore; Jerry Casale and Fred Newman, Boston; Ken McBride, Chicago; Aubrey Gatewood and Bob Sprout, Detroit; Bob Davis and Ned Garver, Kansas City; Truman "Tex" Clevenger, Minnesota; Eli Grba and Duke Maas, New York.

Catchers: Ed Sadowski, Boston; Earl Averill, Chicago; Buck Wilson, Cleveland; Buck Rodgers, Detroit.

Infielders: Don Ross, Baltimore; Jim Fregosi, Boston; Ted Kluszewski, Chicago; Ken Aspromonte and Gene Leek, Cleveland; Eddie Yost, Detroit; Ken Hamlin, Kansas City; Julio Becquer, Minnesota; Steve Bilko, Denver (Detroit).

Outfielders: Jim McAnany, Chicago; Faye Throneberry, Minnesota; Bob Cerv and Ken Hunt, New York; Albie Pearson, Rochester (Baltimore).

Cynics looked at the list and predicted that the Angels would not win 50 games. Autry looked at the list and asked colleague Buttram if he was positive that on the sports pages you never die.

Haney and Rigney knew they had work to do. They returned to Los Angeles, the city displaying great restraint in refraining from a premature victory parade.

Autry set out to round up additional capital, attracting both Joseph Thomas, senior partner in Lehman Brothers, a New York stock firm, and J. D. Stetson Coleman, a wealthy investment associate of Thomas's. Both became minority investors and members of the board of directors. Tire magnate Leonard K. Firestone also joined the board, purchasing 30 percent of the club after Reynolds and O'Bryan had traveled to his Palm Springs estate to make the presentation.

Haney, having moved the organization into offices on Sunset Boulevard in downtown Los Angeles, about a tape-measure home run from Wrigley Field, was busy filling out his staff and deciding on a spring training site. The wisdom of his front office selections could be measured by ensuing developments and the fact that other organizations continually raided Haney's staff.

The late Marvin Milkes, a minor league executive when hired as assistant general manager, went on to become general manager of the Seattle Pilots and Milwaukee Brewers before assuming executive positions with other teams in other sports. The late Cedric Tallis, a minor league executive when hired as business manager, did the legwork on the Angels' selection of Anaheim as their future home and went on to become general manager of the Kansas City Royals and then vice president of the Yankees. Roland Hemond, farm director at Milwaukee when hired in the same capacity by Haney, went on to become general manager of the White Sox and Orioles and is now a senior adviser with the Diamondbacks. Tom Ferguson, equipment manager at Milwaukee when hired as equipment manager of the Angels, became the club's traveling secretary before returning to Milwaukee as a vice president of the Brewers and then a Southern California scout for the Philadelphia Phillies.

The hirings took several weeks. Haney was back from the draft meeting only a day when he closed the deal on a spring training base. It was December 16, less than nine days since Autry and Reynolds had been awarded the franchise. Now there were players and a place for them to train. Haney settled on Palm Springs, a desert resort 120 miles from Los Angeles. It was a decision the club's players applauded for years.

A retreat for the rich and famous, Palm Springs offered a variety of plush golf courses, fine restaurants and neon hunting grounds. There is a pool in every backyard, a bar on every other corner, a bikini on every girl.

While all of the other spring camps were in Florida or Arizona, Haney announced he had selected Palm Springs because of his belief that a California team should train in California and because of its proximity to the Angels' new fans and Golden West Broadcasting's new sponsors.

Years later, retired infielder Bobby Grich would reminisce about those idyllic springs and call it "my favorite time of the year

. . . the intimate crowds, the relaxed atmosphere, the great weather, the chance to see some of the young players, and Gene Autry watching from that tunnel under the stands, right there next to the dugout.

"It was a beautiful place to play, and there was no more wonderful view than to stand out at second base and look at that small grandstand with all those tank tops and shorts, and snow-capped San Jacinto [Mountains] in the background."

If Grich had been in that dugout tunnel under the stadium known as the Polo Grounds during the club's formative years in the early 60s, he might have rubbed elbows with celebrities such as Phil Harris, Phil Silvers, Chuck Connors and Joe E. Brown. He would also have met Dwight D. Eisenhower, a frequent visitor on vacation after leaving the White House.

One day Rigney asked the former President to manage the club for a few innings.

"I don't know how," Eisenhower protested.

"If you can run the country, you can run the ballclub," Rigney said.

"But I don't know the signs," Eisenhower responded.

"Neither do my players," said Rigney.

For 32 years the club spent all or part of each spring there, and every Angels manager in that time wondered just how much and what kind of training his players did. Two-a-day workouts came to have a new meaning. Rigney shook his head once and muttered, "I'm not sure whether my players have a tougher time with fundamentals or the curfew."

The manager walked into the popular Howard Manor one night and prompted an evacuation that rivaled Dunkirk. Players were seen diving under tables and out windows. The Angels initially stayed at the sprawling Desert Inn in the heart of the city. The writers lived in a home designed originally for actress Marion Davies near the front of the Inn. The scribes' lair, known as the Fourth Estate, became a two a.m. haven for bartenders, cocktail waitresses and musicians. There was a party every night. If Rigney had to find his players, he knew where to look. He often found them and fined them.

He also decided in the spring of 1963 that he was going to have the players ride bicycles to and from the workouts. He didn't know if it would help their conditioning, but he speculated that it might keep them so tired they would be reluctant to join the nightly chase. The players, however, showed ingenuity. Buck Rodgers, the second-year catcher then, laughed and recalled how he would have his wife "meet me with the station wagon somewhere along the way. We'd throw the bike in the back and drive to the hotel." The Cowboy himself mounted a bicycle on the first day and led the posse to the stadium, but the plan worked only until that morning when the majority of bikes were found in the bottom of the hotel pool, the culprit never disclosed.

Eventually, restricted to only one diamond in Palm Springs and concerned about the distractions, the Angels first moved the early phase of their encampments to the isolated community of Holtville, about 123 miles from Palm Springs, and then to comparably isolated Casa Grande, Arizona.

However, by the late 80s, as spring training became big business, with new and lavish training complexes dotting the Florida and Arizona landscape, and with the Arizona-based teams complaining about the time and expense involved in flying or busing to Palm Springs for one or two exhibition games, the Angels began a search for a permanent facility.

The search took five years and included futile negotiations with Palm Springs officials on the possible renovation of the former Polo Grounds, renamed Angels Stadium, or construction of a new facility. Ultimately, the Angels signed a 15-year lease to train in Tempe, Arizona, in a renovated stadium formerly the spring home of the Seattle Mariners.

They trained in Palm Springs for the last time in 1992, and pitcher Scott Bailes took advantage of the nostalgic situation to print T-shirts that read "Last Hurrah in Shangri-la"—which he sold for $10. For the first-year Angels of 1961, Palm Springs resembled Shangri-la, indeed. But then, anywhere would have, considering it was a team primarily of castoffs given a second life through expansion.

Second baseman Ken Aspromonte thought about that as he sat

in the small clubhouse at the Polo Grounds in March 1961 and predicted that his new and maligned team was destined "to fool a lot of people. We've been called rinky-dinks and fringe players. Well, that's wrong. A lot of us are guys who only need a break. We're a bunch of angry men."

4

THE FIRST SEASON:
WAGS, GRBA AND SOME TN'T

Those angry men would soon provide Autry with his greatest baseball thrill. But the first order of business at that first spring camp was a "Welcome Angels" banquet at the Desert Inn. Autry was asked to speak. He responded by telling the audience that the club had made a strong attempt to secure Casey Stengel as the manager but had settled for a man the owners were sure would do a good job. He then introduced Bill Rigney as Phil Wrigley.

If Autry had made a similar gaffe when he auditioned for the Fields Brothers Marvelous Medicine Show he might never have gotten out of Tioga. Then again, the owner was to be excused for his celebrative state since this was the first time he had seen his new team together.

At any rate, the humbling start didn't seem to affect Rigney, who was happy to be working, happy to have the opportunity, like his castoff players, to prove he could still do the job, anxious to show Giants' owner Horace Stoneham he had made a mistake.

Rigney had fired a needle in Stoneham's direction on his first day as Angels manager by saying, "Fred Haney has assured me that I'm in charge on the field, that he'll never second-guess me. I don't know if I can manage that way."

Rig quickly became a favorite of the Angels' press corps. He was glib and accessible, capable of providing stories when there were none, which was frequently the case with a team that would lose far more often than it would win, a team that was constantly putting a torch to Rigney's ulcer.

> Example: Rigney's concentration during the critical moments of a game in Washington was shattered by a tap on his shoulder. He turned to find catcher Earl Averill, the same Earl Averill who was responsible for pilfering Rigney's milk and sponge cake. This time, ignoring the status of the game and Rigney's involvement, Averill said, "I just counted, skipper, and there's eighty lights out in this stadium."

> Example: Shortstop Fritz Brickell fielded a double-play grounder and threw it into right field, where Albie Pearson retrieved it and threw it wildly to the middle of the infield, where pitcher Ron Kline retrieved it and threw it wildly to third base. There had been three errors on the same play in this game at Boston, and now the ball was bouncing toward the dugout, where Rigney fielded it, stared at it ("I thought about taking a bite out of it") and finally put it in a secure place, his hip pocket.

> Example: The Mets had Marvelous Marv Throneberry. The Angels had his brother, Fabulous Faye. In the late innings of a tense game, Rigney called on Faye to pinch-hit. He called and called. Faye was asleep in the corner of the dugout.

> Example: The Angels held a slim lead in the late innings of a game in Minnesota. The Twins had loaded the bases against Dean Chance, who delivered a pitch low and away. Catcher Hank Foiles reached for it, then spun and raced to the backstop screen, where he searched in vain for the ball. All three runners scored before Foiles thought to look in his glove. The ball had been there all the time.

"The lunatics," Rigney once observed, "have taken over the asylum."

The takeover had actually begun when 275 "athletes" of all descriptions showed up at a Los Angeles tryout camp in early February 1961. Six were signed to professional contracts. One, pitcher Morris Cigar, performed impressively in spring training before being sent to the minors, where his brief career expired. His Palm Springs roommate was another product of that tryout camp and the first player cut in that first Palm Springs camp. He was a penniless, dispirited infielder who equipment manager Tom Ferguson sent off with a tuna sandwich. His name was Charlie Pride, and he would soon find better days in another area of the entertainment business.

Pride and Cigar, two names that offered intriguing possibilities to the hungry journalists, were gone before Haney began shaping a team that boasted power and little else. The general manager knew he would have to deal and he did. The Angels made 21 transactions involving 30 players in 1961 and 20 involving 24 in 1962. Ryne Duren, Lee Thomas, Joe Koppe, Billy Moran, Art Fowler, Tom Morgan, Leon Wagner—those and other names so important to the Angels during the first few summers—were acquired either through trade, purchase or free agent signing.

Marvin Milkes, Haney's new aide, had broad minor league experience and knew where to look and with whom to talk. Since this was baseball's first expansion, there were only 18 teams and the talent wasn't as diluted as it has become with 30. There were players performing at the Triple A level who were capable of doing a job in the majors.

Joe Koppe and Billy Moran, for instance, were both acquired in minor league transactions. They replaced Ken Hamlin and Ken Aspromonte as the shortstop and second baseman in midseason of that first year and provided important strength up the middle during a surprisingly successful 45–44 second half, with Moran going on to become an All-Star in 1962.

Leon Wagner, who led the Angels in home runs with 28 in 1961, 37 in 1962 (a club record for 16 years) and 26 in 1963, was obtained during the season's first week when Feeney reminded Rigney of the ex-Giant outfielder's potential, and Rigney reminded Haney, who authorized Milkes to open negotiations with Jack Kent Cooke, owner then of the minor league team in Toronto where Wagner was playing.

The new Angel contributed significantly to his team's attack and spirit. He delivered almost as many punch lines as line drives. He also led the club in requests for front office loans. The biggest was applied to a clothing store he opened on Crenshaw Boulevard in Los Angeles. The slogan, "Get Your Rags from Daddy Wags" represented better quality than the merchandise, and the creditors soon foreclosed. Wags told the Angels to deduct the debt from his paychecks. All of the club's favors seemed forgotten when Wagner was traded in a contract dispute after the 1963 season and said Haney was another Khrushchev. Haney responded by calling a unique press conference at which he disclosed the history of the club's financial dealings with Wagner, who quickly issued an embarrassed apology for having compared the general manager to the then Soviet premier, explaining it was only natural for anyone traded to Cleveland to have trouble thinking straight.

The biggest trade of the first season was consummated on May 9 when Haney sent pitcher Truman "Tex" Clevenger and outfielder Bob Cerv to New York for relief pitcher Ryne Duren, first baseman–outfielder Lee Thomas and pitcher Johnny James, the ill-fated right-hander who would soon give a new dimension to the term "breaking ball," breaking his arm while throwing one.

Thomas hit 24 homers, drove in 70 runs and batted .285 while earning the nickname "Mad Dog" because of his temper. Thomas was playing golf with a sportswriter one day in 1961 when he became angered over a poor shot and hurled his driver with such force it tore through a chain-link fence. The Mad Dog was soon joined by another Thomas, an outfielder named George, who was acquired from Detroit. The Thomas boys formed a power package that came to be called TN'T. However, George's career ended early when it was discovered he had trouble releasing throws from the outfield. Twice in one season he lost his grip and threw the ball behind him.

Duren, acquired in the Yankee deal and nicknamed "The Flame" because of his sizzling fastball, became a valuable addition to a bullpen rebuilt entirely that first year, a bullpen that was the backbone of the team's modest success. It included Tom (Plowboy) Morgan, left-hander Jack Spring (one of the few Angels without a nickname) and John Arthur Fowler, known as "King Arthur" and "The Hummer" because of his own lively fastball.

Fowler was a 39-year-old right-hander acquired from the Dodgers. He had helped pitch the Dodgers to the National League pennant in 1959 and was unceremoniously honored by being sent to the minors, prompting an angry response. The veteran pitcher had a simple philosophy on the mound: throw strikes and put a little something on it. He meant movement, but he might also have been referring to saliva or some other banned substance. The theory—and possibly the substance—kept him in the majors at an age when most pitchers are on the golf course. Fowler was extraordinary with the Angels until the freak accident of 1962 (he lost the sight in his left eye when struck by a line drive during batting practice) diluted his effectiveness and perhaps cost the Angels a pennant in only their second year.

No story better characterizes the aplomb with which Fowler went about his job than this one: Pitcher Paul Foytack, having recently been acquired by the Angels, walked the bases loaded in the first inning of his first start in Washington. Fowler was summoned. Foytack handed him the ball and said, "I've been reading how good you are. Let's see you get out of this one." Fowler promptly struck out the side.

Duren also contributed his own chapter to the team's folklore. He was a free-spirited right-hander who wore thick glasses, always threw his first warm-up pitch against the backstop screen in an effort to intimidate the hitter and had the tendency to become obstreperous when drinking, which was frequently. A rehabilitated alcoholic who would later supervise abuse programs in Milwaukee, Duren's exploits included:

- Crashing into the hotel room of sportswriter Dan Hafner, flipping over both Hafner and the mattress he was sleeping on.

- Providing a five-thirty a.m. wake-up call for pitching coach Marv Grissom by chipping golf balls off his hotel room window in Palm Springs, prompting Grissom, accustomed to Duren's eccentricities, to open the door and say, "Got kind of an early starting time, don't you, Ryne?"

- Celebrating a 1–0 win in a rare starting assignment by wading through the ponds of a hotel's Polynesian restaurant in Cleveland. The restaurant manager called Rigney and said, "Mr. Rigney, I've got one of your players . . ." He didn't get a chance to finish. Rigney interrupted and said, "Don't tell me. I know exactly which one. I'll be right down."

The inebriated Duren was always in a fight, suffering more knockouts than the bums Joe Louis confronted on a monthly basis. But he never remembered the next morning, never held a grudge and always gave 200 percent, a characteristic of the Angels during the early years and sometimes a missing ingredient in later years.

The first official step for the "rinky-dinks" and "fringe players" came April 11 in Baltimore on a cold gray afternoon, with Eli Grba facing Milt Pappas, the ace of an Oriole team favored to win the American League pennant.

At a party the night before his team's American League debut, Autry sat next to a longtime friend, Baltimore manager Paul Richards. Richards put his arm around Autry's shoulders and said, "Well, cowboy, you're my pal, but tomorrow the bell rings and I'm going to have to beat your ass."

Autry raised his glass and said, "More power to you, Paul. I imagine you will."

Rigney started a lineup of Eddie Yost at third base, Ken Aspromonte at second, Albie Pearson in right field, Ted Kluszewski at first, Bob Cerv in left, Ken Hunt in center, Fritz Brickell at short. Del Rice was Grba's catcher.

Autry and Reynolds had no sooner reached their seats and buttoned up their overcoats than the Angels exploded in the manner of their owner's six-shooter. Pearson walked and Kluszewski homered to right. Cerv followed with a homer to center, and it was 3–0 after the first inning with more to come. Pearson lined an RBI single in the second, and Klu followed with another homer. It was 7–0 after two innings, and Grba was thinking he was back with the powerhouse Yankees.

The final score: 7–2. The Angels led the American League with an undefeated record, and it was as if they had just won the seventh game of the World Series. They yelled and slapped each other on the back, making sport of the media's critical jabs, the predictions they wouldn't win 50 games.

Publicity director Irv Kaze invited Grba and the writers to his hotel room for champagne, and Grba said that while it wasn't really as big a thrill as being drafted No. 1, he would never forget the emotions he experienced when he handed the ball with which he had secured the final out to Autry in the clubhouse.

Years later, in another clubhouse in another place, with the champagne flowing and the Angels celebrating the 1979 division title, the first title in club history, Autry would say that the victory on April 11, 1961, would always remain his biggest thrill, his greatest moment.

Unfortunately, it was not long before the freshman Angels confronted the anticipated and predicted reality. They returned from that first trip with a 1–7 record, having lost seven in a row after the opening victory while also being rained out eight times. The rain-outs were rescheduled as part of a mid-summer death march of 26 games in 20 days, the Angels winning only seven.

It was never routine.

Duren, for example, tied a major league record by striking out four batters in one inning at Washington, but only after Averill's failure to hold the spitball on the third strikeout led to the run that defeated the Angels.

Lee Thomas went 9-for-11 with three home runs and eight RBIs in a doubleheader at Kansas City and the Angels lost both games.

Tied with the Yankees at 3–3 in the sixth inning of a game in which Duren set a club strikeout record with 12, Rigney, for reasons even the manager couldn't later explain, allowed Duren to bat with two runners in scoring position. Duren responded with a two-run, game-winning single, only his third major league hit.

The Angels lost 91 games that first year. However, they won 70, still an expansion record. The 50th win—a plateau most "experts" predicted was unattainable—prompted a celebration that rivaled that of opening day. Ted Bowsfield pitched No. 50 and two weeks later reached a career high with win No. 10, prompting a personal celebration which included a unique role reversal. Two writers had to help the wobbly Bowsfield back to the team's hotel.

The Angels finished eighth, 38½ games behind the pennant-winning Yankees. But in the year that Roger Maris hit 61 homers and Mickey Mantle 54, the two New York sluggers hit a total of only four at cozy Wrigley Field, where the Angels and their opponents combined for 248, then a major league record for homers in a season at one park. Appropriately, the 248th came in the ninth inning of the season's 161st and last game and was delivered in a pinch-hit role by Steve Bilko, the man who had produced those renowned minor league seasons in Wrigley Field.

The homer was Bilko's 20th, giving the Angels five players with 20 or more, the others being Wagner (28), Hunt (25), Thomas (24), and Averill (21). Hunt, buried behind Mantle in the Yankee system prior to the expansion draft, led the club in RBIs with 84, while Pearson was No. 1 in average at .288. Rigney got 12 wins from Ken McBride, 11 each from Grba and Bowsfield and some strong relief from Tom Morgan (8–2, 2.36 ERA) and Art Fowler (5–8, 3.64 ERA). Duren moved successfully and repeatedly between the bullpen and rotation, setting a then league record, in addition to his other accomplishments, by striking out seven straight hitters in a June 9 start at Boston.

The final month of the first season saw the recall of Jim Fregosi, Buck Rodgers, Dean Chance and Fred Newman, all of whom represented the promise of better days.

The Angels would move to Dodger Stadium in 1962, having drawn 603,510 for that first and last year at Wrigley Field, since torn down to make room for a community center. The Dodgers, playing their fourth and last season at the nearby Coliseum, drew 1.8 million. The Angels escaped the Dodgers' shadow only when Mantle, Maris and the Yankees visited. The nine games with New York attracted 166,522 fans to 20,500-seat Wrigley, twice as many as came to see any other team.

The Angels' attendance was a league low. Yet it was high enough, considering the club's small player payroll, low rent and absence of a farm system, to provide a sizable profit, according to Bob Reynolds, Autry's partner. However, the owners reacted in a curious fashion. Instead of allowing the profit to draw interest, to grow, to be used in the signing of prospects and the development of a farm system, Autry and partners opted to recoup their initial investment.

Ultimately, the bottom line on 1961 was a deceiving loss of almost $1 million, of which Reynolds, years later, said, "It was a mistake, not putting the profit to use. If the decision had been strictly up to Gene and me, we might have decided differently. But we had promised the other investors that they would get their money back as soon as possible, and we felt committed to honor that promise."

There would be other curious decisions carrying significant ramifications, decisions that would begin to take their toll in the mid-1960s, strangling the growth of a promising franchise and extinguishing the glow that became even brighter in 1962, which would be remembered for several reasons, including the arrival of Robert (Bo) Belinsky.

5

BO AND DEAN

No Angel—no major league player ever—received more publicity for accomplishing less. He won the grand total of 28 games during a major league career that spanned six seasons. His highest salary was $18,000.

Five of those wins came in succession at the start of the 1962 season and included a May 5 no-hitter against Baltimore. Years later he would say:

"The night before my no-hitter I met this tall, thin, black-haired secretary out at a place on the Sunset Strip. We had a couple of drinks, and I wound up making it with her at her pad. She wasn't bad. I got home about four a.m. and that night pitched my no-hitter. I went back to look for her after the game and couldn't find her. I never found her again. She was my good-luck pitching charm, and when I lost her, I lost all my pitching luck."

Nothing says more about the way Bo Belinsky went about it, about his philosophy, than that. He also used to say, "If you want a helping hand, look at the end of your own arm."

Bo's hand was most often wrapped around a waist or a glass. He briefly had it all, king of the hill in a manner he dreamed about while growing up on the streets and in the pool halls of Trenton.

He was 5-0 with a no-hitter, having made a mark even before his first win of that first big-league season by staging a contract holdout that ended with a poolside press conference at the Desert Inn. It was an auspicious introduction, and it only got better.

By mid-May Bo was the pal of syndicated columnist Walter Winchell and the hottest stud in Hollywood. He dated Ann-Margret, Tina Louise, Queen Soraya, Doris Duke, Paulette Goddard and a Du Pont heiress, among others. He eventually became engaged and disengaged to actress Mamie Van Doren. There was a party every night, Bo thinking it would never end, his religion being that of night walkers everywhere.

Teammate Dean Chance was his closest friend. A strange alliance: Belinsky, the street-smart left-hander from the big city of the East; Chance, the hayseed right-hander from the farm in Wooster, Ohio. Both were out of the Baltimore organization, where they had barely known each other, only of each other. They soon became inseparable, one's problems becoming the other's, in a way that it was difficult to determine whether Bo was having the most damaging effect on Dean or Dean was having the most damaging effect on Bo.

Each had major league ability. Belinsky's forte was his screwball, and it was frequently written that nothing was more appropriate. Chance had as much talent as any pitcher of his time. His fastball, dispensed from an intimidating full pivot during which Chance did not even look at the plate, featured both velocity and movement. Yet he had it together really for only two full seasons.

Nothing seemed to get through. Autry, Haney and Rigney took turns lecturing both. They were fined repeatedly. Bo was farmed out once (to Hawaii of all places). Ultimately both were traded, the catalyst in Belinsky's expulsion being an incident in which he allegedly used either a can of shaving cream or bottle of hair tonic to slug veteran sportswriter Braven Dyer, a man almost three times his age.

Bo was traded to Philadelphia for pitcher Rudy May and outfielder Costen Shockley in the winter of 1964, his three-year record with the Angels 21–28. The 5–0 start of 1962 ultimately turned to 10–11, followed by 2–9 in 1963, the year he was sent to Hawaii, and 9–8 in 1964, when his earned run average was a very good 2.87.

Chance, a prize plum from the expansion draft and yet a pitcher whom Buck Rodgers described as the "dumbest I ever caught," was traded to Minnesota in the winter of 1966 for first baseman Don Mincher, outfielder Jimmie Hall and pitcher Pete Cimino.

Chance won 74 games in his five seasons with the Angels, a victim frequently of ineffective and inconsistent support, a pitcher whose dominating ability at times could be measured by his 22–4 record at Dodger Stadium during the 1964 and 1965 seasons, when he was 7–0 against the dreaded Yankees.

In 1962, when Bo got off 5–0 and the Angels went on to stun the baseball world by finishing third, the 21-year-old Chance was 14–10, the winningest rookie in the American League. He was 13–18 with a 3.19 ERA in 1963, and he then became the youngest pitcher to that point to win the Cy Young Award, turning in a 20–9 record with baseball's lowest ERA (1.65) in 1964, a year in which he pitched 14 games of five hits or less and manager Rigney called him "the best right-hander I've ever seen."

Chance might have enjoyed the same kind of year in 1965 except for what was described as an "abscessed tooth" but was believed to be an infection of another nature. He appeared in about 15 fewer games than normal, winning 15 of 25 decisions with another good ERA, 3.15.

His ERA (3.08) was even better in 1966 and again more reflective of his performance than a 12–17 record, after which the anemic Angels decided to trade him while his value was still high.

Five years after they had made their major league debuts—the Angels seeing in Belinsky a personality to counter the Dodgers' popularity and in Chance a talent around which to build their future—both were gone, only the memories lingering to be laughed at amid the frustration of what might have been. Even now those memories—who they were, where they came from, what they did— seem fresh, the yesterdays melting away to reveal a tall, thin, good-looking Belinsky surrounded by reporters as he lounged next to the Desert Inn pool on a bright, warm March afternoon in 1962.

He was 25 then, the son of a Polish Catholic father and a Russian Jewish mother. What he learned, he said, he had learned on the streets. He was 10 when he had his first cigarette in the bathroom of a theater, 12 when he had his first relations with a girl, in the elevator of his grandmother's apartment. Hustlers named The Goose, The Farmer, Cincinnati Phil and The Lemonade Man broadened his education, introducing him to the three-cushion bank shot and life on the road.

Baseball then was a diversion, a Sunday sandlot game, a few dollars when his pockets were otherwise empty. The only baseball name he really knew was that of Hal Newhouser, and only because Newhouser was also a lefty. Pittsburgh scout Rex Bowen saw one of those games and offered Bo $185 a month and a bus ticket to Brunswick, Georgia, site of the Pirates' Class A affiliate.

"What the hell," thought Bo, "what else am I doing? I mean, I think I was working in an overalls factory then, playing pool and fooling with the broads."

That was the start of it. Brunswick, Georgia, 1956. A long way from the Sunset Strip.

His route took him to Pensacola, Knoxville, Aberdeen, Amarillo, Stockton, Vancouver and Little Rock. He had modest success, winning 13 one year, 10 another, 9 another, his potential reflected by strikeout totals such as 202 in 195 innings, 183 in 174. His reputation grew in many ways. An 18-year-old Knoxville girl with whom he'd spent a night charged him with rape, and he was smuggled out of town on the floor of a friend's car. He and teammate Steve Dalkowski drilled holes in the wall of a Miami hotel room so they could watch one of the contestants in the 1961 Miss Universe contest, drawing the wrath of the hotel and their manager after Dalkowski shined a flashlight through one of the holes and the woman became aware she was being watched. There was a fight in a Little Rock bar, and Belinsky was accused of having started it.

Bo moved from the Pittsburgh organization to the Baltimore organization. He didn't see much future and considered quitting. Harry Dalton, later a general manager of the Angels but then farm director of the Orioles, talked him out of it. It was the winter of 1961, and Bo was eligible for the annual draft of minor league free agents, having been unprotected by the Orioles, who were rich in pitching talent and skeptical of Bo's behavior.

Fred Haney and scout Tuffie Hashem discussed possible selections, Hashem telling Haney that the one name that kept popping up in his conversations with minor league managers and coaches was that of Belinsky. Hashem said he had seen Bo pitch twice and felt he was a real prospect.

"Why hasn't anybody picked him up before?" Haney asked. "Got a bad arm?"

"No," said Hashem. "He's a wiry guy who can pitch regularly."

"What else is there about him?" Haney asked.

"Well," Hashem said, "you keep hearing the same things. Mention Belinsky's name and people smile at you like you're nuts. They say, 'Sure, we know Bo. He's got a million-dollar arm and ten-cent head.'"

Haney decided to find out for himself. He went to the winter meetings in Tampa armed with his top 20 choices for the minor league draft. He first selected infielder Marlan Coughtry from Seattle. Coughtry played 11 games for the Angels, batting .182 before he was traded. Haney next selected infielder Felix Torres from Buffalo of the International League. Torres would play third base for the Angels for three seasons.

Finally, after the 20 clubs had selected 62 other minor leaguers, the Angels chose Belinsky, then pitching in the Venezuelan Winter League and unaware of his selection. He did not learn about it, in fact, until after he had returned to his Trenton home and opened the contract that called for a major league minimum of $6,000.

"I thought it was a joke," Bo said later, having told Haney the same over the phone. "I had played all those years in the minors, and they were offering me the minimum like I was a kid with no record. I wouldn't sign. I told Haney that if he didn't give me $8,500, then I'd forget about baseball. The hell with it. I had a few things going in Trenton."

The Angels opened camp on February 24. The rookie left-hander wasn't there. Bud Furillo of the *Herald Examiner* called him.

"I'm not coming in for a penny less than $8,500," Bo told him.

"What are you doing to pass the time?" Furillo asked.

"Playing pool and fooling with the girls," Belinsky replied.

Furillo said thank you and broke the land speed record getting to his typewriter. The *Herald* bannered the story of the pitcher who worshiped wine, women and song, and suddenly Bo was a story from coast to coast.

"He was the greatest thing to ever happen to us," then publicity director Irv Kaze conceded years later. "He put the Angels on the map. But I don't think he ever really cared about pitching and winning. He never seemed to care about anything. He had a terrific arm and could have been a star, but he wasn't motivated. I truly think he didn't give a damn if he played in the majors or minors."

Bo's holdout angered Haney, but he sensed the magic, the publicity value in getting Bo to camp. He called and said, "Look, why don't you come out and we'll negotiate here? You can talk to our owners. Maybe they'll give you some more money."

The idea appealed to Bo and he flew west.

"I'm Kaze, welcome to California," the publicity director said, meeting him at the airport.

"Damn," said Bo, "I expected Autry."

Kaze took Belinsky directly to a poolside press conference.

"It was like a movie," Bo said later. "They sat me down, poured me a drink and took off. They wanted names and dates of all the broads I had ever been with. They wanted to know about my pool playing and the fights I had been in. I gave them the answers they wanted to hear. Then they asked about the contract, and I told them I wouldn't sign unless Autry begged me personally."

Three days passed and Haney finally summoned Bo to his room, saying it couldn't go on, that Bo had to sign or go home. Bo decided that he had begun to like the town and the team, and he agreed to sign, providing the Angels would renegotiate his contract in midseason.

"If you make the club we'll take a look at it in midseason," Haney said. "I won't promise anything, but if you don't sign you're gone."

He was almost gone anyway.

The Angels decided a few weeks later that it didn't appear Bo had major league ability and that under those circumstances he wouldn't be worth the aggravation. They offered him back to the Orioles for $12,500, half of the then draft price. The Orioles thanked the Angels for their generosity but said they weren't interested.

Belinsky, reflecting years later, said that while he always considered Haney a good guy, a class guy, he believed that Rigney was always "jealous of all the attention I got" and was determined to prove "he was bigger than anyone on the team. He could manage the hell out of a game, but he was strictly Joe Hollywood, wearing those dark shades and trying to let everyone know just how big a man he was around town."

Rigney wanted to send Belinsky to the minors, but pitching coach Marv Grissom urged that they take a longer look. The Angels headed for the season opener in Chicago with two rookie pitchers, Dean Chance and Bo Belinsky, on the 28-man squad that would be cut to 25 a month later.

It was two weeks later before Bo started for the first time, Rigney being devoid of alternatives for the April 19 day game against Kansas City at Dodger Stadium. Bo prepared in his customary fashion, getting to bed at four or five in the morning.

"Sex always relaxed me, nobody ever died from it," Bo said, ignoring the potential danger of promiscuous relationships.

This time, however, Belinsky knew the importance of the next day's assignment. "I knew it was win or else," he said. "I knew I was just hanging on and that I would have been long gone if the writers hadn't made me a celebrity and front office hadn't pressured Rigney into keeping me."

Bo responded by restricting Kansas City to two runs through seven innings. Art Fowler came on to save Belinsky's first major league victory. Four days later, he beat Cleveland for No. 2, and five days later he went nine innings for the first time, shutting out Washington, 3–0. Within ten more days he would have two more wins, including the no-hitter, which was that much sweeter since it came against the Orioles.

"Everybody wanted me at Hollywood parties," Belinsky said. "Playing baseball seemed only incidental. It was a little too much, even for me. I mean, after hustling in pool halls and living on candy bars, this was something else."

"This" was never going to bed before four a.m., never going to bed alone. It was Walter Winchell and Ann-Margret and Tina Louise and Juliet Prowse. It was the promised raise to $8,500 and a candy-apple-red Cadillac convertible.

Suddenly the record that reached 6–1 began to deteriorate. Bo lost six of his next seven decisions. The girls didn't seem to mind but the Angels did. They warned him about his night life and fined him for missing curfew. Rigney assigned pitching coach Marv Grissom to room with him on the road. Bo never had to look hard for roomies at home.

One night, accompanied by Chance and two girls as he drove home from the customary party, Belinsky lost his cool. It was one of those times when Bo wasn't in the mood to hear his date tell him how much she loved him and wanted to stay with him. He pulled the car over and attempted to pull her out. The girl grabbed the door handle and held on, ultimately suffering facial cuts when her head crashed against the windshield. The melee and its accompanying screams attracted the police, and all four were taken to the nearest precinct, where the police attempted to get the girl to sign a complaint against Belinsky. She considered and then told Bo, " won't sign if you promise to stay with me all week."

Belinsky, understanding the difference between discretion and valor, jumped at the proposition.

Years later, however, he said, "You think she showed any gratitude? Hell, no. She eventually got an attorney and sued me for $150,000. My lawyer had to give her a few bucks to get her out of town, to keep her mouth shut."

The incident created more headlines, and the Angels responded by fining Belinsky and Chance, who was married at the time, $500 each, tip money in baseball's current economy. It was a particularly costly evening, but not one that changed the lifestyles of either Chance or Belinsky.

"Nobody," said Chance, looking back on their careers, "made it with girls the way Bo did. I never learned his secret, but I enjoyed trying."

Albie Pearson roomed with Bo briefly and said he had two jobs, one as a ballplayer and one as Bo's answering service.

"When I roomed with him," Pearson said, "it was like rooming with his suitcase. I'd never see him at night."

Late in the 1962 season, with the Angels making their surprising pennant bid, Haney negotiated the acquisition of relief pitcher Dan Osinski from the then Kansas City A's for cash and a player to be named later, specifically Belinsky.

Trades of that type are made all the time, with the two clubs inevitably agreeing at the time of consummation on who the player to be named will be. In this instance, the Angels saw the need for another relief pitcher during the final weeks of the season. They'd also had enough of Bo's extracurricular activities, but were unable to trade him at that time because of waiver restrictions and because they didn't want to part with his arm during those final weeks.

Bo learned about his involvement in the trade from Kansas City manager Hank Bauer. He had no desire to give up Hollywood for a quiet little city in the Midwest, and he knew by making public the fact that the A's and Angels had already agreed on his inclusion in the deal, and the fact that the Angels had already agreed to trade a player who might be pitching for them in the World Series, he would force the league office to investigate a procedure that goes on all the time.

Thus, after a game in New York, knowing he would get broadest coverage in the media capital, Belinksy announced, "I've been traded to the A's as the player to be named later in the Osinski deal and I'm not going."

Both Haney and Rigney were livid. They knew at once that they could not now trade Belinsky and that they would spend the day making false denials. The then commissioner, Ford Frick, said it was strictly an American League matter, and the American League said it was strictly a club matter. The buck finally stopped at the desks of Haney and the Kansas City owner, Charles Finley. They agreed Belinsky was no longer the player to be announced later; it would be pitcher Ted Bowsfield instead.

Belinsky could keep his Hollywood pad. He was still with the Angels, still rooming with Chance when they celebrated the end of the 1963 Palm Springs encampment with a little party that resulted in their reporting more than an hour late to the final workout. They had started the new season in the same manner they had closed the old one, drawing $500 fines each.

That was the good news. Some two months later, on May 26, Bo got the bad. He was summoned to Rigney's office and told that because of his 1–7 record he was being sent to Hawaii, then the tropical location of the club's Triple A franchise. Some bad news! It was love at first sight.

"I had a chance to pull myself together," he said. "Hollywood had been great, but in Hawaii I could set my own pace. I had also never seen so many beautiful girls in my life. The whole thing was out of this world."

So was Bo's pitching. He was 4–1 with a 2.50 ERA when recalled by the Angels in late August. Belinksy was depressed. He considered not reporting. Then he decided that the Angels still represented the brightest lights and flew back to a royal reception from the Hollywood crowd. He was 1–2 over the remainder of the season and was invited to do two weeks with comedian Hank Henry at the Silver Slipper in Las Vegas, receiving $1,000 a week. Chance flew in to visit him, blew $1,500 the first night and immediately flew home.

Belinsky returned to Hollywood for the rest of the winter and signed a 1964 contract for $15,000, a raise of $2,000 despite his horrendous season. He could also take comfort in a still warm relationship with Mamie Van Doren, would-be successor to Marilyn Monroe as Hollywood's sex symbol.

Bo and Mamie had met in 1962, introduced by her former husband, bandleader Ray Anthony. They were soon seen everywhere together, including the ballpark, where Mamie became a fixture, bringing the Angels the type of publicity that they couldn't attain with their play.

"She's great to be with," Bo told the press, saying her only fault was that she didn't allow him to smoke in the bedroom.

The publicity and constant presence of the actress ultimately prompted Rigney to tell Bo that if he wouldn't spend so much time with Mamie, he might win more games. Bo bit his tongue. He wanted to tell his manager that if he also had more runs and better defense he might win more games.

The relationship with Mamie shifted between hot and cold, on and off, until finally, in April 1963, in an effort, Belinsky would say later, to get the press off their back, Bo told reporter Bud Furillo that they were engaged. Furillo asked Mamie about it, and she said, "If Bo says we're engaged, then we're engaged."

What Bo said was: "Engaged is one thing, married is a different game." Bo wasn't ready to play and the engagement ultimately dissolved, Mamie returning his $2,000 diamond ring only after he had hired a detective to gather evidence that she was being as disloyal as she claimed Bo was.

Remarkably, the end of the engagement created new ardor, and Bo and Mamie remained good friends until she finally was successful in getting a left-handed pitcher to the altar, marrying 19-year-old minor league pitcher Lee Meyers, who was killed several years later in a car accident.

Bo still speaks of Mamie in only the best terms, and they were still good friends in 1964, his last year with the Angels, a year in which he again was twice fined $500. The first fine was levied during spring training when the team's Palm Springs hotel complained about the mess Bo and his female gymnastics partner had created when they failed to clean up a room-service cart they had kicked over at the high point of their exercises. The second was levied when Bo stepped out of a cab in a suit and tie at four a.m. and confronted Rigney and his teammates in their pajamas, having been routed by a fire at their Boston hotel.

The incident, however, that finally ended Bo's career with the Angels took place in the early hours of August 14, 1964, after Bo had been hit hard and victimized by poor defense in a loss to Cleveland at Dodger Stadium the preceding afternoon. Only Charles Maher, then of the Associated Press, went to the clubhouse to talk to Bo after the game. Belinsky was frustrated and discouraged and expressed those sentiments while also saying he was thinking about quitting. Maher reported it all in the context that Bo probably didn't mean it, since he was depressed after a tough defeat.

Maher wrote his story as the Angels and their press corps flew east for a series in Washington, D.C. The team arrived at the Shoreham Hotel about 1:30 a.m. Chance and Belinsky went out to dinner, returning about 3:00. They were in the room only a few minutes when the phone rang. It was Braven Dyer of the *Los Angeles Times*.

"I want to talk to you about that story you gave Maher about quitting," Dyer said, according to Bo.

"I didn't tell him I was quitting," Belinsky responded, "and who are you to tell me what I can and can't tell him?"

"I want to write a story for my paper," Dyer said, "and I want to know if you're quitting."

"Shut up and stay out of my way, you old bastard," Belinsky said.

"Don't you curse me," replied Dyer.

"Look, Dyer, I've had enough of your crap for three years. You've been ripping me ever since I got here. I won't put up with it anymore. Stay the hell away from me. If you ever come within two feet of me again, I'll put your face in the toilet bowl and flush it."

"You're a gutless son of a bitch," said Dyer. "Let's see you do it. I'll be right up."

"You do that," said Bo. "You come up here and I flush your head in the toilet bowl."

Chance and Belinsky sat on the bed and talked for ten minutes. Nobody came. Chance started the water for a bath. Bo called the front desk and ordered all calls stopped until noon. He put the Do Not Disturb sign on the door.

The disturbance followed. Dyer reached the players' room, loosened his tie and removed his jacket, hanging it on the doorknob of the room next door. Chance was in the bath and Belinsky was brushing his teeth when they heard the knock. Bo walked to the door carrying the cup of water he had been using to brush his teeth.

Belinsky later told reporters that Dyer stepped into the room and said, "Now, you gutless son of a bitch, let's see you put my head in the toilet bowl."

The following exchange ensued, according to Bo:

"For crissakes, Braven, go back to your room and sober up."

"Go ahead, tough guy, let's see you put me on my ass, let's see you," said Dyer.

Dyer, according to Belinsky, pushed his way into the room, his chest against Bo's. "I didn't want to have to hit him," Bo said. "I threw the glass of water at him, hoping it would sober him up and make him leave."

Instead, Bo continued, Dyer reached into Belinsky's open attaché case, pulled out a bottle of hair tonic and swung it at Bo, the bottle grazing his face.

"It was at that point," Belinsky said, "that I flattened him with my left hand."

Said Dyer, since deceased, "It was Bo who initiated the phone calls. He had found out that I had written he was quitting, and he wanted me to change the story. I told him it was too late, and he told me he was going to stick my head in the toilet. He called me a nasty name. I wasn't going to take that and I went to his room. We argued for a couple of minutes, and I turned to look for Dean. Bo was holding a can of shaving cream, and it was at that moment he hit me. I never reached for a bottle of [anything], and I never held a grudge against him. The whole thing would have been forgotten if he had been man enough to apologize."

Bo's punch landed on Dyer's right ear. The reporter fell backward, his head slamming against the wall. His mouth was open, his eyes shut and blood covered his face as he lay propped slightly against the wall.

Chance called trainer Freddie Frederico, who called Rigney. Both rushed to the room.

"I thought Braven was dead," Rigney recalled. "I turned to Bo and Dean and told them that I didn't want to hear their lies."

Dyer was revived with smelling salts and went to the hospital for precautionary X rays and treatment of the cuts.

Rigney called Haney and then informed Bo that he was being suspended without pay. He told Bo that the club would return him to Los Angeles and then contact him shortly.

Bo was angry. He believed that Rigney wasn't interested in his side, didn't care why Dyer had come to *his* room, and was so determined to get him off the team that he wouldn't even ask Chance what had happened.

"I was sick," Bo said. "I felt like I was just about to hit the big money. I felt like I was just learning how to pitch, to win in the major leagues. I was on the verge of becoming a big star, and now here I was, guilty without a trial."

Bo left with a 9–8 record and 2.87 ERA. "I was pitching as well as Dean at that point," he said, "and Dean went on to win the Cy Young Award. I'd have gone on to win 15 or 18 games. The Angels hurt me, but they hurt themselves even more."

A week passed while Bo and his attorney, Paul Caruso, studied their options. The Angels then announced they were optioning Bo to Hawaii, additionally angering him. "I'm their best pitcher," he said. "How can they ship me out?"

The Angels decided on the move as a means of countering possible litigation had Bo remained on the suspended list. Bo and Caruso went to New York in a futile attempt to meet with Commissioner Ford Frick, who in the grand tradition of the game at that time said only that it was a club matter.

Bo had a last fling with his Hollywood friends and headed for Hawaii, determined to relax and enjoy it, certain that he was through as a ballplayer.

The Angels, however, weren't high on the idea of Bo simply becoming a beach bum. It wasn't that they were particularly concerned about what happened to him, but rather that they didn't want to lose a 27-year-old left-hander without getting anything in return.

Thus, on the last day of the baseball winter meetings in December, they announced Belinsky had been traded to Philadelphia.

It was the end of one chapter, the start of another. Philadelphia, Houston, Pittsburgh, St. Louis, Cincinnati. A total of eight more wins and a string of empty bottles, empty hopes. Along the way a marriage that didn't work, to former *Playboy* centerfold Jo Collins, the mother of his son, Stevie.

Since then another failed marriage, this to a Weyerhaeuser heiress he met by rescuing her from the surf in Hawaii, where Bo spent several years at the end of his career, ultimately entering an alcohol abuse program and becoming a spokesman for it. He now works for a car agency in Las Vegas but stays away from the neon that once lighted his course.

His former roomie, Ohio farm boy Dean Chance, won 20 games again for Minnesota in 1967, held out for a $60,000 contract the next spring, injured his back rushing to get in shape and was never the same pitcher while also performing for the New York Mets and Detroit Tigers in a career that extended through the 1971 season.

Chance saved some money and bought some Ohio farm land that he leases out. He has managed boxers, including heavyweight contender Earnie Shavers, and he continues to manage several touring carnival shows, describing the state fairs as his World Series.

Regrets? Well . . .

"I came to the Angels as a kid who thought he had been pushed around by life, by minor league baseball," Belinsky said. "I was selfish and immature in a lot of ways, and I tried to cover that up.

"I went from a major league ballplayer to hanging on to a brown bag under the bridge, but I had my moments and I have my memories. If I had the attitude about life then that I have now, I'd have done a lot of things differently. But you make your rules and you play by them. I knew the bills would come due eventually, and I knew I wouldn't be able to cover them."

6

1962: FIRST ON THE FOURTH

The bills were a long way from coming due when Belinsky got off to his 5–0 start in 1962, providing much of the early impetus as the Angels fashioned one of the most remarkable seasons ever by a young expansion team, although the promise was short-lived.

The mood and style were established late in spring training when the Dodgers, flying west from their Florida training base for the season opener in the new stadium at Chavez Ravine, stopped in Palm Springs to play the first of what became an annual series of exhibition games with the Angels, who would come from behind to win in 35 games that year, 18 in their last at-bat.

They set the tone on April 2 before an overflow crowd of 5,181 at the Palm Springs Polo Grounds by winning the "City Championship" via a 6–5 victory over the swaggering Dodgers. Albie Pearson hit a three-run homer off the Dodgers' money pitcher, Johnny Podres, to tie the game in the eighth, and Joe Koppe singled in the winning run off Pete Richert in the ninth.

The teams met twice before the start of the 1963 season and twice before the start of the 1964 season, with the Angels stretching their winning streak to five before the frustrated Dodgers temporarily bowed out of the series. Dodger general manager Buzzie Bavasi insisted that it was impractical for a club that trained in Florida to fly to California for a preseason exhibition game and then fly east again to open the season, but it would be divulged later that owner Walter O'Malley was simply embarrassed over his club's inability to beat the Angels and also angered by the Angels' plan, by 1964, to end their tenancy at Dodger Stadium in favor of constructing their own home in Anaheim.

The two teams would not play again until 1969, when the Dodgers ended the five-game losing streak by beating the Angels at Anaheim Stadium. They have met annually ever since in what is now known as the Freeway Series, with the Angels still holding a 45–40 advantage and clearly prospering from the arrangement. Six times in the period between 1979 and 1987, when Anaheim Stadium seating had been expanded to almost 70,000 to accommodate the Los Angeles Rams, the Angels drew more than 60,000 for games with the Dodgers, helping defray spring training expenses.

In 1962, 35 years before the introduction of interleague play would find the Dodgers and Angels also meeting in regular season games, all freeways led to O'Malley's magnificent new stadium only a few miles from City Hall, where much politicking had been done before the Dodger owner finally was able to build his dream house, overcoming the opposition of a public referendum based on the contention that the city was simply giving away valuable land. The Dodgers and their stadium eventually played a significant role in the downtown renaissance, with a then record attendance of 2.7 million in that inaugural season merely the first indication of a boom that would see the Dodgers become the first team to draw more than three million in 1978 and frequently eclipse that figure in ensuing years.

The Angels also prospered at the start, drawing 1,144,063 in their first season as tenants, almost double what they had drawn in Wrigley Field. The Angels' improbable success on the field that year kept turnstiles humming, particularly when Mantle, Maris and the Yankees visited.

A three-game series with New York in June attracted 146,623, an Angel record at the time, including Marilyn Monroe, who was scheduled to make a presentation before the first game. "You'll do it at home plate," a club official told her. "Where's that?" she asked.

The Yankees attracted more than 120,000 for each of two ensuing three-game visits to Los Angeles, which they looked forward to it as much as the fans did. Johnny Grant, a disc jockey then for Autry's KMPC, held nightly parties for the Yankees at his San Fernando Valley home, with some of Hollywood's loveliest starlets attending. The parties seldom ended before dawn, and the Yankees seldom looked quite as fierce the next night. Grant would never confirm a theory that Autry sponsored the parties in an attempt to weaken his team's most vaunted adversary—as if the second-year Angels needed that assistance during a compelling summer. Eli Grba would look back years later and say the camaraderie and competitive zeal of that season would stay with him always. Fueled by characters such as Ryne Duren, Art Fowler, Leon Wagner, Mad Dog Thomas and Ted Bowsfield, the Angels rode a spiritual high, a bus that came to be known as Desire.

Autry and Leonard Firestone found out about it when they took the team bus to the airport after a game in Washington, D.C. An East Coast air defense test delayed the Angels' flight, and the team spent several hours in Duke Ziebert's restaurant, depleting Duke's beer and wine supply. They were headed for a four-game September series in Yankee Stadium, the pennant on the line, but it was hard to tell. The players made Autry and Firestone sit in the back of the bus and subjected them to the blackest of gallows humor, a trademark during a season in which the club's press corps continually wrote about those wacky rides.

Loose?

"If we win this thing," Rigney said at one point, "they might have to cancel the World Series because they'll never be able to find all my players after the pennant celebration."

In the type of high jinx that characterized the season, Rigney once called on Earl Averill to pinch-hit, and Averill raced to the bat rack, tore off his jacket and ran onto the field wearing a football jersey.

It was definitely another time and place. Economics didn't dominate the industry, agents were known only in Hollywood and the accompanying beat writers were considered almost part of the club. The castoff Angels were happy to have a uniform. They played hard and partied hard.

Fowler and Duren sharpened an Abbott and Costello routine and were featured in every cocktail lounge in the American League. Duren, of course, seldom stopped when the lounges closed. He paraded up and down the corridor of a Baltimore hotel one night, looking for a drinking partner. Finally, concerned that the noise would attract security, Grba, wearing only shorts, emerged from his room and flattened Duren with a solid right. He then hoisted the relief pitcher over his shoulder and carried him down five flights, depositing him in his own room. It was one of the few times starter Grba was credited with a save on behalf of reliever Duren.

Rigney, who displayed a Midas touch throughout the season, emerged as the American League's Manager of the Year. Fred Haney was named Executive of the Year. Billy Moran was the All-Star second baseman, and Leon Wagner the All-Star right fielder and Player of the Game in the second of the two All-Star games that were then played every year. Wags hit his club record 37 homers that year and drove in 107 runs. The leading hitter was a 20-year-old shortstop named Jim Fregosi, who played the final 58 games after being recalled from Triple A to replace Joe Koppe.

That spring Tom Sheehan, a veteran Giants scout, had stood next to Rigney during an Angels workout in Palm Springs and asked, "Who's the kid at short?"

"Fregosi," Rigney replied. "Jim Fregosi. We drafted him from Boston, and he's going to be a great one."

"Don't be ridiculous," Sheehan said. "You can find shortstops like him under every rock in Arizona." Sheehan would eventually apologize, admitting to Rigney he had made a mistake.

Fregosi, a state broad-jump champion and winner of 11 letters at Serra High School in San Mateo, California, ultimately retired in possession of virtually every Angels offensive record to that time, having appeared in six All-Star games. He was Rigney's favorite and Autry's favorite, the team leader on the field and the manager when the Angels ended 19 years of frustration by winning the Western Division title in 1979.

Fregosi had been selected in the expansion draft because the Angels were fortunate to have the Giants' and Dodgers' scouting reports, the information that also produced Dean Chance and Buck Rodgers, among others.

Chance was 14–10 in his rookie season, performing as both starter and reliever, the leading winner on a 1962 staff that also featured Ken McBride (11–5), the irrepressible Bo (10–11) and bullpen requiring reservations, what with Duren, Fowler, Morgan Jack Spring and Dan Osinski fighting for mound time. Rigney used them all. In future years he would develop a reputation as a Captain Hook, the label applied to all managers who are quick to yank their starting pitchers. However, in 1962 he had no choice.

The rules governing the allocating of a save were stricter then Yet Duren had nine, Morgan and Fowler seven each, and Spring six. Osinski arrived late in the year, the man for whom Belinsky was originally to be traded to Kansas City.

Osinski was a 6–1, 195-pound Pole from Chicago, one of the most powerful players ever to perform for the Angels. He proved it during an end-of-the-year party on the road, picking up rotund sportswriter Bud Tucker and dangling him out the window of a 15th-floor hotel suite by his heels.

"I was afraid," Tucker would say later, "someone would hand Danny a drink, and he would drop me and reach for the glass."

Buck Rodgers hailed from Prospect, Ohio, and immediately became the "Prospect from Prospect." He caught 155 games that year breaking the American League's rookie record of 134 set by the legendary Mickey Cochrane in 1925. Rodgers batted .258, drove in 61 runs and was second to Tom Tresh in balloting for the Rookie of the Year Award.

He and Fregosi also began to lay the groundwork for their managerial careers, spending countless hours in countless coffee shops with Rigney, delving into the managerial textbook, acquiring the tools that would allow them to play with intelligence and later become managers themselves. Fregosi would pilot the Angels, Chicago White Sox, Philadelphia Phillies, whom he led to a National League pennant in 1993, and Toronto Blue Jays. Rodgers would manage the Milwaukee Brewers, Montreal Expos and Angels.

"They always cared," said Rigney, speaking of Fregosi's and Rodgers' devotion to the game, which rivaled his own.

The Angels passed their 1961 victory total on August 19 of 1962 and finished the season 86–76, 10 games behind the Yankees and five behind the third-place Minnesota Twins. A doubleheader sweep of Washington had brought the second-year Angels back to Los Angeles on July 4 in first place. Owners Autry and Reynolds were among the 3,000 fans who greeted them at the airport. A headline written by Mal Florence in the morning *Times* read: "Heaven Can Wait! Angels in 1st on 4th."

And they might have stayed there, a magical, mystical blend of prospects and rejects, young and old, registering the most unlikely pennant victory ever, if it hadn't been for three freak injuries of the type that has haunted the club throughout its history.

It was in early April that outfielder Ken Hunt, who had driven in 84 runs and slugged 25 homers the year before, broke his collarbone flexing a bat behind his shoulder while waiting to hit in the on-deck circle. Hunt did not play again until late September and ended the season with only one home run and one RBI. He was limited to 59 games the next year and forced to retire at 30.

Consistent production from Wagner, Moran and Lee Thomas compensated some for Hunt's loss, helping keep the Angels in the race until the devastating loss of pitchers Fowler and McBride on consecutive days in early August.

Fowler went down first, nailed by a line drive off the bat of Ed Sadowski during pregame practice in Boston on August 6. The 40-year-old relief pitcher required nine stitches to close a cut above his left eye and did not pitch again that season, eventually losing sight in the eye.

He appeared in 59 games in 1963, and was still getting minor league hitters out in his late 40s. But the accident in Boston had deprived him of the assuredness that was his trademark, the ability to throw strikes as if blessed with radar.

The irony stayed with Fowler. He was a man who loathed pregame running drills—"I've never seen a guy win 20 games by running the ball to the plate," he liked to say—but he had been unable to escape those drills on the night of August 6, when he was struck on the outfield grass by Sadowski's liner as he headed to the dugout after completing his pregame obligations.

The next day, McBride, who had earlier won 10 straight games, was discovered to have a cracked rib, the apparent result of a prolonged bout with pleurisy. The doctors said McBride would be out only two weeks. It was closer to six. The ace of the staff had only one decision over the final six weeks, and that was a loss.

Nevertheless, the Angels were still only 4½ games behind New York when they went to Yankee Stadium for a Labor Day doubleheader that drew 55,705, the largest crowd to have yet seen the Angels play. The Yankees won the opener, 8–2, and were ahead, 5–0, after seven innings of the second game. The Angels bubble seemed ready to burst, but Albie Pearson hit a two-run homer in the eighth and the Angels scored four in the ninth to salvage a 6–5 win.

They continued to play with persistence the next night, rallying from a 4–0 deficit to again defeat the Yankees, 7–6, and close to within 3½ game of the lead. A 6–5 loss in the series finale made it a deficit of 4½ again, but two wins in an ensuing three-game series at Baltimore and a two-game shutout sweep engineered by Chance (with a one-hitter in which Fregosi hit his first major league homer) and Grba at Minnesota enabled the Angels to return for their final home stand trailing by only four.

Inexplicably, it was at this point that the miracle expired. The Angels lost six in a row to Kansas City, Detroit and Baltimore. They won only four of the final 16 games—an omen, perhaps, in that September has long been one of the Angels' least favorite months.

The bus named Desire was at last stalled, finally on empty, but hardly, it seemed, an outdated model in need of a major overhaul.

And yet it would be several years before the Angels were again a factor in the pennant race, the surprising success of 1962 slowly taking on the appearance of a fluke rather than what it was, what it should have been, a springboard to bigger and better years.

The mistake the owners had made in withdrawing their profits and investments after the 1961 season was compounded when they and others saw more in the 1962 success than was there, believing that since it had come so easily, why pour money into the farm system? They made a waiver deal here, a minor league acquisition there, a patchwork approach to a patchwork team.

"In its final form," co-owner Robert Reynolds said years later, "the effect of 1962 was harmful. From top to bottom, we overestimated what we had and what we had to do. We were lulled into a false sense of security."

7

FRUITION AND FRUSTRATION ON THE FARM

Rooming together in their first spring with the Angels, Rick Reichardt and Tom Egan came to be known as The Millionaires Club. They were far from millionaires, but in baseball's financial context of the mid-60s they had received signing bonuses that attracted national attention.

Reichardt, a 21-year-old outfielder from the University of Wisconsin, and Egan, an 18-year-old catcher from Rancho High in Whittier, California, were two of the country's most coveted athletes among those eligible to be signed in June 1964.

This was at a time when any amateur free agent was fair game for any club. The introduction of the amateur draft was still a year away. Both Reichardt and Egan received bonus offers from all 20 teams. Both signed with the Angels. Egan received a bonus of $100,000. Reichardt doubled that. Some 34 years later, when the amateur draft had truly turned into a millionaires' club, the Angels signed their top pick, infielder Troy Glaus, for $2.25 million.

In 1964, however, Reichardt and Egan were news.

Gene Autry, who personally led the hunt for both players, noted that the Reichardt bonus was more than the studios used to budget for one of his movies and far more than the star generally received.

"As soon as I hand him the check," Autry said, "I'm going to ask for a loan."

The benefits the Angels hoped to accrue never materialized. Reichardt retired at 30, having spent only three-plus seasons with the Angels and six-plus in the majors. Egan also retired at 30, having never been anything more than an irregular for either the Angels or Chicago White Sox. Both were victims of the type of physical misfortune that has plagued the club. Both, to some measure, characterized the frustrations that have long haunted a scouting and developmental system victimized at times by limited financial support and an inconsistent philosophy.

The revolving door on the general manager's office led to sweeping changes in the scouting and farm staff and frequent changes in the club's direction. The system's best products were frequently traded in an effort to win today. The division titles of 1979, 1982 and 1986 featured lineups dominated by players obtained from other organizations.

It was not until the 90s, in fact, as Gene and Jackie Autry tightened the saddle bags to prevent further debt and payroll escalation, that the Angels made a total commitment to their system and stayed with it, producing and maintaining with multiyear contracts an impressive lineup of homegrown talent, including shortstop Gary DiSarcina, outfielders Darin Erstad, Garret Anderson, Tim Salmon and Jim Edmonds, pitcher Chuck Finley, and closer Troy Percival.

"Was there a lot of short-term thinking?" said Tony Tavares, the club president under Disney, reflecting on the club's history in 1999. "I think so, and I think that was the result of frustration. Of course, if I had been president when the 'win one for the Cowboy' concept was prevalent, I might have been just as guilty. It's human nature to look for short-term solutions when you don't win year after year. Was that done too much? Historically we can say it was. They traded away a lot of good young talent in pursuit of a championship.

"If we're smart, we should learn something from that history. I firmly believe that the way to win championships in hockey and baseball is off the small foundation that you build through the draft, making solid moves and not trading away a lot of prospects. You have to have answers from within—otherwise you are constantly chasing free agents and you are constantly hoping that the free agents you sign are going to perform as opposed to using their contracts as a retirement package."

And building from within, Tavares added, is the best way to deal with the black cloud that has hovered over the franchise.

"I don't believe this franchise is always destined to have something go wrong," he said. "I think you can work your way through those kinds of things, but you have to be able to find answers from within the organization. A lot of the problems over the years have been injury-related, and the club was always forced to go outside the organization to try and find solutions with free agents. There just wasn't a lot of player development, and it was a very damaging process."

It wasn't that the Angels didn't produce bona fide major leaguers. The hurt was that few started and finished their careers with the Angels. Many reached their potential and/or sustained their careers elsewhere.

Among the best who fit in those categories: First basemen Wally Joyner, Willie Aikens, Lee Stevens and Bruce Bochte. Second basemen Damion Easley, Mark McLemore and Jerry Remy. Shortstop Dickie Thon. Third baseman Carney Lansford. Outfielders Devon White, Dante Bichette, Tom Brunansky, Gary Pettis and Ken Landreaux.

The purpose of a farm system is twofold: to supply talent to the major league club and to supply talent for the major league club to trade. Relying on the 20–20 of hindsight, it can be said the Angels traded wisely in a few cases, but prematurely, impetuously and foolishly in too many others, giving up on young talent out of frustration, impatience and that desire to get Autry a ring.

Among the aforementioned, for instance:

- Bichette became one of baseball's best power hitters after being traded for a washed-up Dave Parker.
- Brunansky established his power credentials in Minnesota after being traded for relief pitcher Doug Corbett, a bust with the Angels.
- Lansford, on the verge of winning an American League batting title and the best position player developed by the Angels to that point,

was traded for an All-Star shortstop, Rick Burleson, who blew out his shoulder a year later.

- Easley became an All-Star after being traded for pitcher Greg Gohr, nothing before and nothing after the trade.
- White remained a premier center fielder and became a consistently productive hitter after being traded for two utility types, Luis Sojo and Junior Felix.
- McLemore developed into a regular on contending teams in Baltimore and Texas after being traded for a backup catcher, Ron Tingley.

"You've got to give your young players a chance to mature," said Jim Fregosi, the man who piloted the club to its first division title in 1979 only to be fired less than 20 months later.

"With the Angels, they were always building through the farm system one year, then going with free agents the next. It's different now. They have some stability, but for a long time they never had the same six or seven [front office] people working together over the years for the same goals. They had it for a time in the early years but weren't willing to put their money into the development of a foundation."

The scouting and drafting of high school and college players is an inexact science. There are no guarantees. Every club has a litany of hits and misses. The list of players selected by the Angels who have reached the major leagues is not unimpressive, but many realized their potential or sustained their careers after having been traded or allowed to leave as free agents, and it is a list woefully short on pitchers—often forcing the Angels to deal in a suspect market of fringe veterans and injured arms.

Through almost four decades the Angels have produced only two 20-game winners—Clyde Wright and Andy Messersmith—and only a few others, Jim McGlothlin, Frank Tanana, Mike Witt, Chuck Finley, Kirk McCaskill and Jim Abbott, who had significant success in a starting capacity. Amid the expansion-diluted process of the 80s and 90s, the Angels chose 24 pitchers in the first five rounds of the 1989 through 1996 drafts, but only eight made it to Anaheim, and only four—Brian Anderson, Joe Grahe, Phil Leftwich and Jarrod Washburn—won more than a game.

"It definitely would be nice if you had a crystal ball," said Bob Fontaine Jr., forced to resign as the Angels' respected scouting director in another front office shakeup after the 1999 season and a man who otherwise filled the 90s lineups with homegrown talent, creating stability despite budget restrictions—particularly in the final years of the Autry ownership.

In 1994, for instance, the Angels passed on Jaret Wright, the hard-throwing right-hander who went to high school in the shadow of Anaheim Stadium and who is the son of Clyde Wright, a familiar name in Angel history. The senior Wright pitched a no-hitter for the Angels, set a club record with 22 wins in 1970 and is a member of the club's speakers bureau. Nepotism and need gave way to signability in the case of his son.

Instead of Wright, the Angels used their sixth pick on high school outfielder McKay Christensen. The Cleveland Indians selected Wright, now one of baseball's best young pitchers, with the 10th pick and signed him for $1.2 million. The Angels invested a comparatively modest $700,000 to sign Christensen, who promptly left on a two-year Mormon mission and was traded to the White Sox even before he got back.

"I don't think our philosophy or commitment changed," said Bill Bavasi, Buzzie's son and a member of the front office from 1984 through 1999, when he resigned as general manager. "The attitude has always been, 'Let's go out and try to win now while protecting our farm system.' Naturally, when a trade doesn't work, it looks like you've mortgaged the future, but I don't remember seeing any deal that said, 'to hell with the future.' The only thing that resembled that was Brunansky for Corbett (in 1982), and then only because Corbett failed.

"I mean, there may have been an instance or two where we backed off drafting a player recently because we knew he was going to ask more than we wanted to pay, but I think we changed with the industry and our recent commitment was greater than ever because we expanded our international operation.

"You have to be in the international market if you want to be a major player in major league baseball. We had always thrown in just enough to say we were involved [internationally], but never enough to really say we were developing. It's an area where the better franchises have excelled developmentally and where we failed by a wide and glaring gap. We had begun to turn that around."

The Angels under Disney have a revived and expanded presence in Latin America and the Caribbean, a fertile and mandatory hunting ground in an era of expansion-diluted talent and intense domestic competition from football, basketball and other sports—but an area long neglected by the Angels, who have never signed, developed and benefited from a Hispanic impact player. Now the club has as many as 10 scouts working internationally, and the improved budget can be characterized by the $900,000 signing of 17-year-old Venezuelan pitcher Francisco Rodriguez in the winter of 1998. In addition, the Angels top prospect entering the 1999 season was 23-year-old pitcher Ramon Ortiz of the Dominican Republic, and the club had high hopes for two Dominican shortstops, Nelson Castro and Bienvenido Encarnacion, as well as infielder Carlos Gastellum of Mexico and Trent Durrington from Australia.

"It's still a ways away," Fontaine said in reference to reaping the rewards of the international operation prior to his resignation. "We had only worked heavily in that area for the last two years. It's probably a five- or six-year process. We were hoping that by the fifth or sixth year we might start to have a flow of people ready for the big leagues."

Venezuela, of course, is a long way from the mother lode that the Angels might have mined in Southern California during their formative years if the success of 1962 had not created that false sense of security and the owners had not withdrawn their initial investments from the profits of 1961.

The free agent draft wasn't initiated until 1965, meaning the Angels had four years in which to sweep their own backyard for talent, offering as a new team a quicker route to the majors, a potentially shorter wait for youngsters who might be backed up and lost in organizations such as the Dodgers and New York Yankees.

The opportunity was squandered. The Angels signed 289 college and high school free agents in the four years before the draft, but only three or four had any impact on the club.

Jim McGlothlin, signed in 1961, pitched successfully for several seasons and was traded in 1969 for the controversial Alex Johnson. Tom Satriano and Paul Schaal, also signed in '61, gave some early solidarity to the infield. Ed Kirkpatrick (1962) and Jay Johnstone (1963) fashioned long careers but had their best years with other teams, both leaving in trades that proved less than memorable.

"Haney's approach," said an Angel scout a few years later, "was based on quantity. He'd spend $100,000 to sign ten players, but he hated the idea of giving it all to one. He came from the old school and had difficulty coming to grips with the idea of big signing bonuses. He believed in numbers alone there was always the chance of finding that diamond in the rough."

While area scouts such as Tuffie Hashem and Rosey Gilhousen were considered among baseball's best, Haney had also assembled a staff of older cronies who tended to be outhustled in an area dominated by the Dodgers, compounding the frustrations of farm director Roland Hemond, who looked back and said it was difficult for the Angels to establish an identity.

"We were second fiddle to the Dodgers in every regard," he said. "Our scouts not only had to introduce themselves, they had to explain who the Angels were."

The major scouting successes were at the minor league level. Operating frequently with limited funds and on the patchwork philosophy that followed the 1962 success, the club's scouts scoured the minors to effectively plug holes the farm system couldn't keep plugged, helping the Angels win 80 or more games four times in the first seven years. Billy Moran, Joe Koppe, Felix Torres, Bob Lee, Minnie Rojas, Bo Belinsky and Aurelio Rodriguez were among the minor league players acquired via trade, purchase or the December draft, with Haney's assistant, Marvin Milkes, providing significant insights and connections.

Rigney called Milkes his special weapon. He would soon need others, since the stopgap approach adopted by all expansion clubs was never designed as a panacea. The Angels' inability to construct a foundation during those early, pre-draft years was compounded later when Autry established a revolving door to the front office and Haney, who retired after the 1968 season, was followed in an eight-year span by Dick Walsh, Harry Dalton and Buzzie Bavasi—

each new general manager bringing in a new farm director, new scouts and new philosophy.

Walsh replaced Haney and attempted to streamline the scouting system, dismissing some scouts, reassigning others and placing the Angels in a scouting co-op with the Chicago Cubs, Atlanta Braves and Yankees. Roland Hemond quit to become a vice president with the White Sox and was replaced by Tom Sommers, a former player in the Angels' system.

That system, Walsh said when he took over, was devoid of talent. There was no question about it after Walsh finished negotiating a series of trades that cost the Angels Jay Johnstone, Tom Egan, Tom Bradley, Doug Griffin, Ken Tatum, Jarvis Tatum, Lloyd Allen, Jim Spencer, Rick Reichardt, Aurelio Rodriguez, Pedro Borbon, Jim McGlothlin, Tom Satriano, Bobby Knoop and others. Veterans and youngsters alike were traded by Walsh, who said there was no time for a five-year plan when you are competing with the Dodgers.

"You've got to go for broke every year," he said.

Walsh was fired at the end of the 1971 season, a few months after the club had enjoyed one of its most successful drafts, obtaining pitcher Frank Tanana, second baseman Jerry Remy and third baseman Ron Jackson, among others.

Harry Dalton, architect of the Baltimore dynasty, replaced Walsh and sang the same song, insisting there was nothing in the system. He brought in Walter Shannon, his scouting director at Baltimore, and a number of his key Baltimore scouts.

Dave Collins, Dave Chalk and Bruce Bochte were among the players drafted and signed in 1972; Julio Cruz and Thad Bosley came in 1974; Willie Aikens, Carney Lansford, Bobby Clark, Dickie Thon, Paul Hartzell and Danny Goodwin were obtained in 1975, and Ken Landreaux, a future .300 hitter for Minnesota, was acquired in 1976.

Dalton believed he was on schedule in reconstructing the farm system, but Autry surprisingly disagreed. He hired Buzzie Bavasi as executive vice president and chief financial officer late in the 1977 season and ordered Bavasi to tighten purse strings.

Despite the owner's desire to reestablish the farm system, Bavasi told Dalton to trim $400,000 from his player-development budget, which prompted Dalton to leave. He became general manager of the Milwaukee Brewers, taking Shannon and his scouts with him.

Those tightened purse strings yielded to another round of contradictions as Bavasi became general manager and, under Autry's urging, continued the free agent spending spree that Autry had initiated with the signing of Joe Rudi, Don Baylor and Bobby Grich—all emancipated by the 1976 changes in the reserve system, which created the new world of free agency.

The farm system that Autry didn't think Dalton was developing fast enough provided Bavasi with sought-after trade material in Thad Bosley, Richard Dotson, Willie Aikens, Danny Goodwin, Ken Landreaux, Ron Jackson and Dave Engle, among others. The new general manager cut into the scouting and instructional staffs. Son Bill ultimately contributed to the rebuilding as farm director, but the absence of continuity, the now you see it, now you don't brand of philosophy, had—and to an extent would continue to have—a damaging impact on the Angels.

Roland Hemond had seen it from the start. Exasperated by the club's failure to take a more affirmative approach to its farm system in the formative years, the initial farm and scouting director went to co-owner Robert Reynolds in the spring of 1964 and told him it was time to get more active or he was gone.

Hemond told Reynolds that this seemed to be a key year, with young talents such as Reichardt, Egan and Willie Crawford (who would ultimately sign with the Dodgers) available and that "if we're going to make strides we have to get more aggressive."

Reynolds agreed and authorized Hemond to begin an all-out pursuit of any or all of those three. Hemond called Autry and asked the Cowboy to head the pursuit of Reichardt, who would later say that the personal involvement of Autry and Reynolds was one reason he signed with the Angels.

Reichardt could have signed anywhere and, in fact, was offered considerably more by the Yankees and then Kansas City A's. The A's owner, Charles Finley, a man used to getting his way, was told by the young player that he could offer $1 million and "I still won't sign because I want to play in an area like Los Angeles or New York."

Reichardt represented Jack Armstrong, the All-American boy. He was the son of a noted surgeon and a premed major himself. He was the only player in Big Ten history to that point to lead the conference in batting for two consecutive years, and he was the Big Ten's leading receiver in 1963 as a star end on the Wisconsin football team that lost to USC in the Rose Bowl, 42–37. He was articulate and accessible, and he filled notebooks with comments such as:

- "My greatest fault is a lack of concentration. It's just that my mind is so active, it's conditioned to think quickly of many things."
- "The game requires a crystallization of thought. It requires dedication, discipline and determination."
- "The general jokes of the clubhouse [Reichardt was frequently needled and criticized about his fielding] don't bother me. Actually, it's a healthy situation, although I am concerned that sometimes a thing said in jest can be carried too far. We have a tendency to project our own inadequacies on others."
- "One or two shaky games are not indicative. It takes time and experience before you master the intricacies of each park."

Intricacies? Inadequacies? Reichardt brought a new language to the clubhouse. He received that record bonus and generated some record hype.

He was flown to Los Angeles for the signing ceremony and walloped an array of home runs during a special batting practice at Dodger Stadium. It was June 24, 1964.

"You think I wasn't impressed," manager Bill Rigney said. "He hadn't slept in 36 hours and he's rocketing balls out of here. The only other kid who impressed me that much was Willie Mays."

Mays? It got better. Rigney was soon saying he would be surprised if Reichardt wasn't the American League's next superstar. A *Sporting News* headline read: "Rigney Sees Reichardt Cast in Mantle Mold." It was 1966, the spring of Reichardt's first full season, and Reichardt soon showed he might live up to the fanfare.

He hit the Angels' first home run at Anaheim Stadium. He hit two home runs in the same inning of an April 30 game at Boston. He had 16 homers and 44 runs batted in at the All-Star break.

Unfortunately, he was also suffering severe headaches and periodic fainting spells. Reichardt saw a battery of doctors and was examined at the Mayo Clinic. The diagnosis was that a congenital blockage of the ureter had created high blood pressure of such severity that a kidney would have to be removed.

The operation was performed in midseason, and Reichardt did not return until the season's final game, when he drew a standing ovation from an Anaheim Stadium crowd in a pinch-hitting appearance.

A year later, *The Sporting News* had a headline of another sort. It read: "Erratic Rick Tests Angels' Patience." And now Rigney was saying, "You can't play baseball and study the market at the same time. I want him to be a superstar and he can be. But he hasn't approached the job with the dedication it demands."

Reichardt hit 17 homers and drove in 69 runs in 1967. He led the Angels with 21 homers and 73 RBI in 1968. His batting average in the years 1967 through 1970 fluctuated between .253 and .265. The next Mays or Mantle? Reichardt was again healthy, free of headaches and fainting spells, but it was as if some of his three D's—dedication, determination and discipline—had been removed with the kidney. A certain timidity replaced his customary aggressiveness. The drive was gone, and Reichardt with it.

Dick Walsh and his manager, Harold (Lefty) Phillips, traded Reichardt and third baseman Aurelio Rodriguez to Washington for third baseman Ken McMullen on April 26, 1970. Phillips, who spoke a language akin to Stengelese, couldn't communicate with Rodriguez, who spoke only Spanish. He also didn't understand much of what Reichardt said.

Reichardt spent one season with the Senators, two with the White Sox and retired to the field of insurance. Egan, his former partner in the Millionaires Club, the once coveted catcher, retired after the 1975 season, still convinced he would have lived up to expectations if he had ever received the opportunity to play regularly and if Earl Wilson hadn't broken his jaw with a 1969 fastball.

It was still the early years of what would become known as the Angels curse, but momentum was building.

8

A TOLL ROAD TO ANAHEIM

One of the first visitors Gene Autry received after being awarded the franchise in St. Louis was Branch Rickey, former general manager of the Brooklyn Dodgers, an astute baseball thinker known as the "Mahatma."

Rickey congratulated Autry, wished him well and told him not to forget that aspect of the game's history which showed how difficult it was for two clubs to survive, to peacefully coexist, in the same stadium. Rickey used as his examples the Browns and Cardinals in St. Louis, the Phillies and A's in Philadelphia and the Red Sox and Braves in Boston.

"I advise you to get out from under as soon as you can," he said. "It just doesn't work."

That was December 1960, a year before the Angels would move into Dodger Stadium. The new team had yet to play its first game. There were other problems to be attended to, and Autry didn't have to be told about the largest obstacle of all. He was aware of what had happened in St. Louis and Philadelphia and Boston, and he was aware from that first night in Walter O'Malley's suite, when the details of the Dodger Stadium lease were hammered out, that it would be difficult merely surviving in the same city as the Dodgers, let alone the same stadium.

He knew that a search for a new, permanent home would have

to be initiated early and that he didn't have the resources to build his own stadium, that he would have to have municipal help. He also knew he had no alternative but to move in with O'Malley, who was without alternatives himself.

In future years, long after the Angels had gone elsewhere in search of their identity, O'Malley's associates would confide that their boss had neither really wanted the Angels as roommate in his dream house, nor to provide another club with that kind of stepping-stone to the potential riches of Los Angeles. O'Malley, they said, was pressured into it, knowing that to demand $350,000 in territorial indemnification and then force the new club to find refuge on the street would be to risk arousing public animosity toward the Dodgers, who were still trying to heal the wounds stemming from the referendum. It would also risk arousing public sentiment on behalf of the Angels, who carried a name long familiar to minor league baseball fans in Los Angeles.

At the time Autry was awarded the franchise, the rights to the name Angels actually belonged to the Dodgers since the Dodgers had purchased Wrigley Field and the minor league club—the Los Angeles Angels of the Pacific Coast League—as a first step in moving to Los Angeles. That the Angels simply usurped the name without asking permission was one more thing eating at O'Malley.

Instead, he appeared to roll out the red carpet, on which Autry trudged hesitantly, knowing that to remain amid the limited seating capacity of Wrigley Field for more than a year was to risk the loss of significant revenue and that he had no choice but to risk the permanent loss of his club's identity by becoming a tenant of O'Malley.

Four years later, on the eve of the club's move to Anaheim, Robert Reynolds said that all their fears had come true, and now the Angels had no alternative but to get out.

"We are like a boxer whose hands are tied," Reynolds said. "We have not been able to get out of our corner in the fight for the baseball dollar.

"We have been restricted in areas of promotions, merchandising, pay-TV and sponsors. We play in a park that advertises Union

Oil, and one of our sponsors is Standard Oil. We are cast under the Dodgers' shadow as long as we remain in Chavez Ravine."

The Dodgers, with their rich tradition and history, were attracting two million annually on their way to three million, a milestone. They were attracting more stars than attend an Oscars ceremony. The Angels had only Mamie Van Doren, and then only when Belinsky pitched.

Attendance, declining at a pace comparable with the Angels' artistry, went from 1,144,063 in 1962 to 821,015 in 1963 to 760,439 in 1964 and to 566,727 in 1965.

Only 945 fans turned out for the last day game the Angels played at Dodger Stadium, and one player said, "We're getting out of here just in time. I can't even give my passes away anymore."

Even Belinsky knew it would come to that, though he learned his lesson the hard way. Bo, having recently been recalled from Hawaii in 1963 and scheduled to make his first start against Baltimore, said, "If I don't draw 15,000, they should send me right back to Hawaii."

Bo had drawn at least 12,000 for each of his starts on the island, but he failed to consider that this was a Thursday afternoon in late September, the Angels were in ninth place and he wasn't exactly the prodigal having returned. Bo pitched a five-hit, complete-game victory, but only 476 fans, the all-time smallest crowd at Dodger Stadium, saw it.

"I wouldn't be so upset," Bo said later, "but it was obvious I wouldn't even have gotten 476 if 200 or so hadn't wanted to come out and boo me. What sadists."

Bo had been traded by the time the Angels decided against renewing an option that would have kept them in Dodger Stadium through the 1968 season, at which time, had they maintained the attendance pace, they would have been drawing about 100,000 annually and Autry would have long since hocked the saddles.

"I couldn't have even interested my own station in the games," he said.

Approximately one month before expiration of that option clause, in the spring of 1964, the Angels notified O'Malley of their intention to move. The original agreement tied the Angels to Dodger Stadium for four years with an opportunity to stay for three more. Autry agreed to pay 7.5 percent of his attendance gross in rent. The Dodgers took all of the parking revenue and 50 percent of the concession gross. O'Malley even insisted on a clause by which the Angels, who televised 20 regular season road games, would have to compensate the Dodgers for the loss those telecasts created at Dodger Stadium. And if the Angels ultimately became interested in pay-TV, it could only be through the pay-TV company O'Malley was at the time developing—but which never got past the developmental stage.

"Every department head in the Dodger organization," O'Malley said when the Angels moved in, "is available to help the new club. There will be no sabotage, no sniping. It's our desire they be successful. It's rare when a young married couple can move in with their in-laws and be happy. But this may be one of those rare occasions."

Right.

"They dollared us to death," Autry said later.

Amateur horticulturist O'Malley sent the Angels a bill for half the stadium's landscaping, a considerable sum since there was a considerable area to be landscaped. The Angels complained, arguing that the plants weren't going to be uprooted and replanted each time the Angels left town, that the Dodgers were going to landscape the stadium no matter how many tenants they had.

The Angels received a bill for window cleaning and again promptly complained, pointing out that the only windows were in the Dodger offices.

The Angels received a bill for the resurfacing and striping of the parking lot. They filed another complaint, suggesting that since they received no revenue from parking, they shouldn't be expected to pay for parking improvements.

The Angels were billed for half a season's supply of toiletries. They angrily complained again, saying the bill should be prorated on the basis of attendance, that no matter how bad a team the Angels were, the Dodgers still went through more toilet paper because of their greater attendance.

All of the complaints were arbitrated by the Dodgers' vice president in charge of saying no, Dick Walsh, a man who would later serve three seasons as general manager of the Angels, stirring up a storm of the type he was constantly responding to at Dodger Stadium. Walsh was a cold, efficient businessman who would be nicknamed "The Smiling Python" by Angel players while serving as their general manager. He had several shouting matches with the executives of both clubs then sharing Dodger Stadium, and there were many times that old friends Bavasi and Haney, the respective general managers, had to mediate the differences.

Nothing upset the Angels more than the location of their ticket office. While most of the club's executives worked out of a building in downtown Los Angeles, tickets were handled out of a windowless dungeon at Dodger Stadium. The office was in the left-field corner, near the place where the groundskeeper kept his equipment. The only avenue for customers buying tickets in advance, for those interested in group purchases, took them past the towering manure piles, always a pleasant experience during the heat of summer or, in the words of a Dodger executive, the appropriate preparation for watching the Angels.

All of it served to put greater stress on the relationship and convince the Angels they would ultimately have to move. Autry knew it, and others sensed it. In the three years before the move to Anaheim was formally announced, the Angels received fifteen to twenty "feelers" from cities interested in building a stadium for the club.

Had the Angels been able to sustain their momentum of 1962, had management seen it for what it was instead of overestimating its significance, had the club finished better than ninth, fifth and seventh in its next three years at Dodger Stadium, and delayed or permanently forestalled the attendance skid, it is difficult to say whether the Angels would have picked up the option on the next three years at Dodger Stadium.

In an interview years later, Autry couldn't say. He said it was doubtful, however, that anything could have convinced him that coexistence was possible or that the Angels could have stayed anywhere in the metropolitan area and established their own credentials in the face of the Dodgers' enormous popularity.

He put business manager Cedric Tallis in charge of the relocation project and told Tallis that three points were essential. Autry wanted (1) to remain accessible to the Los Angeles market and the areas of major growth; (2) to receive an appropriate lease that would give the Angels a share of both parking and concessions and in no way inhibit their involvement with television, including pay-TV; and (3) to have the type of stadium in which the fans were on top of the action, with seating as close as possible to the foul lines.

The first time Tallis got back to Autry was to inform him he would probably need a new car, since his old one was certain to disintegrate before he was through investigating. Ultimately the Angels selected Anaheim, but only after negotiations with the city of Long Beach collapsed, leaving Tallis to think "all was lost."

Long Beach, 30 miles to the south of Los Angeles, a city believed to be home for more Iowans than Iowa itself and a city then of considerable tideland oil wealth, had invited Tallis to investigate its potential late in 1963. While restricted on the west by the Pacific Ocean, Long Beach offered an immediate attendance market of about four million. It proposed the El Dorado Park area in the northeast section of the city as a possible stadium site, citing its proximity to several freeways and to the metropolitan Los Angeles area.

Tallis was intrigued and so was Autry. The negotiations had almost reached the yes or no stage when two problems developed. The first was the possibility that Long Beach could not obtain tideland money for an inland project. The city told the Angels not to worry, since the financing could be resolved. The second was that Long Beach insisted the club be called the Long Beach Angels. The Angels told the city to forget it, since under no circumstances would the club be called anything except Los Angeles or California.

Autry simply had been a corporate cowboy too long to underestimate the importance of Madison Avenue. He realized there was little chance of marketing the Long Beach Angels in New York or selling it to potential radio sponsors. He had Tallis explain the club's predicament to Long Beach officials and tell them the club would not object if Long Beach was part of the stadium name.

The city, however, remained firm, saying for all that money and all that land, it had a right to name the baby.

Among those watching and intrigued by the collapse in negotiations was a man named Rex Coons, the friendly and progressive mayor of Anaheim, home of Disneyland but still known best for the Jack Benny routine in which Anaheim, Azusa and Cucamonga first came to prominence. The 1963 population of Anaheim was only 150,000, but there were seven million people within a 50-mile radius. And the area, the county known as Orange, was exploding unlike any in the country, the fruit and vegetable fields giving way to housing tracts and industrial developments at a dizzying pace. The per capita income was among the nation's highest and the politics among the most conservative.

Autry and the Angels were aware of Anaheim. Walt Disney, it will be recalled, had been lobbying his friend for some time to explore the area. The Angels had also read a Stanford research study predicting a population belt from Santa Barbara to Mexico with Anaheim at the center. The Angels spent $23,000 on a study of their own and got the same information.

At about the same time in late 1963 that Tallis and Autry had concluded that Long Beach was out, and that they'd have to start from scratch elsewhere, Rex Coons was knocking on the door. Coons was aware of the Long Beach situation and firmly believed that a professional sports team was about the only thing Orange County was missing in its emergence from more than a century as a sleepy agricultural area, a pleasant spot for Los Angeles residents to visit on Sunday afternoon.

Coons had recently returned from Washington, D.C., where he and a hundred other Orange County politicians and businessmen had successfully petitioned the Bureau of the Budget to have Orange County designated a standard metropolitan statistical area, permitting its employment, economic and population figures, among others, to be listed separately rather than lumped with Los Angeles–Long Beach.

The trip to Washington had allowed Coons to thoroughly in-doctrinate himself in the development of his and other counties, and he became convinced that a professional sports team would be more than an additional impetus for the nation's fastest-growing county, that it was the required frosting.

Concerned that public knowledge would send land prices soar-ing and blow the deal before there was one, Coons kept his con-victions basically to himself. He did tell Bill Phillips, chairman of the Orange County board of supervisors, and Keith Murdoch, An-aheim's city manager, but until he received the Angels' informal approval, he acted independently of his city council, holding clan-destine meetings with Tallis and Reynolds. It was early 1964, and the clock was ticking for both club and city.

The mayor realized he couldn't keep it quiet forever, and the Angels knew if they wanted their own stadium in 1966, if they didn't want to be trapped in Dodger Stadium until 1968, a decision had to be made soon. Coons and Phillips met with Tallis and Reyn-olds at the Los Angeles Country Club.

"We have to know, Bob," Coons said.

"Does it matter what we call ourselves?" Reynolds asked.

"I don't give a damn," Coons said. "Why should I? I know every broadcast, every dateline will have Anaheim in it."

Reynolds gave his approval, and a meeting was scheduled for Palm Springs in late March, at which time Anaheim would formally make its proposal to the club's board of directors.

A significant problem ensued—temporarily. A. J. Schute, senior member of the city council and the man who owned the land where Coons and Murdoch wanted to put the stadium, had by now learned what the land was to be used for and raised the price so drastically that the mayor and city manager considered it beyond the city's reach. Ten days before the Palm Springs meeting, Anaheim had everything except the land on which to build a stadium.

The solution was offered by a man who insisted he communi-cated with God and had been working behind the scenes to prove Anaheim and the Angels were a match made in heaven. His name was C. J. Gill, a veteran real estate broker. He had gotten wind of the attempt to bring the Angels to Anaheim and of the problems with the original site.

"I'm a Christian Scientist," Gill said in a later interview, "and I talked with the Supreme Being—it helps clear my mind—to seek His help in trying to determine the logical site for a stadium. I pray before any business deal—'If this be right for all, please let it happen.' I have a sound knowledge of Orange County real estate, and as I prayed and reviewed the pieces of land, it came to me."

Gill envisioned a stadium on land then used for the growing of alfalfa, oranges and corn, a site, he would learn, that encompassed approximately 157 acres some two miles south of the original.

Did the Supreme Being tell Gill there was the possibility of a $150,000 commission if he was successful in getting the owners to agree to the sale? That was never ascertained. What is certain is that Gill came to city manager Murdoch at the propitious moment, having put together the package that would cost the city approximately $4 million (a bargain compared to current Orange County land values), in addition to a lifetime pass to the Angel games, a bonus Herman Bruggeman insisted on when he committed his 21 acres of orange trees to the Gill package for $565,000.

Roland Reynolds paid for his own season tickets with the $1.3 million he received for his 70 acres of alfalfa. "A lot more fun than baling it," Bessie Reynolds said, watching a game at Anaheim Stadium years later.

The Angels filed their intention to move with the Anaheim City Council on April 9, 1964. The council and the board of supervisors met the next day, at which time the county officials, under pressure from conservative constituents such as R. C. Hoiles, publisher of the *Orange County Register*, backed out of the project, leaving the city of 150,000 to go it alone—"not at all afraid," as Coons said.

A nonprofit board was established to supervise negotiation of the contract with the Del Webb Construction Company, to prepare and handle the sale of private bonds to finance the project and to administer the 35-year lease with the city. Architect Noble Herzberg was hired to design a compact stadium of about 50,000 seats. The ground breaking was held in the middle of a cornfield on August 31, 1964. There were bands, balloons and all of the Disney characters, who would return to stay in about 30 years, when the Disney Company bought the team and, with financial help from the city, renovated the stadium for $118 million, almost five times the original $24 million.

While the Dodgers had taken half the concessions and all the parking, the Anaheim Stadium lease permitted the Angels to keep half the parking and two-thirds of the concessions net. The club paid a minimum of $160,000 in rent each year or 7.5 percent of the admission gross up to $2 million, 10 percent after $2 million. It was an attractive arrangement when the club moved in 1966, but it became a source of contention in the late 80s and early 90s as payroll escalated and the Autrys began to realize they might have to sell.

"It was a fabulous lease in 1964, but 30 years later it was one of the worst," Jackie Autry said. "A lot of new stadiums had come on line, and a lot of old leases had been renegotiated. We ended up with one of the worst leases in baseball, and it put us behind the eight ball as far as the revenues we could generate and our expenses as a tenant. I mean, we were paying an extraordinary amount of rent. Where you had some clubs generating $16 million and more from the stadium, we were generating $2 to $3 million. When you consider that kind of spread in stadium revenue, even before discussing peripheral assets, you are at a distinct disadvantage to go out and get the type of player you need."

The industry's recent stadium renaissance tended to separate big and small markets, haves and have-nots. Luxury suites became a major source of revenue, but not for the Autrys. Anaheim Stadium had been enclosed, with 112 luxury boxes and seating expanded to 70,000, when the Rams moved out of Los Angeles in 1980, but the Angels basically received little of the suite revenue. They benefited from the expansion, attracting 27 crowds of 60,000 or more in ensuing years, but the enclosed stadium had lost much of its appeal and attraction and was neither a baseball nor football arena, a situation that the Disney Company was adamant about correcting before finalizing its purchase.

The Rams' arrival also reminded the Angels of the familiar pitfalls of joint tenancy. The city's agreement with the football team gave the Rams developmental rights in an area of the parking lot, cutting into the 12,000 spaces that the Angels were guaranteed. The Autrys filed a $100 million suit that was litigated for almost a decade and ultimately settled out of court. The Angels preserved their parking guarantee and "only the lawyers got rich," said Jackie Autry. The Rams put off any development when the real estate market sagged and ultimately moved to St. Louis after the 1994 season, by which time the Autrys were already in the process of selling, having decided that their pockets weren't deep enough amid baseball's soaring costs.

In reflection, the move had been a case of survival and a good one for the Cowboy. His season ticket sales jumped from 2,600 in the final year at Dodger Stadium to 5,000 in their first year in Anaheim to more than 18,000 in 1982, a league record at the time. Critics would suggest that with improved continuity—on and off the field—and stronger marketing in Orange County and the booming Inland Empire of Riverside and San Bernardino, the Autrys might have withstood the industry inflation—despite the rampant toll on family ownership. Late-season collapses and misplaced optimism tended to leave Angel fans wary, but the club still drew two million or more 15 times between 1979 and 1998, an impressive show of faith considering it finished better than .500 only eight times in that span while also winning the three division titles.

Peter Ueberroth, the former commissioner and a member of the Angels board of directors, said he was motivated to bid against the Disney Company when the Autrys posted the sale sign in the early 90s because he felt that the protracted suit of the 80s had created a sense of stagnation at the stadium and that the team and area still boasted a "significant upside."

He said he considered the Angels "one of the few undeveloped major market teams" in the sense that "I don't believe they ever really worked on attracting the Latino market, and I don't think they ever really engrossed themselves in a Riverside-Orange County campaign to develop a feeling of home spirit. I think they should have drawn better and should draw better."

Said Jackie Autry: "Orange County is an interesting area.

There's a lot of entertainment and recreational choices. Fans tend to be fickle, but that's the same everywhere. In years we had good ballclubs, we had pretty good attendance. The stadium in later years was not conducive and warm enough to make people want to be there, but Gene had promised the city in 1966 that he would make every effort to work with it in getting a football team. So when they were finally successful, Gene had to enthusiastically support the changes at the stadium, but it clearly took away a lot of the charm. I mean, when you look at it, the county never really supported the Rams from the start, and while the Ducks have done well, who knows how long that will last?"

In time, rising debt, payroll and expenses took a toll. The Autrys operated one of baseball's smallest front offices in the late 80s and had to pick their spots when it came to advertising and promotions. Richard Brown, the club president from November 1, 1990, to May 14, 1996, said it was as if marketing was a whole new concept. The Autrys, he pointed out, spent $17,000 on their last opening day festivities, while Disney came in and spent millions on their first.

But with all of that, with the ongoing reality that the Dodger shadow continued to stalk the Angels and affect decisions at times as the Angels seemed to play to the marquee, one thing is certain: The Angels helped put Anaheim and Orange County on the national map, and former Disneyland president Jack Lindquist, at the time of the Cowboy's death, said Autry deserved to be ranked with Walt Disney, Walter Knott, who founded the Knott's Berry Farm amusement park, and others "who in many different ways played an important role in the development of [the area] in the last half of this century. What [the Angels' decision signified] was that this area had arrived. It was growing up. Anaheim was now a major league city, and there aren't a lot of those in the United States."

It was a beaming Autry himself, wearing alligator boots and a tan suit cut in Western style, who turned the first shovel at the 1964 ground breaking. His team still had two long years left in Dodger Stadium, two long years before Buzzie Bavasi, still the Dodger general manager, presented the Angels with a cake that carried a frosted replica of Anaheim Stadium and the inscription "Good Luck."

The Autrys didn't always have it in Anaheim, but they enjoyed a larger slice of income and identity, and their ticket office was out front, a long way from the groundskeeper's manure.

9

1963–65: Expansion Blues

The Angels weren't so much lame ducks during their final three seasons in Dodger Stadium as dead ducks. The misleading euphoria of 1962 faded rapidly as the Angels finished ninth, fifth and seventh, their attendance falling from 821,015 to 760,439 to 566,727. A sarcastic Rigney reflected on that crowd of 945 that saw the Angels lose to Baltimore, 4–2, in their next-to-last game at the Stadium, an afternoon make-up of a rained-out night game, and said: "My players planned on this being a day off, and they can't adjust their thinking that quickly."

Rigney and Haney would no sooner plug one hole than there would be another somewhere else, typical of the expansion blues. One season it would be a lack of pitching, the next a lack of hitting. Bo Belinsky took a black Labrador retriever (the canine's name was Bimbo) with him to spring training in 1963, and it was soon being suggested that all the Angels had gone to the dogs.

A team that won 86 games while almost winning it all in 1962, the Angels won only 70 in 1963, 82 in 1964, and 75 in 1965. They finished 34 games behind the Yankees in 1963, 17 behind the Yankees in 1964 and 27 behind Minnesota in 1965.

Rigney's ulcer put him in the hospital twice during the 1965 season, and a review of his quotes illustrates his frustration during the course of the three years. For example:

- "It looks like it's even an effort for my players to swing the bat. It looks like they want a vacation."
- "We've been bluffing our way, going through the motions. If they'd really rather be somewhere else, we can accommodate them."

It became increasingly difficult to find substitutions on the waiver lists or in the minor league systems of other organizations. Impatience and frustration ate at the relationship between Haney and Rigney. The manager received a one-year extension at the end of the 1964 season and another at the end of the 1965 season, even though he was at times publicly second-guessed by Autry, who had said he would never do that.

Haney, who some believed was left bitter and envious because of the acclaim Rigney received in the wake of the 1962 success, ultimately charged reporters with trying to create a rift between himself and the manager.

The situation was compounded by rumors that the Giants wanted Rigney to return, a possibility that never reached the point of a definitive offer. Finally, prior to a game on September 5, 1965, Haney held a press conference in Rigney's office and announced the one-year extension.

"Bill had no reason to say we haven't talked with him about the situation," Haney said emotionally. "And I said the same thing to his face, isn't that right, Bill?"

Rigney was about to respond when Haney continued, "I gave him my word three months ago that he would go to Anaheim as the manager. We hadn't had time to work out the details, but there's never been a question about it."

Rigney shrugged and smiled, wondering why, if there had never been a question about it, Autry had been quoted repeatedly during the previous week as saying a decision had not yet been made. But the manager bit his tongue. He was happy to be working and was committed to developing the Angels into a winner. Asked repeatedly over the years about his relationship with Haney, he would always answer the same: "Naturally, two men working together are going to have their differences. Ours have never been that serious, and Fred has never second-guessed anything

I've done on the field. A manager can't ask for anything more."

Which wasn't exactly true. Rigney kept asking for one more pitcher and/or one more hitter, pleas made by every manager since Doubleday. The plea was more desperate in the case of the expansion Angels since there was no farm system to fill the gaps and little the Angels could offer in the way of trade bait.

Rigney went into the 1963 season saying the Angels were happy to accept the challenge of trying to prove that 1962 wasn't "a flash in the pan," saying, too, that "we improved 16 games last year and I'll be delighted to add 16 more."

He emerged from the season saying that while it wasn't the most disappointing year he had ever experienced as a manager, "it certainly was the most frustrating. I had great expectations. I wasn't sure we could finish third again, but I was positive we could win 85 games again."

The magic that had produced 35 come-from-behind wins, 18 in the Angels' last at-bat, was gone. This time the Angels lost 28 games in the last at-bat and lost 60 of 106 games decided by three runs or less.

Mad Dog Thomas, who years later would become general manager of the Philadelphia Phillies, went down without a whimper in 1963, batting .220 with 55 runs batted in after having hit .290 with 104 RBI the previous year. Buck Rodgers, the promising rookie catcher of 1962, was introduced to the realities of his position, suffering a broken finger early that year and later a sprained ankle. He caught only 99 games after catching the rookie record 155 during the previous year, and drove in 20 fewer runs. Leon Wagner, who still led the Angels with 26 homers and 90 RBI, drove in 17 fewer.

Albie Pearson became the first Angel to hit more than .300, hitting .0004 more, but the inseparable Dean Chance and Bo Belinsky went from a combined 24–21 to a combined 15–27, and there was inconsistent relief pitching from the celebrated bullpen, of which the one-eyed Art Fowler became the ace almost by default, the renowned depth of 1962 having virtually disintegrated.

Rigney faced one of his toughest jobs of a tough season in spring training when he had to inform the 34-year-old Ryne Duren that he had been sold to Philadelphia, the Angels having tired of his behavior off the field. There was another tough task in May when an unhappy Eli Grba had to be told he was being farmed out.

"I just got married and I just bought a home," Grba said. "I don't understand how a guy can be good enough to pitch the opening game two years in a row and then isn't even good enough to pitch in the bullpen."

The old guard kept changing, and the relief burden fell on the 40-plus Fowler, who dismounted from one of the bicycles the Angels were forced to ride between their hotel and practice field in spring training and said, "A man my age should be excused from such nonsense."

The Angels got one of their few lifts in the season opener when Ken McBride pitched a four-hit 4–1 victory. The club then scored just two runs in the next 21 innings, leaving 16 runners on base, to set the pattern for a season that ended with a 4–3 loss to Boston in which Felix Torres appropriately bunted into a triple play.

It was a season in which Haney complained that the Angels seemed to lack spirit and seemed to be interested only in individual pursuits.

The most individual of the Angels was again the left-hander named Belinsky, who announced in April that he was going on a health-food diet prescribed by a veteran Los Angeles hippie named Gypsy Boots, who provided Bo with a daily supply of organic oranges. Mr. Boots regularly joined Miss Van Doren and Mr. Winchell in the dugout box seats at Dodger Stadium, producing a scene that was often more interesting than anything that transpired on the field.

Bo was optioned to Hawaii in May 1963 and said he was considering applying for the voluntary retired list so that he could accept one of his many movie offers. The Angels quickly put Bo on the disqualified list, terminating his salary and influencing him to catch the next plane to Hawaii.

Mamie at this time received a call from Ray Johnson, owner of the Dallas–Fort Worth team of the Pacific Coast League. Johnson asked her if she would be willing to appear with Bo when the Islanders visited Texas.

"What are you willing to pay?" she asked.

"This is the minor leagues," Johnson replied.

"You may be the minor leagues, but I'm the major leagues," Mamie said, terminating the proposal.

Bo ultimately returned, but appeared in just 13 games, losing nine of 11 decisions, prompting his rejection of organic oranges in favor of his customary diet of wine, women and song.

This was also the season in which the Angels signed another individual who tended to dance to his own music, outfielder Jim Piersall, then a veteran of 12 major league summers. Piersall was 35 and had been released by the Mets because of a series of leg injuries and because the Mets manager, Casey Stengel, hadn't laughed when Piersall ran the bases backward after hitting a home run.

A marvelously gifted player whose struggle with mental illness was chronicled in the book and movie *Fear Strikes Out*, Piersall produced laughter and tears throughout his career. He had played for four other major league clubs, and he said he was happy for the opportunity to join the Angels because he knew that next to Belinsky, Chance and Mad Dog Thomas, "I'd look sane."

Piersall spent three and a half years with the Angels, after which he briefly joined the club's promotions department. He won the Comeback of the Year award for his .314 average in 1964, and he came back again in 1965 and 1966, making liars of the doctors who said he wouldn't play again after shattering a kneecap when he ran into the Dodger Stadium foul pole early in 1965.

"I can't sign a contract promising I'll stay within the lines of baseball as written by Abner Doubleday," Piersall said when he first signed with the Angels.

Two days later, Piersall proved it. He became embroiled in a pushing match with umpire Bill Kinnamon while zealously protesting a strike call. He was no sooner back in uniform than he was out of it, fined $250 and suspended for four days.

Piersall called his wife, Mary, to see if she had any advice. She told him to stay away from Mamie.

A year later, responding to Charles Finley's plan to book the Beatles into the Kansas City ballpark, Piersall went to bat there wearing a Beatles wig.

"He can get me for a lot cheaper than the $150,000 he's giving those bums from Liverpool," Piersall said.

"Okay," umpire Frank Umont told him, "I'll give you two minutes to do your act."

"Relax, Frank," Piersall said. "We're on national TV. I'll get you more camera time than you've ever had."

In August 1963, pitcher Paul Foytack was tagged for four home runs in the same inning by Cleveland's Woodie Held, Pedro Ramos, Tito Francona and Larry Brown. It cost the Indians, then playing in cold, cavernous and almost always empty Municipal Stadium, $350 to set off the center-field fireworks after each blast, and publicity director Nate Wallick responded to the third of the four homes by telling the trigger man, "No more, we can't afford it."

Piersall greeted Foytack in the clubhouse later with earplugs and a stretcher.

The Angels limped out of the 1963 season and soon lost another familiar face when Leon Wagner was traded to Cleveland in a major winter transaction.

"I have nothing against Cleveland," Wagner said, "but I'd rather have been traded somewhere in the United States."

The Angels obtained pitcher Barry Latman and first baseman Joe Adcock, the imposing slugger who had been a catalyst in Haney's pennant-winning seasons as manager of the Milwaukee Braves.

"I already have an assignment for Adcock," Rigney said at the time of the trade. "The big guy will room with Chance, and Joe will keep the only key."

Adcock was 37 and conceded that his best years were behind him. Nevertheless, he led the Angels with 21 homers in 1964, hit another 14 in 1965 and led the Angels again in 1966 with 18 homers and a .273 batting average.

He was the conscience of the clubhouse, a fundamentalist whose drive for perfection plagued his one attempt at managing, with the Cleveland Indians in 1967. Adcock retired then to his quarter horse ranch in Coushatta, Louisiana.

Latman had a brief and unsuccessful tenure with the Angels, but did not have to worry about his future. He was the son-in-law of Leon Schwab, who owned the Hollywood drugstore of the same name, the place where Lana Turner and other actresses were discovered.

Latman was 6–10 in 1964, another desultory season highlighted only by the one-hitter that Ken McBride and Julio Navarro combined on in the presidential opener in Washington, D.C., the marvelous pitching of Cy Young Award winner Dean Chance, a club record 11-game win streak in June, the all-around fine play of All-Star Jim Fregosi (18 homers, 72 RBI and a .277 batting average), the arrival of relief ace Bob Lee and the departure of veterans Lee Thomas and Billy Moran.

Thomas was traded in early June for Boston outfielder Lou Clinton. Moran went to Minnesota ten days later for first baseman Vic Power, a stylish defensive performer who was Adcock's late-inning replacement.

Chance seldom needed a replacement. This was the one season it all came together for the talented farm boy, who was easily the game's best pitcher in 1964. He set club records for wins (20), ERA (1.65), shutouts (11), complete games (15), strikeouts in a game (15), strikeouts in a season (207), innings pitched (278⅓), consecutive scoreless innings (28) and consecutive shutouts (3). Five of his shutouts were by a 1–0 score, a major league record.

Chance went into the season angry that he had not received a raise from his 13–18 season in 1963, and it was his constant source of motivation, a carrot that Haney kept dangling in front of him and then withdrawing when Chance seemed certain to take a bite. He got the raise only after the 1964 season ended, only after he had become the youngest pitcher to that time to win the Cy Young.

His dominance was best illustrated by a 4–0 record and incredible 0.18 ERA against the powerful Yankees. On the few occasions when Chance needed relief, Rigney found a new stopper in Bob Lee, an intimidating right-hander who stood 6-foot-3 and weighed 230 pounds—when he was in shape.

The Angels drafted Lee for $25,000 from Batavia of the Pittsburgh system, where he had won 20 of 22 decisions, striking out 240 in 185 innings. Lee challenged hitters with the same vigor he challenged the curfew rules. The Angels couldn't seem to escape his type. He once drew a whopping fine when Haney discovered him romancing a young lady in the bullpen golf cart. He played hard and lived hard, and he expressed the opinion that his best years might have extended beyond the three he spent with the Angels if Rigney had not burned out his arm by calling on him at the first sign of trouble.

Lee's 1964 emergence came at a time when the venerable one-eyed Art Fowler had been assigned to pitch strictly batting practice. Lee responded with 17 saves before breaking his hand on September 5 when he hit an iron railing as he swung at a drunk, taunting fan near the bullpen in Boston's Fenway Park. He appeared in 64 games that year, 69 in 1965 and 61 in 1966, after which he was traded to the Dodgers for pitcher Nick Willhite.

The major trade of the winter of 1964 sent Belinsky to Philadelphia for pitcher Rudy May and first baseman Costen Shockley, who did not report until late in spring training because of a contract dispute with the Phillies. Shockley quit halfway through the 1965 season because he was unhappy being so far from his Delaware home, and also he felt he could earn more as a construction worker. May spent five seasons with the Angels, never quite realizing the potential he would later fulfill with Baltimore, Montreal and the New York Yankees.

Belinsky, familiar with Philadelphia because of his years in Trenton, said, "It's a hip town. They know what's happening. Whenever we were looking for fun, we'd go to Philly."

As Bo's career moved toward a premature death, the Angels were fortunate they didn't have to play their 1965 season in Philadelphia, where fans were known to boo Santa Claus and the Easter Bunny. It was their last season in Los Angeles and the lamest of their lame-duck seasons. They were rained out of the season opener, lost to Cleveland, 7–1, while making three errors the next day and then had it turn worse.

Lee's 21 saves helped retain a measure of respectability, but Haney addressed the team in midseason and said, "We either get one hundred percent hustle, or some of you won't go to Anaheim."

The tragic death of pitcher Dick Wantz in May left the team in a persistently somber mood. Ken McBride, the most consistent pitcher during those early years but the victim of a series of injuries during the 1964 and 1965 seasons. was sent to the minors in August and did not return.

Frustrated by the voids in his own farm system, Haney's youth movement took a strange turn. Pitcher Jack Sanford, 36, was purchased from the Giants, and pitcher Jim Coates, 34, was obtained from Seattle. Cy Young Award winner Dean Chance went from 20–9 to 15–10. This time Chance said he wasn't motivated so much by the prospect of a raise but by his desire to avoid a cut.

The season's highlight might have been a beanball brawl with Boston, triggered by Chance. It was more than a customary waltz, and the Red Sox emerged saying they would ultimately "get" Chance, a vendetta never fulfilled. Buck Rodgers was fined $100 for throwing the first punch and said it represented $50 a swing.

"Don't be upset," Piersall cautioned him. "If you had my reputation, you would have gotten 10 days and $500."

The Angels formally announced on September 2 that henceforth they would be the California Angels. That night they played like the Los Angeles Angels, losing to New York, 8–1.

With all the misgivings and complaints during their Dodger Stadium tenancy, the Angels were 46–34 during that final year there and an overall 170–153 for the four years. The hitters now talked of getting to a park with fairer dimensions while pitchers bemoaned the departure from the spacious Ravine.

Asked if it would be a more difficult transition for the players or manager, Rigney said, "It will definitely be more difficult for the players. I'll have to do only one thing differently, and that's manage better."

Jim Fregosi, Rigney's leader among the players, said, "The important thing is that having our own park with our own fans will mean a great deal for team pride. There won't be 10,000 people in the stands listening to the Dodgers."

10

1966–67: OLD-TIMERS DAZE

That strange youth movement initiated by the purchase of seniors Jack Sanford and Jim Coates continued as the Angels waited out their Anaheim debut. During the winter of 1965, Haney signed pitcher Lou Burdette, 39, and third baseman Frank Malzone, 35, as free agents, traded outfield prospect Dick Simpson to Baltimore for first baseman Norm Siebern, 32, and purchased catcher Ed Bailey, 34, from the Chicago Cubs.

It was an indictment of the young Angels' farm system, and it was soon being written that the Angels would not play just one Old-Timers Game in Anaheim, they would play 162.

Haney responded by saying that the club had to get off to a good start in their new stadium, that they were shooting for a big year and that the poise, polish and spirit of the new veterans might rub off on the young players.

"We must make a good showing," the general manager said, "and that constitutes a first-division finish. From the stands we looked dead last year. We have to recapture the spirit and attitude of three years ago."

Haney referred to the third-place finish of 1962, which the Angels clung to as some sort of talisman, hoping to regenerate a magic that had long since faded.

Bill Rigney greeted his team in spring training and said, "We may be beaten this year because the other club is better, but it will not be because we didn't go to bed at night. I will not allow this team to leave its desire on the golf course or in a bar.

"We displayed a consistent lack of initiative last year, and we can't play in Anaheim the way we closed out Dodger Stadium. Some of the players think this is a one-way street. We allowed them to be masters of their own fate. Now the twenty-four hours of each day will be done my way."

If Rigney hoped to convert the Angels from country club to chain gang, the results were not evident. The Angels' first season in Anaheim was their sixth overall, and it was not much different from those that had come before. Some may have questioned the Angels' dedication and attitude, but it seemed more a matter of talent—the lack of it—as the Angels finished sixth, 18 games behind pennant-winning Baltimore, with an 80–82 record.

The Angels went to work in Anaheim with only five players remaining from the 1961 expansion draft—Dean Chance, Fred Newman, Buck Rodgers, Jim Fregosi and Albie Pearson.

They also went to work with only five farm products among the 28 players on the opening-day roster—Jim McGlothlin, Tom Satriano, Paul Schaal, Ed Kirkpatrick and Rick Reichardt.

The Angels did get an unexpected bonus in 1966 when second baseman Bobby Knoop, the personification of "good field, no hit," slugged 17 homers and drove in 72 runs, both career highs.

Knoop, drafted from Denver in 1963, joined with Fregosi to form the American League's best double-play combination and four times in his six years with the team was voted the Owners' Trophy by his teammates as the club's most valuable and inspirational player.

Coach Del Rice said Knoop was the best second baseman he had ever seen and "I've seen Joe Gordon, Bill Mazeroski and Red Schoendienst."

"Every pitcher who gets a raise should give it to Knoop," the veteran Malzone said.

Knoop enjoyed his finest all-around year in 1966, when the Angels made their formal debut at Anaheim Stadium on April 19, losing to Chicago, 3–1, before a crowd of 31,660.

The game was delayed in starting 25 minutes when a water main burst in downtown Anaheim, creating a traffic jam that extended into Azusa and Cucamonga. The visiting manager, Eddie Stanky, was also enraged when an electrician could not be located, forcing the White Sox to take batting practice in the dark, when a cluster of lights blew out.

"Twenty-four million for a park," Stanky roared, "and they won't spend three dollars to give us lights."

Stanky made headlines again later that year when he categorized the theatrical Rigney as a "TV manager" and said Kansas City's Alvin Dark "and myself are the game's only serious managers."

"Eddie never liked guys from California," Rigney said of his former Giant teammate, "but I don't really know what he means and I don't really care. I just consider the source."

The "TV manager," a suggestion that Rigney played to the cameras, might have done one of his best jobs in 1966, keeping the Angels in first-division contention by pleading, pushing, cajoling and maneuvering. Eleven of Rigney's hitters batted under .250 and the team average was .232.

The offense was so offensive that when the Angels scored 12 runs in the eighth inning of a 16–9 victory over Boston, Rigney, confined to his hotel room because of the flu and watching on television, said, "We've gone months without totaling 12 runs."

It was seldom easy for Rigney. There was seldom a laugher, baseball's term for a rout. He was constantly dealing with players who had learned their fundamentals in other organizations, rejects, fringe and utility players on whom he couldn't rely.

A measure of the futility and frustration encountered by Haney's five-year plan was that retreads led his club in virtually every category in 1966.

Adcock was the batting (.273) and home run (18) leader, while Sanford was the pitching leader at 13–7. Pearson retired after injuring his back in April, Reichardt underwent kidney surgery in July, and Chance, suffering from his mysterious infection, slumped to 12–17.

The Angels at least had their own home now, and attendance

almost tripled, soaring from 566,727 in 1965 to 1,400,321 in 1966, which did not include the 40,735 who watched an April 9 exhibition with the Giants. The Angels lost that first ever game in Anaheim Stadium, 9–3, but came back to defeat the Giants, 6–5, the next day when Fregosi homered in the 10th inning, inspiring a crowd of 23,061.

The new stadium was quickly dubbed the Big A in reference to the giant A-framed scoreboard behind the left-field fence, which featured a halo at the top that was lighted after Angel wins—and in many seasons did not cost the Angels much for electricity.

"The first chill I ever received in this game came when I walked into the [New York] Polo Grounds for the first time," said Rigney. "I received another when I walked into this park."

Dean Chance watched batting practice the first day, noted how the ball carried in Anaheim, and said, "I thought they were hitting golf balls. We've got three guys who are a cinch to hit 30 homers each—Jim Fregosi, José Cardenal and Paul Schaal."

Cardenal hit 16 homers, Fregosi 13 and Schaal 5.

Rigney was criticized for his tendency to display a quick hook with starting pitchers, to burn out hot relievers, but he consistently seemed to draw more out of the Angels than they were capable of giving. His strategic moves were seldom questioned, and he was definitely a newspaperman's manager, providing stories on games that otherwise weren't worth more than a sentence.

He ripped players, managers and umpires. He exhibited emotion, sensitivity and humor. He worked hard to provide something other than a cliché. He enjoyed being with the writers socially.

The camaraderie between Rigney and the media was such that one morning the entire press corps arrived at a Palm Springs work-out wearing uniform tops with the number 18½ on them, a half digit above Rigney's 18.

There is this story reflective of his gregarious nature and love of repartee, no matter where or when: Rigney was seated with a writer at Toots Shor's famous bar in New York when an eaves-dropper heard the bartender ask "Mr. Rigney" if he would like another drink. The eavesdropper, believing that the bartender had said Wrigley instead of Rigney and that he was sitting next to the owner of the Chicago Cubs, pardoned himself and said, "Mr. Wrigley, could you tell me please why you've never put lights in your park?"

Rigney carried off the charade perfectly, luxuriating in the opportunity to spend twenty minutes explaining that "we just don't believe in night baseball." The eavesdropper thanked "Wrigley" profusely and scurried to a phone to inform family and friends of his experience.

Rigney's own phone rang constantly. He received frequent job offers from other clubs, a measure of his appeal and ability. The most tempting came in September of that first season in Anaheim. Detroit general manager Jim Campbell received Haney's permission to speak with Rigney and then flew to Anaheim to meet personally with the Angels manager.

Campbell offered a three-year contract at a total close to $200,000, a significant sum at that time. Rigney spent several days considering it, during which period the Angels offered a one-year extension at $65,000. Rigney ultimately called Campbell and said he had a job to finish with the Angels and that California was still his home.

The Angels announced that Rigney would be back in 1967 but that his coaches—Del Rice, Jack Paepke, Marv Grissom and Salty Parker—would not be rehired, scapegoats for the string of sad summers, temporarily snapped in 1967 when the Angels played a significant role in one of the American League's most exciting pennant races ever, after mounting their own pennant challenge in midsummer.

Bob Lemon, Billy Herman, Mike Roarke and Don Heffner joined Rigney's coaching staff. General manager Haney then visited the trading market, where he found spirited interest in Dean Chance, whose deteriorating performance and inconsistent behavior in 1966 prompted the Angels, seeking hitting help, to make him expendable.

The best offer came from Minnesota, and on December 2 the Angels traded their Cy Young Award winner of 1964 for first baseman Don Mincher, outfielder Jimmie Hall and pitcher Pete Cimino.

"I'm not sure we'll ever find another arm like Dean's," Rigney said, "but we had to do something about our first base situation and overall hitting."

"I'm not surprised to be traded," Chance said, "but I am shocked that the Angels would trade me to an American League club. I'm shocked that they'd run the risk of letting me come back to haunt them."

Chance did come back, winning 20 games in 1967 and 16 in 1968, after which he injured his arm and was never again the same talent.

Hall and Cimino never fulfilled their promise, but Mincher led the club with 25 homers and 78 RBI in 1967 before succumbing to the club jinx. He was beaned during the opening week of the 1968 season, his last with the Angels, and retired at the end of the 1970 season at 32.

The Angels headed for spring training in 1967 without Chance, without Belinsky, without 26 of the 30 players they had selected in the expansion draft. Rigney believed this would be "the best club we've ever had, the best [starting] eight. This is the first time I've ever felt this good about our prospects."

The opening-day lineup read: Paul Schaal, 3B; Jim Fregosi, SS; Rick Reichardt, LF; Don Mincher, 1B; Jimmie Hall, RF; José Cardenal, CF; Buck Rodgers, C; Bobby Knoop, 2B, and George Brunet, P.

The Angels beat Detroit's Denny McLain, 4–2, that day, Anaheim's ceremonial first pitch having been thrown by a right-hander named Ronald Reagan, and the optimistic glow became that much brighter on April 24, when a doubleheader sweep of Cleveland put the Angels in sole possession of first place for the first time since that memorable July 4, 1962.

The clubhouse celebration made it seem as if this was September 24 instead of April 24, and what followed was almost predictable. The Angels lost their next three games and then lost six in a row in mid-May. They were eight games under .500 on May 23, when Haney said, "It looks like we're dead. I haven't seen the spirit to battle back."

Unwilling to let what was expected to be their best season get away, Haney and Robert Reynolds held a unique clubhouse meeting with the team on May 24, Haney impersonating a football coach delivering his halftime oratory.

"Rig has talked his heart out," Haney told the press. "Maybe it will have some new meaning if it comes from someone else."

Rigney wasn't happy about the front office intervention. He said the clubhouse was his, the executive wing theirs.

"I believe the morale is good, damn good," he said heatedly.

There was no immediate improvement. The Angels were still eight games under .500 on June 2, when Reynolds said, "It's too early to make radical changes, but it's a blessing that Gene Autry has been in Japan and hasn't been here to see the way the team has played."

Three days later, Rigney, Haney and Reynolds held a summit meeting, after which Haney repeated his 1964 vow, saying Rigney would be "the manager for as long as I'm the general manager."

The Angels finally began to move, winning five in a row, then 18 of 24 to reach .500 on July 1. They were now only seven games out of the lead, and Rigney, his confidence restored, was again saying he had a pennant contender.

The impetus was provided by a stable pitching staff that lacked the big winner but got 12 wins for the season from both Jim McGlothlin, who set a club record in midsummer with 33 consecutive scoreless innings, and Minnie Rojas, the Cuban right-hander, who set a club record for appearances (72) and saves (22). Rojas, paralyzed in the tragic car accident that followed the 1968 season, had the best ERA (2.51) among the regular pitchers on a staff that led the league in ERA (3.19).

The Angels were 4½ out and five games over .500 on July 10 and within 1½ games on August 14, when the first five teams were separated by only 2½ games.

The league-leading Minnesota Twins moved into Anaheim for a three-game series on that day, and it was the beginning of the week that was for the Angels, the week that destroyed their pennant aspirations.

A throwing error by Fregosi and two RBI by an unlikely hero, reserve shortstop Jackie Hernandez, a throw-in in the deal that sent

Chance to Minnesota, gave the Twins a 2–1 victory in the opener of the series and seemed to strip the Angels of their heart.

Jim Perry shut them out, 4–0, and Dean Chance beat them, 5–1, sending the Angels limping to Boston, where they lost four straight games, emerging 6½ games behind the Twins, a stunning and sudden disparity that proved insurmountable.

The Boston series was the one in which Tony Conigliaro, one of the game's best young players, a hitter of unlimited potential, suffered his almost fatal beaning when a fastball thrown by Jack Hamilton, a pitcher who made his living with the spitball but who in this case insisted he had not put saliva on the ball—an assertion supported by catcher Rodgers and most of the Red Sox—struck Conigliaro on the left side of his face, catching both bone and batting helmet, then devoid of an ear flap.

Those who were there in Fenway Park and heard that sound will never forget it.

The pitcher and batter were never the same.

Hamilton, a journeyman right-hander who had been obtained from the Mets in a June trade that sent Nick Willhite to New York, seemed haunted by the incident and was out of baseball within two years.

Conigliaro, 22 at the time, a strikingly handsome Italian who had hit 104 homers in his first three and a half seasons with the Red Sox, suffered a broken cheekbone and dislocated jaw and lost significant vision in his left eye. He sat out the 1968 season, came back to hit 20 homers for the Red Sox in 1969 and 36 in 1970, but then suffered additional deterioration in his sight and retired abruptly in midseason in 1972, having been traded, ironically, to the Angels during the previous winter. Conigliaro would suffer an incapacitating heart attack on January 9, 1982, and die Febuary 25, 1990, at 45, his life never the same after the beaning.

The Hamilton-Conigliaro incident took place on a Friday night in the first game of a trip that remains one of the Angels' most memorable. Boston won the next day's Fenway special, 12–11, and then swept a doubleheader on Sunday, the Angels blowing an 8–0 lead in the second game, highlighted by a verbal and physical exchange between umpire Bill Valentine and Boston manager Dick

Williams in which almost the entire Boston team was called on to restrain Williams.

The Angels moved on to Cleveland, where Jim Coates and Tony Horton of the Indians exchanged punches during a 6–4 Angels win; Luis Tiant struck out 16 in pitching a 3–2 Cleveland win; the Angels got 25 hits in a 16–5 romp; and Sam McDowell struck out 10 Angels in a 3–2 Cleveland win.

The club next headed to Baltimore, where a Friday night doubleheader was rained out, the second game of a Saturday night doubleheader was rained out after Mincher had won the opener with a three-run homer in the ninth, and the Sunday doubleheader was also rained out.

The Angels continued to play aggressively, but were unable to improve on their fifth-place standing. They did, however, turn what was called the Great Race in favor of Boston by winning two of three from Minnesota (beating Chance in the final game of the series) and two of four from Detroit during the final week of a season in which the top three clubs were separated by only 1½ games entering the final day.

A six-run rally—ignited by Fregosi's single and capped by Fregosi's two-run single—in the eighth inning of the second game of a doubleheader with Detroit on the season's next-to-last day had wiped out a 4–2 Detroit lead, leaving the Tigers in a position where they had to sweep the Angels on the last day in a doubleheader to gain a tie with either Boston or Minnesota, who were playing at Fenway Park.

The Tigers won the opener 6–4 as Boston beat Chance and Minnesota, but in the emotional nightcap, in the lingering twilight of a cold and gray afternoon at Tiger Stadium, Rick Reichardt and Don Mincher hit clutch home runs and George Brunet came out of the bullpen in the ninth inning, for only the third time in 40 appearances, and got Dick McAuliffe, who had grounded into only one double play all year, to ground into another with two on and one out, preserving an 8–5 Angels' victory that gave the pennant to Boston.

The Angels finished 5½ back with an 84–77 record.

Johnny Podres, the former Dodger star who was wrapping up

his career in Detroit, sat in the silent Tigers clubhouse and said, "If the Angels had played like this all season, there wouldn't have been a great race. The Angels would have won it easily."

Rigney concurred, but said that his team's play during the final week had provided a foundation for 1968.

"We learned what it takes to win the pennant," he said. "We learned the meaning of guts and what you have to stand up to emotionally. What we learned we won't forget. They'll never forget what they went through that final week."

So much for long memories. The 1968 season was one of the Angels' most disappointing. The Angels went from 84–77 to 67–95, finishing eighth, 36 games behind the Tigers, who finally achieved the goal they had come so close to achieving the year before.

It all went bad for the Angels, who could have guessed as much on opening day, when they lost in New York, 1–0, and then had to flee a burning plane at La Guardia Airport just after taking their seats.

Mincher was beaned by Sam McDowell a few days later and appeared in just 120 games, hitting only 13 homers. Third baseman Paul Schaal was beaned by Boston's José Santiago in June and appeared in just 60 games, batting just .210.

Minnie Rojas, suffering from a sore arm, the result perhaps of his 72 appearances in 1967, appeared in just 38 games, saving but five, 17 fewer than the previous year.

Rick Reichardt hit 21 homers and drove in 73 runs, but the team batting average was a league-low .227.

George Brunet was the leading pitcher with an unattractive 13–17 record.

The Angels heard Gene Autry deliver a rare clubhouse pep talk on August 30, but Autry should have saved his voice for another recording. The Angels finished the year with a 32–49 record in Anaheim, losing seven of their last eight games.

Marvin Milkes, Haney's important right arm, left to become general manager of the Seattle Pilots (who would later become the Milwaukee Brewers), while Cedric Tallis, the most important cog in the move to Anaheim, left to become general manager of Kansas City's expansion team.

Rigney would have left, too, since he received managerial offers from the Giants, Twins, White Sox and Royals, but Autry's offer of a two-year contract influenced him to stay. It was a vote of confidence for the manager that would not be repeated ten months later.

11

1968–70: THE SNAKE PIT

The future of Bill Rigney was not the only boardroom discussion during the 1968 season.

The Signal Companies, a Los Angeles conglomerate, approached Gene Autry with a proposal that allowed Golden West Broadcasting minority shareholders to sell out while Autry retained majority control. Signal ultimately acquired 49.9 percent for $25 million. The arrangement also gave Signal first option on obtaining Autry's 50.1 percent for approximately the same amount at the time of his death. It was indicative of Autry's cowboy code that when the broadcasting industry was struck by an ensuing recession, he decided that the contract wasn't fair to Signal and called in the reluctant lawyers to rework it.

The $25 million option was reduced to $20 million. Autry, seeking to improve his immediate cash position as part of a complicated transaction, agreed to a yearly payment of $250,000 tax-free, with the amount applied to the purchase price. He also waived rights to a percentage of Signal's profits, which had been part of the original transaction.

Leonard Firestone, who owned 30 percent of the Angels in 1968, objected to Signal's corporate invasion and offered his holding to Autry and the other investors, who bought him out for $9 million. The remainder of the investment group sold their percentages to Golden West Broadcasting in 1974. Robert Reynolds, Autry's longtime partner, received $7.5 million.

The Reynolds and Firestone figures now seem modest, of course, but both sold before national and local television contracts and the stadium renaissance of recent years contributed to skyrocketing franchise values.

Autry and Signal were left as the only shareholders, and Signal bowed out in another complex arrangement in 1982. Kohlberg Kravis Roberts & Company, a firm specializing in leveraged buyouts, paid Signal $225 million and received KTLA, Autry's independent television station in Los Angeles, and the transmitting tower on Mt. Wilson. Autry, who turned down a $235 million deal with Cap Cities because he had already shaken hands with KKR, emerged with sole ownership of the Angels, $20 million in cash, an improved contract to televise Angel games on KTLA, the Sunset Boulevard building which housed Golden West Broadcasting, and radio stations in Los Angeles and Seattle. He also emerged with two radio stations in Portland, two in Detroit, a TV station in Oklahoma City and a radio station in San Francisco, but those, as required by trust, were placed under the umbrella of the Autry Foundation, the charitable wing established by Ina Autry, his late wife.

The transaction was a major step in Autry's estate planning, but the boardroom decision that had the more significant impact on the club's operation was reached in September 1968 and involved Fred Haney, who had turned 70 in April of that year.

Frustrated by the inability of the Angels to manufacture a series of solid seasons and believing the farm and scouting systems had not produced in the anticipated manner, Autry and Reynolds decided it was time for a younger man to carry on as general manager, for close friend Haney to step down.

They met with Haney and told him they still retained confidence in him but they believed age had become an issue. They offered him a position as club consultant at his same salary.

Haney was disappointed. He knew that the consultant's position translated to a title without substance, and he tried to talk Autry and Reynolds out of their decision while not saying anything that would impair their long relationship or sound ungrateful for their years of support.

"Fred knew that Gene and Bob were under pressure to make a change," Haney's widow, Florence, said years later, "but Fred wouldn't think of saying anything that would hurt anyone. He would have done anything in the world for Gene and Bob."

Haney agreed to become consultant to a general manager not yet selected. The three candidates were Giants' general manager Chub Feeney, Mets' general manager Bob Scheffing and former Dodgers' vice president Dick Walsh, then in the third year of a five-year contract as commissioner of the North American Soccer League.

Both Feeney and Scheffing demanded stock arrangements that the Angels were unwilling to meet, leaving Walsh the primary candidate. It seemed an improbable alliance, since the Angels and Walsh had argued frequently during the four years in which the Angels were tenants at Dodger Stadium, where Walsh, Walter O'Malley's vice president in charge of saying no, had served as director of stadium operations.

In that time, Reynolds said later, the Angels developed admiration and respect for Walsh's knowledge and energy, for his unyielding, uncompromising and no-nonsense approach, traits soon described in a far less flattering manner.

Golden West executives Bert West and Stan Spero were dispatched to New York to sound out Walsh, who responded with enthusiasm to the proposal that eventually took the form of a seven-year contract. The announcement was made on September 23, 1968, the same day it was announced that Rigney had been rehired for two years.

"I look upon this as the start of a new era for the Angels," Reynolds said. "I'm confident that under Dick Walsh and Bill Rigney our team will attain the capabilities that we still believe it possesses."

Rigney was fired eight months later. Walsh was fired with four years remaining on his contract. The new era became the most tumultuous in Angels history to that point, the capabilities disintegrating under a cloud of controversy.

How it happened is more easily explained than why. Richard Bishop Walsh Jr. was a man of unquestioned ability and intelligence. He emerged from the reputation-shattering experience with the Angels to resume his schooling, received a law degree and ultimately became director of the Los Angeles Convention Center.

He had previously been an All-City third baseman at Los Angeles High School, his desire to play professionally frustrated by World War II. He was 17 when he received an officer's commission and 18 when he became an infantry platoon leader in the Pacific conflict with Japan. He was hired by the Dodgers when the war ended and assigned to learn the business literally from the ground up, sweeping out stadiums, punching tickets, selling advertising.

He had been with the Dodgers for 18 years when he accepted the offer from the North American Soccer League, reasoning he had gone as far as he could with the Dodgers, since there were two heirs on the horizon, Peter Bavasi, son of the then general manager, and Peter O'Malley, son of the owner.

"I'm returning to my first love," Walsh said at the time of his hiring by the Angels, a statement some soon questioned, appalled that anyone would treat their love with Walsh's callousness.

The belief that Walsh would supply a direction and discipline previously absent soon gave way to the realization that Walsh's discipline represented dictatorship and his direction was leading directly to doom.

His relationship with the city of Anaheim dissolved in the same manner as his relationship with players and front office associates. City officials accused him of lies and broken promises. A former club executive said, "He was always trying to set traps and catch you in lies. He was always using his own lies to set the traps."

Traveling secretary Tommie Ferguson left to become vice president of the Milwaukee Brewers. Farm and scouting director Roland Hemond left to become vice president of the Chicago White Sox. Speakers Bureau director Johnny Lindell left to become security director at Santa Anita racetrack.

Ferguson recalled the day close friend Rigney was fired. "Walsh sent me to his hotel room with the airline ticket for Rig's flight home," Ferguson said. "When I got back to the stadium, Walsh asked me if I had brought the club suitcase Rig had been using."

Stunned by Walsh's cold pettiness, Ferguson said, "No, I'll leave that up to you."

Walsh had a hand in every department. He was accused of failing to delegate authority.

"There was no organization when I arrived," he said. "I had to build one. I made sure I was in the middle of every department at first. Once we had a format, I stayed clear. I had regular staff meetings, and I even had meetings just for the secretaries. I felt they had a right to know what was going on."

Of the conflicts with the city, Walsh said, "We were being charged indiscriminately, such as the salary for a maintenance man on a twelve-month basis rather than simply the duration of the baseball season. That's minutia perhaps, but it added up."

Little things seemed to eat at Walsh. He sent a letter to the equipment man saying the players had been using too many towels. The players responded with a sign that read: "2 Towels for Regulars and 1 for Extra Men. Pitchers Who Are Not Used Must Shower at Home."

The players believed Walsh was attempting to use fear as a motivation. Personalities meant nothing. It was all about production.

"I don't want to get close to the players because I don't want to lose my objectivity," Walsh said. "The players aren't entertained in my house, and I'm not entertained in theirs."

Walsh's dispassion was seen in 1971. Six-time All-Star Jim Fregosi, the club leader, a man to whom Walsh had just given a three-year contract, which was designed, he said, to eventually help Fregosi become the Angels' manager, developed a tumor on his foot. Walsh, with several other players hurt and his team in tatters, refused to let Fregosi undergo the required operation. It was not until midseason, when Fregosi checked himself into the hospital, that the shortstop left the lineup.

The players' distaste for the man they called the "Smiling Python" manifested itself in 1971 when, spotting Walsh standing in foul territory down the left-field line during batting practice, they moved up in the batting cage and purposely tried to hit line drives in the direction of Walsh's back. Manager Harold (Lefty) Phillips soon caught on and canceled the rest of batting practice, sending the players to the clubhouse in the manner of misbehaving youngsters.

It was in 1971 that the A in Big A came to stand for "Agony." It all fell apart, and manager Phillips said, "I'm afraid there's going to be real violence in the clubhouse. Somebody is going to hit somebody else over the head with a stool . . . or worse."

The "worse" referred to the guns and knives that many of the players began to carry as the symptoms of disintegration became acute. The clubhouse became a place where Angels feared to tread. There were fights, arguments and a continuous process of internal decay, much of it stemming from Alex Johnson, the talented but temperamental outfielder who seemed to carry a deep-seated hatred for all humanity.

Johnson had been acquired in one of a series of trades that left Hemond shaking his head and saying it was "chaotic." Walsh said he didn't really believe in building a team through trade but that there was no time for a five-year plan, that he had to go for broke when competing with the Dodgers and that there wasn't anything in the Angels' farm system when he took over.

Those who watched Walsh, a man with little experience in the area of personnel, do his wheeling and dealing could have sworn he was using farm talent to put across his trades.

Aurelio Rodriguez, a brilliant third baseman fresh out of the farm system, was coupled with Rick Reichardt and traded to Washington in 1970 for Ken McMullen. This wasn't entirely Walsh's doing, since he was prodded by Phillips, who found it difficult communicating with the Spanish-speaking Rodriguez, who was still a major leaguer ten years later.

Phillips' forte was execution, not elocution. He once said, 'Our phenoms ain't phenomenating." Another gem was "It's all water under the dam." Phillips had a tough time communicating with everyone, no matter what language they spoke.

Pedro Borbon, who spoke mostly Spanish and threw mostly fastballs during a distinguished career as a big league relief pitcher, was lifted out of the farm system and packaged with Jim McGlothlin and Vern Geishert in the 1969 trade by which Walsh acquired Alex Johnson, who had already created a legacy of problems in Philadelphia, St. Louis and Cincinnati.

A year later, pitching prospect Greg Garrett went to Cincinnati for veteran pitcher Jim Maloney, who never won a game for the Angels. Outfielder Bill Voss went to Milwaukee for pitcher Gene Brabender, who was optioned to the minors even before the season began.

Pitching prospect Tom Bradley was coupled with Tom Egan and maturing outfielder Jay Johnstone in a trade with the White Sox that brought Ken Berry, who batted .221 with the Angels, seldom-used infielder Syd O'Brien, and pitcher Billy Wynne, optioned before the season began.

Those lamentable trades were all in the future when the Angels gathered in the "Carrot Capital" of Holtville for spring training in 1969. Rigney and Walsh were anxious to correct the eighth-place finish of the season before, and Rigney knew he was not really the new general manager's man. That, of course, was Phillips, hired initially as director of player personnel and then assigned to Rigney's staff as pitching coach, a move that surprised Rigney but which he did not entirely object to since he respected Phillips knowledge of the game. Rigney had asked Phillips, a pitching coach under the Dodgers' Walter Alston, to assist him on a part-time basis during spring training, and Walsh responded by putting Phillips in uniform on a full-time basis, wasting no time in getting one of his own people in the clubhouse.

The pressure on Rigney was evident from the first day of spring training when, after chatting with the press prior to the initial workout, Rigney walked away and Walsh said, "That gray-haired gentleman has only a two-year contract and I have a seven-year contract."

The American and National Leagues split into Eastern and Western divisions in 1969, and that was the reason the Angels lidn't finish eighth again. They finished third in the West, 13 games behind Minnesota, with a 71–91 record.

The Angels' team batting average of .230 was last in the league, and they were also last in home runs, RBI, runs scored, hits and total bases. Johnstone led the club with a .270 batting average, but he could not prevent the Angels from being shut out 19 times, a league high.

Andy Messersmith, one of the best starting pitchers ever developed by the Angels, was 16–11 in his first full season, but his 0–5 start contributed to Rigney's firing, as did the absence of a relief pitcher. Rigney kept asking for Ken Tatum, a right-handed relief pitcher then at Hawaii, but Walsh did not respond until after Phillips had taken over. Tatum had 22 saves, a 7–2 record and an ERA of 1.36 after his recall, helping Phillips go 60–63.

The inevitable began to close in on Rigney with the first pitch of the new season. The Angels stranded 10 runners and lost to the new expansion team from Seattle, 4–3.

A 15–1 loss on May 5 to the expansion team from Kansas City prompted Walsh to say, "When we fall behind we just go through the motions. This is a unique experience for me, and I don't like it."

"At least," Rigney said, "no one got hurt."

Two weeks later, Walsh again talked about the "defeatist attitude" and traded the most respected and best-liked Angel, second baseman Bobby Knoop, to Chicago for second baseman Sandy Alomar, father of future major leaguers Sandy Jr. and Roberto.

Knoop's former teammates reacted angrily to the trade, but it was one of Walsh's best, since Alomar, 26, was five years younger than Knoop and had more offensive weapons, including speed. He stole 20 of the Angels' 54 bases that year and 35 in 1970. He had 22 game-winning hits in 1970 and extended what would become a club record for consecutive games played, a streak that reached 648 before Alomar broke his leg in 1973.

The Alomar deal was consummated on the day that the Angels left on the trip that led directly to Rigney's firing.

There had been the 8–18 death march of 1961 and a 1–8 excursion in 1967, but there had never been an exercise in futility to match the 0–10 trip which ended with Fregosi, aware that Rigney's firing had to be imminent, saying the manager wasn't to blame. Fregosi's pleas were too late.

Walsh had already called Autry and Reynolds to tell them, "Rig has lost control of the team. I don't feel we can win. I don't think we can turn it around with him in there."

Reynolds received Walsh's call while on a vacation in India. He reacted by sending his wife to visit the Taj Mahal with friends while he paced the hotel room for two days, trying to digest what Walsh had told him.

Autry was on a business trip to New York when Walsh called. "Perhaps I knew it was inevitable," Autry said in reflection, "but it was still a blow. I told Dick that Rig was not only the only manager we had ever known, he was our friend. I told him that if he was convinced a change had to be made, then let's do it at once since there's no sense in waiting. I asked him who he had in mind."

Walsh's answer was Lefty Phillips. Autry would concede years later that it was at this juncture he made a serious mistake by not insisting Walsh elevate Chuck Tanner, a communicative fireball who would later lead Pittsburgh to a world championship. Tanner was then managing the Angels' Hawaii farm club, having been in the system as player and manager almost from the start, a man totally familiar with the players then on the Angels' roster.

"I suppose," Autry said, looking back, "there are three kinds of owners. One is the type who puts up the money and runs the club himself, serving as his own general manager. The second is the type who hires a professional to run the club, then stays out of the way and keeps score. The third is the type who keeps such a low profile that the players and fans hardly know he exists.

"I like to think I belong to the second category. I have tried hard not to interfere with the men on the firing line. I am consulted on major decisions and the final approval is mine, but I don't recall ever overruling someone who felt strongly his way was right. I have made an effort to know the players. I drop by the clubhouse from time to time, and I try to write personal notes to each player who is traded away after long service with the club. I have never had

ny desire to go on the field or be in the dugout. I have wondered often why a manager did this or that, but I have always
ried to restrain my second-guessing. I have never ordered a manager to play a certain player, and I have never called a manager at
hree in the morning to ask why he didn't play the infield back
with one out.

"Lefty Phillips was a fine man with a solid reputation as coach
and scout, but he was a disaster as manager and I will accept the
blame for not insisting Tanner be hired. I will also accept the blame
for not dealing promptly with the Alex Johnson situation, but again
thought we had professionals running the show."

Rigney was fired on May 26, 1969, Autry announcing, "We
simply don't believe the Angels are a last-place team."

Almost every reporter who had covered the club during its
eight-plus years went to Rigney's Anaheim hotel room to share a
drink with him following the announcement. There was no anger
or bitterness on Rigney's part. He had a contract that entitled him
to be paid for three more years, and he would soon be in a situation
that would allow him to enjoy a last laugh of sorts.

"Sometimes a change in managers is what it takes," Rigney
acknowledged as he packed the suitcase that would ultimately be
returned to Walsh. "It gives the players a reason for why they have
been bad. The saddest thing about this is that, in the eight years,
the organization really didn't improve any."

Said the Smiling Python, "I said this spring that we are capable
of contending, and I still believe that. I had to move now or forgo
the entire season. The club was down and beating itself too often.
It was waiting for lightning to strike. It was waiting to be beaten."

With a .216 team batting average and a 4.10 ERA at the time
of Rigney's firing, it seldom had to wait long.

Phillips understood the scapegoat implications of Rigney's dismissal. "He was a very sound manager," the new manager said. "I'd
say that 95 percent of the time I agreed with the way he did things.
The other 5 percent you could go either way."

In another time and place, Harold Phillips may not have been
the disaster Autry perceived. He was a slow-moving, slope-
shouldered, pot-bellied man of whom Johnny Podres, the Dodgers'

pitching star, once said, "No one looks worse in a uniform or knows as much about baseball." A student of pitching and fundamentals, and a man credited with signing many of the Dodgers' top players of the 1960s, Phillips knew and cared little about syntax, or about the players' alleged need for communication. He made his points in brief bursts of shattered English, waving an unlit cigar, a chaw of tobacco dirtying his uniform and making it that much more difficult to understand what he was saying. The cigar was never lit because Phillips was an asthmatic. He was only 53, in fact, when he died suddenly of an asthma attack on June 12, 1972, having been fired along with Walsh during the previous winter.

The story is told with compassion of the night in 1969 when pitcher Phil Ortega, a Yaqui Indian who couldn't handle his alcohol, appeared in the lobby of the Muehlbach Hotel in Kansas City wearing only underwear. The call went to manager Phillips, who piled out of bed and boarded an elevator, failing to notice that every floor had been punched. By the time an angry and excited Phillips had reached the lobby, he was wheezing so badly that he could barely walk or talk. He found Ortega, however, and had no trouble making the pitcher understand he had just been fined $1,000.

In another time and place, without the distractions created by an Ortega, an Alex Johnson, a Tony Conigliaro, Phillips might have been able to put his knowledge to work. He might have been able to do it with the Angels except that he received virtually no support from Dick Walsh, his friend. Phillips became the fall guy, hearing only sounds of silence from Walsh, Autry and Reynolds. Good friends Phillips and Walsh seldom even talked during their final days with the Angels.

The man who pushed both over the brink, who did even more, perhaps, to tear the organization apart than the man who traded for him, was Alex Johnson. He was acquired from Cincinnati in November of 1969, the Angels also getting utility infielder Chico Ruiz and seldom used pitcher Mel Queen in the deal.

Walsh, either through naivete or total disregard for Johnson's track record for disruptions, said, "I'm elated. Alex will answer many of our problems."

And, in some measure, Alex did, at least in 1970. He became

the first Angel ever to collect 200 hits in a season, two coming on the final night when he went two for three to finish with a .329 batting average, edging Boston's Carl Yastrzemski for the league title by .003.

Johnson was the catalyst as a team that had the league's lowest batting average in 1969 rebounded to set club records for hits (1,391) and average (.251) in 1970. Jim Fregosi, batting ahead of Johnson, had 16 game-winning hits, 22 homers, 82 RBI and a .278 average. Jim Spencer, batting behind Johnson, hit .274.

Rib and shoulder injuries diluted Messersmith's effectiveness between May and August, but left-hander Clyde Wright, a farm system product out of Carson-Newman College in Jefferson City, Tennessee, went from two wins in 1969 to a club record 22 in 1970, including a no-hitter against Oakland, the Angels' first no-hitter since Belinsky's in 1962. Another promising pitcher, Tom Murphy, won 16 games, while Tatum saved 17. Tatum, however, was never the same pitcher after he beaned Paul Blair of Baltimore, at Anaheim Stadium in August. The hard-throwing right-hander, a man who saved 39 games in his first two seasons, became reluctant to throw his best fastball inside, and this was a key reason for his inclusion in the trade for Conigliaro.

The Angels were only three back of Minnesota on September 4, 1970, when the Twins, managed then by a man named Rigney, initiated a three-game sweep of California, plunging the Angels into a nine-game losing streak during which Phillips said:

"I watch us play now and feel like patting myself on the back. I must have been a mastermind for three-fourths of the season."

Phillips also said, "We finished 26 games out last year, and it would mean quite a bit to the franchise as well as to each man if we could finish second. However, from what I've seen, I've got some players who are too dumb to realize it. There is a definite lack of maturity."

The Angels frustrated Phillips by tailing off to finish third, 12 games behind Rigney's pennant-winning Twins. The 86–86 record was 15 games better than in 1969, and attendance spiraled from an Anaheim low of 758,388 to 1,077,741. Walsh and Phillips had reason to believe they were doing a few things right—though not enough reason, perhaps, to disregard the time bomb that was Alex Johnson.

Johnson at times in 1970 had angered his manager and teammates with an inexplicable lack of hustle, and had strained nerves with his taunting of teammates and writers. In other words, displaying again the temperament that had made him a liability in Cincinnati, St. Louis and Philadelphia.

Alex Johnson had it all—strength, speed, instincts—but it was impossible to quell the fires that raged within him. A Prince Charming away from the park, his behavior when he put on the uniform once prompted his wife to apologize to the wives of the other Angel players.

In one of his few coherent interviews, one of his few interviews of *any* kind, Johnson said his attitude was a response to racial injustice.

"Hell, yes, I'm bitter," he said. "I've been bitter since I learned I was black. The society into which I was born and in which I grew up and in which I play ball today is anti-black. My attitude is nothing more than a reaction to their attitude. But they [the whites] don't keep their hatreds to themselves. They go out of their way to set up barriers, to make dirty little slights so that you're aware of their messed-up feelings."

Johnson never tried to hide his own. He and Chico Ruiz exchanged punches by the batting cage in September 1970, and there were constant confrontations with the media. He poured coffee grounds into the typewriter of the *Los Angeles Herald Examiner*'s Dick Miller, and he daily delivered obscenity-laced tirades that made it impossible for the writers to interview Johnson or anyone else in the Angels' clubhouse. The club's press corps ultimately filed a formal complaint with the league office, prompting the Angels' publicist, George Lederer, on behalf of Johnson, to send each writer a telegram in which Johnson said, ". . . in the future I will not talk with you in any manner, offensive or otherwise."

The 1970 season was a mere prelude to the nightmare of 1971, when Johnson's antics were compounded by the players' mounting unhappiness with Walsh, by the front office's belief that the trades for Berry, Conigliaro and Maloney had ensured a pennant, and by the performance of Conigliaro, who settled into a Newport Beach apartment next door to actress Raquel Welch.

If that alone was not enough to create envy among his teammates, Conigliaro, who had been acquired in a six-player trade with Boston in September 1970, soon created annoyance and the suspicion that he was malingering as he missed games with a nagging string of little injuries. He returned from one hospital trip and found a stretcher in front of his locker with his uniform laid out on it, a pair of crutches tied together as a coat of arms, and the whole thing splashed with catsup for blood.

"If Conigliaro does for us what he did for Boston," Walsh had said at the time of the trade, "then I can't help but think in terms of a pennant."

What Conigliaro had done for Boston in the second year of his comeback from the near-fatal beaning of 1967 was hit 26 home runs and drive in 116 runs. What he did for the Angels in 1971 was hit four home runs and drive in 15 runs. He appeared in only 74 games before the new deterioration in his left eye prompted him to hold a five a.m. press conference on July 10, announcing his retirement. The unusual hour stemmed from the fact that the Angels had gone past midnight before losing a 1–0, 20-inning decision in Oakland. Conigliaro had been unable to sleep because of his hitless effort and two run-ins with umpire Merle Anthony. The weight of the season and the uncertainty with his vision prompted him to summon the writers at a time when they are generally comatose.

"This is something I had to do," he said, referring to his retirement, "or I'd end up in a straitjacket with the other nuts.

"I almost lost my mind out there tonight. I was doing things on the field and saying things on the bench that I didn't know I was saying or doing. I was saying good-bye to baseball."

Manager Phillips, devoid of any sympathy, responded by saying Conigliaro belonged in an institution. The Angels placed him on the voluntary retired list and terminated his salary. Conigliaro later filed a grievance through the Major League Players Association seeking his second-half wages. He argued that the Angels should have been aware of his eye problem and placed him on the disabled list before he reached a mental state that led him to retire. An arbitrator ruled in favor of Conigliaro, and the Angels were forced to pay an additional $40,000.

The decision was reached after Walsh had been fired. He responded by saying, "There was not much I could have done differently in the Conigliaro situation. Boston had guaranteed that he was physically sound, that there was no problem with his eye. If I had remained as general manager I'd have demanded compensation from the Red Sox."

Phillips' problems with Johnson had flared again in spring training of 1971 when the batting champion leaned against the outfield fence and stood in the shade of a light tower while on defense during an exhibition game and was then benched when he failed to run out a ground ball in the eighth inning. He was benched again the next day when he again failed to run out a ground ball, establishing a pattern that hounded the Angels for the next five months. Johnson was in and out of the lineup, in and out of the doghouse. The lingering crises undermined morale, cost Phillips what respect he had with the team and created a rift between Phillips and Walsh as they disagreed over who should have done what and when with Johnson.

Remarkably, the outfielder viewed it all as some sort of conspiracy and said he would rather be playing in hell than Anaheim. There were those who insisted that Anaheim had become just that.

"I'm not writing about baseball," complained one reporter. "I'm writing about World War III."

Walsh could have initiated an armistice simply by supporting his manager on any of the numerous occasions when Phillips told the team that Johnson "will never again play for the Angels."

But that kind of support never came—until it was really too late. The taunts, the lack of hustle, led the Angels to take things into their own hands. An enraged Ken Berry charged at Johnson in the clubhouse, forcing teammates to intervene, knowing neither Berry, nor anyone else really, was a match for the muscular Johnson.

Clyde Wright threateningly raised a clubhouse stool after Johnson had thrown a Coke at him, prompting Johnson to say, "Go ahead. You get one swing with the stool. Then you're mine."

Wright backed off.

Ultimately, however, Chico Ruiz, one of several armed Angels and a favorite target for Johnson's obscene diatribes, allegedly pulled a gun on his tormentor during a clubhouse dispute, and it was a few days later, on June 26, 1971, that the Angels finally suspended Johnson for "failure to hustle and improper mental attitude."

Johnson responded with a grievance filed through the Players Association. Executive director Marvin Miller argued that Johnson had been seeing a psychiatrist for emotional stress and should have been placed on the disabled list. The arbitrator agreed, ruling in September that the Angels had to put Johnson back on their roster and provide him with his salary. Johnson was back, but not for long.

The Angels began their postseason housecleaning by trading Johnson and catcher Jerry Moses, unhappy over his lack of playing time ("He ain't exactly Gabby Hartnett," Phillips said at one point), to Cleveland for outfielder Vada Pinson, infielder-outfielder Frank Baker and pitcher Alan Foster.

Only Pinson made a significant contribution in 1972, but this was a trade that represented addition via subtraction. Johnson's departure eradicated a malignancy, removing the man who had stripped the Angels of any chance of living up to their preseason role of favorite in the American League West.

The Angels had won their first seven games in 1971 and were then heard from again only because of their clubhouse chaos. Andy Messersmith won 20 games and Clyde Wright 16, but with Johnson (who batted just .259), Conigliaro and Fregosi frequently out of the lineup, the team batting average fell to .231.

The Angels finished fourth with a 76–86 record, 25½ games behind Oakland after playing at a 44–43 pace following Johnson's suspension.

The firing of Phillips and Walsh was as inevitable as the trading of Johnson. Phillips and his coaches—Pete Reiser, Norm Sherry, Rocky Bridges and Fred Koenig—got the word on October 7, when

Autry announced that a move had to be made for the good of team morale.

Phillips refused to blast Walsh for his lack of support. "Too much has been said already this year," he said. "I feel I did the best job I could considering what I had to work with and the circumstances that surrounded the season."

Autry again cited team morale (several players had said they would ask to be traded if Walsh remained) when he announced on October 21 that Walsh was being terminated with four years remaining on his contract, one of many multiyear mistakes the Cowboy was forced to saddle during his ownership.

Walsh would reflect on the traumatic summer of 1971 and say, "It's impossible to describe what it was like to live through." He said his greatest regret was not trading Johnson after his batting title of 1970, "but he had played like hell during the final month of that year and I thought he had seen the light, that he would take pride in the batting title and continue to play that way. I should have known there are no panaceas for the Alex Johnsons of the world. He strained the relationship between himself and the other players, between the players and the manager, between the manager and myself."

Of his failure to intervene, Walsh said, "My philosophy is that until a player signs his contract, he's the general manager's responsibility. After he signs, he belongs to the manager. The more the front office interferes in the clubhouse, the more likely the chance of morale problems.

"I stepped into the Johnson situation only after Lefty came to me and said he'd had it. We were in Oakland and I said, 'Okay, have him in my room this afternoon.'

"I talked for an hour with Alex, and he promised to give 100 percent. At the same time, Lefty was holding a clubhouse meeting during which he told the team that Alex would never again play for the Angels. I couldn't understand Lefty's reasoning, since he'd just asked me to sit down with Alex and see if I might have some influence. At any rate, I asked that he be returned to the lineup."

Those words set the stage eventually for what even Walsh concedes was a lie, a lie that convinced Autry a change would have to be made.

Walsh said at the time of the Ruiz clubhouse incident he had no evidence a gun was employed. He then stated under oath at the grievance hearing that a gun *had* been used, prompting Autry to tell reporters he was stunned by his general manager's failure to advise him of all the facts.

"I had known Ruiz had a gun," Walsh said, "but I did not know if he had threatened Johnson with it, and since Ruiz was not a U.S. citizen, I felt it would jeopardize his status to admit there was a gun.

"I gave this information to the commissioner and to the American League president. I also called Autry, but when I was told he wasn't available, I gave the information to Bob Reynolds. I asked Bob to relay it to Gene, but I can only assume Reynolds didn't do it or Autry forgot having talked to Reynolds."

One thing Autry and his organization would not quickly forget was the abbreviated tenure of Dick Walsh and what had been labeled a new era.

12

1972: DALTON AND HIS GANG

New era II was less traumatic than its predecessor, but no more successful. The professional in whose hands Autry entrusted it this time was Harry I. Dalton, who left a position as director of player personnel with the Baltimore Orioles to become executive vice president and general manager of the Angels.

Dalton served in that capacity for six years, during which time the Angels employed five field managers, never finished higher than fourth and never reached .500, getting closest in 1973, when the record was 79–83.

The new general manager took over a dispirited organization sadly in need of stability, one that required rebuilding from the ground up. Dalton needed time and Autry gave it to him, extending his original five-year contract.

The task was made more difficult by a new wave of injuries and misfortune, the plague that has haunted the Angels since their inception. Dalton resisted predictions and refused to employ the traditional cliché, the stock and solemn pronouncement of a five-year plan.

Scouting director Walter Shannon and a number of men who had worked under Shannon and Dalton in Baltimore joined the California migration. The farm system took on a new look. A trickle of potential players appeared. A few made it. A few made it elsewhere. The majority failed—not unusual in what is the inexact science of drafting high school and college players.

Dalton was accessible to club and city officials and did not share Walsh's fear that a general manager's presence in the clubhouse would lead to morale problems. He visited the clubhouse before and after almost every game, making himself available to the players and manager.

The Angels reacquired the look and feel of a major league organization—everywhere except on the field. Dalton's inability to find the man he perceived as the right manager seemed an indictment of his ability to judge character and an attempt to shift responsibility for the club's poor performance.

The hirings and firings became an annual rite, serving in some measure to tarnish a reputation Dalton had established with Baltimore, where in his six seasons as personnel director the Orioles won four American League pennants and two World Series.

Dalton, 43 at the time of his hiring by the Angels, had spent 18 years with the Orioles following graduation from Amherst College. He was an assistant farm director before becoming farm director, then personnel director. Autry and Reynolds pursued him vigorously, making an initial contact in September 1971, during the final days of the Walsh nightmare.

Autry, in fact, probed Dalton's interest before asking the Orioles for permission to talk with him, raising the ire of Baltimore's then owner, Jerold Hoffberger, who rejected the formal request when it came just prior to his team's confrontation with Oakland in the American League championship series of 1971.

Autry waited until after the World Series, in which Pittsburgh defeated Baltimore, and then called again. This time he received the owner's approval, though grudgingly.

"What difference does it make?" Hoffberger said in an interview with the *Los Angeles Times*. "They talked to him once without my permission, and I assume they'd do it again.

"I turned them down the first time because it was right before the playoffs and series, and Harry had important obligations to the club and to our fans, but it would be wrong for me to stand in his way now. He knows how I feel. He knows how badly I want him to remain with the Orioles."

Dalton would laugh at that. He would reflect later and say Hoffberger had given him no clue as to how he felt, that when he asked permission to meet with the Angels, Hoffberger made no attempt to talk him out of it. Dalton admitted he was hurt by that. He said it made him feel as if his 18 years spent helping to contribute to a successful organization had not been appreciated.

The Orioles left for a tour of Japan two days after the World Series ended, but Dalton flew to California and met with Autry, Reynolds, and attorney Clair Stout at Lakeside Country Club, outlining the prospective job.

He then returned to Baltimore, at which time Hoffberger said he would be willing to give Dalton the same title the Angels would, meaning that Dalton would receive a raise and assume complete authority over the Orioles' operation, an authority he formally shared with Frank Cashen, a management expert from Hoffberger's National Brewery Company.

The offer came too late to dissuade Dalton, who had wanted to hear it a week earlier. He returned to California on the following Saturday and met with Autry in Palm Springs, putting the finishing touches on a contract calling for $75,000 a year, another almost meager amount when measured against current salaries—on and off the field.

Dalton called Hoffberger and told him he had decided to leave, forsaking a championship team in favor of a team that had never won a championship and seemed unlikely to win one soon. That alone, he said, was a significant part of the Angels' attraction, the opportunity and challenge to develop another winner. Dalton said he was also attracted by a significant increase in salary, by his belief that the Anaheim area could become one of the league's best, and by the affection that wife Pat and their three daughters shared for the West Coast.

"As one of the architects of the Orioles' success," Robert Reynolds said, "Dalton is used to winning. After the disappointment of last summer, we are determined to build a winner."

Dalton's hiring was officially announced on October 27. The new general manager said it would probably be several weeks before a manager was hired, since his first obligation was to analyze the organization's playing talent. His first trade then came before the hiring of his first manager.

Attending baseball's winter meetings in Phoenix, Dalton sent relief pitcher Dave LaRoche to Minnesota for shortstop Leo Cardenas, whose age was somewhere between 33 and 43 and who had set a major league record in 1971 for fewest errors in a season.

The Angels would learn that Cardenas didn't make many errors because he didn't reach many balls. The disheartening discovery would be made during the ensuing summer after Jim Fregosi, made expendable by the acquisition of Cardenas, had also been traded.

"In 11 years the Angels have never finished higher than third," Dalton said, attempting to explain the acquisition of Cardenas, and the availability of Fregosi. "I believe Fregosi [who had undergone foot surgery in 1971] can still be productive, but I'm determined to put the 25 best players in uniform.

"We had to have a shortstop, and now we've achieved one of our objectives. Our bullpen is a little thin [LaRoche had a 5-1 record and nine saves in 1971], but it is much easier to develop a relief pitcher than a shortstop."

Dalton would find that it was not easy to do either. The Angels had critical problems both at shortstop and in the bullpen during the 1972 season, making the job of new manager Del Rice almost impossible.

Cardenas was acquired on December 1, 1971, kicking off a tumultuous two-week period in which the Angels dominated the headlines.

December 6: Forty days and 40 nights after his own hiring, Dalton hired Rice as the Angels' third manager. The job had been offered to no one else, though an attempt had been made to negotiate with Yankee manager Ralph Houk.

Responding to Autry's urging, Dalton had called Yankee general manager Lee MacPhail, who refused to give the Angels permission to talk with Houk. MacPhail also told Dalton that Houk would not be interested in joining the Angels.

Dalton then turned to Rice, 49, the 17-year major league catcher who had been the first player ever signed by the Angels. Rice spent only the one year on the club's player roster before joining Bill Rigney's coaching staff for five years. He went on to manage at virtually every stop in the Angels' farm system and was elevated to the job he "had always wanted" after guiding Salt Lake City to the Pacific Coast League pennant, being named Minor League Manager of the Year by *The Sporting News*.

"His managerial record is excellent," Dalton said. "In four years in that capacity, he's sent nine players to the majors with a possibility of four or five more next spring. He is a firm, knowledgeable leader who fits our needs completely."

December 8: The Angels announced a coaching staff of Peanuts Lowrey, Tom Morgan, John Roseboro and Bobby Winkles, the latter having decided to give up the security of his position as head baseball coach at Arizona State to pursue the goal of a managerial position in the majors.

Winkles, 41, had spent 13 years at Arizona State, winning NCAA championships in 1965, 1967, and 1969 while compiling a career record of 524–173. Among his pro products were Reggie Jackson, Rick Monday and Sal Bando.

"I suppose," Winkles said, "that some players might be leery of a college coach, but I'll accept the challenge. I'm sure that by the end of spring training they'll all admit that Winkles knows baseball. They'll all realize that to be a successful college coach, it can't be otherwise. You have to know every phase of the game. You're it. You don't have a staff with specialized instructors."

Winkles had known Rice for almost 10 years, but it was Dalton who lobbied for the hiring of a man who had received pro offers virtually every year while at Arizona State, but never previously had the opportunity to step in at the major league level.

"I didn't hire Bobby on the basis that he was the heir apparent," Dalton said, "nor was I trying to be a pioneer. Bobby had a solid reputation for instruction and fundamentals, and I believed that with a young organization his enthusiasm would rub off. I saw him as the perfect complement for Del."

Winkles would become more than a complement. He would

eventually become the manager, a position in which he heard few compliments.

December 11: Jim Fregosi, the six-time All-Star and only remaining Angel from the 1961 expansion draft, was traded to the Mets for pitcher Nolan Ryan, outfielder Leroy Stanton, pitcher Don Rose and catcher Francisco Estrada.

An angry Fregosi, the clubhouse leader and unnamed captain, said he was a better player than Cardenas and that he was traded only because Dalton wanted to sever ties to the past and establish his authority.

Dalton said Fregosi was traded because he did not believe the shortstop could regain his mobility after the foot surgery of 1971 and he had the chance to acquire one of baseball's best arms in Ryan.

"Sure," Fregosi said, "I'll be leaving some of my heart behind, but after last year this is the perfect year to make the move. It's obvious the Angels didn't want me and I'm happy to go.

"I'll be playing for a pennant contender, and that's what I've always wanted. I'll be playing for fans who get excited and emotional. I can concentrate on playing baseball. I don't always have to be the man in the middle [a liaison between Angel managers and the other players]."

Regardless of motivations, it proved to be Dalton's best trade for several reasons:

- Fregosi, who would return to the Angels in another time and another capacity, went on to demonstrate Dalton had been right, that he had lost mobility and that his best years *were* behind him.
- The fringe players proved useful. Stanton supplied a degree of power during seasons otherwise almost devoid of it, and Ross was traded to the Giants in 1973 for pitcher Ed Figueroa, who won 16 games for the Angels in 1975 and was then traded to the Yankees for a bona fide power hitter, Bobby Bonds.
- Above all, Ryan soon lived up to his awesome potential, producing a string of high-strikeout and low-hit games that did not always result in victories, since he was a consistent victim of poor support and his own wildness. However, he created a volume of new records with his

overpowering fastball, established a close relationship with a fellow Texan named Autry while laying the groundwork of a Hall of Fame career, and became an authentic gate attraction, attaining a plateau comparable to Mickey and the other heroes at Disneyland, just down the street.

The Angels, in the worst mistake in club history, would ultimately allow Ryan to leave as a free agent, joining the Houston Astros as baseball's first million-dollar player, but that was eight exciting years away, and Ryan still represented untapped potential in the winter of 1971.

The civic wounds were still festering in that winter following Walsh's firing, and Dalton tried other means to bind the breach and regenerate interest. He hired former Dodgers and Cincinnati Reds executive Tom Seeberg as director of community relations and initiated an "Industrial Caravan" on which club executives and players visited businesses and industries in the Anaheim area.

The Angels were a hit at every stop, drawing crowds that often exceeded those they drew during a season in which attendance dipped to 744,190, the all-time low in Anaheim. Ryan worked only once every fourth or fifth day. In between, the crowds averaged 5,000 to 10,000 less than when Ryan was scheduled.

The nightmare of 1971 was over, but the disintegration continued. The Angels finished fifth, 18 games behind Oakland. They finished with a 75–80 record, having never been at or over .500 after the second week of the season, when they lost five in a row, including four straight to Texas, a series, Dalton said, that "put us on the wrong road for the rest of the year."

Rice talked of having the best pitching staff he had ever been associated with and then saw injuries restrict the availability of Ryan, Wright and Messersmith during the first half, after which the four-man rotation that also embraced Rudy May compiled a dazzling 1.80 ERA over the last two months.

Each of the four starters finished with an earned run average under 3.00, a remarkable accomplishment when measured against today's array of four and over mediocrity, but each was handicapped by an offense that produced only 78 home runs and averaged fewer than three runs per game.

It might have been even worse had Dalton not negotiated a May trade in which pitcher Tom Murphy went to Kansas City for first baseman Bob Oliver, who led the Angels with 20 homers and 76 RBI.

Cardenas batted only .223. He didn't know if witches inhabited Anaheim Stadium, as Gary Gaetti would later believe, but he considered driving through a cemetery with his bats in the trunk of his car so as to chase out the evil spirits that had wormed their way into the wood.

Messersmith, the 20-game winner of 1971, suffered a broken finger early and won only eight games. The bullpen, known as the Arson Squad in future seasons because of its inflammatory performances, challenged the ineffectiveness of the offense by saving only 16 games.

Rice frequently brought his team out early—sometimes as early as nine in the morning—in an attempt to review fundamentals and awaken the offense, but the only real spark in an otherwise lethargic season came from Ryan's arm.

The right-hander, whose fastball was timed at 100.9 miles per hour by scientists from Rockwell International, produced a 19–16 record. He had a 1-hitter, two 2-hitters, four 3-hitters and four 4-hitters. He registered 329 strikeouts, the fourth highest total ever at that time. His 1-hitter against Boston included eight straight strikeouts, an American League record. He tied another record in that game by striking out the side in one inning on nine pitches.

Ryan also issued 157 walks, hounded again by the control problems that would plague him in his early years with the Mets and Angels. Now, however, he had begun to learn how to use that wildness to his advantage. He had become baseball's most intimidating pitcher. Reggie Jackson was among the many who said Ryan was the only pitcher he actually feared. Many sought refuge, a night off, by claiming they were victims of the Ryan flu, an illness that conveniently appeared when Ryan was scheduled to work.

He delivered 18 wild pitches in 1972, enough to keep the bravest of hitters wary. He also displayed the low-key, easygoing, un-affected demeanor that made him a favorite of the media.

Amid the luxury cars in the players' parking lot, Ryan's truck seemed out of place. He wore jeans and boots before it was the thing to do. A Texan who loved the places and spaces of his native state, he loathed New York, both from a standpoint of environment and what he said was a lack of help and support offered by Mets' manager Gil Hodges and pitching coach Rube Walker.

The Mets' rotation, Ryan said, was designed strictly for Tom Seaver. It was Seaver, and Seaver alone, Ryan said, who worked every fourth day. A hard-throwing young pitcher with control prob-lems, with a weekend-a-month military obligation, found it difficult getting the consistent work and assistance required for his devel-opment.

There were moments, Ryan conceded, when he considered quitting, periods when he didn't believe there was a future. The trade, he said, came at a propitious time.

Ryan found in Anaheim a more comfortable pace, a lifestyle to which he could adjust. It wasn't his ranch in the Houston suburb of Alvin, but it also wasn't the New York jungle. He also got a chance that wasn't always provided by the Mets, the opportunity to come back in four or five days from a start that might include seven walks, two wild pitches and a hit batter.

Manager Rice, pitching coach Tom Morgan and catcher Jeff Torborg worked constantly with Ryan, who would say later, "I don't know how to thank them for the chance they gave me. I may not have always made the most of the opportunity. I may not have had the ability to do so. But at least they gave me the chance that everyone is entitled to."

The late Morgan was of particular help, providing Ryan with a sense of rhythm and timing, a delivery with which he could make best use of his comparatively short, muscular legs, his base of power. Morgan was Ryan's pitching coach for three years, after which Ryan continued to seek his help and advice in a clandestine manner, mak-ing either phone calls or visits to the Morgan home.

Ryan would ultimately throw seven no-hitters and strike out 5,714 batters, both major league records. He would win 324 games and pitch 27 seasons, retiring at a still effective 46. He was elected to the Hall of Fame in 1999, his first year of eligibility, with the second highest percentage ever—second, ironically, to Seaver, who so often took his starts when the frustrated Ryan was still with the Mets.

He would look back late in his career and say that it was in the otherwise undistinguished summer of 1972, his first year with the Angels, that he became convinced he could win in the major leagues, certain he could support his family through baseball.

"The big thing was that there was a difference in organizational attitude [between the Mets and Angels]," Ryan said. "With the Angels at that point, the game wasn't as critical as allowing the talent to develop. There wasn't the pressure to win, at least I didn't feel it. I knew I would be given a chance to work in and out of jams, that one or two bad starts wouldn't put me in the bullpen. That's not a criticism of the Mets, it was just the circumstance. The Mets were looking to repeat 1969 [and their surprising World Series victory], while the Angels were in that rebuilding mode and could be patient with young players. It was a fresh start, and my experience there turned my career around."

Though a fresh start for Ryan, 1972 turned stale in a hurry for Del Rice—"a good manager with a bad team," said Ryan. Rice had only a one-year contract, and his rehiring was clouded by uncertainty. He conceded that there were things he would do differently if given another chance.

"I hadn't seen most of the guys play regularly before," he said. "Through the course of the season I learned a great deal about them. If we were to go back to spring training, I'd probably be stricter in a number of areas. We ran the bases poorly, for example, and our bunting was even worse.

"These are things you learn only by watching people play. I couldn't guess in the spring that some veterans would be the worst offenders.

"On the whole, I'm satisfied with the job I did. Under the circumstances I don't see how I could have done anything differently. We simply didn't score many runs. And yet, if we have Andy Messersmith healthy, winning 15 to 20 games instead of going 8 and

11, we're right in the thick of it. I'm a patient man, and I can only hope that Dalton is, too."

Hope was all there was for Rice. "I'm disappointed," Dalton said. "I thought we were capable of playing over .500 and scoring more runs. We also didn't play very good fundamental baseball. We missed cutoff men, threw to the wrong base and ran poorly. We failed to do a lot of things that don't show in the box scores."

It added up to a pink slip for Rice—a firing, Dalton said, that was in Rice's best interest, since his health had deteriorated during the long season, his customary scotch and water replaced by milk and Maalox.

"Del had lost control of the club some," Dalton said, "but I'm not sure we'd have made the change if it hadn't been for his health. We had to make a change both for the club's and for Del's best interest."

Rice died of cancer at 60 in 1983. He never managed again.

Dalton was one year into the job and looking for his second manager. He had only just begun.

13

1973–76: THE GREAT EXPERIMENT— AND OTHERS

In considering a successor to Rice, owner Autry investigated the availability of Oakland manager Dick Williams. Autry received permission from A's owner Charles Finley to talk with Williams, who was still basking in the glow of a World Series championship, his first of two straight with the A's, who would win three in a row—the third with Alvin Dark as manager. Williams had one year left on his contract and told Autry he wasn't interested in a move.

On October 12, 1972, less than a year since he had left Arizona State, Bobby Winkles became the first man in baseball history to receive a major league managerial job after having previously managed only at the college level.

In reflection, Autry said, "Harry and I both felt it was something of a gamble to give the job to a man with so little experience, but we also felt that because of his rapport with the young players and his reputation as an instructor, he might give the club a real spark.

"Walter Alston had great success with the Dodgers after a big league career that consisted of one at-bat. Joe McCarthy never played in the majors but was a legend as manager of the Cubs and Yankees.

"We believed in Bobby and felt he could pull it off. I still believe he might have except that he was victim of one of those no-win situations. We acquired Frank Robinson, who had been a great player in both leagues and whose goal was to become a manager, a position no black had yet attained. Robinson reached his goal [with Cleveland in 1975], but before that, some thought he was managing the Angels. Many of our players went to Frank instead of Winkles, and there was growing friction and tension."

The hostile atmosphere eventually forced the Angels to make another managerial move, but that was not until midseason of 1974. Of Winkles' appointment Dalton said, "The fact that at times there was a noticeable lack of enthusiasm [last year] was an important factor in my decision. I don't expect a constant rah-rah attitude, but when you're playing 162 games there has to be an unbroken thread of determination. I don't think Bobby's enthusiasm and aggressiveness can be challenged. Winning is in his background. Some people will say that college is different, but I feel that baseball is baseball."

Winkles' hiring became known as the "Great Experiment." Some wondered if the third base coach would give signals with pom-poms and if there would be card stunts between innings. The players called him Joe College and talked about his playbook, 70 pages titled "The Winkles System of Playing Baseball."

The new manager initiated hair and dress codes and announced a series of fines for any player showing up a coach or manager. His enthusiasm and drive seemed to win the respect of the Angels, though a frequently unorthodox approach to strategy earned him the nickname "Dr. Strange Moves." The feeling also grew slowly that communication was not one of his strengths, this despite the fact that the Angels seemed to lead the league in meetings.

Among the players who sat in on those meetings were five obtained from the Dodgers in a November 1972, a trade that was the biggest ever between the Southern California rivals. It was consummated at the winter meetings in Hawaii, the tropic breezes softening the hardline approach the two clubs generally exhibited toward each other.

The Angels packaged pitcher Andy Messersmith and third baseman Ken McMullen in exchange for pitchers Bill Singer and Mike Strahler, infielders Bobby Valentine and Bill Grabarkewitz and outfielder Frank Robinson, the only man ever to win the Most Valuable Player award in both leagues.

It was the second time Robinson had been involved in a major trade negotiated by Dalton. The first was in 1966 when Dalton acquired Robinson from Cincinnati in his initial transaction as the Orioles' personnel director. Robinson soon became the cornerstone of a dynasty, the Orioles winning pennants in four of the six years he and Dalton were together.

The right fielder hit for average and power, played his position respectably and was the team leader, setting an example via a competitive and aggressive style.

Robinson was also candid and outspoken, and those traits, coupled with the fact that at 37 he had been the victim of a series of leg injuries, restricting his effectiveness and availability in his one year with the Dodgers, led Los Angeles to trade him. It was a trade he had asked for if the Dodgers did not intend to play him regularly.

Dalton had no compunction about taking him back, saying he was convinced that Robinson's pride would enable him to rebound from 1972 and that his leadership qualities were an important consideration. Dalton said he saw Robinson as an adjunct to Winkles and not a rival or threat.

Dalton was right, at least on the matter of Robinson's ability to regain his batting stroke. Used both in the outfield and as a designated hitter, Robinson slugged 30 homers and drove in 97 runs, both club records for a right-handed hitter until then.

It was a relatively peaceful period for Robinson and Winkles, whose team set club records for hits and batting average en route to finishing fourth in 1973 with a 79–83 record, 15 games behind Oakland.

The Angels were in first place on June 26, but lost 19 of their next 28 games, the absence again of a bullpen and shortstop proving critical. Bobby Valentine, a multi-talented and charismatic prospect, had opened the season at shortstop and was scheduled to play there on the night of May 17 when center fielder Ken Berry came down with the flu, and Winkles responded by shifting Valentine to center. It was an ill-fated decision, for in the fourth inning, chasing a drive hit by Oakland second baseman Dick Green, Valentine leaped against a chain-link fence, devoid of padding, caught his right cleats in the links and broke his leg so severely that his career was ruined. The 27-year-old player, who would later resurface as manager of the Texas Rangers and New York Mets, was carried off the field on a stretcher and never regained his speed or mobility, joining the long list of jinxed Angels.

Former Dodger teammate Bill Singer proved more fortunate, at least during the 1973 season. A 20-game winner with the Dodgers in 1969, Singer became only the 12th pitcher in baseball history to win 20 games in both leagues, fashioning a record of 20–14. He also combined with Ryan to register 624 strikeouts, breaking a major league record for two pitchers on the same team, a record set in 1965 by the renowned tandem of Sandy Koufax and Don Drysdale.

Ryan pitched complete-game victories in his last seven starts to finish with 21 wins against 16 defeats. It was a season of remarkable accomplishments for the man whose fastball earned him the nickname "The Express," a takeoff on the movie *Von Ryan's Express*. Ryan became only the fifth pitcher in baseball history to throw two no-hitters in a season. He struck out 12 while no-hitting Kansas City on May 15 and struck out 17 while no-hitting Detroit on July 15.

The Tigers' futility was characterized by first baseman Norm Cash, who carried a piano leg as he went to the plate in the late innings. which proved as useless as his Louisville Slugger had. Ryan later said his stuff that day was the "most dominating" of the four no-hitters he pitched with the Angels, "one of those special days when everything came together."

Incredibly, Ryan should have thrown *four* no-hitters that year alone. He lost two others through fielding mistakes.

In his first start after the no-hitter against Detroit, with a chance to become the only pitcher aside from Johnny Vander Meer to hurl no-hitters in consecutive starts, Ryan kept it alive until the eighth inning, when the weak-hitting Baltimore shortstop, Mark Belanger, blooped a single to center, the ball falling just in front of a charging Ken Berry, who, for reasons he couldn't explain, had been playing Belanger as if he were Babe Ruth. It was the only hit Ryan allowed until he lost the game in extra innings.

In an August 30 start against New York, Ryan watched Thurman Munson loft a first-inning pop-up into shallow center, where second baseman Sandy Alomar and shortstop Rudy Meoli each called for it and then backed off, believing the other would make the catch. The ball fell for a single, the only hit Ryan allowed in a 5–0 victory.

Ryan averaged 10.57 strikeouts per nine innings, and joined Sandy Koufax and Rube Waddell as the only pitchers to record 300 or more strikeouts in consecutive seasons.

He also broke Koufax's single-season record with a total of 383. Ryan got the record in his final start, needing 16 as he went to work against Minnesota at Anaheim Stadium, where a crowd of 9,100 offered vocal support on each pitch. He tied the record by fanning Steve Brye in the eighth inning, tearing a calf muscle in the process. Trainer Freddie Frederico and Dr. Jules Rasinski worked on the leg between innings, and Ryan finally generated enough velocity to claim Rich Reese on a swinging third strike in the eleventh.

Ryan finished the 1973 season with club records for complete games (26) and innings pitched (326). He led the league again with 162 walks, 15 wild pitches and seven hit batters, but he also boasted an ERA (2.87) that was among the league's best.

It was a disappointment to Ryan that he only finished second in voting for the Cy Young Award, which went to Baltimore's Jim Palmer, but he was angered more when Palmer said the voting was justified because he pitched for putouts while Ryan pitched only for strikeouts.

"I always thought they were the same thing," Ryan said.

Ryan's feelings were soothed some by a raise to $54,000 and the gift of a new truck as a bonus for his no-hitters. The generosity helped him to retain confidence and momentum as he relaxed in the wake of the old season and prepared for the new.

It was another good season for Ryan in 1974, when he was 22–16, the anemic Angels scoring just 22 runs in his defeats. The pathetic nature of the Angels' attack was illustrated by the fact that

Ryan had only one win to show for a three-game streak in which he registered a major league record of 41 strikeouts. He recorded 367 for the year, becoming the first pitcher ever to accumulate 300 or more in three straight seasons, and he hurled his third no-hitter against Minnesota in his final start.

The Angels won their final five games to avoid their worst record ever. As it was, they finished last for the first time, a record of 68–94 leaving them 22 games behind Oakland in another star-crossed season.

Pitching prospect Bruce Heinbechner was killed in a spring training car accident; Singer, 7–4 in a bid to win 20 again, underwent back surgery in June; and leadoff man Mickey Rivers, a fleet-footed and scatterbrained center fielder (the Angels called him "The Chancellor"), who led the club with a .285 average, missed the last six weeks of the season with a broken hand.

Robinson hit 10 fewer homers and drove in 34 fewer runs and still led the Angels in both departments. He also led the team in intrigue, since he appeared to be at the heart of a deepening clubhouse rift that split the players into those supporting Winkles and those supporting Robinson. A losing season tends to magnify the little disruptions and distractions that happen on all clubs, and that seemed to be what happened in 1974, when the suddenly sensitive Robinson said Winkles wasn't communicating with him and Winkles said Dalton wasn't responding to either the growing tension or the manager's recommendations involving players. The media fed on it, looking everywhere except at the lack of talent for reasons for the Angels' poor play.

The absence of a bullpen, the inconsistent nature of the offense, the significant string of injuries—all seemed overlooked amid an epidemic of bruised egos and feelings.

The overriding suspicion was that Robinson, critical of Winkles' communicative and strategic skills, had been attempting to create a situation in which close friend Dalton would ultimately hand him the managerial reins.

Dalton, who watched the situation fester while refusing the peacemaker's role, denied it would ever come to that, and those close to the organization tended to believe him, since it was unlikely that a franchise located in a conservative hotbed such as Orange County would hire the first black manager.

Robinson finally reached a point that he refused to discuss the situation, saying, "I've been made to look like the goat in this whole thing." He had already fueled the flames with a series of public criticisms of Winkles, and he had allowed himself to become involved in a shouting match with the manager in the lobby of a Milwaukee hotel. The public debate stemmed from a clubhouse meeting in which Winkles told the team he had asked Dalton to trade Robinson.

In mid-June, amid the mounting belief that a change was inevitable, Winkles said, "I work for the hardest-working general manager in baseball, but I'm a little disappointed that he's become a middle-of-the-roader with me. I truthfully believed Harry would take a stronger stand about me, one way or the other."

Dalton finally made his stand on June 26, 1974. He fired the manager.

"It was a mistake on my part to believe he could manage a major league team without more experience," Dalton said. "It was a mistake on my part not to insist that he go to Triple A for a year first. Bobby was fine around the kids, but he just wasn't sure of himself with the veterans. He was obviously uncomfortable in Robinson's presence, though I never felt Frank made any covert or overt attempt to undermine him."

Winkles responded with a bitterness that he later expressed regret for, though much of what he said in the initial wake of his firing would be repeated by his successor. "Dalton made all the decisions on players, and I think everybody knew I was uncomfortable with Frank Robinson around," Winkles said. "I admitted openly I couldn't handle him. Maybe they should have fired the general manager. The thing that disappointed me was that [Dalton] seldom paid any attention to any recommendations. I've always delved into the hearts and souls of my players. I feel I know them better than anybody, including the general manager. But somehow Harry and I could never get together on who should be on the ballclub."

Winkles later said he hadn't meant to put the blame on anyone except himself. "The Robinson situation," he said, "was my own fault. I did a lousy job of handling him. I might have kept my job if I had done a better job. I'm basically a disciplinarian but I didn't have enough discipline. I did a _____ _____ job."

In his book *The Other Game*, Nolan Ryan told author Bill Libby that there was guilt on both sides. "[Robinson] tried to manage the Angels while he was playing with them, and he was a disruptive factor on the team. . . . Winkles was a fine person who had been a great manager at Arizona State, but he was not prepared to deal with professionals or to manage in the majors. He knew fundamentals, but he didn't know the players, and he didn't know the majors.

"Winks tried to treat everyone well, but you don't motivate major leaguers with the same rah-rah spirit as you do collegians. We're married men making big money out there, and we play or try to play professionally through a long, hard schedule of 162 games, night after night, with few days off. You simply can't sustain a college spirit through that traveling grind.

"Winks insisted on details like the players having short hair and wearing ties on the road. The players merely laughed at him. Today's players wear long hair and mod clothes. I don't, but most do. The rules didn't bother me, except that I saw they bothered most of the others. You can't treat a man like a child and get away with it.

"Whatever their troubles, they turned to Robinson. He's always been a leader, especially among black players. He's a powerful personality, and players have always respected him. I lost a lot of respect for him in that situation. Instead of backing up Bobby, he turned the players against him. Robinson's not a bigot, but because of the situation, he created a black-white rift on the team. He split the team right down the middle, black and white. You were either Robby's player or you were Bobby's."

Dalton had met with Autry and Reynolds on June 15, eleven days before Winkles' firing, and set the wheels in motion. Autry emerged thinking that the club couldn't again go for an untested or second-best manager. He felt he had to have the best, a strong-willed disciplinarian. He and Reynolds flew to Oakland to meet with A's owner Charles Finley, seeking permission again to talk with Williams.

It had been almost two years since they last talked. Williams had become fed up with the phone calls in the middle of the night, the middle of the game, the constant interference from a dictatorial owner who believed he knew more than his managers about selecting a lineup and roster. Williams received a managerial offer from the New York Yankees and attempted to accept it. He believed Finley would let him out of a contract that had a year to run, since Finley had said as much on national TV after the 1973 World Series.

Williams' belief was misplaced. There was no way to predict Finley's thinking, no matter what he said, a fact Williams discovered again when the A's owner went to court in an effort to block Williams' bid to manage the Yankees. The result was a long litigation which ended with Bill Virdon being named to manage New York, Alvin Dark becoming manager of the A's and Williams, still receiving paychecks from Finley, going to work for multimillionaire John D. McArthur, a Florida insurance and real estate mogul. Williams' primary job was to address businessmen on the art of motivation, a subject with which he was familiar, since in six years as a major league manager with Boston and Oakland he had led his teams to two world titles, three American League pennants and three divisional crowns.

Finley, who viewed his managers as nothing more than middlemen and always believed he could find another manager on the next street corner, had obstructed Williams' move to the Yankees more out of a distaste for the Yankees than anger over Williams' desire to leave the A's. He sat in an Oakland bar with the owners of the Angels for more than six hours, talking about everything except the reason for their trip. He then finally told them that since they had been supportive of his decision to move the A's out of Kansas City, he would give them permission to talk with Williams.

Autry agreed to give the A's $50,000 in compensation if Williams accepted his offer, which he did. Williams signed a three-and-a-half-year contract at $100,000 a year and took the reins of the Angels on July 1, 1974.

That night, in an obvious bid for unity on a divided team, Williams appointed Robinson as his captain, the first captain in the Angels' history.

"I'm glad Dick has this much faith in me," Robinson said. "Now I can give advice to somebody without thinking, 'Am I doing the right thing?' "

There was little Robinson or Williams could do to stop the Angels' tailspin. The season's pattern had been set. Too many players had stopped caring. Too many had been injured. There was no relief—in either the bullpen or the farm system. The Angels lost their first 10 games under Dick Williams, waived captain Robinson to Cleveland in September and finished the year with a 36–48 record under their new manager.

Tom Morgan, Salty Parker and John Roseboro were released as coaches and replaced by Jerry Adair, Billy Muffett and Grover Resinger, Williams' first lieutenant. Whitey Herzog, later a successful manager of the Kansas City Royals and St. Louis Cardinals and an Autry favorite who would return to the club as general manager in the 90s, remained as third base coach. Williams also retained Jimmie Reese, whose baseball career had started in 1917, when he was hired as a batboy with the Los Angeles Angels of the Pacific Coast League. At 69, he was a former roommate of Babe Ruth, the game's foremost exponent of the fungo bat, and a confidant and friend to Nolan Ryan.

The off-season's boldest move—the club's only move, really—was made by Autry, who responded to Robert Reynolds' decision to leave the organization by initiating a search for a new club president, a man who would be on the job full-time, giving the Angels a more visible face in the community, taking some of the administrative load off Dalton and inaugurating a more marketable program of promotions and public relations.

Autry sought the advice of several people, including Arthur (Red) Patterson, longtime vice president of the Dodgers and a public relations specialist acknowledged to be the father of many of the game's most popular promotions, such as Bat Day, Ball Day and the Old-Timers Game.

Autry called Patterson in mid-winter to ask his opinion on three people: St. Louis Cardinals vice president Richard Meyer, former Cincinnati Reds owner Bill DeWitt, and A. Ray Smith, a Tulsa oilman who owned the minor league club in that city and was a lifelong friend of Autry's.

The Cowboy listened to Patterson's opinions, thanked him for his help and hung up. Patterson thought about the conversation, then told club president Peter O'Malley about it.

"Hell," O'Malley said, "what he's really asking is, 'Are *you* interested?' I hate the thought of losing you, but it's the chance of a lifetime. Call him back."

Patterson shook his head, finding O'Malley's interpretation of Autry's call hard to believe. He returned to his office, thought about it some more, then made the call.

"I know that I just attempted to answer your question," he said to Autry, "but in thinking more about it, I realized that I had interest in the job myself and wondered if we could talk about it."

Autry and Patterson met at Lakeside Country Club the next morning and reached an agreement within five minutes. The announcement was made that night at the Baseball Writers Association banquet. Patterson and Dalton insisted they could work together, though Patterson, as club president, would be kept aware of Dalton's moves and serve as a liaison with Autry.

"Harry will develop the product and I'll help sell it," said Patterson, who at 65 had the energy of a man of 35, a devoted baseball executive who thought nothing of delivering three speeches a day, and of whom it was once said, "He could sell snowballs to the Eskimos."

Patterson received the same $75,000-a-year salary as Dalton and a contract that covered the same number of years. The Angels had drawn 917,269 in 1974, and Patterson said, "If there are fifty guys in Hemet or Encino who are potential ticket buyers, I'm going. I'll quit if we ever draw less than a million again."

Williams made a comparable promise. Remarkably self-confident and a disciple of Dr. Norman Vincent Peale, the guru of positive thinking, Williams held a team meeting on the opening day of spring training in 1975 and said, "I guarantee you that as long as I'm the manager, you will never again finish last."

Among the believers was Nolan Ryan. "There's a pride and stability here that's never been here before," he said.

The pitcher would eventually have other things to say about Williams, but March is a rose-tinted time of optimism and high hopes.

The Angels had decided to dedicate the 1975 season to new growth, to the best of their often criticized farm system. Among the relatively untested starters were first baseman Bruce Bochte (signed in 1972, Dalton's first year), second baseman Jerry Remy (signed in 1971, Dick Walsh's last year), shortstop Orlando Ramirez (1972) and third baseman Dave Chalk (1972).

The "Incubator Infield" was a classic example of force feeding, an attempt, some said, by Dalton to prove that his developmental system was in gear and producing. It seemed to be Dalton's only real course, since he had little to trade, and it might have been a profitable one had the entire organization not been burdened with the futility of the past, the pressure to win immediately. The players felt it, the manager felt it, the general manager felt it. Time, patience and consistent run production were in short supply.

Mickey Rivers led the league in 1975 with 70 stolen bases, and the Angels stole a total of 220, the most by any team since 1916, but the bats consistently had trouble getting the legs home from second. The Angels hit a league-low 55 homers as Williams finished under .500 for the first time in his managerial career and failed to fulfill his spring training promise.

A 72–89 record left the Angels last again, 25½ games behind the A's, Williams' former team. The powder-puff attack prompted Texas manager Billy Martin to say that the Angels could take batting practice in a hotel lobby and not break anything. Boston pitcher Bill Lee picked up on that theme after a May victory in Anaheim, saying that not even the lobby chandelier would be in jeopardy.

Williams decided to put that to a test. He purchased a supply of plastic bats and balls and conducted batting practice in the lobby of the Sheraton-Boston Hotel on May 24. The Angels damaged nothing except their own reputation, which suffered yet another blow that night when Lee shut them out, 6–0.

"He popped off and backed it up," Williams said. "He embarrassed the hell out of us."

The Angels embarrassed themselves in many ways. The arson squad saved only 16 games, and four shortstops combined to make 50 errors. Leroy Stanton led the club with 14 homers, and no one hit more than .285.

The inconsistency of the offense and defense served to dilute a relatively strong performance by the pitching rotation. Rookie Ed Figueroa won an unanticipated 16 games. Sophomore Frank Tanana, a 14-game winner as a rookie in 1974, was 16–9, led the majors in strikeouts with 269, tied a league record for left-handers by striking out 17 Texas batters on June 21 and had a stylish earned run average of 2.62.

The son of a Detroit cop, Tanana had been the Angels' No. 1 draft choice in 1971, the year Walsh also drafted and signed second baseman Remy and a modestly successful third baseman, Ron Jackson.

Tanana made it first, a cocky left-hander who considered himself without equal, on or off the field. The numbers in his black book were believed to be as impressive as those that followed his name on the statistics sheet.

"I went to an all-boys high school and now I'm making up for it," Tanana said.

He also said, "My idol as a kid was myself," and, "My ambition is to become the best pitcher in baseball. I may have already achieved it."

Tanana was definitely the Angels' best pitcher in 1975, this despite the fact that Nolan Ryan earned a $3,000 bonus and tied Sandy Koufax's career record by hurling his fourth no-hitter on June 1, dispatching Baltimore, 1–0.

Ryan again flirted with the Vander Meer feat of consecutive no-hitters by pitching 5⅔ hitless innings against Milwaukee in his next start. He emerged with a two-hit, 6–0 victory, the no-hitter having expired when home run king Henry Aaron, then 41 and a .200 hitter in the twilight of his distinguished career, singled cleanly to right field.

Ryan was 11–3 with that win, but he won only three of his last

12 decisions while suffering a series of arm and leg injuries. Ryan's string of three straight seasons with 300 or more strikeouts ended when he struck out only 186.

The frustrating summer came to an appropriate close when four Oakland pitchers combined to no-hit the Angels in the last game, after which Ryan entered the hospital for the removal of bone chips from his right elbow.

Dalton put the Angels under X ray that winter and decided that a change in philosophy was needed. It had been the general manager's theory that Anaheim Stadium wasn't conducive to power, that his club should be built on pitching, speed and defense.

Now, suddenly, in the wake of a season in which the Angels had hit just 55 home runs, he went the other way.

Continuity be damned.

Figueroa and Rivers, two young players who rose above the mediocrity that surrounded them in 1975, were traded to the Yankees for right-fielder Bobby Bonds, a player with superstar ability and only the fifth major leaguer to that point ever to hit 30 home runs and steal 30 bases in the same season.

Dalton also traded two other young players, first baseman Jim Spencer and outfielder Morris Nettles, to the White Sox for third baseman Bill Melton, the American League's home run leader in 1971 and a man who had not hit less than 15 homers in any of the past three seasons.

Williams sized up his team in spring training of 1976, overlooked the continued absence of a bullpen, dismissed the absence of a replacement for Figueroa, and said it was the best he had ever managed, better than the championship clubs of Oakland and Boston.

Williams' textbook case of spring fever was compounded by the fact that he also overlooked the jinx, the curse, the hex—the mysterious spell that had gripped the Angels from the start and could be counted on to strike again in 1976.

Bonds was the victim this time, injuring the middle finger of his right hand when he collided with Dodgers catcher Steve Yeager in an April 3 exhibition game.

Bonds, determined to give the Angels what they had traded for, continued to play, but was unable to generate his customary power. While Figueroa and Rivers were helping the Yankees win an American League pennant, Bonds ultimately underwent surgery in August and finished the year with just 10 home runs and 54 RBI—surprisingly, club highs.

Melton, too, was injured early, pulling a leg muscle in April. He appeared in only 118 games and hit just six homers, with 42 RBI and a .208 average.

The anticipated power wasn't there as the Angels batted a league-low .235 and increased their home run production by a modest eight. Tanana had another fine season (19–10 with a 2.44 ERA), and Ryan came back from surgery to win 17 games (he lost 18) and lead baseball in strikeouts (327) and walks (183). Yet that was virtually all there was. As Dave Distel wrote in the *Los Angeles Times*: "Tanana, Ryan and a lot of cryin'."

The Angels finished fourth with a 76–86 record, 14 games behind Kansas City. Williams was there for only half of it, having been fired on July 23 with a year remaining on his contract.

Dalton removed his third manager in four and a half years because he believed Williams "isn't ready to come to grips with the needs of a young club. His frustration grew amid adversity. He reached a point where he didn't believe in the organization, the talent or the system. He put so much pressure on the young players that they were unable to be themselves. And he reached a point where he felt he was above the losses, that they tainted him personally."

"I learned a lesson," said Williams, who went on to manage the Montreal Expos and later became an adviser to Yankee owner George Steinbrenner. "I learned that you take a hard look at an organization's talent before you jump at their offer. The Angels came after me with a contract that allowed me to become the first six-figure manager. I jumped at it instead of waiting to analyze what they had and what kind of a job I could do with it. It wasn't until later, until I had spent a considerable time asking players to do things they weren't capable of doing, that I realized the only player of substance was Remy and the only pitchers were Ryan and Tanana. It was a great place to work, but they didn't have any players."

And Dalton, Williams believed, didn't respond to the needs, to his field manager's requests for changes. It was a charge similar to that delivered by predecessor Winkles.

"There were never any serious arguments," Williams said, "but the fact that Autry had hired me, that I wasn't really Harry's man, didn't help at all. We weren't as close as we should have been. There wasn't the communication there should have been."

In June 1976, with Autry in New York on business, Williams and former Dodger teammate Don Drysdale, then a member of the Angels' broadcasting team, had attempted a palace coup. They visited Autry in his suite at the Waldorf-Astoria and recommended Dalton be fired, saying he wasn't responsive to the needs of his manager or club. They suggested Drysdale be moved into an executive capacity.

A man who places a high premium on loyalty, Autry's response to the visit was negative. He listened to both, told them he would discuss the situation with Dalton, and then invited them to leave, only the distaste remaining. Autry, in fact, carried it with him until 1980 when, executives at Golden West Broadcasting say, it was a significant reason that KMPC did not meet Drysdale's contract demands. A year later, faced with the possible loss of advertising revenue in response to lower ratings, Autry relented and rehired Drysdale. The owner was not making as many changes in the broadcasting booth as in the manager's office, although the club would later change broadcasters at a brisk rate as well.

Williams, a self-confessed sore loser, dug his grave in another way, putting relentless pressure on the young Angels while failing to restrain his drill instructor, Grover Resinger, whose intensity was such that he often walked the streets until dawn after a losing night game.

Williams and Resinger would storm at the Angels in the dugout, and Resinger would often be up on the top step, responding to mistakes by screaming at the young players even before they got off the field.

"They should wear swastikas on their collars," ex-Angel Joe Lahoud said after being traded.

In his book *The Other Game*, Ryan told author Libby that Williams was sarcastic and very hard to play for. "Dick was always ridiculing his players behind their backs, but they'd hear about it, and they hated him for it. If he wanted to tell them off face to face, he did it in front of the other players, as if to embarrass them. I know he won a pennant at Boston, but those tactics turned the players against him before long, and he was fired. He won pennants and championships at Oakland, but anyone who plays for Charlie Finley is used to tough tactics. They were tough, experienced players, anyway, and they won for Williams, but I think they would have won in spite of anyone.

"We had scared, inexperienced players; they didn't play for Dick and didn't win with him. He is good at the game, but bad with young players. He murdered our morale."

The catalyst in Williams' firing was an incident on a bus carrying the Angels from the Los Angeles airport to Anaheim Stadium in the early hours of July 23.

The team was 20 games under .500 and coming off a long road trip. The frustrated Williams, sitting in the front of the bus, reacted to singing and laughter by turning and saying, "Quiet, all you winners."

"_____ you," responded a voice.

"Who said that?" demanded Williams.

"I did, you _____," said third baseman Bill Melton, meeting his manager in the middle of the bus as coaches and players attempted to separate them.

"You're suspended," Williams said.

"This is the happiest day of my life," responded Melton, who ultimately drew a three-day suspension and the congratulations of his teammates for having made the key contribution of his injury-riddled season.

Williams was fired that afternoon and replaced by coach Norm Sherry, whose relaxed, low-key style was in direct contrast to the authoritative Williams.

"We had reached the point," the new manager said, "where we couldn't do anything right. The players were trying so hard to please Dick that they were putting a monkey on their backs. Dick's from the old school. It was just his way.

"At the first meeting, I told the players not to worry about pleasing me. I said, 'You'll make mistakes and so will I, but if we can cut down on the number of mistakes we'll make progress.' They had to stop thinking a pop-up or error or wild pitch was the end of the world."

The Angels responded with a 37–29 record over the second half, and Sherry was rewarded on October 4 with a one-year contract, becoming the Angels' sixth manager and the first under the game's new rules. Baseball became moneyball in the winter of 1976, and Gene Autry demonstrated he knew how to play.

14

1977: A NEW GAME—FREE AGENCY

On the eve of spring training in 1977, Norm Sherry thought back to July 23, 1976, the day he replaced Dick Williams as manager. It was an off day for the Angels, and Sherry had just returned home from taking his family to the beach.

The phone rang at four p.m. "Can you get right down to the stadium?" Red Patterson asked.

"Anything wrong?" a worried Sherry said.

"Yes, but not with you," Patterson said.

Sherry arrived at the park and found the doors locked.

"I had to pound away for about ten minutes before I caught someone's attention. When I finally got upstairs, Red handed me a press release. I had just started to read it when Tom Seeberg came into the room and said, 'It's on the air.'

"'What's on the air?' I asked him.

"Then I read on and found out I was the manager. I never had a chance to say no, as if I would have. I'm still pinching myself about that, let alone the caliber of team I now have."

Sherry's Angels entered the 1977 season favored to win the American League West. It was suddenly as if there had never been a string of futile and frustrating summers. The Angels might never have finished higher than third, and might have finished better than

.500 only four times in 16 years, but it was as if 1977 represented a fresh start, the start certainly of something big.

The expectations stemmed from a decision by Gene Autry, exasperated by the failure to farm his own winner and overlooking the progress Dalton was making with that farm system, to contribute to the economic revolution that swept baseball in the winter of 1976.

At the end of the 1975 season, arbitrator Peter Seitz, in a decision upheld by a federal circuit court, declared that pitchers Andy Messersmith and Dave McNally had become free agents, since they had played the 1975 season without signed contracts but under the renewal clause uniform in all contracts. Owners had long argued that the renewal clause tied a player to one club forever. Seitz ruled that a club could exercise the renewal clause only once, after which the player became a free agent. The owners' lifetime stranglehold on players was over. Clubs would have to compete for players eligible for free agency.

McNally promptly retired, having proven a point on behalf of the players union. Messersmith, the former Angel, jumped from the Dodgers to the Atlanta Braves, signing a three-year, $1 million contract. The owners fired Seitz, but his ruling stood. In July 1976, owners and players reached agreement on a new bargaining contract that established ground rules for free agency. Players who had contracts renewed before August 9, 1976, were allowed to count that season as their option year and became eligible for free agency when it ended. Anyone who had signed after that date would have to play for six major league seasons before becoming eligible.

Under the initial process, since eliminated, eligible free agents went through a reentry draft in which they could be selected by a maximum of 12 clubs interested in their services. A player's original club did not have to draft the player, but had to inform the player by a certain date whether or not it intended to retain negotiating rights.

The initial salaries evolving from this process now seem like only a blip when measured against the $105 million contract that pitcher Kevin Brown received from the Dodgers in the winter of 1998 and the $80 million contract that first baseman Mo Vaughn received from Disney's Angels that same winter. But the procedure triggered the escalation leading to contracts of that magnitude, triggered the owners' collusion of the mid- and late 80s (the conspiratorial attempt to restrain salaries by forcing free agents to return to their original clubs) and triggered a series of labor disputes in which the owners kept looking for a system that would cap or slow salary growth—basically asking the players to put limitations on the free market and protect the owners from their own lack of restraint.

A's owner Charles Finley characterized the way it was in that first reentry draft in New York, when he told reporters that his fellow owners resembled a "den of thieves trying to cut one another's throats."

Harry Dalton wielded the machete on behalf of Gene Autry. The Cowboy had driven in from his Palm Springs hotel in October 1976 to have lunch with Dalton and Patterson and discuss what role, if any, the Angels would take.

"Gene was against the whole concept," Dalton said. "He knew what effect it would have. But when he asked me if I felt our restraint would help create restraint throughout the game, I had to answer negatively. I told him that I believed it would only put us further behind, since most of our competitors wouldn't demonstrate the same restraint."

Autry later told the media that while he opposed the changes and was apprehensive about the game's future, he had an obligation to the Angels' fans, players and sponsors to do everything he could to produce a winner. He authorized the spending of $4 million and told Dalton he was particularly interested in Oakland outfielder Joe Rudi, considered one of baseball's best clutch hitters and defensive players.

The draft was held in mid-November in New York, and Dalton then flew to Providence, Rhode Island, the lair of agent Jerry Kapstein, who represented 10 of the two dozen players in that first draft, and the players Dalton most coveted. What followed was a spending spree that made the $2.1 million Autry and partners had spent on 28 players in the 1961 expansion draft seem like a pittance.

Dalton and Kapstein first agreed on a contract for former Baltimore and Oakland outfielder Don Baylor, a power hitter and clubhouse enforcer whose defensive play was limited by a shoulder injury suffered playing high school football. Dalton, then with the Orioles, had signed that same 17-year-old high school player for a $7,500 bonus. Now Dalton signed Baylor again for six years at $1.6 million and handed him a check for $580,000, his signing bonus. Baylor, who had made $34,000 with the A's the year before, put the check in a hotel vault and invested $500,000 in Treasury bills the next morning. The Angels' investment would become one of their best, but not immediately.

The signing of Rudi, another Kapstein client, was announced the next day. The A's outfielder received a signing bonus of $1 million and a five-year, $2.01 million contract. Dalton thought he was through at this point and headed to California happy with the additions. As Dalton flew home, Bobby Grich, a Kapstein client and All-Star second baseman with the Orioles, heard about the Baylor and Rudi signings while driving through New Mexico en route to his Long Beach home.

Grich grew up a fan of the nearby Angels, an admirer of middle infielders Jim Fregosi and Bobby Knoop. He was happy for former Baltimore teammate Baylor but a little envious. He knew the Angels had only one signing slot still available—most teams were limited to signing two free agents but the Angels could sign three because they had lost three (Paul Dade, Tim Nordbrook and Billy Smith) in the draft—and he immediately pulled over and called Kapstein in Providence. Dalton had left, but Kapstein reached Angel scouting director Walter Shannon, who was still in Rhode Island, and Shannon contacted Dalton as soon as he landed in California.

Dalton called Patterson, who snared Autry just before he walked into the press conference where Baylor and Rudi were to be introduced.

"Are you willing to spend a few dollars more?" Patterson asked.

"What's a few?" Autry replied.

"About a million and a half," Patterson said.

"Sure," Autry said. "I've already hocked the horse. I can always hock the saddle."

Patterson called Dalton, who flew back to Providence and reached a five-year, $1.55 million agreement for Grich on the same day that Autry had told reporters at the news conference, "I still don't believe all this is good for baseball. I'm not happy about it."

In a three-day period he had authorized the spending of $5.2 million. He might not have been happy about it, but the Angels now dominated the headlines, spurring an increase in the sale of season tickets from 3,718 to 5,879, helping defray the suddenly inflated payroll. The entertainer in Autry understood the value of the marquee, which led in ensuing years to additions such as Reggie Jackson, Rod Carew, Fred Lynn and others. The cost at times was considerable in money and/or prospects, but it wasn't a matter of competing with the Dodgers for publicity as much as her husband's belief in the star system, Jackie Autry would say years later.

"Gene's philosophy of a marquee player had nothing to do with the Dodgers or any other ballclub," she said. "His philosophy was related to his show business career and the understanding that you needed that star to make something happen. I think that's why he went into the free agency market in 1976. He knew the value of star names, star quality. I don't think he thought about the Dodgers one way or the other. They were there. He respected the O'Malley family and thought they ran an outstanding organization, but he also thought he could do something different from what they did."

Buzzie Bavasi, the longtime Dodger executive who would soon replace Harry Dalton, disagreed with that perception. Bavasi said that Autry and the Angels always had their eye on the Dodgers— at least that one redheaded Dodger in the broadcasting booth.

"We weren't competing with Cleveland and Detroit," he said. "We were competing with the Dodgers every time. I mean, the Angels now have a team that is as good as the Dodgers and don't have to do that, but I always felt our biggest competition was [Dodger broadcaster] Vin Scully. We couldn't put anybody on the field as popular as Scully. The point is that in Anaheim, you've got to have the marquee players. It's why we [traded for] Carew, why we signed Jackson. Our season ticket sales jumped from 6,500 to 12,000 when we [traded for] Carew and to 18,000 when we signed Jackson."

Las Vegas responded to the 1976 winter spending spree by installing the Angels as an 8–5 favorite in the American League West.

Manager Sherry responded to the rampant optimism by expressing a need for caution, saying the Angels still had to do it on the field.

His was now a set lineup, the most attractive in the club's history. Nolan Ryan reflected on the anticipated improvements in the offense and said, "I don't expect to have to go out there anymore with the feeling that every pitch is life-and-death, that with every pitch the game is in the balance."

The easygoing Sherry, a former Dodger catcher credited with the technical advice that helped Sandy Koufax shed the control problems that plagued his early years, knew the Angels still were not without questions. He knew it was still a game of pitching, and there was a question as to how much pitching the Angels had after Ryan and Tanana.

A number of people close to the club could not believe Dalton had spent $5.2 million of Autry's money on three offensive players, totally disregarding the club's pitching needs, particularly in the bullpen. The Angels made no attempt to sign Rollie Fingers, the game's premier relief pitcher, another Kapstein client who had been available in the reentry draft.

Dalton also made no attempt to improve the bullpen through trades. Dick Drago, Mickey Scott, Don Kirkwood and Sid Monge, who had combined for a 22–27 record and just nine saves in 1976, returned to form the heart of the arson squad.

It was not until May 11, 1977, with the Angels already four games under .500 and the team earned-run average over 4.00, that Dalton responded, knowing that by then the other clubs would put a gun to his head as he talked trade.

He eventually assembled a hefty package of Bruce Bochte, Sid Monge and $250,000, dispatching it to Cleveland for relief pitcher Dave LaRoche. This was the same LaRoche he had traded to Minnesota in 1972 for the inept shortstop Leo Cardenas. Dalton, it will be recalled, said at the time, "It is much easier to develop a relief pitcher than a shortstop."

The reacquired LaRoche responded with 13 saves and six wins, but it was again a season in which there were problems more painful than pitching.

Tragedy had again visited the Angels in January. Mike Miley, a 23-year-old former Louisiana State University quarterback who was expected to fill a reserve role with the Angels en route to becoming the future shortstop, was killed in an auto accident near his Louisiana home.

Then, on Valentine's Day, lifting an air-conditioning unit at his new apartment in Long Beach, Bobby Grich felt a pain in his lower back. The doctors called it a herniated disc. Grich spent three weeks of spring training in traction, losing a chance to prepare for a season in which the pressure of their new contracts would weigh on each of the free agents and in which Grich, a four-time Gold Glove winner at second base, would move to shortstop, leaving second to Jerry Remy.

None of those problems or pressures seemed to matter on opening night, when the Angels helped the new Seattle Mariners open the Kingdome before an SRO crowd of 57,762. Joe Rudi drove in five runs and Frank Tanana pitched a 7–0 shutout.

The Angels won three of the five games in Seattle, but then went to Oakland and lost four straight to the once proud A's, whose championship team had been decimated by free agent defections.

Rudi drove in 27 runs to tie the American League's April record, but Baylor, used primarily as the designated hitter, a position he detested initially because it demeaned his conviction that he was an all-around player, struggled through the early weeks, compounding the frequent absence of Grich and the inconsistency of the pitching.

Baylor, who would hit 16 homers and bat .281 during the second half, hit just .223 with nine homers during the first, creating a new form of pressure, that of fan abuse. The heat became so intense that the personable Baylor, who won the respect and admiration of the media by retaining his accessible and frank posture, was forced to provide his family with security when they attended games at Anaheim Stadium, where the normally dispassionate fans of that era, many transplanted to Orange Country, got excited only when cheering the visiting team.

The touted Angels hovered at or near .500 through April and May, unable to generate momentum. Then the disintegration that had characterized previous summers began.

Grich, batting .243 with only seven homers and 23 RBI, made his last start on June 8 and underwent back surgery on July 3.

Rudi, batting .264 with 13 homers and 53 RBI, attempted to ward off a fastball thrown by Nelson Briles of the Texas Rangers on June 26 and broke his right hand. Rudi did not make another start and underwent surgery on September 2.

Dalton attempted to repair the pitching wounds with cosmetic surgery in mid-June, acquiring Gary Nolan from Cincinnati and Ken Brett from the Chicago White Sox. Nolan reported with a sore arm and lost all three of his decisions with the Angels. Brett lost 10 of 17 decisions.

On July 11, with the Angels 39–42 and 9½ games out of first place, Dalton made his annual managerial change, firing Sherry and replacing him with coach Dave Garcia, an anonymous veteran of more than 35 years in the game, 15 as a minor league manager.

Dalton had fired Dick Williams a year earlier because he was too overbearing. Sherry was fired because Dalton believed he was too much the other way. The Angels, he said, were flat, listless and "not fully motivated." He also said that Garcia, whose personality seemed to be strikingly similar to Sherry's, had the capability to be more direct and assertive.

Sherry, under whom the Angels were 76–71 overall, said he had been made a scapegoat.

"I felt I had done all I could do and that it wasn't my fault," he said. "We had been unable to use either Rudi or Grich, and we hadn't been getting help from Baylor. You take those three guys away, and you have pretty much the same team you had last year."

Second baseman Jerry Remy, whom Sherry had appointed captain, concurred, saying, "It never changes. The manager gets blamed for the shortcomings of the players and the mistakes of the front office."

Baylor, who had played on championship teams in Baltimore, saw it another way. He said he was stunned to join an Angel team lacking "a major league attitude," seemingly caught up in the laid-back Southern California atmosphere. "Win or lose, it did not seem to matter to some of those guys," Baylor wrote in his autobiography, co-authored by Claire Smith.

"That loose atmosphere could have been fixed if the Angels had a strong manager," Baylor said. "We did not. We had Norm Sherry." And the change to Garcia, he added, was strictly superficial. "The players did not respect Garcia any more than they had Sherry, so discipline remained nonexistent," Baylor said.

Garcia was Dalton's fifth manager in five and a half years, and he said, "No one will ever have to worry about firing me. I'll be the first to know when I'm not doing a good job and I'll quit."

The firing of Sherry was accompanied by the firing of pitching coach Billy Muffett and the hiring of Frank Robinson, who had been fired as Cleveland's manager and baseball's first black manager earlier in the season. Robinson, the first acquisition by Dalton when he was building the Oriole dynasty and a major player in the controversy that split the clubhouse when Bobby Winkles managed the Angels, returned as the batting instructor, with the possibility he could be activated as a designated hitter if the Angels became involved in a pennant race, an eventuality that did not occur.

Robinson's presence proved to be a major lift for Baylor, his former Baltimore teammate. He and Robinson worked overtime to correct Baylor's first-half batting breakdown, enabling the man known as Groove to find one in the second half of another jinxed and disappointing season for the team.

Garcia's Angels went 35–46, finishing fifth with an overall record of 74–88, 28 games behind Kansas City.

The best numbers again belonged to Ryan and Tanana, in addition to Bobby Bonds, who returned from his hand injury to set a then club record with 115 RBI. He also stole 41 bases and slugged 37 homers, tying a club record Leon Wagner had set in 1962.

Ryan missed three starts with leg injuries, pitched hurt in four others and still completed 22 of 37 assignments, fashioning a 19–16 record and an impressive ERA of 2.77. He struck out 341 batters in 299 innings, walked 204 and created a midseason controversy when he refused to accept an appointment to the All-Star game.

American League manager Billy Martin selected Ryan only after Tanana, one of Martin's original choices, had bowed out because of an injury. Ryan's pride was injured and said he would spend the All-Star break at the beach, as he had planned.

Martin responded by saying, "I'll never again pick Ryan, even if he has 40 wins by the All-Star break."

Tanana approached the 1977 break as baseball's best pitcher, a swaggering and free-spirited southpaw who combined over-powering stuff with a knowledge of his art beyond his experience. The Angels had signed Tanana to a five-year, $1 million contract (not including $600,000 in deferred money) before the start of the 1977 season, and he made it look like a bargain.

He was 10–2 with a 1.84 ERA at midseason, and he was in the process of pitching 14 straight complete games, a remarkable but debilitating streak that brought on an inflamed triceps tendon, the injury that took him out of the All-Star game and left him an ir-regular starter over the second half.

Tanana did not work again after September 9, completing the year with a 15–9 record and the league's lowest ERA of 2.54. He was only 24, but he had already pitched 1,081 innings. And he was already beginning to pay a price. The tendon injury was the first of several he would suffer in quick succession, his physical skills eroding at the height of his career, forcing Tanana to become a finesse pitcher long before he envisioned making that change.

How could the Angels jeopardize a valuable young talent with that kind of workload? There were several factors:

A designated-hitter rule that kept starting pitchers in the game longer; a string of managers whose insecurity was such they were interested only in protecting their jobs; a failure by Dalton to strengthen the relief pitching and provide his managers with reason and confidence to lift Tanana earlier; a consistent unwillingness to shift from the four-man rotation Ryan favored to the five-man ro-tation favored by Tanana.

The two aces of the Angels' staff were not close, despite having lockers only a few feet apart in the Anaheim Stadium clubhouse. A difference in lifestyles was compounded by the sharp difference in regard to which rotation best served theirs and the club's needs.

When Tanana reacted to his 1977 injury by saying it was the result of a four-man rotation, Ryan said, "As far as I'm concerned, he hasn't pushed himself since the All-Star break. There is more to pitching than just going out there every four or five days and throw-

ing a baseball. You have to prepare yourself mentally and physically."

Tanana responded to that criticism by saying the value of a
five-man rotation in the face of a long season had been proven by
other clubs, and it was time the Angels stopped "glorifying" their
two-man staff, stopped giving in to Ryan's whims and desires.

"In the overall picture," Tanana said, having been asked if coexistence was still possible, "it doesn't matter who does or doesn't
get along. He'll do his job and I'll do mine. That's all I really want
to say. I'm of the opinion that if you don't have something good
to say about someone, don't say anything."

There was little good being said about the 1977 season, which
ended with the Yankees, who had also invested significantly in the
free agent market, defeating the Dodgers in the World Series to
prove they were "The Best Team Money Can Buy."

The great expectations had again turned to frustration for the
Angels. Autry's $5.2 million purchased him his "most disappointing
season yet." There was even a lack of satisfaction, of solace, when
he reflected on a club record attendance of 1,432,633. Autry found
it difficult equating that record with an alleged loss of $600,000.

He could see how the increased payroll was part of it, how the
attendance increase compensated some for the amortized bonuses
and salaries. But he was still too much of a businessman to understand and accept a $600,000 loss in a season of record attendance.

Autry met with Dalton late in the season and said he was dis-
tressed by seemingly unchecked expenses and the distribution of
$300,000 in complimentary tickets, mostly through youth programs
initiated by Patterson at Autry's urging when Patterson was hired
as president with the mandate to put people in the seats.

Autry said he was considering the hiring of Emil (Buzzie) Bavasi
as a finance director. Dalton said he had no objections but didn't
think there was room for both Bavasi and himself in the baseball
department.

Autry assured him that Bavasi wouldn't interfere, and Dalton
said, "It's your club and your money. You're entitled to hire anyone
you want."

Autry had admired the gregarious Bavasi for many years. He

had offered him Fred Haney's position as general manager when the Angels moved to Anaheim in 1966. Bavasi, still general manager of the Dodgers at that time and looking for a situation in which he could gain a measure of stock control, rejected Autry's bid and later became a president and part owner of the new San Diego Padres of the National League.

There was no other offer from Autry until he invited Bavasi to lunch in October 1977. Bavasi had left the Padres a month earlier. He was 61 and ready to retire to his ocean view home in La Jolla, not far from San Diego.

"I had no desire and no intention to return to a full-time position," he said, reflecting on his emotions as he met with Autry at Mr. Stox, a restaurant in the shadow of Anaheim Stadium.

Autry, who had outlined his thinking in several telephone conversations with Bavasi, again explained that the club's financial situation had to be corrected, controlled, streamlined. He invited Bavasi to join the Angels as a chief operating officer, with specific control of economics.

Dalton, Autry said, would remain in charge of player personnel. Patterson would forfeit his title as president (which chairman of the board Autry would assume) but retain his role as a community liaison and unofficial director of promotions and public relations.

It seemed improbable that the Angels or any organization could function smoothly with three men of the ambition and ego of Bavasi, Patterson and Dalton sharing power and responsibility, but Bavasi decided to accept the challenge. He went back to work under a complicated formula which based part of his salary on bonuses for increased attendance and decreased expenses. And it was not long before people were saying that the E in Emil stood for Economy.

"I found the Angels to be a country club money-wise," Bavasi said. "I told Dalton I wasn't going to tell him what player to get or how to go about it, but I was going to have control over the finances, and all departments would have to come to me before they spent anything."

Patterson considered quitting. He had worked with Bavasi in the front office of the Dodgers and felt he could get along with him on a personal basis. However, he was hurt by the reduction in power (Patterson emerged as assistant to the chairman of the board), since he believed it was unjustified, his accomplishments having been hard-won. Attendance had risen approximately 500,000 in his three years as president, and no other club executive had ever made as many speeches or established comparable visibility in the community. He had begun to help make the Angels competitive with the Dodgers at the gate and on the sports pages. But now he was no longer president, no longer in charge of the administrative purse strings, no longer permitted to stimulate the growth of future fans via complimentary tickets to Little League and straight-A students.

He was hired to do a job, did it, and was then stripped of his role in the type of management decision that consistently haunted the Angels as the Singing Cowboy responded to what one former club executive described as "the whims of the moment or the last person to have his ear."

Amid the curtailments and cutbacks, a disappointed Patterson decided to stay, to resist the temptation to look elsewhere. It was a decision based on his age (68 when Bavasi was hired), his salary (which remained intact through Bavasi's first year and was then reduced), his affection for where he was and what he was doing, and his conviction that despite reduced power, he could still make contributions.

Dalton reached a different decision. Bavasi informed him that $400,000 would have to be trimmed from the player development budget, and Dalton knew what that meant—the firing of scouts and instructors and the possible loss of a farm team. He knew it meant that he would be unable to do the job he had set out to do.

"As far as I was concerned," Dalton said, "Bavasi was now trimming muscle instead of fat. I didn't see any way of accomplishing our goals if player development was going to be curtailed. The timing was particularly bad because we were starting to make some real progress. It wasn't all at the top yet, all at the major league level for Gene to see, but it was definitely there."

Dalton's six-year tenure produced major league players in Carney Lansford, Willie Aikens, Ken Landreaux, Julio Cruz, Dave Collins, Bruce Bochte, Dave Chalk and Brian Harper, among others. The system was recovering from Walsh's rape, but Dalton felt it couldn't continue with Bavasi controlling the budget. He had two years left on a contract that had been extended twice. He didn't like the thought of leaving a job unfinished, of leaving with a 444–520 record and the knowledge many people would remember only that he had employed five managers in a continuous series of clubhouse disruptions and distractions, but he liked less the thought of staying amid restricted circumstances.

It was early November, and Dalton was thinking of placing himself in the job market when he received a call saving him the trouble. Milwaukee Brewers owner and future commissioner Bud Selig, having recently fired Jim Baumer as his general manager, sensed in the Angels' hiring of Bavasi the possibility that Dalton would be available. He called Autry and received permission to talk with Dalton. The negotiations were brief. Dalton was offered a six-year contract and explained to Autry he couldn't refuse the money or tenure. Autry, satisfied with the Bavasi budget, made no effort to retain the man whose initial attractiveness had led the Angel owner to risk a tampering fine by approaching Dalton before he had the Orioles' permission.

Dalton became executive vice president and general manager of the Brewers. Bavasi, who a month earlier had expressed no real desire to return to a full-time position, became executive vice president and general manager of the Angels. Then the economy move took a strange turn—yet another shift in philosophical direction and continuity.

15

1978–79: Triumph and Tragedy

While belting up the saddle bags and enforcing the new farm controls in the winter of 1977, Autry and Bavasi paused long enough to sign free agent outfielder Lyman Bostock for $2.2 million. Bostock had batted .323 and .336 in his last two seasons at Minnesota and came to the Angels via the recommendation of Minnesota manager Gene Mauch

"Gene told me that Bostock was the second best hitter in the American League," Autry said, "and that he'd definitely win a batting title someday."

Bostock would have won the American League crown in 1977 except that his Minnesota teammate, Rod Carew, the league's best hitter in the estimation of Mauch and most others, batted .388.

Autry, of course, was hungering for a winner, his appetite growing by the year. The $5.2 million he had spent on Baylor, Grich and Rudi during the previous winter had not achieved the anticipated results—artistically, at least—but he was anxious to believe he was getting close, one player, maybe two, away.

Bostock was signed for a deferred bonus of $250,000 and a five-year contract calling for $400,000 per year. He had become available because of Minnesota's inability and unwillingness to participate in baseball's new salary escalation. The Twins, knowing Bostock would leave at the end of the 1977 season, had cut his salary 20 percent that year, the maximum allowed by baseball's bar-gaining agreement. The man who would be paid $400,000 by the Angels was paid only $20,000 by the Twins.

Bavasi's ensuing decision to trade Bobby Bonds, his home run and RBI leader, was also a concession to the game's new economics.

Bonds had earned $180,000 in the final year of a two-year con-tract and was committed to the Angels in 1978 because of the op-tion year of that contract. The Angels knew that if they didn't satisfy his desire for a new multiyear, multimillion-dollar contract he could opt for free agency at the end of the season, leaving the Angels with nothing in return.

Bavasi decided to act before that happened. In a trade roasted by the club's fans, but a trade beneficial to the Angels, Bavasi sent Bonds and two promising youngsters, outfielder Thad Bosley and pitcher Dick Dotson ("A future Tom Seaver," the Angels had said when making him their top selection in the amateur draft a year earlier) to the Chicago White Sox for two pitchers with a combined major league record of 13–8 and a catcher who had experienced elbow and shoulder injuries while performing as a reserve during most of the 1977 season.

The catcher, Brian Downing, would develop into a power-hitting catalyst in the Angels lineup, while the pitchers, Dave Frost and Chris Knapp, would make important contributions. Bonds, meanwhile, did not receive the coveted multiyear contract from the White Sox, either. The father of future major league star Barry Bonds was traded from Chicago to Texas to Cleveland to St. Louis, extending a strange odyssey that found him playing for seven teams in eight years.

The trade in which he left Anaheim was recommended by special-assignment scout Frank Lane, a former major league gen-eral manager whose reputation had been that of a precocious trader. Lane was in his twilight years, having lost much of his vi-sion. He would sit in the press box, a radio at his ear, the local an-nouncer helping him identify the shadows on the field. The man he worked under with the Angels was new to the American League. Bavasi had spent his career in the National and was open to advice in his new assignment. Lane was among those who provided it, pushing for the Downing, Frost, Knapp package. He also supported a trade Bavasi consummated 24 hours later. At that point there was no way of telling how much dealing Bavasi would do if Lane's radio held up.

This time Bavasi sent team captain and farm product Jerry Remy to Boston for Don Aase and $75,000, which the Angels immediately applied to the signing of free agent center fielder, Rick Miller, a defensive standout.

Miller received a three-year contract totaling $450,000, meaning Autry had now spent close to $8 million on five free agent acquisitions since ordering Bavasi to cut $400,000 from Dalton's player development budget.

It still did not get Autry his pennant, though it helped move him a step closer than he had ever been.

The Angels finished second in 1978, winning a club record 87 games while losing 75 and finishing five back of the Kansas City Royals, who won their third straight title in the American League West and lost their third straight pennant playoff to the Yankees.

It was a season of triumph and tragedy for the Angels, a season in which the free agent acquisitions helped attract club record attendance of 1,755,386 and helped produce club records for hits and average.

It was also a season in which the owner helped undermine the authority of his manager. Autry had done it first during the final days of the 1977 season when, during the course of an interview concerning the status of Dave Garcia, he innocently expressed a particular fondness for Kansas City manager Whitey Herzog, who had been the third base coach under Bobby Winkles and Dick Williams and, like Chuck Tanner before him, should never have been allowed to leave the organization.

Autry did not say he was going to attempt to hire Herzog and did not say he was going to fire Garcia. But he did draw a $5,000 tampering fine from Commissioner Bowie Kuhn and did create the impression he wasn't satisfied with Garcia.

Any doubt was removed a few weeks later. Gene Mauch, still under contract in Minnesota but unhappy with owner Calvin Griffith's refusal to stop the exodus of key players by meeting their contract demands, told Autry he understood the Angels were considering a managerial change and wondered if he could discuss the position with him if he first received Griffith's approval.

Autry responded affirmatively, telling his staff he had to have a more dynamic leader and personality than Garcia, that he had to have a man who could compete for media attention with Dodgers manager Tom Lasorda, a renowned extrovert who bled Dodger blue and prayed to the great Dodger in the sky and was in the process of leading the Dodgers to National League pennants in 1977 and '78.

Autry and Mauch both called Griffith and received his permission to talk contract. "If Gene doesn't want to work here," Griffith said, "I see no sense in trying to keep him."

A stormy reaction by the Minnesota fans, already angered over the loss of a number of star players, changed Griffith's mind. He called Autry and said he could not let Mauch go without compensation. The Angels responded by giving Griffith a list of secondary players, from which he was invited to choose one or two. The Twins' owner was not satisfied. He said he would require a frontline player for a manager of Mauch's stature.

The Angels balked. "We have high regard for Mauch," Bavasi said, "but we are not going to tear up the team to get a manager. What sense would there be in trading for a manager when you would then have to turn around and trade for the type of players you just gave up?"

Mauch remained in Minnesota and Garcia remained in Anaheim, Bavasi conceding, "The situation should have been handled better. Dave should have been told if he was or wasn't coming back. The point is, he's going to spring training as our manager. Mr. Autry and I support him 100 percent. A lot of skeptics are going to be surprised."

Among the skeptics was Frank Tanana.

"The Angels more than told Garcia he wasn't in control," Tanana said, "that he was only a hole card. It's a crime. They've created a sticky situation that has trouble written all over it."

Garcia didn't agree. He didn't believe his authority had been diminished or the pressure increased. There was no pressure, he said, comparable with the pressure of being the teenage support for your mother and four sisters, no uncertainty comparable with ending a minor league season as the manager in Oshkosh or Danville or Mayfield and not knowing where, or even if, you would open the next. Dave Garcia was simply happy to have the job, the opportunity.

"Managers have *won* and gotten fired, so why worry?" he said. "Pressure is for the manager who walks into the park knowing his club doesn't have a chance. I'm lucky. I don't have that pressure. My club can win and I'm not afraid to say it. I don't see why we can't beat anyone in our division. I really feel we might win a hundred games. On a position-by-position basis, I think we're better than Kansas City or Texas."

Garcia didn't really get a chance to prove it. He was ultimately fired on June 1, 1978, with his team four games over .500 and only 1½ games out of first place.

The manager, as usual, paid a price for his players' failures. Bostock, for instance, opened the season in such a protracted slump that he donated his April salary to a Los Angeles church after Autry rejected the outfielder's request that the club retain his salary for that month.

"We wouldn't give him a raise if he had a good month," Autry said, "so I'm not going to withhold his pay just because he had a bad one."

Bostock opened the season with one hit in his first 23 at-bats and two in his first 39. His frustration was so intense he began hallucinating at the plate; so intense there were days he drove to the stadium and simply sat in his car, unwilling to venture inside until talked in by teammates; so intense that the popular player nicknamed Abdul Jibber-Jabber by his teammates because of his constant chatter became a virtual mute.

Bostock was hitting 127 points below his 1977 average when Garcia was fired, and he said, "I'm the one who should go."

The manager had been handicapped in other ways as well. A calf injury caused Rudi, coming back from his broken hand, to miss 22 of the first 41 games and drive in just six runs through June 1; a hamstring injury took Ryan out of the rotation for three weeks;

Grich, who batted .216 in April and May, was undergoing a pro-longed struggle to regain his timing in the wake of back surgery; a case of nerves affected the new shortstop, rookie Rance Mulliniks.

The 22-year-old Mulliniks played erratically in the field and had only five hits in his first 46 at-bats, forcing Garcia to bench him. Dave Chalk was moved from third base to shortstop, opening third for another rookie, Carney Lansford.

Lansford, probably the best player to come out of the Angel system to that point, had a season of the type expected from Mulliniks, but Garcia was not there long enough to enjoy it, his firing having been almost preordained.

When Autry wasn't coveting other managers, Bavasi helped set the stage by second-guessing a series of Garcia's strategic moves and by asking Baylor to take a stronger leadership role.

A seven-game losing streak capped by a 17–2 loss to the White Sox on May 31 provided Autry and Bavasi with their final stimulus.

Autry, listening to that game on radio in Palm Springs, some 2,000 miles from the action, heard announcers Dick Enberg and Don Drysdale question Garcia's failure to leave the dugout and argue with the umpires over a debatable decision, enforcing the owner's belief that a more aggressive leader was required.

Autry called Bavasi and suggested the hiring of a man he had once thought would become player-manager of the Angels, a man Autry had always been fond of, the former shortstop Jim Fregosi.

"I didn't know Jimmy that well myself," Bavasi said, "but I knew Gene admired him and I knew of a lot of baseball people who were high on his knowledge and aggressiveness. The funny thing is, the day Gene invited me to lunch at Mr. Stox, Jimmy was also there, having lunch at another table. And on his way out, he stopped and said, 'If you ever think about a managerial change, keep me in mind.' "

Bavasi responded to that thought soon after he was hired, calling the Pittsburgh Pirates, with whom Fregosi was a utility player, and asking their permission to talk with Fregosi regarding the managerial position at Salt Lake City, site of the Angels' Triple A farm club.

It had long been Autry's belief that Fregosi would someday

become the manager. Salt Lake City seemed the perfect stepping-stone, since it would put Fregosi in the wings while Autry fulfilled his contractual obligation to Garcia.

The Pirates, however, rejected the Angels' request, on the basis that Fregosi was an important adjunct to their bench and spirit (he once responded to a week of regular employment by telling the Pirates, "Bench me or trade me"). The Pittsburgh decision did not disappoint Fregosi, who said later he would have refused the Angels' offer because "I didn't feel I had to go to the minors to manage in the majors. I had already spent two seasons managing in the Puerto Rican Winter League, and that was comparable to managing in Triple A. Bill Rigney had always advised me to continue playing as long as I could. It was his belief that I could gain as much experience playing, listening and watching at the major league level as by managing in the minors."

It was different when Bavasi called again on the first day of June. The Pirates said they couldn't stand in the way of Fregosi's opportunity to manage in the majors, and Fregosi said he had now played long enough, that he couldn't reject a major league offer, particularly from the team with which he had spent 10 seasons, the team that had provided him with the opportunity to play in the majors.

"In my heart," he would later say, "the Angels have always been my organization."

Fregosi thought about that when Bavasi's call reached him in Cincinnati. It was an off day and the Pirates had scheduled a team party, putting Fregosi in charge. He had just delivered the ribs and beverages, in fact, when he was summoned to the phone.

Here was a man who had once played 952 of the Angels' 972 games in a six-year span, playing hard and then leaving it behind him. He didn't brood into the night. He seldom missed a party. This time he didn't get his first drink. He bid adieu to his now former teammates and left for the airport to catch a flight to Los Angeles. He was baseball's youngest manager at 36, having been preparing for more than a decade. He asked the flight attendant for stationery and reflected on some of the men for whom he had played: Bill Rigney, Billy Martin, Chuck Tanner. He wrote down the qualities he most admired, the qualities he hoped to incorporate as manager of the Angels.

The plane landed and Fregosi tore up his notes.

"The hell with it," he said. "I'm just gonna be myself."

It proved to be enough, for in addition to an air of command, a sense of when and where to communicate, a feel for what he had done and how he had acted as a player, Fregosi represented the prodigal returned.

"When I got here," Don Baylor said, "pitchers did what they wanted to do, regulars did what they wanted to do. There was no control in the organization. In doubleheaders, pitchers would leave the park once they were taken out of the game. The first time it happened, Ryan said, 'That's the way we do it. That's part of it.' Jimmy said, 'No, that's not part of it. That's not the way we do it.' He stopped it right there.

"The players had been in charge and that was it. Dave [Garcia] wasn't a disciplinarian at all. Sherry wasn't either. Fregosi had been hired by Autry himself. We knew he was going to be around for a while. We knew he was going to be in charge."

Fregosi protected his authority by limiting its use. He asked his players only to show up on time and play hard. There were no rules governing dress and curfew. He had few meetings, believing the more often you said the same thing, the more meaningless it became.

The relationship with Autry was a security blanket, the foundation of his authority, at least at the start.

"I think everybody feels he's more like a permanent fixture in the organization," Nolan Ryan said of Fregosi. "More than that, he's a product of the organization. He was very successful. He's very popular in the community. He's the first homegrown manager the organization ever had. He's not somebody else's reject."

Fregosi wouldn't be around as long as Ryan and others suspected, but he made an impact when it was needed.

He returned the slumping Rudi to the regular lineup and made Downing his regular catcher. Baylor, disgusted with his role as the designated hitter, met with the new manager and was told that anyone who didn't want to stay, who would prefer to be traded, would be accommodated. Baylor had made an off-season request to be traded to the Texas Rangers, but Bavasi had been unable to work out a satisfactory deal, primarily because the Rangers demanded Nolan Ryan as part of the package. Now Baylor told Fregosi that he wanted to stay but wanted the opportunity to play in the field. Fregosi replied that he had an obligation to the 25 players to field the best possible lineup every day. If that put Baylor as the DH, that's the way it would be, but he also promised his proud player that he would take a hard look at him in the outfield and perhaps first base.

"Jimmy told me I could live with that or ask for a trade again," Baylor said years later. "I told him I could live with it as long as I felt I was given a fair shot. He and I became friends. He used me a lot as the DH, but he also allowed me to play the field. He understood the way I felt and didn't hold it against me that I just wanted to play. He also made the transition [to full-time DH] easier by instilling a leadership quality in me and convincing me I could be an asset no matter where I played."

The Angels finished the season 62–54 under Fregosi, a pace comparable with that established under Garcia. They were in first place by a half-game on August 25, but were then swept in a three-game series at Boston, lost five in a row, and held on for second. The last month might have been different if—a familiar refrain throughout Angel history—Ryan (rib separation), Dave Frost (muscle spasms in the small of his back) and Ron Jackson (sprained wrist) hadn't spent most of it on the disabled list.

Ryan completed his injury-plagued season with a 10–13 record. Frank Tanana, 11–3 at one point, won only seven of his last 16 decisions and finally conceded his arm was as sore as it had been the year before.

Dave LaRoche supplied 10 wins and 25 saves out of the bullpen, but there was no other relief, and no one to step into the rotation when Chris Knapp, 10–6 at the All-Star break and scheduled to pitch the first game of the second half, walked out in a contract dispute. He returned apologetically two weeks later, but the Angels had lost each of the three games he had been scheduled to start.

The offense, warming up for 1979, was the best in the club's history. Baylor was second in the league in homers (34) and fifth in RBI (99). Rudi came back from his wretched start to drive in 79 runs and hit 17 homers. Grich batted .356 for the month of September to finish with a respectable .251. The unheralded Lansford led all American League rookies with a .294 batting average. Bostock regained his stroke and personality, batting .331 as the league's hottest hitter the final four months to lead the Angels with a .296 average, a 149-point increase from his mid-May low of .147.

The resurgence might even have taken him to .300, since there were seven games remaining on the night of September 23, when Bostock left the team's Chicago hotel to visit with friends and relatives in Gary, Indiana. He would not return. According to police reports and later court testimony, Bostock went to a dinner party in Gary with his uncle, Ed Turner, and two women—Barbara Smith, a childhood friend of Bostock's, and Smith's sister, Joan Hawkins.

Leonard Smith, the estranged husband of Barbara Smith, stalked the group by auto. When Bostock's uncle stopped at a traffic light, Leonard Smith pulled alongside and fired a shotgun into the backseat, where his wife was sitting. She was hit by one pellet. Bostock caught almost the full force in his face and died three hours later.

Leonard Smith was tried twice for first-degree murder. The first ended in a hung jury. The second jury decided he was innocent by reason of insanity. He was institutionalized for seven months and freed just 22 months after Bostock died. The public reaction, according to lawyers involved in the case, prompted Indiana to change its judicial tenets. A person found mentally impaired can now be found guilty and sentenced to jail.

The Angels were devastated.

"I had a late dinner and got back to the hotel about midnight," Jim Fregosi recalled. "Ken Landreaux and Danny Goodwin were standing in front of the lobby. I was about to say that it was a little late to be going out when I noticed they both were in tears."

Another tragedy—the most devastating yet—had struck Gene Autry's team, claiming one of its most popular and talented players. A series finale with Chicago the next afternoon was suddenly with-

Gene Autry had a Midas touch with virtually all of his entertainment and business endeavors, but he wasn't quite as fortunate with his ownership of the Angels, the one enterprise he loved most.

Angels' owner Gene Autry shares a moment with longtime friend Fred Haney, his first general manager.

Two baseball fans, Gene Autry and former President Richard Nixon, autograph a baseball for a young admirer.

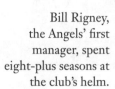

Bill Rigney,
the Angels' first
manager, spent
eight-plus seasons at
the club's helm.

Angels' owner Gene Autry presents a trophy to young shortstop Jim Fregosi in 1963, the club's third season. Fregosi would later manage the Angels, winning a division title in 1979.

Leon Wagner, known as Daddy Wags, hit 37 homers and drove in 107 runs in 1962.

ABOVE: Angels' shortstop Jim Fregosi discusses batting technique with former Boston Red Sox star Tony Conigliaro before a game in 1971.

RIGHT: Rick Reichardt, Bobby Knoop and Jim Fregosi chat with a youngster during spring training in Palm Springs in 1965.

LEFT: Dean Chance and Bo Belinsky, more hellions than Angels, pose at an Anaheim Stadium Oldtimers Game. *(Photo by David Hawkins)*

BELOW: Hall of Fame outfielder Frank Robinson, who played with the Angels in 1973 and '74, poses with two teammates during spring training.

ABOVE: Slugger Reggie Jackson and Angels' owner Gene Autry at the news conference announcing Jackson's signing by the Angels to a four-year contract as a free agent in 1982.

RIGHT: Reggie Jackson, who hit 39 homers as the Angels won the 1982 division title, unleashes his powerful swing.

Angels' owner Gene Autry presents Don Baylor with the 1979 award as the club's most valuable player. Baylor also won the American League's MVP Award that year.

Rod Carew, who would collect more than 3,000 hits in his career and be inducted into the Hall of Fame, waves to the crowd on a night in his honor at Anaheim Stadium in 1986.

ABOVE: Bobby Winkles, who went almost directly from a long coaching career at Arizona State to a managerial opportunity with the Angels in what was called the Great Experiment, addresses the media at the news conference in 1973.

RIGHT: Buzzie Bavasi, after a long and successful career as general manager of the Dodgers, became GM of the Angels in 1977 and saw the club win two division titles before he retired after the 1984 season.

LEFT: Doug DeCinces, who played a key role on the Angels teams that won division titles in 1982 and '86, scoops up a grounder at third base.

BELOW: Second baseman Bobby Grich, who was among the first free agents to sign with the Angels and played an important role on the club's three division winners, hurdles a runner as he completes a double play throw to first base.

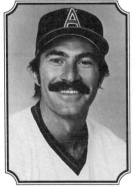

Gene Mauch, known as the Little General and remembered for his controversial decisions in the 1982 and 1986 playoffs, managed the Angels in five different seasons.

Angels' owner Gene Autry and manager Gene Mauch are interviewed before the opener of the 1982 playoff with the Milwaukee Brewers.

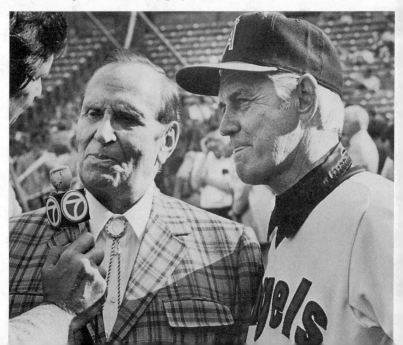

Dave Winfield, a star performer with the New York Yankees, generated two productive seasons with the Angels in 1990 and '91, the twilight of his career.

Don Sutton, who had his best years with the Dodgers, spent two-plus seasons with the Angels and recorded his 300th win in Anaheim in 1986.

Angels pitcher Nolan Ryan, sidelined by an injury in 1974, sits with Richard Nixon and Gene Autry in the owner's box at Anaheim Stadium.

Nolan Ryan, who threw four no hitters during eight years with the Angels, speaks to the crowd on a day in his honor at Anaheim Stadium in 1992. *(Photo by John Cordes)*

RIGHT: Jim Abbott, who was born without a right hand and became a successful major league pitcher and widespread inspiration to thousands of people coping with physical disabilities, unleashes a fastball in 1996. *(Photo by V. J. Lovero)*

BELOW: Wally Joyner hit 56 homers and drove in 217 runs during his first two seasons as Rod Carew's replacement at first base. Joyner left the club as a free agent amid controversial negotiations after the 1991 season.

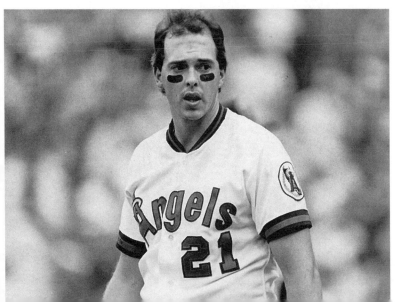

ABOVE: The 1999 season was Chuck Finley's 13th as one of the Angels' most dependable pitchers and their top left-handed winner of all time. *(Photo by John Cordes/Lovero Group)*

RIGHT: Center-fielder Jim Edmonds won a second straight Gold Glove for his fielding prowess in 1998 and was one of the Angels' most consistent power hitters after a breakthrough season in 1995 when he slugged 33 homers and drove in 107 runs. *(Photo by John Cordes)*

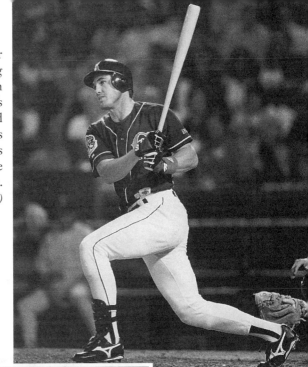

RIGHT: Right-fielder Tim Salmon, driving the ball in 1995, won the American League's Rookie of the Year Award in 1993 with 31 homers and 95 RBI and has remained one of the club's top power threats.
(Photo by V. J. Lovero)

Darin Erstad, the Angels' first draft choice in 1995, hit .299 and .296 in his first two seasons with the Angels and won admirers with his hustle and tenacious play.

Terry Collins succeeded Marcel Lachemann as the club's manager in 1997 and led the team to second-place finishes in his first two seasons before injuries and clubhouse friction took a toll in 1999, when Collins resigned. *(Photo by John Cordes/Lovero Group)*

ɔut meaning. The Angels dressed amid sounds of silence. The red-
ɛyed manager sat in his office and said, "We're professionals and
ɔhis is our business. We'll play this game like it should be played."

He breathed heavily and the tears came again. "Right now,"
Fregosi said, "the team has to be secondary. A man has lost his life.
A good friend is gone. Lyman Bostock had a super feeling for the
game. He was close to everyone. I'll hold a meeting, but there's not
much I can say. Everyone knows what kind of guy he was."

The Angels won five of their last seven games, staving off math-
ematical elimination until the start of the season's last series. Fregosi called it a "show of character." Bostock's memory permeated
the thoughts of both players and club officials, one of whom, Buzzie
Bavasi, was enraged by a call from Bostock's agent, Abdul Jalil,
within hours of the accident, requesting money from Bostock's salary for an unfinished business deal of which his widow was unaware.
Bavasi, as part of the original contract, had already given Jalil a
check for $145,000 to cover his agent's fee. Now he vowed never
to deal with the agent again, a decision that carried consequences
for Jalil's three other clients on the team—Ron Jackson, Ken Landreaux and Danny Goodwin. All would soon be traded.

Bostock's $2.2 million contract, meanwhile, was covered by an
insurance policy with Lloyd's of London, but while his widow,
Yuovene, received the guaranteed provisions, it was subject to a
significant tax because Jalil had rejected the Angels' original recommendation that Bostock take out an insurance policy instead of
the team. The benefits, if he had done so, would have gone to his
wife free of tax. Instead the beneficiary was the club, and Bostock's
wife received the money as taxable income. Jalil, people familiar
with the situation said, saved Bostock about $10,000 by rejecting
the club recommendation but cost his widow about $500,000 in
taxes.

The best season in the organization's history suddenly carried
new implications. What Bostock represented in talent was uninsur-
able, seemingly irreplaceable. The tragedy forced the Angels back
into the trade and free agent markets.

"We're in a state of shock," Bavasi said. "We've suffered a physical and spiritual loss that will force us to restructure our entire

thinking in regard to our needs. We had reached a point where we really needed only one other hitter, maybe one other pitcher. We didn't plan to go into the free agent market, and we didn't envision a major trade. Now we're looking at major needs again."

The restructuring began in early December 1978, with the purchase of Jim Barr, an irregular starter and relief pitcher whose seven-year record with the San Francisco Giants was a less than convincing 81–90. The Angels saw Barr as the right-handed complement to left-handed relief pitcher Dave LaRoche. Barr saw dollar signs. The free agent received a four-year contract calling for $150,000 a year, a $50,000 signing bonus, a $210,000 deferred commitment and a life insurance policy costing the Angels $150,000.

The next day Bavasi filled Bostock's outfield position with a close friend of the late outfielder, former Minnesota teammate Dan Ford, known as Disco Dan because (1) he had a financial interest in one and (2) tended to march to his own beat. The anxious Angels agreed to a contract extension that allowed Ford to earn $200,000 a year for five years. The Twins received infielder Ron Jackson and catcher Danny Goodwin in exchange—two of agent Jalil's clients.

The Angels had harbored high hopes for Goodwin when they made him the No. 1 selection in the 1975 amateur draft and gave him a $100,000 signing bonus out of Southern University. He was sent to their El Paso farm club and soon joined by instructor Vern Hoscheit. The young catcher had not thrown in a competitive situation for several months and was attempting to bring his arm along slowly. Hoscheit, a regimental assistant to Dick Williams, thought Goodwin was malingering and demanded he throw hard for nearly 20 minutes. Goodwin's arm was never the same and neither was the Angels' investment, though as a down payment on Ford he brought a dividend of another type.

Ford and Barr represented a mere prelude to the February acquisition of Minnesota's seven-time American League batting champion Rod Carew, who painted the penurious Griffith into a contractual corner and then received the Twins' permission to make his own deal.

It was a complicated situation. Carew, a .334 lifetime hitter who had won more batting titles at the time than any player except Ty

Cobb, Honus Wagner, Rogers Hornsby and Stan Musial, was scheduled to become a free agent after the 1979 season, during which the Twins would pay him $220,000, loose change compared with what he could make on the open market.

The Twins, having already suffered significant player losses because of their inability to cope with baseball's inflationary economics, knew they would be unable to satisfy Carew's contract demands and knew they would get nothing in return if he was allowed to play out his option with them in 1979.

They invited Carew to reach a contract agreement with the club of his choice, at which point the Twins would then attempt to consummate a trade with that club. Carew didn't require urging, for in addition to the financial considerations, the last of his affection for the Twins had been erased when Griffith delivered a speech containing racial slurs while at a suburban Lions Club meeting.

Carew immediately looked toward Anaheim, expressing an interest in the laid-back lifestyle, the cleanliness of the ballpark, the potential of the team and the size of the contracts the Angels had been handing out. The flattered Angels did not intend to disappoint the All-Star first baseman. Bavasi and his assistant, Mike Port, went to the airport to greet Carew and his attorney (brother-in-law Jerry Simon) on their arrival in Los Angeles. The four huddled at a nearby hotel and required only the one negotiating session. Carew agreed to a five-year contract for a basic $4 million before cost-of-living increases. Autry had again lit up the marquee.

The announcement was made on January 18, 1979. It was not until February 3 that the Angels and Twins consummated the trade that officially brought Carew to Anaheim. It wasn't easy. The Twins kept demanding third baseman Carney Lansford, and the Angels kept telling them Lansford wasn't available. Carew turned to the Giants and Yankees. It seemed that the "Best Team Money Can Buy" was about to get even better. Then suddenly the Yankees withdrew their trade offer. Owner George Steinbrenner explained that critical remarks Carew had made regarding the fans and city of New York had made it clear he "doesn't understand the privilege of playing for the New York Yankees."

Said Carew: "Had [the Yankees] been willing to match the California contract, I probably would have gone there, even though I didn't like the idea of playing in New York as much as I did the thought of playing in California. I really didn't want to get involved in all of the fighting and controversy that goes on in the Yankee clubhouse."

It was three weeks before the start of spring training, and the Twins were getting nervous. The Yankee withdrawal came as a surprise. They liked the New York proposition better than that of the Angels, but now, since Carew had said he would not go to the National League, they had only the Angels. Twins vice president Howard Fox called Bavasi early on the afternoon of February 3 and resumed negotiations. A few hours later the Angels agreed to give up outfielder Ken Landreaux, the Minor League Player of the Year in 1977; pitcher Paul Hartzell, pitcher Brad Havens and catcher Dave Engle.

Landreaux would spend two years with the Twins and seven with the Dodgers, a productive player. Hartzell, Havens and Engle would all contribute at the major league level, but Carew, of course, was in a higher league.

"We hate to give up young players," Bavasi said, "but with the addition of Carew we have a chance to win it all. Right now we can put eight legitimate major leaguers out there, guys who can play. I think Carew is a winner. He knows what it is to play hard in September."

Carew paid off long before that. The announcement of his acquisition was made on a Saturday afternoon, and lines began forming at the Anaheim Stadium ticket windows almost at once. The offices, normally closed, were opened on Sunday. Season ticket sales jumped from 6,530 to 11,043. Season attendance jumped from a club record 1,755,386 to a club record 2,523,575 in 1979.

Fans rocked the Big A, which frequently in the past had resembled a mausoleum. The chant of "Yes We Can" became the theme as the Angels marched to their first title. The crowds' exhortations and the confidence of Jim Fregosi, who never wavered after predicting a pennant in the spring, helped the Angels overcome 47 injuries that forced Fregosi to use 81 lineups and helped overcome the ineffectiveness of a shell-shocked pitching staff that compiled an ERA of 4.34, highest in club history.

The Angels did it primarily with the most explosive attack in the major leagues. One hot hitter ignited another. The Angels batted .282, which was 23 points higher than the previous club record, and scored 866 runs, an average of 5.5 per game.

Don Baylor won the American League's Most Valuable Player Award as he hammered 36 homers, drove in 139 runs, stole 22 bases and batted .296. The Angels' board of directors voted him a $100,000 bonus and the privilege of negotiating a contract extension, despite a club policy against it.

The disco craze even swept Anaheim Stadium, as Dan Ford drove in 101 runs, hit 21 homers and played right field in award-winning fashion, compensating on a statistical basis at least for the absence of Bostock.

Bobby Grich came all the way back from his back surgery, establishing career highs for homers (30) and RBI (101). Carney Lansford supported Bavasi's wisdom in refusing to trade him—for the time being—and stamped himself as the best player ever to emerge from the Angels' farm system, committing only five errors as he batted .287, hit 19 homers and drove in 79 runs. Another farm product from the Harry Dalton regime, Willie Aikens, spelled Rod Carew at first base some, was used some as a DH and responded with 81 RBI, 21 homers and a .280 batting average. Carew battled a hand injury but batted .318. Brian Downing altered his stance, lifted weights ("How come you're wearing your chest protector under your shirt?" Nolan Ryan asked when he saw the now muscular Downing for the first time), and compiled a .326 batting average, highest among the league's right-handed hitters.

"We just pummeled everyone," said Baylor, looking back. "Every day we went to the park, we had it in our minds that we were going to win."

Baylor played in all 162 games despite a variety of injuries and was the acknowledged leader.

"He was the enforcer," Carew said. "He wasn't a loudmouth or anything. He'd pick guys up in a professional way. . . . He had this sixth sense of when something needed to be done, and he did it."

It was that rare team, Carew said, on which players would not hesitate "getting in each other's face if you didn't execute. And no matter how far behind we were, people would stay around in the eighth and ninth innings because we had this habit of coming back to win. Every day someone different would start it and someone else would finish it. I can still hear the chant."

To the beat of "yes we can," the Angels were never behind by more than 4½ games and never ahead by more than 5. Kansas City, seeking its fourth straight division title, was 10½ games behind on July 19 and a half game ahead on August 31, when the Angels beat Cleveland, 9–8, to take a lead they did not relinquish.

Nine to eight was a characteristic score. The ferocity of the hitting and inconsistency of the pitching was best illustrated during a pair of three-game series with Kansas City in July. The Royals swept the first, getting 45 hits and 27 runs. The Angels swept the second, getting 38 hits and 28 runs.

Any self-doubt the Angels harbored was erased during a mid-July series with the Yankees at Anaheim Stadium. Nolan Ryan pitched eight no-hit innings in the opener before emerging with a two-hit, 6–1 victory. The Angels fell behind, 6–0, early in the second game and were still trailing, 7–4, with two out in the ninth. The Yankees had relief star Rich Gossage on the mound when Lansford and Ford singled consecutively and Baylor homered off the left-field foul pole for a sudden and dramatic tie. Merv Rettenmund won it for the Angels with a double in the 12th, a stunning victory. The Angels trailed Cy Young Award winner Ron Guidry, 4–0, early in the series finale and were still down, 4–3, in the ninth when Bobby Grich hit a two-run homer for an equally stunning victory and an improbable series sweep.

The hysterical crowd forced Grich to return from the clubhouse for a curtain call of the type that became habit over the second half of a season in which the Angels continually responded to predictions that they were on the verge of folding.

Critics examined the Angels' pitching staff and forecast an inevitable collapse. Nolan Ryan and Dave Frost each won 16 games, but there were long periods when both were unavailable because of injuries; Frank Tanana did not pitch between June 10 and September 4 because of his recurring arm injury and won only seven games; Chris Knapp did not pitch between mid-June and mid-August because of a back injury and won only five games; five farm products summoned in emergency situations combined for only four wins; Dave LaRoche, the anticipated relief ace, compiled a 5.57 ERA while losing 11 of 18 decisions; Mark Clear, the unanticipated relief ace, struggled through the second half, totaling 14 saves and 11 wins, 8 in the first half.

An August charge by Kansas City brought another from Don Baylor. He criticized Bavasi for a failure to respond to the pitching problems, suggesting to a reporter that Bavasi would rather let the pennant slip away than spend a few dollars on the required repairs. Bavasi responded by engaging the writer of the article, Jim Ruffalo of the *Orange County Register*, in a press box wrestling match, prudently avoiding a physical confrontation with the powerful Baylor. He then made another prudent move, purchasing John Montague from Seattle. Montague won two games and saved five during the final five weeks.

The key series of the final month started in Kansas City on September 17. The Angels were three games ahead when the four-game series began, and three games ahead when it ended.

Someone asked Jimmie Reese, the senior coach and senior citizen, about the pressure and how he was adjusting to it. "I've been able to take nourishment," he said.

The Royals won two of the first three games and were within two games of the lead when Autry fed the Angels some incentive before the finale. He sent Fregosi a tape recording of an interview between a Palm Springs radio station announcer and Kansas City owner Ewing Kauffman, in which Kauffman said he didn't care who won the American League West as long as it wasn't the Angels.

Kauffman's remarks stemmed from his conservative financial philosophy. The Royals seldom participated in the free agent auction, and Kauffman wasn't happy with those who did.

Fregosi played the tape in a locked clubhouse before the game, and the Angels then defeated the Royals, 11–6, to regain a three-game lead with nine to play.

The race ended five days later when the Angels officially eliminated the Royals, beating them 4–1, at Anaheim Stadium as Tanana overcame his physical problems to pitch a four-hitter, his virtuosity adding a Hollywood touch to the game that ended Autry's frustration and helped ease Tanana's.

The left-hander had returned to the Angels in early September after not being expected to pitch again in 1979. Keith Kleven, a Las Vegas physical therapist, had helped send Tanana back to work when some doubted he would ever work again. The crowds chanted, "Yes We Can," and Tanana proved he still could, proving it most dramatically in the game that clinched the division title, his first complete game since June 5.

"For us to win it and for me to pitch the clincher," he said, waving a bottle of champagne exultantly, "well, hell, it's unbelievable. I've never been this happy. It's like a script. It takes some of the sting out of all the B.S. I've had to go through this year, out of all the frustration of the last six years."

Tanana took a hearty swallow from his bottle and poured the rest over his head. He grabbed another and sprayed Autry, who paraded from player to player, beaming like a new father. The Angels had won their first title and the price didn't matter. The long wait was forgotten. The mistakes and misfortunes yielded to the satisfaction of the moment. The memory of the years when the Angels simply didn't have the talent was washed away by the domestic champagne.

Nolan Ryan took one look at Autry, who had former President Richard Nixon with him and who would invite the entire team to his San Clemente estate for a celebration, and said, "I imagine he's 'bout as happy right now as he can remember being."

He added: "There's been more spirit on this club than any I've ever been associated with. These guys never knew when to quit. We didn't have any real cheerleader types, but we had a lot of guys who wanted to win."

Bobby Grich had won before. He had experienced the feeling as a member of the Baltimore Orioles. This was different, he said. "This is a dream come true. I've been an Angels fan since I was a kid. I used to come out to this park when Fregosi and Knoop were playing. I'd sit in the stands and say, 'I'd like to be out there some-day.' Now here I am. It's unbelievable."

The dream ended there. The bid to turn Autry's half pennant into a whole pennant failed.

It was probably not surprising, since the Angels had left a mea-sure of their emotion in that wet clubhouse. Also they entered the best-of-five playoff series with Baltimore at a disadvantage.

Willie Aikens had strained ligaments in his left knee during the September series in Kansas City and was unavailable. Hard-luck Joe Rudi was still sidelined by a strained Achilles tendon suffered in mid-August. Jim Barr had broken the little finger on his pitching hand when he took a swing at a plastic toilet seat marked "A Royal Flush" during the Angels victory party at a bar near the stadium. Barr thought it was papier-mâché. It turned out to be the real thing.

The pitching-rich, fundamental-minded Orioles, a team whose strength, manager Earl Weaver said, was in its depth, took advan-tage of California mistakes to win the first two games in Baltimore: 6–3 on a 10th-inning homer by John Lowenstein and 9–8 when Don Stanhouse finally choked off an Angel rally that began with Baltimore leading, 9–1.

The series moved to Anaheim, with the Angels encountering turbulence en route. Broadcaster Don Drysdale, a fierce competitor during his years as a Hall of Fame pitcher with the Dodgers and convinced that Barr was capable of pitching and would have made a difference in the 9–8 loss the Angels had just suffered, got into the pitcher's face on the flight home. Drysdale screamed that Barr was malingering and that Fregosi should have called on him, broken finger or not. As Barr and Drysdale advanced on each other, Fregosi got out of his seat, pushed Drysdale, and it took Baylor and coach Bobby Knoop to separate them, the raised voices carrying through-out the plane. Ultimately, Bavasi, something of a surrogate father to Drysdale when both were with the Dodgers, ordered Drysdale back to his seat, and Drysdale went in the manner of a scolded son.

The plane landed without additional problems, and Drysdale called Fregosi the next morning to apologize. "I heard something I didn't like, and I said something I shouldn't have," Drysdale said.

"It shouldn't be misunderstood. We are all on edge. It was a momentary disagreement, and I take full blame."

The Angels displayed some fight of their own that night, scoring two runs in the ninth for a 4–3 win in Game 3, their only win of a series that ended in Game 4 when Scott McGregor, an Angel nemesis throughout his career, pitched a six-hit, 8–0 shutout. The Orioles led only 3–0 in the fifth when third baseman Doug De-Cinces, who would soon join the Angels, turned away the only Angel threat and possibly saved the game and series by making a brilliant backhanded stab of Jimmy Anderson's wicked grounder with the bases loaded, turning it into a double play and taking the heart out of the Angels.

The zealous fans brought the Angels out of the dugout for one final curtain call when the game ended, the long and loud salute providing the team with a warm remembrance to carry through a winter that turned cold in a hurry.

16

"The Worst Mistake"

Even before that 1979 season had started, some three weeks before the first pitch of a summer that produced the Angels' first division championship, Nolan Ryan had predicted it would be his last with the Angels.

Ryan was approaching the final year of a three-year contract that called for a signing bonus of $200,000, a yearly salary of $250,000, a $20,000 payment each year for five years after the contract ended, and a $50,000 interest-free loan to be deducted from his salary and paid Ryan each January of the contract's life.

At the end of the 1978 season, through attorney Richard Moss, Ryan wrote a letter to Bavasi in which he said that if the Angels would like to extend his contract past the 1979 season, he would be receptive to negotiations. But, Moss wrote, if those negotiations were not consummated by the start of the season, Ryan would declare his free agency in October.

"The one thing I want to make clear," Ryan said in the spring of 1979, "is that I don't want to be distracted by trying to negotiate a contract during the season."

Bavasi responded to the letter by asking Moss and Ryan to submit a proposal in January 1979. The proposal was for a four-year contract at $550,000 per year. Bavasi took it to Autry, who decided that since Ryan was 31 and coming off an injury-plagued,

10–13 season, the Angels should allow him to play out the year and then perhaps retain negotiating rights by selecting him in the re-entry draft.

It was a cold and curious decision in that Autry seemed to be turning his back and bidding adieu to the most spectacular pitcher of the 1970s, a friend and fellow Texan, and a man whose drawing power was worth a minimum of approximately 1.4 million fans during his seven years with the team—1.4 million above what the club would otherwise have drawn.

Ryan expressed disappointment. "The Angels don't owe me anything," he said, "but I do feel that I've given them everything I've got and that I have made contributions at the gate and on the field. I've been totally loyal, and I would expect the same from them. Buzzie has said he might be willing to look at the situation somewhere around the All-Star break, but that's unsatisfactory. I don't expect an offer, and I don't expect my attitude to change."

It didn't. Ryan played out his contract, contributing 16 wins and 223 strikeouts to the championship summer, and then became baseball's first million-dollar-a-year pitcher, signing a four-year contract for $1.1 million a year with the Houston Astros, who at that time played indoor baseball some 30 minutes from Ryan's home in Alvin, Texas.

A personality clash between Bavasi and attorney Moss marred the final, fragile attempts to keep Ryan in Anaheim. Bavasi's last offer was for the same amount Ryan had been seeking at the start of the year. By then, however, Ryan knew he could double it in the market, and his pride had been injured by the Angels' attitude.

"Buzzie tried to embarrass us," Moss said, "by saying we made a final proposal for a million a year. Hell, it was strictly a bargaining position. We sat and waited for a counterproposal, and it never came. Buzzie still thinks this is the mid-fifties and he's the general manager of the Dodgers and the name of the game is trying to sign a player for $15,000 when he's been authorized by Walter [O'Malley] to give him $16,000. All the talk about Buzzie getting a piece of the action, I don't think that's what it's about. He has to win in negotiations. He has to beat people."

Plagued by wildness early and inconsistent support throughout,

Ryan was 138–121 with the Angels, a .533 percentage compared to the .481 percentage of the Angels, who finished at .500 or better in only two of those years. He won 16 or more games six times and 19 or more four times, including 21 in 1973, when the Angels were four games under .500, and 22 in 1974, when they were a dreadful 68–94. He led the American League in strikeouts in seven of the eight years, topping 300 five times, and pitched four no-hitters along with five one-hitters, 13 two-hitters and 19 three-hitters.

A failure to communicate between infielders Rudy Meoli and Sandy Alomar Jr. on a first inning pop fly in a game against the Yankees cost him a possible fifth no-hitter with the Angels, and a questionable scoring decision cost him a possible sixth. He was a no-hit threat every time he went to the mound. Above all, he chewed up innings, averaging 250 per season, taking the load off a series of suspect bullpens.

"I used to hear a lot of comments about being only a .500 pitcher [with the Angels]," Ryan said prior to his Hall of Fame induction in 1999, "but it wasn't as if those Angel teams were only one player away. You could have added Babe Ruth and it wouldn't have made that much of a difference. When you look at the type of clubs those were, my control problems were very detrimental to me. I could walk three or four guys, give up four or five hits, and it would cost me the game. If I had been on a team that scored five or six runs a game, it would have been nothing. On the other hand, pitching for those Angel teams made me a more focused and better pitcher since I didn't have the luxury of making a mistake. I consider those years the foundation of my career."

What a career. He would pitch 27 years, win 324 games, strike out a record 5,714 batters and pitch seven no-hitters.

He would pitch for 14 more years after leaving the Angels, at which point Bavasi strained plausibility by insisting that Ryan's departure did not represent a serious loss since "all I have to do is find two pitchers capable of going 8–7 each." It was an attempt at humor, a reference to Ryan's 16–14 record in his final season with the Angels, but it was gallows humor at best. Fregosi and his players weren't laughing, and neither was Bavasi after a time. He would soon admit that the failure to retain Ryan was the biggest mistake of his tenure—to be compounded, he would also admit, by the failure to retain Baylor after the 1982 season.

"I think it's been hard for any old-timer to justify the present-day salary scale," Bavasi said in reflection. "I just can't see anybody 60 times better than Jackie Robinson. Or name a pitcher 30 times better than Sandy Koufax. If Dick Moss had forced me into it a little harder I might have given in, but remember that Ryan was basically a .500 pitcher his last two years with us. There's no doubt that he's now a Hall of Famer, but I had to look at wins and losses, whether we were winning pennants with a pitcher who wanted $1 million, and it wasn't happening."

Bavasi never found those two 8–7 pitchers, the pursuit costing him the kind of money in wasted free agent signings that could have gone a long way toward signing Ryan. Fans of the team still bemoan his departure, and Autry, for many years after that, rued the fact that he hadn't become more involved in the negotiations, "but again I put trust in the people I trusted well enough to put in that job."

When Ryan threw his sixth no-hitter with the Texas Rangers in 1990, Bavasi sent a telegram that read:

"Nolan, some time ago, I made it public that I made a mistake. You don't have to rub it in."

Ryan did, however. He frequently said that, despite his affection for Autry, a fellow Texan, he would not have returned to the Angels as long as Bavasi was associated with the team. "The truth was that I had not asked for a million dollars. I had asked for much less than that," Ryan said at the time of his Hall of Fame induction. "If Buzzie had given me what I'd asked for, he would have had a bargain, and I'd probably still be pitching for the Angels. What Buzzie did was make it possible for me to move on and make a lot more money."

Ryan, however, did almost renew his relationship with the Angels before signing with the Rangers as a free agent after the 1988 season, lured back by Autry, long one of his favorite people.

"I love Gene, and I really thought I'd end up in Anaheim, but I didn't anticipate the [home state] Rangers getting involved," he said. Ryan could have signed with the Angels for more, but the Rangers' involvement meant he did not have to uproot his family. Said Mike Port, the Angels' general manager at the time, "The only thing we were unable to do, and we respected Nolan in this regard, is move Alvin, Texas, to Orange County."

As Fregosi and staff contemplated the 1980 season without the workhorse Ryan, they had other concerns as well. They worried about the injuries that had sidelined Chris Knapp and Frank Tanana in 1979, about the uncertain nature of the bullpen, about the suspect status of a staff that had permitted almost 4.4 runs per game en route to a division title.

"We overpowered people last year," Don Baylor, the league's MVP, said, "but that's not the way to build a club or win consistently. You do it with pitching and defense, but I'm concerned again that our front office has been lulled to sleep by the success of last year and again won't respond to what are obvious needs."

Handicapped again by the shallow farm system, Bavasi did respond, but in a manner vulnerable to second-guessing.

He first spent another $2.4 million to sign Pittsburgh free agent Bruce Kison as a replacement for Ryan—a replacement in body only.

Kison had averaged only 140 innings during his nine years with the Pirates, never winning more than 14 games in a season. His availability was often curtailed by hand and elbow injuries, and he would become unavailable to the Angels in midseason of 1980 because of a nerve condition that required elbow and wrist surgery. He was 3–6 that year, 1–1 as he rehabilitated in 1981 and 10–5 for a 1982 team that won the division title.

The beleaguered Bavasi responded to Kison's 1980 injury loss by shifting blame, saying he had been signed on the recommendations of Fregosi and pitching coach Larry Sherry, both formerly employed in Pittsburgh.

Kison received a $750,000 signing bonus, a deferred commitment of $800,000, a $15,000 relocation allowance and a five-year guaranteed contract for $160,000 per year.

Bavasi then went to baseball's winter meetings in Toronto and negotiated a trade that would have sent his productive but expendable first baseman, Willie Aikens, to the New York Mets for Craig Swan, a proven pitcher who might have helped fill the Ryan void.

Bavasi and Joe McDonald, the Mets' general manager, shook hands on the deal, but New York owner Lorinda de Roulet, on the verge of selling her club, decided it would be unfair to the new owners to make a trade of that magnitude. Bavasi, who was headed to the press room to make the announcement, described the Mets' withdrawal as "the worst thing that's ever happened to me in baseball."

Whether it was that momentous or not, the loss of Swan seemed to affect the Angels' perception of their needs. Instead of continuing to use Aikens as the bait in a bid for pitching, Bavasi promptly traded Aikens for Kansas City outfielder Al Cowens. Bavasi's explanation was that the Angels also required outfield protection, since Joe Rudi was coming off his Achilles injury and Dan Ford had undergone postseason knee surgery. The Angels obtained Cowens on December 6, 1979. They traded him on May 27, 1980, just five months later, for Detroit's Jason Thompson, a left-handed-hitting first baseman like Aikens.

"We seem to be back where we started," said Baylor, whose relationship with Bavasi was starting to unravel in the manner of Ryan's.

Thompson was acquired with four months remaining on the 1980 schedule, but the season had already ended for the Angels, the bid to repeat as division champion wiped out by what Bavasi called the worst injury wave he had ever seen. At one point seven Angels were on the disabled list. Five, including Ford, underwent some form of surgery. Baylor, Ford and Brian Downing, who had combined to hit 69 homers and drive in 315 runs in 1979, combined to hit 14 homers and drive in 102 runs in 1980. Baylor broke his wrist, and Downing his ankle. Ford never regained strength and confidence following knee surgery. The decimation of the offense placed the burden on a pitching staff unable to shoulder it. The decimation of the pitching staff put the burden back on the decimated offense. The Angels scored 168 fewer runs than in 1979. The team ERA climbed to 4.52, a new club record. Kison won three games and Dave Frost four. Of the 10 pitchers on the opening-day roster, none had a winning record when the season ended.

The champion Angels fell to fifth, 31 games behind once again dominant Kansas City. The record was a disturbing 65–95, and it was accompanied by the inevitable displays of backbiting.

Baylor and Tanana criticized the club's response to the pitching crises, and Baylor said the club had prepared for the season complacently. Tanana and LaRoche said Fregosi lacked confidence in them, and asked to be traded. Rod Carew, who was unfazed by the ruin around him and batted .331, stopped talking baseball with the press because, he said, his quotes were being twisted and used against him in what was tantamount to a lack of respect. Ford said that the obvious inability to repeat as division champions should have eliminated the need to push his knee by rushing him back to the lineup, prompting Bavasi to say, "Someone should give Ford a fat lip, and I would do it if I was twenty years younger."

There was also the inevitable pressure on Fregosi, a Manager of the Year candidate the year before. This time the second half of the 1980 season was played amid rampant rumors of his imminent firing. Bill Rigney, Fregosi's former manager and tutor who had returned to the club as special assignment scout, raised eyebrows throughout the league by frequently second-guessing Fregosi. There was speculation that Rigney was attempting to create a scenario in which he would be rehired as manager—an unfair indictment, perhaps, given Rigney's stand-up character and long relationship and fondness for Fregosi.

Nevertheless, the disagreements between Fregosi and Bavasi over player personnel, the disagreements all managers and general managers experience, were seen in a different light. Nolan Ryan, now a member of the Houston Astros, saw it from a distance and said the rift between manager and general manager was widely known and that, in his view, "the only thing holding that club together is Jim Fregosi." Ryan said that it was strictly Harry Dalton who was responsible for putting the 1979 division winner together and added that Bavasi's profit-sharing arrangement affected his approach to adding needed players and spending money.

Ryan, of course, had an ax to grind with Bavasi, but there was no question that Fregosi's "favorite son" stature with Autry wasn't what it had been. The unhappy owner asked Bavasi to join the Angels in Detroit in August and use his own discretion in regard to Fregosi's future. Bavasi tried to defuse the situation, saying he couldn't justify a managerial change because injuries had made it impossible to tell what kind of team the Angels really had.

However, the long summer continued to weigh on Autry, who had seen only the promise and now searched for solace in the fact he had not been alone. The allegedly knowledgeable odds makers had favored the Angels to repeat. The eager fans had purchased 17,514 season tickets, an American League record. Anaheim was alive and roaring, but there was a sense of betrayal in the Angels' performance. The memory of 1979 faded and the cheers turned to boos. The Singing Cowboy provided an accompaniment.

He spoke frequently about his disappointment and frustration. He blasted the players for their lethargic play and said the pitchers lacked guts. He said the smart thing would be to call up his Salt Lake City farm team as a full-scale replacement for the varsity. He called the 1980 team "the worst we've had in our 20 years and it can't go on."

The frequency and intensity of his criticisms were uncharacteristic and might have stemmed from the disheartening loss of his wife, Ina, who died suddenly in May 1980. They had been married for 48 years, but now Autry rode alone through that hard season, headed for another in 1981.

17

1980–81: The Surrogate Son's Firing

A 50-day players' strike prompted major league owners to split the 1981 season into two abbreviated halves. The Angels, 65–95 during what Autry called the worst season yet in 1980, improved in 1981 but only slightly. They were 31–29 in the first half and 20–30 in the second, when they were last in the West. The overall record of 51–59 put them 13½ games behind Oakland, the overall leader in the division.

Enough said? Hardly.

The period between the end of the 1980 season and the start of the 1982 season was one of the most active and tumultuous in club history as the Angels went from one policy to another, from one personnel shake-up and/or controversy to another, from one headline making trade and/or free agent signing to another. Whether caught up in the attempt to (1) win one for the Cowboy, (2) compete with the Dodgers, or (3) simply put another star on the marquee, the span produced a significant series of events that did little to save the 1981 season but helped provide the foundation for a second division title in 1982. Some of the highlights:

- In two blockbuster trades with the Boston Red Sox prior to the 1981 season, the Angels sacrificed Carney Lansford, the best position player to come out of their farm system; Mark Clear, one of the best relief pitchers to come out of the system; and veteran Frank Tanana, among others, in exchange for All-Star shortstop Rick Burleson and All-Star center fielder Fred Lynn. Burleson and Lynn were signed to multi-year, multimillion-dollar contracts, and soon confronted the dreaded Angel hex.

- In what became an ongoing attempt—and one that has now spanned decades—to solidify the pitching staff, particularly in the immediate aftermath of Nolan Ryan's departure, the Angels traded another promising player in the winter of 1980, shortstop Dickie Thon, for veteran Ken Forsch and signed journeyman pitcher Geoff Zahn as a free agent. Forsch and Zahn would prove to be productive additions, but the search for those "two 8–7 pitchers," as Buzzie Bavasi had put it, to replace Ryan also produced expensive busts in free agents Bill Travers, John D'Acquisto and Jesse Jefferson, all signed prior to the 1981 season.

- Inevitably, Jim Fregosi, Autry's surrogate son, was fired in May and replaced by Gene Mauch, the man Autry had been coveting before Fregosi was hired to replace Dave Garcia.

- Don Baylor, the clubhouse leader, and general manager Buzzie Bavasi engaged in several verbal skirmishes, prompting Baylor, in April 1981, to retire—for a few hours anyway. He was ultimately coaxed into returning by Fregosi, Mauch and teammates—a fortunate development considering Baylor's catalytic role in the title success of 1982.

- Having ended the 1981 season with a declaration that they were no longer going to participate in free agency, the Angels promptly took one of their biggest plunges, signing the celebrated Reggie Jackson, while also trading for catcher Bob Boone, shortstop Tim Foli and third baseman Doug DeCinces, all between the end of the 1981 season and start of the 1982 season.

- With all of that, an even more meaningful event for the team occurred on July 19, 1981, when Autry married his banker—14 months after the death of his first wife.

Jacqueline Ellam, a self-described tomboy from New Jersey, had gone to work as a 17-year-old switchboard operator at a Security Pacific branch in Palm Springs. She was on her way to the

University of California at Berkeley and simply looking for a summer job, but at $225 a month, she decided, who needed a higher education? She rose to assistant manager at 24, manager at 30 and vice president at 32. She had been supervising much of Autry's desert portfolio for 16 years, including the Palm Springs hotel that carried his name, when he summoned the courage and invited her to a 1980 New Year's Eve party. He was 73, she was 40.

"It was the first time in almost 50 years he had asked a woman to go on a date, and he was obviously nervous," she recalled. "He called about two weeks before and said he'd like me to be his guest and that I could bring my date if I had one. I'm not sure if he knew I was married or dating, and I sensed his timidity. We had a terrific time, and our personal relationship proceeded from there."

The new Mrs. Autry immersed herself in baseball, broadcasting and the business side of an empire, employing her experience in banking. Autry called her an "owner in training," and she gradually became a force in the industry—a member at one time of baseball's powerful Executive Council—and, of course, a force with the club.

As Autry battled a series of physical problems in the 80s and 90s, the self-assured and protective "Mrs. A" took on a more visible and influential role, which often put her in conflict with media and fans.

She made sense, arguing against those quick-fix solutions because "you can only mortgage the future for so long" and "we can't afford to put nine corporations on the field or we'll price fans out of the game," but she was perceived by many of those long-suffering fans and many in the media as cold, calculating and only interested in the bottom line.

Profits over pennants seemed to be the perception, although Mike Port, who succeeded Bavasi as general manager, said that was unfair and untrue.

"The way I'd put it is that Jackie brought a tempering element," he said. "There was still a lot of wild, unbridled spending when she married Gene. She brought a perspective that you can win games, but there has to be a business side to it as well."

It was in the early 80s that the new Mrs. A hired a consulting firm to analyze and help streamline a front office that tended to resist streamlining because of the changing philosophies and personnel.

It was in the early 90s, amid mounting debts, that she summoned beat reporters during spring training, provided the financial numbers on operating losses, and first hinted that the club would have to be sold.

"Gene's too old to go back to work, and I have no desire to," she said, trying to smile through the pain.

Was there a gender gap?

No one questioned the care and comfort she provided the Cowboy, extending his life by 10 years or more, many close to the Autrys believe.

No one questioned her role through the 80s and 90s in carefully and competently reorganizing his estate.

No one questioned her contribution to the cultural landscape by spearheading development of the Gene Autry Western Heritage Museum in the Griffith Park area of Los Angeles.

There were times, however, when both media and fans reacted skeptically to her financial numbers, bemoaned her reluctance to expand the payroll and put her in the same castigated company with Rams owner Georgia Frontiere, before Frontiere took her team to St. Louis.

There were times when people in and out of the organization wondered . . .

Well, Jackie Autry knew what they wondered.

"They wondered, What the hell does she know about the game of baseball? How the hell is she making decisions? Well, what the hell does any owner know?" she said, reflecting at her Palm Springs home in 1999, a few months after her husband's death. "If truth be told, does [New York Yankee owner] George Steinbrenner know any more than I do? Does [Baltimore owner] Peter Angelos?

"Because I'm a woman, should I know any less than a man does? Can I tell you whether this player is going to be a superstar and this player is going to be a failure? No, I can't tell you that. Neither can the scouts who pick the top draft choices every year, and 10 percent or less make it to the major leagues.

"Can I tell you what's happening in a game? Yes, I can tell you what's happening in a game.

"Baseball is a business. As sad as it is, we've all come to the realization that it has to be operated like a business.

"Beyond that, my philosophy has always been the same. You have to build through your farm system, and never once, like Gene, did I say to the people we had running the club that I think you should sign this player or that player.

"Did I help them if they were interested in a player because of some connection I had? Yes. Were there times I told them we didn't have the resources to sign a certain player? Yes. Was I in touch, involved and available for advice on a daily basis, and did I follow up if my husband asked me to do something on behalf of the club? Of course. Did it ever go beyond that? No."

Tim Mead, who began his career with the Angels in 1981 and is the club's vice president of communications, endorses the theory that Jackie Autry was simply lumped with Georgia Frontiere to an often malicious and unfair extent.

She was not vampira, as portrayed by some, Mead suggested.

"I can't recall one tirade or one instance when she second-guessed someone," he said. "She was hands-on and aware from the standpoint that she wanted the final say on big issues and she disdained learning about a major development after the fact, but she wasn't walking the halls every day and wasn't in the middle of every decision.

"I think it was to the club's credit that the Autrys let their general managers run the operation. They were in touch by phone, but I don't think they ever wanted to be at the stadium eight hours a day, and they weren't.

"I also think it was to Jackie's credit that she strongly believed the club should focus on the farm system and develop from within. She deserves much of the credit for the homegrown nucleus of the 90s, because she encouraged us to go that route. She never drastically cut or pulled the plug on the payroll, as a lot of other clubs did when the salaries and payrolls began to get out of hand; she just insisted that we focus on the farm and not continue to sign high-priced free agents."

Former club president Richard Brown believes that Jackie Autry became a target for the media after she asked reporters covering the club to meet with her in Palm Springs in March 1992 and outlined the Angels' financial woes, insisting the club had lost $3.6 million in 1991 and would lose more than $8.5 million in 1992 and that it was operating in constant debt.

She said that she and her husband could not continue to sustain the losses and that escalating salaries and costs were ultimately going to drive a club into bankruptcy—labeling it a dreadful prospect for baseball.

"Everything Jackie said was absolutely true," Brown said, "but there was a tremendous credibility gap between the players union and baseball and between the press and baseball, and people weren't prepared to believe her.

"Jackie was naive in thinking she could say, 'Okay, let me educate you, say what I have to say, straighten you out,' and that she could then sort of disappear. Once you interject yourself into the media arena, you can't then step away. The press is entitled to say, 'Hey, you came into the arena, now you're fair game.'

"If she was going to be out front on an unpopular issue, she had to stay out front, and I told her that it was a mistake to think otherwise. What happened was that she became a target for all the failures of the Angels, the acrimonious point of attack."

Jackie Ellam was still working in the Cathedral City branch of Security Pacific when Bavasi emerged from the wreckage of the 1980 season and traded Carney Lansford, Mark Clear and Rick Miller to Boston in December for shortstop Rick Burleson and third baseman Butch Hobson.

Bavasi thought back to his Dodger days and described Burleson as his "new Pee Wee Reese." Said Autry: "We've had a void at shortstop since Jim Fregosi was traded [at the end of the 1971 season]. Now we've filled it with one of the best shortstops in all of baseball. I would expect that an infield of Carew, Grich, Burleson and Hobson is one of the best in baseball."

Fregosi had pushed for the trade, although he had recently called the homegrown Lansford an untouchable.

"I was sincere, but what we have done is trade one untouchable for another," he said. "It comes down to a choice between an out-standing shortstop and an outstanding third baseman. I'd rather have the shortstop."

The Angels soon signed Burleson to a six-year, $4.65 million contract, the largest ever for a middle infielder to that point. As Lansford moved to Boston and won an American League batting title in 1981, only one of the highlights in a 15-year major league career that eventually saw him become a cornerstone of the Oak-land A's dynasty of the late 80s and early 90s, Burleson responded with his best season. He batted .293 and stabilized a pivotal posi-tion, but only temporarily.

Having thrown too often too early under Mauch's supervision during spring training in 1982, Burleson blew out his shoulder on a long throw from deep short in the first game of that season and never played regularly again, another victim of the Angel curse.

Fred Lynn, his former Boston teammate and a winner in 1975 of both the Rookie of the Year and Most Valuable Player awards, fared better—but only after an inauspicious debut. A month after the Burleson acquisition, Bavasi went back to the Red Sox and ac-quired Lynn and pitcher Steve Renko for Frank Tanana, Joe Rudi and a young pitcher, Jim Dorsey.

Lynn, available because of his imminent free agency, received a four-year, $5.3 million extension and promptly injured his knee on a May slide, was in and out of the lineup, had September surgery and batted .219, 89 points below his career average—another body blow for the star-crossed Angels,

While Lynn would come back in 1982 to repay the investment en route to the team's second division title, his 1981 injury was only one of the setbacks during a season in which Bavasi and his players openly sniped at each other and Autry made his seventh managerial change in eleven years.

Fregosi was fired on May 28, less than a year and a half after leading the Angels to their first division title. He was replaced by Gene Mauch, whom Autry had hired in January as director of player personnel after failing in the attempt to hire him as manager in 1977.

Autry insisted that Mauch had been hired only as a possible

successor to Bavasi, hired to give the club the benefit of a field man in the front office, but Fregosi suspected otherwise.

"I have to believe he was hired because Gene [Autry] questioned my ability right from the start," Fregosi said after his firing.

Mauch, 55, had quit as Minnesota's manager in August of the previous year, frustrated by Griffith's financial inability to retain his best players. He was known as the Little General because of his intensity and military demeanor, and he was considered one of the game's top strategists, a trim, tanned, silver-haired man who knew the rulebook by heart and had dedicated his life to the game.

In 21 seasons managing mostly bad teams in Philadelphia, Montreal and Minnesota, he had compiled a record of 1,524 wins and 1,705 losses at the time of his resignation, going 21 seasons without winning a title of any type. Only Connie Mack, John McGraw, Bucky Harris and Casey Stengel had lost more games than Mauch, but all are in the Hall of Fame, having won 32 pennants and 17 World Series.

"I've had enough of building bad clubs," Mauch said at the time he quit in Minnesota. He also said he would never manage again, but he was soon tempering that, saying he would manage only in a winning environment, only with a club that had a chance to win.

When he accepted the front office invitation extended by Autry, a Palm Springs neighbor, Mauch said, "Not for one instant am I thinking of managing the Angels. I have no designs on Jimmy's job. I have even asked Buzzie to include a clause in my contract that would prevent me from managing the club as long as Buzzie is here."

Bavasi refused, saying, "Things change."

Things did change, as the cynics thought they would and as Fregosi's intuition told him they would.

The pressures mounted as the Angels' touted offense got off to a sluggish start in 1981. Oakland won its first 11 games and 17 of its first 18. Bavasi played ill-advised mind games with Fregosi's designated hitter and clubhouse leader, Don Baylor. The press, responding to a series of damning statements from Autry and Bavasi, created an atmosphere of uncertainty surrounding Fregosi. And Autry delivered ultimatum after ultimatum, culminating in his firing of a man frequently portrayed as his surrogate son.

Of that pressure during Fregosi's final weeks, a veteran Angel said, "They've laid so much B.S. on Jimmy that he's now finally given up."

Fregosi waited several months before saying he would never work for Autry again. "They brought me back as a 36-year-old man and treated me as if I was still the 17-year-old kid," he said, adding, "The one thing I'll never understand is this: If the man wanted to fire me, why didn't he fire me? Why did he create a day-to-day situation in which he was too embarrassed to walk into my office and look me in the face and which made the conditions that much harder to work under? How could I walk into the clubhouse and kick a player's rear when he could say to me, 'Hey, what does it matter? You're not going to be here tomorrow anyway'? I learned a lot and I now know I wouldn't work under those conditions again. I put enough pressure on myself without having to put up with people in my own organization putting it on me."

His firing, Fregosi contended, was an act of panic by a management that did not understand how Oakland's improbable start had led to a false imbalance in the West and did not understand that the Angels—with eight new pitchers (from opening day of 1980) and with a new shortstop, third baseman, left fielder, center fielder and catcher—needed more than 47 games to develop cohesiveness, faith in each other, and a belief that as a team they were as good as everyone said they were.

"I'm also not sure," Fregosi said, "if it was recognized or accepted [by management] that when you build a team on hitting, you live when it hits and die when it doesn't. When you build a team on pitching and defense, you have a chance to win no matter how many runs you score. You win with pitching, defense and speed. Hitting comes fourth. When we won in 1979 it was with [a comparatively low] 88 wins and with the hitters mashing the ball. Those things aren't going to happen every year. You can't expect hitters to have the best year of their careers every year."

Fregosi had repeatedly drawn Autry's criticism for failing to bunt more, to hit and run, to steal. He was expected to play for a run at a time, even though he didn't seem to have the kind of pitching that could win low-run games or the speed to allow him to play a running game. Mauch changed the style but not the substance. The lack of hitting put an obvious burden on the pitching and defense (the Angels led the league in errors). A frustrated Mauch held a September clubhouse meeting and said his players were quitters. The Angels responded by losing 14 of their next 15.

Fregosi, listening via radio and watching via television, cited a lack of front office direction and continuity. He said the pressure to win a pennant for "poor old Gene Autry" before he died, coupled with Autry's belief in the star system and a philosophy that you can buy a pennant, had prevented the Angels from "adopting a policy and sticking with it." He spoke from the experience of 14 years in the Autry organization.

"No championship club could have survived the injuries we had in 1981," Fregosi said, "and that was the year the inadequacies of the farm system really showed up. You've got to give your young players a chance to mature, but they had traded away a lot of the kids who seemed close to playing in the big leagues or had already proven they could.

"My goal when I came back was to win a championship, and we did that at least on a division level. We not only had to beat the other teams, but had to tear away the reputation of always having been a loser, of being a hard-luck organization. No matter what happened to me later, I'll never forget the thrill of finally seeing that stadium filled, the look on the faces of the people who had been with the club for a long time when we finally won, and the positive reaction of the fans when we lost to Baltimore in the playoffs. You can live a lifetime and never be fortunate enough to experience any of that."

The firing by an organization in which he had grown up, by an owner he considered a second father, was an emotional jolt for Fregosi. His biting comments in the aftermath of his firing represented a message the organization needed to hear, but time would ease his personal pain. He would go on to manage the Chicago

White Sox, Philadelphia Phillies (winning a National League pennant) and Toronto Blue Jays. He would return to Anaheim to embrace Autry, have his No. 11 retired and join Baylor, Carew, Grich, Ryan and longtime coach Jimmie Reese as the first inductees into the club's Hall of Fame.

"We had a veteran club in which Gene had invested a lot of money, and he felt that we needed a more experienced manager," said Bavasi, reflecting on Fregosi's firing.

"Jimmy went on to become an outstanding manager who recognized that you can't get as close to the players as he had, but I think at the time he was too much of a players' manager and we needed some stronger direction and discipline."

Said Baylor, who would go on to manage the Colorado Rockies and the Chicago Cubs:

"Jimmy's firing had nothing to do with his managerial ability. It came back to the players not doing the job, as it always does. That '81 season was a disaster, and you could see it wearing on Jimmy. The pressure is always there, and it becomes worse when the rumors start. We knew something was up because Mr. Autry wasn't around, and he was always in the clubhouse when the team was home, but it was still a shock. I mean, it had seemed like the perfect marriage. We knew Jimmy had been a special player in the club's history and a favorite of Mr. Autry's, and we all respected him for that."

Rod Carew might have felt otherwise. His and Fregosi's relationship was tenuous at best. Some felt it went back several years to an incident in which Carew, then with Minnesota, had put a hard slide on Angel second baseman Bobby Knoop, resulting in a severe spiking. Knoop was Fregosi's former double play partner and best friend, and there was a rumor Fregosi had put a $500 bounty on Carew. When Fregosi became manager of the Angels, Knoop was his third base coach. Carew batted .318, .305 and .331 in three seasons under Fregosi but said he went to the plate, ran the bases and played generally in fear.

"I had the feeling that what I did was never right, that I could never do enough for him," Carew said of Fregosi, claiming that he kept hearing little needles from the manager, such as:

- "The reason we're leading you off is to get you out of the way."
- "If the ball is popped up, we don't want you near it."
- "You've got no range at first base. We've got to hope the ball is hit at you."

Carew said he welcomed the hiring of Mauch, his former Twins manager.

"Gene knows I'm not perfect and knows how to use my capabilities. Jimmy didn't take advantage of my ability to do a lot of things. I felt pressured into doing things I wasn't accustomed to. If I stay healthy, you're going to see me do a lot of the things I had done previous to the last three years."

Carew would play three more seasons with the Angels, collecting his 3,000th career hit in 1985, but the problems that cost Fregosi his job remained under the new manager—at least over the remainder of the 1981 season. A lineup that featured three former winners of the American League's MVP award and six hitters who had driven in 100 or more runs in a season generated an average of just over four runs per game, never establishing any consistency in the strike-interrupted year. The pitching was better than expected, but incapable of producing the occasional shutout or low-run game required to end a losing streak and the subject of criticism from several position players, who ripped Bavasi at times for building a staff with quantity instead of quality.

In the two years since he had refused to meet the contract demands of Nolan Ryan, Bavasi had spent $7 million on free agent pitchers Bruce Kison, Geoff Zahn, Bill Travers, John D'Acquisto and Jesse Jefferson. While Ryan was recording 22 wins and pitching a fifth no-hitter and more than 380 innings in his first two seasons with Houston, the five Angels were totaling only 19 wins, 10 by Zahn. Travers, given $1.5 million despite a history of arm troubles, developed tendinitis during spring training and pitched only 9⅔ innings for the Angels in 1981, was out all of 1982 and was 0–3 in 1983, his final year with the club. D'Acquisto, given $1.3 million despite a career record of 34–50, was sent to the minors in May and did not return. Kison, given $2.4 million before the 1980 season (despite having never won more than 14 games in a season), won seven games in two years and was out a full year while recovering from elbow and shoulder surgery.

Bavasi, more familiar with an era in which it was possible to play mind games with players and enjoy a facetious repartee, responded to the criticism by saying the problem with his team in 1981 might have been that the players were trying to do two jobs—run the club and play ball. His biggest spat came with the man he could least afford to anger—the respected Baylor, his 1979 MVP and clubhouse leader, whose contract would expire after the 1982 season.

Baylor and Bavasi got into it on April 1 of the 1981 season when Bavasi traded Jason Thompson to Pittsburgh for catcher Ed Ott and pitcher Mickey Mahler not long after Dickie Thon had been dealt to Houston for Ken Forsch.

"Some of the guys are upset, no question about it," Baylor said when asked about the trades by the *Los Angeles Times*. "I don't think you can really tell what kind of trades they are until the season is over."

The Thompson trade sealed Baylor's fate as the full-time designated hitter, with Juan Beniquez moving into left field, and Bavasi reacted to Baylor's comments by saying, "Player rep, my ass. He's got no guts. If he doesn't like what we're doing, then he should come see me. He can go to the press, but he should come see me first. What do you think Forsch, Ott and Mahler are going to think when he says things like that? If he played left field the way it should be played, Jason Thompson would still be here."

Baylor was stunned by Bavasi's overreaction, but it got worse two weeks later. Bavasi, insisting he was merely joking in a conversation with *Orange County Register* columnist John Hall, noticed Baylor in a picture with Rod Carew and Fred Lynn on the cover of a club program and said, "What's Don doing in that picture with the two hitters?"

Baylor, nursing a sore wrist at the time and frustrated with his hitting, as well as the failure of the Angels to produce a meaningful contract extension while bringing in more and more free agents at more money than their own MVP was making, saw nothing funny in the comments when he read them in Hall's column.

He stormed into Bavasi's office and told the general manager that if that was what he thought of him, he must not want him on his team, so he was going to retire. Baylor went to the clubhouse, packed his equipment and left, returning a few hours later only because he felt he owed Fregosi, his manager, an explanation.

They talked for 30 minutes about sensitivity and loyalty in an emotional meeting in which Fregosi attempted to convince Baylor that Bavasi's comments meant nothing to him, that he and the team needed him, and he asked Baylor to put his uniform on for him—no one else but him. Baylor was still uncertain, but teammates echoed Fregosi's plea, and Gene Mauch, in his front office position at the time, came to the clubhouse to tell him, "Little people do little things, and big people do big things. You are not a little person."

Baylor, who would ultimately leave the Angels after the 1982 season and become a coveted player and clubhouse influence on a succession of championship teams, knew he couldn't walk out on a contract and responsibility. He unretired, but the incident left scars on a player who had hoped to finish his career with the Angels, and it characterized a controversial and disappointing season interrupted by the long strike.

A frustrated Autry, who had virtually underwritten the free agent system, announced in August 1981 that he was through with that system, that the club would now build from within. He said bitterly that all the lucrative long-term contracts seemed to have diluted some of his players' intensity and aggressiveness, and he added that the next time there was the hint of a strike the owners should just shut down the season for a year.

"I'm sure there was a time when the pendulum was all on the side of the owners and that they took advantage of the players," he said, voicing a theme that has remained constant among management though a long series of labor disputes. "Now it's all on the players' side, and it may be that the only way to get it back in the middle is through a one-year moratorium. It would be all right with me because I personally don't get any money from baseball anyway."

Said Bavasi, reaffirming the Angels' intention to withdraw from free agency, a decision akin to Safeway announcing it was no longer into fruits and vegetables: "We simply believe that we now have the nucleus of a good club and that the money would be better spent in the farm system, where we have a group of youngsters who seem ready to play in the majors. If, in the future, there's one free agent who would definitely make the difference in our winning or losing the pennant, we might be interested, but we're firm in our conviction that we're now in position to build from within."

So much for good intentions.

That one free agent did become available, and the Angels embarked on another active winter of trades and signings, leading to a successful summer under the manager known as the Little General.

18

1982: A CLASSIC FALL

The Angels would win their second division title in 1982. They would win the first two games of the American League's best-of-five championship series from the Milwaukee Brewers, but they would not win the decisive third game. Their bags were packed for St. Louis and a World Series engagement with the Cardinals, a young Gene Autry's favorite team, but they would return, defeated and dejected, to Anaheim instead—what Don Baylor would describe years later as a "World Series–caliber team" that had not gone beyond a division title.

They were swept by the Brewers in the final three games of the 1982 playoff in Milwaukee as Gene Mauch, the Little General, made a series of command decisions that would be vulnerable to second-guessing—controversial, and ultimately costly, decisions of the type he had been accused of making while managing the Philadelphia Phillies in September 1964 and would be accused of making again in the American League's 1986 championship series with the Boston Red Sox when the Angels were one strike away from finally getting Autry to the World Series. A tantalizing third strike that proved to be as elusive as that third win had been in the 1982 playoff.

Gene Mauch's managerial career would span 26 years and 3,943 games. He would consistently prod seriously deficient teams in

Philadelphia, Montreal, Minnesota and Anaheim to play above their level, but it is a career that will always carry the star-crossed memory of the Phillies' pennant collapse in 1964 and the wrenching defeats of the Angels in the 1982 and 1986 playoffs.

If a handful of games provides an unjust and unfair evaluation measured against 26 years, there is no questioning the fact that Mauch was the central figure in the Angels' history of the 80s, although he managed for only four years in two different stints. There is no questioning the fact that he believed in himself to the point of arrogance.

"If we win, it will be because we have quality players, but I also don't argue when I hear someone say I'm the best manager around," he said in a 1982 interview in which he also told this writer, seeking to explore his emotions as the Angels closed in on the division title and his first managerial title, "You and your colleagues aren't smart enough to analyze me."

Perhaps he was right. Sparky Anderson, who managed the Cincinnati Reds when they were the dominant team of the 70s and later won a World Series championship with the Detroit Tigers, once called Mauch the smartest manager ever. Intelligent, cunning, innovative. One of the first, if not the first, to employ a five-man infield against certain hitters in certain situations. A rulebook expert who at times corrected or reminded umpires what the right call should be. A driven workaholic who was as intense, Pulitzer Prize–winning columnist Jim Murray wrote, "as a lightbulb, as explosive as six sticks of dynamite in a bouncing truck."

Mauch excelled at games that required patience, such as bridge and golf, but he was as impulsive as he was calculating. He raged, seethed, carried losing games in the pit of his stomach and wanted his players to have that same intensity. He threw fists, tipped over clubhouse buffet tables in his early managerial years. The rap was that he tended to overmanage, as if attempting to prove he was really the genius people said he was. The one certainty is that no one worked harder or cared more passionately about a game that had been his life for 40 years, a onetime gritty and gutty infielder who played in an era of sharpened spikes and hard slides and head-high fastballs, a star in the minors and a role player in his brief major league opportunities, the type of player who had to be a student of the game to survive, a manager in training.

Asked in the spring of 1982 if he would feel pressure managing a star-studded team, Mauch said: "A man feels pressure only when he doesn't know what he is doing. I don't know everything there is to know about baseball, but there isn't anyone who knows more. I've been at this for 30 years and have never had to ask for a job. I worked hard. I was willing to do the physical work because I felt it rubbed off on the players, and I was willing to do the mental work because I felt it would help me find a way to make the players better, to win a game."

If he didn't win the biggest games, if haunted by the demons of 1964 and 1982 and 1986, a 73-year-old Mauch, sitting on the patio of his condominium at Sunrise Country Club in Rancho Mirage long after his retirement following the 1987 season, said he is not the tormented soul he is often portrayed to be.

"I've been disappointed, but I've never disappointed myself and never bored myself," he said. "I don't give myself a pep talk this way, but in any of those years you'd have to find me some SOB who could have gotten the '64 team or the '82 team or the '85 or '86 teams to the point I did, to a position where he *could* be disappointed. I knew I didn't always make the right decision, but I knew I had the best chance of anyone I knew of being right."

As he emerged from the strike-mangled 1981 season and his disappointing return to a major league helm after the firing of Jim Fregosi, Mauch knew there had to be some pivotal decisions made.

After all those years of managing building and rebuilding projects in Philadelphia, Montreal and Minnesota, he had told himself that he would manage again only in an environment where he had a chance to win. The Cowboy, frustrated by his experiences in the free agent market, came out of the 1981 experience determined to go another route, to build from within, saying the farm system was ready.

Mauch suspected otherwise. He knew there was a decent core, but to succeed in 1982, to avoid another reclamation project, "there had to be an influx of not just talent, but an influx of winning people." Autry and Bavasi, for all of their good intentions, did not require arm twisting. Mauch's relationship with the general manager was such that "if I went in adamant about something, I think Buzzie trusted me enough to get it done. He was absolutely great that winter."

In quick succession Bavasi traded Dan Ford to Baltimore for third baseman Doug DeCinces to replace the erratic Butch Hobson; sent cash to Philadelphia for veteran catcher Bob Boone; traded catching prospect Brian Harper to Pittsburgh for versatile infielder Tim Foli in a move that proved providential when Rick Burleson blew out his shoulder in spring training and Foli became the regular shortstop, and, in the biggest free agent signing yet, landed Reggie Jackson in mid-January.

The celebrated Mr. October, the self-proclaimed straw that had stirred the New York Yankees' drink for five stormy and successful seasons, was signed to a four-year contract at $900,000 per year, with a clause that netted him 50 cents for every admission over 2.4 million. It was a money-maker for both Jackson and the Angels. Season sales, having initially been spiked by the acquisition of Rod Carew, jumped from 12,000 to 18,000 after Jackson's signing, and attendance doubled to a club-record and league-leading 2.8 million.

"From the standpoint of excitement and drawing power, Reggie and Pete Rose are in a class by themselves," Autry said of his decision to reenter the free agent market after saying he wouldn't. "I've long admired the way [Jackson] hustles and handles himself, and while we already have a number of players who have been on championship teams, Reggie adds yet another dimension. His desire should rub off."

Said Bavasi: "I don't know how many home runs Reggie will hit, but we're in the entertainment business and he's an entertainer. Either you love him or you hate him. The man has charisma. If we draw well, he has a chance to make a great deal of money, and so do we."

Jackson was 35 and ready for some peace after a tumultuous tenure with the Yankees, seldom far from a tabloid headline as he feuded with owner George Steinbrenner or manager Billy Martin while also helping power the Yankees to three American League pennants and two World Series victories, dramatically hammering three homers in Game 6 of the 1977 Series.

"I don't know if Reggie Jackson will ever know total serenity," Jackson said at his introductory news conference, talking in the third person as he frequently did, "but I recognize that about myself and I do believe that to a greater extent than ever before, I'll be able to relax here and do my job.

"I don't want trouble. I just want to play well and reach a third World Series with a third different team. Being that lightning rod in New York, the center of attention, beat me down. There's still pressure, of course. There's the pressure of proving to the fans that I can still play and the pressure of justifying the money, but there's always pressure and I hope it stays that way. Besides, what's pressure when you've just come out of Three-Mile Island?"

One of Jackson's first acts after signing with the Angels was to call Mauch.

"I don't want you to worry about what you may have heard about my attitude or my personality," Jackson told his new manager in the type of call he never made to Yankee manager Billy Martin— his frequent sparring partner. "I'm willing to do whatever you want me to do. I'll play right field, I'll DH. It's your call, your team. You just point me in the right direction."

Replied Mauch: "I don't need to hear anything like that. I appreciate you calling me like this, but all I want you to do is play for me the way you did against me."

Jackson respected Mauch for that, and they had only one minor disagreement during that first year together.

There had long been doubt about Jackson's ability to play right field on a full-time basis, but Mauch went with him there, replacing him with better defensive players in the late innings. Jackson would feel frustrated and helpless if those games ended up tied and he was unable to contribute, and he discussed it with Mauch at an early juncture, saying, "I want to be out there when we win."

Mauch wasn't deterred. He looked hard at Jackson and said:

"You've got to trust me on this. It's my way of giving you rest and keeping you strong. I want you to be right there for me in

September and October, because this team is going all the way and I'm going to need you."

In another time and place a younger Jackson might have created a confrontation, but this time he went with the flow, and on the last day of the regular season, after hitting 39 homers to tie Gorman Thomas for the American League lead and driving in 101 runs with a .275 batting average after a slow start, he went to Mauch and said, "You were right and I was wrong. You handled me perfectly."

Jackson provided the Angels with an identity as they labored in the Dodgers' shadow, but he was only one of the bellwethers on a team that also featured four former winners of the Most Valuable Player award—Carew, Lynn, Baylor and Jackson—and did not have a homegrown player in either the starting lineup, which averaged 33.1 years of age, or rotation, which averaged 34.1.

Mauch reflected on Bavasi's off-season acquisitions and said of Jackson, DeCinces, Foli and Boone: "They weren't ex-Yankees or ex-Orioles or ex this or that. They were a bunch of proud guys who came to the club and wanted to show each other how good they were. I felt from the start of that season, if they simply had normal years we would win."

Left fielder Brian Downing, having been switched from the catching position, looked on it differently, saying the Angels had better win.

"What we have here is a very talented team that can't afford to let this opportunity get away," he said.

"Many of us don't have a lot of years left."

The Angels won the West with a 93–69 record, beating Kansas City by three games. The Royals, who otherwise dominated the division during the late 70s and early 80s, lost 10 of 11 at one point in September, including three in a row to the Angels in Anaheim. The Angels wrapped it up by sweeping three games from the Texas Rangers on the final weekend.

Five regulars hit 20 or more homers, with Bobby Grich just missing at 19. In addition to Jackson's 39, Doug DeCinces emerged from the shadow of Brooks Robinson in Baltimore to slug 30 and drive in 97 runs; Downing had 28 and 84 in the leadoff role; Baylor 24 and 93, and Lynn 21 and 86. Mauch combined big ball with what he called little ball. Some of the manager's players thought he did too much of it, but Foli and Boone, batting in the eighth and ninth positions, combined for 49 sacrifice bunts and were frequently asked to hit and run when they weren't bunting. The Angels batted .274 as a team, but while the offensive statistics were impressive, it wasn't as easy for the Angels as the numbers would make it seem.

Mauch had no team speed, patchwork pitching and a proud and sensitive group of veterans requiring consistent rest. The Angels lost seven in a row at one point, eight in a row at another.

A May trade in which, at Mauch's urging, the Angels gave up one of their top young outfield prospects, Tom Brunansky, for Minnesota closer Doug Corbett, proved to be a bust. Brunansky went on to play 14 seasons in the major leagues and hit 20 or more home runs eight times. Corbett, an effective closer for Mauch when he managed the Twins, couldn't do it with a pennant on the line in Anaheim, going 1–7 with eight saves, and was seldom used down the stretch, when Mauch had to rely on left-hander Andy Hassler and the erratic Luis Sanchez.

"A lot of people didn't like what we gave up," Mauch said of Brunansky. "He was a nice player who could hit a home run, but he wasn't going to lead anyone anywhere. And by those years, you actually started to build a pitching staff backward. I'm not minimizing the importance of the starting pitchers, but you better get the guy to close it. I expected Corbett to be one of the best in the game. He showed me in Minneapolis he was capable, but lots of players do things short of first place."

If Brunansky for Corbett reflected the urgency of a now-or-never year, there were also those in the organization who privately held Mauch responsible for arm injuries to shortstop Rick Burleson, catcher Ed Ott and relief pitcher Don Aase.

Both Burleson and Ott developed shoulder pain when the regular infielders were kept on the field for every inning of two consecutive intrasquad games soon after they reported to the Arizona training base. When they went to Mauch to reveal their pain, they were told to work it out with long throws in the outfield, an outdated and ineffective therapy for sore arms. Burleson, so impressive in his first season with the Angels, was still nursing the condition when he blew out the shoulder on a long throw from deep shortstop in the season opener. He and Ott ultimately had rotator-cuff surgery and were lost for the season, their careers virtually ended.

Aase, the league's best relief pitcher through mid-May and the projected short man, was employed for 4 ⅔ innings in the season's third game, for six in the seventh and was on the disabled list with a season-ending arm injury by mid-July. The trade for Corbett would not have been necessary if Aase had not been overused, but Aase was not heard from during the second half except for a clubhouse shouting match with Mauch after the manager questioned his fortitude.

The Little General also had a clubhouse shouting match with Bruce Kison in July when Kison said he was fine and refused to accept a rehabilitation assignment to the minors after being hit on the leg by a line drive.

Mauch, in what seemed to be retribution, did not start Kison for 82 days after the incident, prompting many of his players to say the manager was cutting his nose off to spite his face. Kison, coming back from his arm problems of the previous two years, was one of the Angels' most effective pitchers before and after his inexplicable inclusion in the manager's doghouse. He opened the season with a 4–0 record, was 3–0 in September and 10–5 overall.

Despite the incidents with Aase and Kison, Mauch seemed determined to restrain his emotions to match those of his veteran team.

"Gene is just as fiery and competitive as ever," said Foli, a Mauch disciple from Montreal, "but with this group he doesn't have to scream about it or look for as many different ways to win. These guys know how to prepare themselves and how to play. There's more latitude to Gene's direction."

Said Mauch: "I burn inside just as much when we lose and I'll do anything to prevent it, but I'd hate to think I couldn't adjust to suit a team. This group knows how to play. Every regular has been on at least one division winner. I said from the start that there was so much talent that they only had to have normal years. I said from the start that if they play their A game, no one can compete with them.

"All those things I had to do with other teams wasn't to create a reputation but to try to keep from getting buried. I don't have to assert myself as much with this team."

The Angels kept their intense manager on edge by coming from behind to win 42 games. Pitching was a consistent adventure, but the Angels got a career-high 18 wins from Geoff Zahn, 13 from Ken Forsch and 11 from Steve Renko. A patchwork staff led the league in team earned-run average, and on August 31 Bavasi gave up another piece of the future to enhance the club's 1982 hopes, trading young left-hander Dennis Rasmussen, the Angels' No. 1 draft choice in 1980, to the New York Yankees for left-hander Tommy John.

The deal would have seemed improbable four years earlier when John, leaving the Dodgers as a free agent, hoped to move down the freeway to Anaheim so that he could maintain his Orange County home, only to have negotiations with Bavasi end bitterly and angrily. Bavasi sent John a letter calling him a "Phony with a capital P." John responded by saying he would never want to pitch for the Angels because he would spend all his time "batting Bavasi's bald head around."

That was the winter of 1978. John, whose career had been resurrected in 1974 when he pioneered a surgical process in which a torn elbow ligament is replaced by a tendon from the other arm, a process that came to be known as Tommy John surgery and which has salvaged the careers of many pitchers, ultimately signed that winter with the Yankees. The breach with Bavasi remained until the summer of 1981, when John and his wife, Sally, were moved by a compassionate letter Bavasi wrote them during the uncertain hours after their son, Travis, who would recover fully, accidently fell from a second-floor window.

John went 52–26 in his first three seasons with the Yankees, winning 20 games twice, but at 39 he fell out of favor, was in and out of the 1982 rotation and ultimately asked to be traded.

"The basic fact is that the people who make the decisions didn't think I could pitch anymore," John said after joining the Angels with a 10–10 record. "I loved New York, but the conditions weren't conducive to a healthy future for me.

"They seemed to think I was too old, my stuff was gone. I came here and felt appreciated immediately. Gene Autry called me the first night in Detroit and said he had wanted me for a long time. The first thing Gene Mauch said was that he didn't expect me to win every game, but he did expect me to keep the club in every game.

"My only regret is that the trade wasn't made a month earlier. It would have been more relaxing for me. There would have been less pressure. As it was, happening at the start of September, I almost had the feeling that I was expected to be the savior. I couldn't help thinking that one bad game and people might wonder why the Angels would make the investment."

The investment proved to be a winner. John won four of six decisions during the final month, helping the Angels overtake the Royals and win going away, prompting management to reward him with a three-year contract extension through the 1986 season, when he would be 43 with a bionic arm of only 12.

John's performance in September also influenced Mauch to select him to pitch the playoff opener against Milwaukee, whom he had defeated, 5–2, with a complete-game performance in his first start for the Angels on September 3. He had an 8–4 career record against the Brewers and was playoff-tested. In four previous playoffs with the Dodgers and Yankees, John had compiled a 3–0 record and 1.02 ERA.

The Brewers, however, were every bit as menacing as the Angels. They were managed by a one-time great hitter named Harvey Kuenn and known as Harvey's Wallbangers, having led the league in homers and hits. Their lineup included Gorman Thomas, who had tied Jackson for the home run title with 39 and drove in 112 runs; future Hall of Famer Robin Yount, who had 29 homers, drove in 114 runs and was voted the league's most valuable player; Cecil Cooper, who hit 32 homers with 121 RBI; Ben Oglivie, who hit 34 with 103 RBI; and Paul Molitor, who had 19 and 71.

"The best offensive team I ever pitched against was Cincinnati's Big Red Machine in the 70s," John said, "but Milwaukee doesn't have to take a backseat to anyone. They are an awesome offensive club, the best I've seen since the Reds."

John was up to the challenge. He yielded a two-run homer to

Thomas in the second inning, a solo run in the third, and then pitched six shutout innings, allowing only three more hits as the Angels won the playoff opener, 8–3, before an Anaheim Stadium crowd of 64,406.

Don Baylor, who had led the league with 21 game-winning RBI, drove in five runs to again put the spotlight on his uncertain contract status and the possibility he could be in his final days with the Angels. The six-year contract that Baylor had signed in the first winter of free agency and which paid him $186,000 in 1982, the lowest salary among Autry's mercenaries, would expire when the season ended, and he had not had any meaningful negotiations with Bavasi—often his verbal sparring partner.

Baylor, responding to repeated questioning after the Game 1 victory, said his only goal was to get the Angels to the World Series and that he wasn't thinking about the contract. Friend and team-mate Reggie Jackson, however, said that Baylor had been under considerable pressure, a pressure similar to what Jackson experienced during his final year in New York, an almost daily evaluation.

"It's as if his life is hanging in the balance," Jackson said, "and he's been uncomfortable with it most of the year. He's been un-comfortable with it until the game gets to a point where the out-come depends on his production, and then he seems to get his mind straight just like Paul Newman in *Cool Hand Luke*.

"The whole thing has been difficult for both of us because we're close friends and I've got to be the DH [Baylor's position] sooner or later. My hope right now is that he stays [with the team] and that I stay healthy enough to play another 140 games in the out-field."

As effective as John was in the opener, Kison was even better in Game 2. The powerful Brewers collected only five hits in a 4–2 defeat, their last 13 batters going down in order. Milwaukee had now scored only 5 runs on 13 hits through 18 innings in which the Angels had not been forced to employ their bullpen even once. Reggie Jackson, Mr. October, homered, Tim Foli and Bob Boone played little ball, and the Angels were one win away from a sweep, one win away from putting the Cowboy in the World Series—with staff ace Zahn scheduled to pitch when the series resumed two days later in Milwaukee. In the 13 years of division play, no team had ever come back from an 0–2 playoff deficit, and Fred Lynn said:

"When you look at the super pitching we've been getting and the way we've been playing for the last month. I think it's a pretty tall order for any team to win three in a row from us. It's not impossible, but it is improbable. The way we've been playing, we're just not going to give anything away. They're going to have to take it."

The off-day flight to Milwaukee was comparable to a club picnic. The Angel charter was crammed with family and front office people. Players who should have known better kept asking when the victory party would be. Reggie Jackson, who did know better, was concerned, thinking that some of his teammates were putting the cart before the horse.

"I thought it was the wrong way for a supposedly hungry team to go about things," he said. "No one was putting enough emphasis on closing the Brewers out. There was a lot of World Series talk. We didn't read the 'Beware of Dog' signs that were all around us. The dog was the Brewers, and the dog bit."

The series resumed on a flawless fall afternoon at County Stadium. The dog still wasn't doing much biting, but veteran Don Sutton, who had been acquired for September insurance much as John had been acquired by the Angels, hurled seven strong innings in a 5–3 Milwaukee victory that kept the Angel celebration on hold. Mike Witt, a young right-hander who would develop into one of the best pitchers to come out of the Angels system, yielded a decisive two-run homer to Molitor in the seventh inning after the Brewers had scored three runs off Zahn in the fourth.

The Angels still led the series, two games to one, and still needed only one more win, but Mauch now faced a difficult choice, one that would stir the demons and rekindle memories of 1964, when Mauch attempted to turn Chris Short and Jim Bunning into mechanical pitching machines, starting them 13 times during the final 20 games of a race in which the Phillies blew a 6½ game lead with 12 to play, losing 10 in a row at one point.

Mauch had put a Philadelphia team that had set a modern major league record with 23 straight losses only two years before in position to win a pennant, but critics tended to remember only the September collapse.

"Some people think that's the only year I ever managed," he frequently said, with a hint of bitterness.

Mauch had previously announced that Ken Forsch would start Game 4 of the Milwaukee series if it went that far.

But now, with the ghosts of Short and Bunning on his shoulder, he decided to start the 39-year-old John on three days' rest rather than the usual four.

The result: A 9–5 loss in which the Angels trailed 6–0 before getting their first hit off Moose Haas in the sixth and 7–1 before Baylor slugged a grand slam homer in the eighth.

Control specialist John, who had defeated Philadelphia twice as a member of the Dodgers on three days' rest in the 1977 playoffs, walked five, threw three wild pitches, gave up four hits, permitted six runs in 3⅓ innings and said he knew the rest factor would be an issue "unless I had a perfect game."

Asked if he had visions of 1964 or second-guessed himself, Mauch said he was impervious to the second-guessing.

"I do what I have to do," he said. "I do now and I did then. There's not enough room for me to second-guess myself. It's all taken up."

He also seemed to put the onus on John.

"The man thinks he pitches best [on three days' rest]," Mauch said. "He's our most experienced and successful playoff pitcher. If he feels he pitches best that way, I'm going to try and take advantage of it."

The next spring, however, John said the decision was strictly Mauch's.

"Whether it was the right or wrong move is not for me to say," John said. "I do think that if it was his intention to start only three pitchers, he should have announced it at the start of the playoffs like [Dodger manager] Tommy Lasorda did in '77. A pitcher can be ready physically, but there's a lot more to it than that.

"There's enough pressure in the playoffs without being put in a situation where it comes as news to you the night before and where you then go out there thinking, 'It's up to me, it's all on the line, I've got to have a good game.'

"There has to be time to get your mind ready. If Gene had announced it at the start, the questions and the media pressure would have been up front and out of the way. As it was, the media descended on Kison [who would be brought back to pitch Game 5 on three days' rest] and me as if it was our decision as soon as the third game ended. There were suddenly 95,000 questions. 'How do you pitch on three days' rest? Will you eat differently? When will you go to the bathroom?'

"Like I said, there's enough pressure in a playoff without having all that thrown at you, but I'm not using that as an excuse. I have no excuse. I had good stuff, my ball was moving, but I was just missing. I should have called time, regrouped and simply challenged the hitters. I got locked in a groove instead and couldn't break out of it."

Then and now, John said, "the guy I felt sorry for was Forsch. I thought he handled it much better than I would have."

Forsch had won 13 games with a 3.87 ERA. He had pitched a 2–1 complete-game victory over Kansas City on September 21, but had failed to go more than three innings in each of his last two starts.

Now, with John having failed on three days' rest, Mauch made another pivotal decision, scrubbing Forsch again to start Kison in the decisive fifth game—his first start on three days' rest since 1979 and a start no one was even sure he could make because he had pitched the final four innings of Game 2 with a blood blister on the tip of his right middle finger.

"I don't know if he can make it," Mauch acknowledged, "but adrenaline often takes the place of a lot of things, including medicine."

Forsch, currently the Angels' assistant general manager, said he was bitterly disappointed when bypassed in Games 4 and 5.

"Rather than take my whole season into account, Gene apparently based his decision on the two bad games at the end," Forsch said. "In fairness to Gene, he tried to explain it to me, but I was so upset that I told him, 'You're the manager, it's your call, I don't need an explanation.' Still, I couldn't understand the rationale. Kison had absolutely no skin on that one finger."

A dogged competitor who was 4–0 over his last five starts after spending those 82 days in solitary, Kison went five innings, allowing only three hits and two runs, before yielding to the blister and fatigue. He left with a 3–2 lead that should have been more, but the Angels failed to take advantage of four Milwaukee errors in the first five innings and nine hits and two walks off Brewer starter Pete Vuckovich in a high-wire stint of six innings during which the Angels had 12 base runners but scored only the three.

After a Brian Downing double and Lynn single produced one run in the first, Mauch went to little ball—giving up an out when he seemed to have Vuckovich on the ropes. He sacrificed after an inning-opening single by Boone in the third and did it again after DeCinces opened the fourth with a double. Mauch got a run each time, but Vuckovich and the Brewers were still alive, still trailing only 3–2 in the seventh when they had the bases loaded with two outs and a two-strike count on Cecil Cooper, who rocketed a two-run single to left field off Luis Sanchez for the 4–3 lead that would prove decisive as 54,968 fans rocked County Stadium.

Mauch had southpaw Andy Hassler, probably the most consistent and effective Angel relief pitcher in the first half but forgotten and frustrated in the second, up and throwing in the bullpen as the left-handed-hitting Cooper walked to the plate, but in a fatal decision he allowed the right-handed-pitching Sanchez to remain—impervious, as he noted, to the percentages and the risk of second-guessing.

"I remember sitting in the bullpen, and we were all kind of stunned, especially Andy, who was really upset," said Forsch of the decision to stay with Sanchez. "It's probably not what I'd have done, but it's easy to second-guess. The manager has the best feel for how to work the bullpen, and I have a lot of respect for Gene."

Hassler, who would come in to strike out Ted Simmons to end that inning and then pitch a flawless eighth, had struck out Cooper in a Game 3 relief appearance, but Mauch said he didn't call on him in the bases-loaded situation in Game 5 because he tended to get most of his outs on pitches in the dirt or out of the strike zone, and he didn't want to put Hassler in a situation where he would have been forced to throw strikes over the heart of the plate or risk a wild pitch that might have tied the game.

"Andy gets 90 percent of his outs on balls, and I didn't want to narrow him down like that," Mauch said. "Any manager can take himself off the hook by bringing in another pitcher, but I do what I have to do, and the rest of the world can think what it wants."

Hassler was livid at the explanation.

"I'm not going to let that _____ put the monkey on my back," he said of Mauch. "If he's not man enough to say he made a mistake, then I'll say it."

So did Cooper.

"When Robin [Yount] walked [to load the bases], I really thought I'd see Hassler," Cooper said. "He has a tailing fastball that's tough on left-handers, and he's really been tough on me. Sanchez is a power pitcher. I knew what he'd been throwing and where."

The manager sits on the hot seat. He is hired to be fired, paid to make the critical decisions. In the late chill of that gray afternoon, a future manager named Don Baylor, with the clock ticking on his Angel career, watched Cecil Cooper walk to the plate and wondered where Andy Hassler was.

"I think most of us thought, 'Lefty vs. lefty, we'll take our chances,' " Baylor said of the matchup that didn't happen. "Gene said he didn't want to risk a wild pitch, but that would have been only one run. The hit was two. I had a lot of hurtful things happen in my career, but losing that series with that team . . . well, that one really hurt."

It is the nature of baseball, of course, to illuminate those special moments. The decisions of October are magnified. The Mauch résumé will always include Philadelphia in 1964 and California in 1982. He would be at the heart of other controversial decisions as Angels manager, but what is overlooked about the decisions involving John and Kison and Andy Hassler, what tends to be forgotten about that fifth game in particular, are a number of events that also affected the outcome.

They included: the opportunities that the Angels blew in the early innings, a perfect throw from right fielder Charlie Moore that cut down Reggie Jackson going from first to third and nullified a potentially huge inning in the fifth, a bloop single by Moore—"the finest dying quail I've ever hit"—that fell behind Sanchez and barely out of the reach of a diving Bobby Grich in that pivotal seventh, a leaping catch by center fielder Marshall Edwards to take a tying home run away from Baylor in the eighth and ground outs from Downing and Rod Carew with the tying run at second and Reggie Jackson on deck in the ninth.

What is also overlooked as the Angels went from 2–0 to 2–3 and out is that Jackson was only 2 for 18 in the series, Carew 3 for 17, Downing 3 for 19 and Grich 3 for 15. Mauch felt he had to revert to little ball, even bunting with his big ball players, and Jackson said, "I can't fault the manager. When you've got guys struggling like we were, you try everything."

The potent Brewers batted only .219 for the five games but were headed to the World Series.

Not Mauch, who called the setback his biggest disappointment to that point.

"The only way I wanted to go was in the best company in the world," he said, referring to his players.

Said Forsch: "I could visualize the championship ring, we were so close. It was a brutal feeling not to get it."

A disconsolate Bavasi walked out of County Stadium with Gene and Jackie Autry and later said the outcome hurt worse than the events of 1951, his first year as Brooklyn Dodger general manager.

That was the year the New York Giants came back from a 13½ game deficit on August 12 to tie the Dodgers for the National League pennant and ultimately beat the Dodgers in a playoff on Bobby Thomson's dramatic home run, the "shot heard 'round the world."

"As much as it hurt in '51, I think we knew we'd have other opportunities," Bavasi said. "We wanted it so bad for Gene in '82 and we had it right there, but the Cowboy was amazing. All he said was that we'd start over in the spring and do it better."

As the Angels quietly and sadly gathered for the flight back to

Anaheim the next morning, Jackson appeared wearing an eye patch. He would insist that a piece of dirt had lodged under his eyelid on that slide into third in Game 5, but there were also rumors that he had been in a bar fight after the game and that he might have even been slugged by Baylor, which both players denied.

It made for a rare headline of the type Jackson had avoided since leaving New York and momentarily took the focus off the series defeat, which had been captured in a *Los Angeles Times* headline that read: "A Fall Classic for Kuenn; A Classic Fall for Mauch."

The vision-impaired Jackson was helped onto the team bus by Joe Ferguson. Reggie knew he would be back with the Angels in 1983.

The manager and his designated hitter wouldn't be.

19

1983–84: MCNAMARA'S BAND

Shortly after the All-Star break in 1982, general manager Buzzie Bavasi made a rare trip to the clubhouse. The Angels were on a roll, playing good, hammering opponents, and Bavasi couldn't resist needling manager Gene Mauch.

"I'm not having any fun," Bavasi complained with a straight face.

"What do you mean? What's wrong?" replied Mauch.

"You haven't given me a chance to second-guess you all year," Bavasi said, smiling.

"Well," said Mauch, "be patient, just be patient."

Mauch would reflect on that exchange years later and say, "I didn't know how prophetic I was being."

A shroud of silence enveloped the Angels front office in the aftermath of the stunning playoff defeat.

While a player or two continued to vent frustration by sniping at the decisions Mauch had made during the Milwaukee series, the Autrys and Bavasi said nothing, which in some ways spoke volumes. The perception seemed to be that they weren't happy with the leadership during that series and were going to let Mauch cool his heels before inviting him back for 1983, which they had to do considering that he had led a less than complete team to within a game of the World Series.

Nevertheless, the Angels created an atmosphere of uncertainty. Calls to the front office went unanswered. The usually accessible and gregarious Bavasi said only that he and the Autrys were still coping with the pain of the defeat, still sorting out their emotions. A decision on the manager would be made in time.

Ultimately, in late October, Bavasi said, "If we had to make a decision today it wouldn't be a good one. The atmosphere isn't right. Every time we pick up the papers and see it's the Brewers in the World Series and every time we think about the money we're losing by not being there, we become that much more disappointed. I don't think we should make a decision while there's still doubt in anyone's mind."

A 90-minute meeting with Mauch on October 30 convinced Bavasi that Mauch shared those doubts.

"He's annoyed and disappointed by things that have been said by management and the players [critical of his decisions in Games 4 and 5]," Bavasi said. "He wanted to tell me how he felt about coming back, but I told him I didn't want to hear it yet, that we should both take another 72 hours to think about it. After all, we played 167 games this year. If we'd won one more, we'd have been in the World Series."

The Angels eventually made the anticipated move, offering Mauch the opportunity to return, but now Mauch was coping with a more intense and private pain. His wife, Nina Lee, his friend since junior high school, was dying of cancer, and baseball didn't seem as important to the man who had made it his life, who couldn't have envisioned anything being more important.

Mauch has never talked in depth about his emotions during that difficult winter. But flattened by his wife's illness and annoyed by managerial critics who ignored how he had taken an aging team of no speed and inconsistent relief pitching, a team that failed to hit in the anticipated manner against the Brewers, to within a game of the World Series, he opted to resign.

"There were just some things that were more important," he said, referring to his wife's condition. "For the first time in my life I didn't care about anything. What was worse, I didn't care that I didn't care. I was indifferent about being indifferent."

The Angels were suddenly back in the managerial market, looking for the man who would be their 10th manager in 22 years, the ninth in the last 15. Ten days after Mauch informed Bavasi he would not be back, the Angels gave a one-year contract to John Francis McNamara, who had previously managed the Oakland A's, San Diego Padres and Cincinnati Reds—like Mauch, a baseball lifer at 50.

Bavasi said there was some initial consideration given Bob Lemon, who was under contract to the New York Yankees, but that McNamara was the only real candidate, particularly after Autry became intrigued with the interest other clubs—Milwaukee, Oakland and the Baltimore Orioles—were showing in McNamara.

"I've known John for many years," Bavasi said, "and he's always been a solid baseball and organization man. When Gene brought his name up, I threw my support behind it. He has the qualities that an established, veteran club should respond to. We have a team that knows how to play, and I imagine John will let it play. It's a team similar to the one he won with in Cincinnati, but then they took his horses away and he had no chance."

McNamara had replaced Sparky Anderson as manager of the Big Red Machine prior to the 1979 season and produced a 245–186 record in 3½ years at the helm, the best in the majors over that span. He won a division title in his first year, finished third in his second and was a frustrated 66–42 in 1981, when the Reds had the best overall record in baseball but were deprived of a playoff berth because they failed to win either half of a season split by the players' strike. A penurious approach deflated the budget and the Reds' hopes in 1982, and McNamara was fired on July 21 after he voiced displeasure with the arbitrary roster moves of general manager Dick Wagner. The Reds were 34–58 when McNamara was fired and 27–53 under successor Russ Nixon.

Asked if he was apprehensive about the pressure that awaited him in Anaheim, the "World Series or Bust" environment, McNamara said: "I thought about it, but I'm not unfamiliar when it comes to dealing with it. Replacing a manager as popular and successful as Sparky Anderson with a team that was expected to win wasn't exactly a walk in the park. I don't feel that in coming to the

Angels there could be any greater pressure. I know they want a winner, but not any more than I do."

McNamara managed from a foundation of common sense. Low-key and soft-spoken but capable of getting his Irish up. A former seminary student who felt he wasn't cut out to be a priest, but soon realized that listening to the confessions of his players was part of a manager's responsibilities. He played, coached and managed for 18 years in the minor leagues. A young Reggie Jackson, then in the Oakland farm system, played under McNamara at Birmingham and forever became an admirer and supporter in return for the support McNamara had provided on trips through a racist South, ordering his club back on the bus when restaurants wouldn't serve Jackson.

Sal Bando, another future Oakland star, also played under McNamara in the A's system and said, "If I could pick one guy I'd like to play for on the basis of personality, it would be Johnny Mac."

Charlie Finley, the eccentric Oakland owner, handed the reins of his budding dynasty to McNamara in 1970. The A's finished second, which wasn't good enough for Finley. Dick Williams was hired to take the A's to the World Series. McNamara ultimately spent three-plus years managing the formative Padres when Bavasi was club president, and he was a member of Dave Garcia's 1978 coaching staff with the Angels after Bavasi had joined the front office.

"Like everyone else," he said, "I was startled when Gene Mauch decided he wasn't coming back. I had talked to a lot of clubs, but from the time Buzzie first called, the Angels were my choice. I've worked with and for Buzzie before, I know how Mr. Autry supports the operation, and I was attracted by the outstanding talent. Position by position, the Angels have more bona fide stars than any club I've ever managed. The regular lineup is solid, but we may need some pitching help."

McNamara considered patience, consistency and the ability to handle pitching as his strong suits. He was attractive to the Angels because he was experienced and available, had won with teams that had the talent to win, and had never attempted to prove he was a genius, basically allowing established teams to play without interference from the bench. He came to the Angels, however, at a time when management pulled in the financial reins and elected not to build on the 1982 success. He never got the required pitching help—or any real help, period.

It didn't take long for McNamara to learn the way it would be. Soon after accepting the Angel offer, he spoke publicly about his hope that Don Baylor would be re-signed. The designated hitter had 93 RBI, 24 homers and a league-leading 21 game-winning RBI in 1982. He had driven in 10 runs in the five-game playoff with the Brewers, and had averaged 23 homers and 87 RBI in his six seasons with the Angels—one shortened by a strike and another by injury.

Beyond his offensive production, McNamara knew from his coaching experience with the Angels in 1978 that Baylor was the clubhouse enforcer, a consistent voice of reason and a liaison between the manager and players.

"Don is definitely a factor in the clubhouse, and I'd like to be able to count on him to help me a lot, more than strictly with his bat," the new manager said. "Contracts are not in my domain, but I'd like to have him with us. I'd like to be able to use his insights into some of our players and to rely on his respect off the field."

The plea went nowhere. Bavasi has long acknowledged that failing to keep Nolan Ryan with the Angels was his biggest mistake. His second, he has also acknowledged, was not re-signing Baylor. Unlike Ryan, Bavasi said years later, the problem was not so much the money Baylor demanded but a series of incentive clauses that "would not have been fair to the other players."

Incentive clauses? Baylor said he didn't know what Bavasi was talking about.

"I asked the Angels for a $6 million, five-year contract, and Buzzie offered $3 million for five years," Baylor said. "I later offered to compromise. I reduced the $1.2 million a year to $875,000 a year, but Buzzie still wouldn't give in. I didn't want to leave, but there was a principle involved. I had stood by my original contract, and I wanted a show of appreciation for that and the good years I'd given the team and community. Buzzie not only wanted to pay me less than Carew, Lynn and Jackson, he wanted to continue paying me about $300,000 less than Rick Burleson, who would probably never play again. I'd had problems with Buzzie over the years and I could swallow all that, but he obviously figured I had no self-worth at all. It hurt to leave, hurt probably more than I let on, but there were teams out there that wanted me. I had to close the book on my Angel career and move on."

Baylor would play seven more seasons, a coveted addition as hitter and clubhouse influence on a series of championship teams with the Yankees, Red Sox, Twins and A's. He would also come back in 1986 to haunt the Angels as a member of the Red Sox in probably the most famous game in Angel history—ironically at the expense of Mauch while helping McNamara, then managing Boston, to reach the World Series.

"I was reminded in '86 of just how strong a leadership role Don filled," McNamara said. "We could have used him in '83."

Baylor's departure set the tone for what McNamara called the most frustrating season of his career. A team that won 93 games as division champion in 1982 almost lost that many in 1983. The Angels were tied for first on July 10 but went 26–55 over the remainder of the season to finish in fifth place at 70–92, 29 games behind the division-winning Chicago White Sox.

With the planets misaligning again, 14 Angels ended up on the disabled list at various times, and McNamara said he never employed his regular lineup even once. Baylor took a large chunk of the offense with him, but Doug DeCinces, Brian Downing, Bobby Grich, Fred Lynn and Reggie Jackson, who had totaled 137 homers in 1982, hit only 89 in 1983.

"When the catcher plays 30 or more games than anyone else, it tells you what it has been like," catcher Bob Boone said of the injury wave. "It may not tell you why we've been as bad as we have, but it tells you why we didn't win."

An old team was a year older, and no one appeared older than Jackson, who plummeted from his 39 homers and 101 RBI in his first year with the Angels to 14 homers and 49 RBI and a .194 average in his second and worst season.

"You have to be terrible to hit .194, and I was," Jackson said the next spring. "I never had a good swing, never felt comfortable after the first couple weeks. I had hopes right up until September that I'd find it, but I never did. I'm used to being the dominant personality on the field when I'm in the batter's box, but that wasn't there last year. I was Reggie Jackson in name only. All slumps start in the bat and end up in the head. I broke down mechanically and then fought it so long that it became mental."

Jackson was 35 in 1983. Rod Carew was 37 and in the final year of his five-year, $4 million contract, a span in which assorted injuries kept getting in the way of his acknowledged artistry and march on 3,000 hits, an automatic passport to the Hall of Fame. Carew appeared in 138 games and batted .414 during a 25-game hitting streak in April and May of the division-winning season of 1982, but a persistent hand injury ultimately impacted his performance and he finished at .319. He came back in 1983 to rip off an astounding 48 hits in his first 96 at-bats and was hitting .402 at the All-Star break, but nagging injuries again reduced his availability to 129 games and he finished at .339, the 15th straight year that the seven-time American League batting champion had hit .300 or more.

With the team batting average slipping from .274 in 1982 to .260 in 1983, the team ERA rose from a league-leading 3.82 to 4.32. Geoff Zahn, an 18-game winner the year before, fought injuries and finished at 9–11. No one won more than 11 games, and there was no significant move by the front office to improve the rotation or the bullpen. The Angels lost 27 games in the seventh inning or later in 1982 and 32 in 1983.

Said Ken Forsch, who at 37 was 11–12: "We still had an absolute All-Star team, but it was getting old and more susceptible to injuries. I can't speak for anyone else, but no one had to tell me that I simply didn't have it anymore. I mean, I don't know that the change of managers made any difference that year because that was a veteran group that didn't really need a manager."

On August 12, cognizant that there was little McNamara could have done differently to compensate for the decimating injuries, the Angels announced his rehiring for 1984.

"The timing factor is very important for me and for the club," McNamara said. "When a club is playing as badly as we're playing, rumors start to surface, and this puts them to rest before the turmoil starts. I've been through it and it's not pleasant."

Said Bavasi: "Our thinking was that we wanted the public to realize that we realize that Mac had a very hard time with all the injuries. It's not his fault, and we want him to have a chance with a healthy team."

With the Angels, of course, things have never been that simple.

In mid-September, about three months after the death of his wife, Gene Mauch agreed to rejoin the club as director of player personnel. Mauch said he had no intention of managing again, which is what he had said after leaving Minnesota to join the Angel front office while Jim Fregosi was manager.

In early October, about two months after he had been offered the 1984 managerial reins, McNamara had yet to sign a contract or agree to terms, and in a move ultimately forestalled by peace talks with Mauch and Bavasi, he submitted his resignation on October 6.

McNamara was angry on two counts:

1. He and his coaching staff were concerned with Mauch's appearances on the field and possible interference with their work both before and after Mauch's rehiring by the club.
2. He and his coaching staff were concerned with a *Sporting News* column by the *New York Post*'s Dick Young in which Young, while ignoring the Angels' 1984 commitment to McNamara, wrote that Mauch's long friendship with Don Zimmer, who had resigned as a New York Yankee coach because he was unable to get along with then Yankee manager Billy Martin, might result in Zimmer becoming an Angels coach or possibly the manager if McNamara wasn't rehired.

McNamara, seeking clarification and communication from both Mauch and Bavasi, the reestablishment of his own authority on the field and in the clubhouse, and a better understanding of the chain of command, met with both men on October 8 and emerged satisfied with the situation.

"I was serious," he said of his offer to resign, "but I don't anticipate any problems. I'm comfortable with the way it sits."

Mauch admitted that he had talked to Zimmer with Bavasi's concurrence about joining the Angels, but he had not made an offer and he was left with the impression that Zimmer planned to join the coaching staff of the Chicago Cubs.

Mauch reiterated that he did not intend to manage again and would not be interfering in the manager's domain since "I never allowed anyone to interfere in mine."

McNamara agreed to terms on October 11, and Bavasi said:

"Nothing has really changed from the time [Mauch] was hired. John will run the club on the field and take overall orders from me. He'll communicate with Gene as to what he needs, and it will be Gene's job to lay the groundwork for trades and acquisitions. No one man makes all the decisions. This is not a one-man organization. There had been a lack of communication that was corrected. Both have their areas of responsibility. They are intelligent men with respect for one another. I expect them to get along."

There was no evidence that they didn't during a season in which the Angels improved to 81–81 and finished in a second-place tie with Minnesota, three games behind Kansas City.

What evidence there was, however, suggests that Bavasi and Mauch did little to bolster McNamara's chances. The 1984 team was basically the 1982 and 1983 team, only a little older—while also a little healthier after the 1983 injury wave. The Angels were locked into multiyear contracts with veteran players, leaving the front office with little flexibility. Bavasi talked about the need to improve the pitching, but it never happened. Shortstop Dick Schofield and center fielder Gary Pettis came out of the farm system to become regular players in 1984, improving the defense, but Schofield hit .193 and Pettis .227 while stealing 48 bases. When Schofield was lost with an injury in midseason, Bavasi and Mauch allowed McNamara to operate for a month with only 24 players, one less than permitted.

"We never had strong enough pitching or that one horse in the bullpen," McNamara said years later. "People talk about pitching being 70 or 75 percent of the game. Hell, it's 90 or 95 percent. I mean, it was a frustrating situation trying to patch a staff together, always hoping you had enough healthy arms."

Goose Gossage, the renowned Yankee relief pitcher, had been available as a free agent during the previous winter but signed with the San Diego Padres and helped pitch them to their first National League pennant in 1984, a fact that weighed on Tommy John in September, when the Angels were eliminated from division contention.

"If we'd had Rich Gossage, we might be the ones sipping champagne right now. All Gene Autry had to do was ask, and the starting pitchers would have chipped in to help pay for him. I really believe that."

In the history of the Angels, it was always the road not traveled or the one wrong turn. In this case Autry insisted he had pursued Gossage and that he had not been dissuaded by his wife, who was new to the business but talking of a change in the club's philosophy from buying players in the market to doing a better job of growing them on the farm.

"We've needed a real stopper in the bullpen the last three years," Autry said during the 1984 season. "In '82 I think we would have been in the World Series if we'd had one. We made pitches for Gossage. We made an offer of $1.1 million for five years, and when you guarantee five years to a pitcher, you never know. It's a gamble."

The Angels did give Rod Carew a two-year contract extension before the 1984 season, but Carew battled a cervical nerve problem, and batted .295, ending his streak of 15 consecutive seasons at .300 or more.

"If I kept stats or worried about stats it would be important to me, but I don't think I have to prove I can hit .300, and I don't think batting .290 at 38 is too bad," Carew said. "I am disappointed with my year as a whole, but I think we went as far as we could with what we had."

Reggie Jackson, the arrogant, defiant Mr. October, went to spring training in 1984 filled with self-doubt after hitting only .194 with 14 homers in 1983.

"The fact that I've accomplished a lot doesn't matter now," he said. "I'm human. The thoughts drift through my head. I've got a mental fight on my hands. I'm in the same situation I was in in '82, when I read so much of the negative stuff from Steinbrenner that I started to believe it and I had to prove I could play again. This time I'm in even more deeply."

Jackson responded. He batted only .223 but drove in 81 runs and hit 25 homers. His 22nd, coming off Bud Black in the seventh inning of a 10–1 loss to the Royals on September 17 at Anaheim Stadium, a loss that dropped the Angels 1½ games behind Kansas City in the division race, enabled Jackson to become only the 13th player to have hit 500 in his career, ensuring his Hall of Fame election.

The 500 did not include the 18 he had hit in playoff and World Series competition as one of the most productive hitters in post-season play.

"Think about what 500 means," Jackson said with typical verbal flair. "It means you have hit 30 home runs a year for 15 years, and you're still 50 shy. That's some hittin', pal.

"I feel like I have an E ticket at Disneyland. I feel like there are eight pieces of pie at a party, eight people at the party, and I've got more than one slice. I've got more than I can ask for."

Jackson was not the only Angel hitter to rebound in 1984. DeCinces hit 20 homers and drove in 82 runs, Downing hit 23 and drove in 91, and Lynn hit 23 and drove in 79. However, the Angels hit only .249 as a team, next to last in the league, and not enough to compensate for a pitching staff that lost Forsch for the season with a dislocated shoulder in April and scrambled for a reliable closer until Aase returned from the arm problems that surfaced from his overuse early in 1982 and went 4–1 with eight saves over the second half of 1984.

Rookie Ron Romanick was an impressive 12–12 in a starting role, but veterans John, Kison and Zahn were a cumulative 24–28. Mike Witt, developing into one of the best pitchers to come out of the system, was 15–11 in a breakthrough season and ended it in a spectacular fashion. On the last day of the season, with nothing at stake for the Angels and Texas Rangers except an early start on a long winter, Witt became one of only 13 pitchers in major league history to hurl a perfect game. He retired all 27 batters in a 1–0 victory at Arlington, Texas, the seventh no-hitter in club history, four of which were pitched by Nolan Ryan. There were no difficult plays in Witt's perfect game, and only four balls were hit to the outfield. He needed only 94 pitches and struck out 10.

"I used to think no-hitters were thrown by guys who won 20 games and struck out 300 hitters a year," the 24-year-old Witt said. "I have to think now that I may be in that class."

The perfect game definitely put the 6-foot-7, 190-pound right-hander, selected on the fourth round of the 1978 draft out of Servite High in the shadow of Anaheim Stadium, in a richer class.

Although only 23–29 in three seasons prior to his 15–11 of 1984, he received a three-year, $2.1 million contract in the winter after his no-hitter, one of the first of two in which he was a participant. Witt would come out of the bullpen to finish off a no-hitter by Mark Langston in the opening game of the Angels' 1990 season, but neither that game, nor his perfect game, is remembered as the most memorable game of Witt's career with the Angels.

He and Mauch will be forever linked by the events of Game 5 of the 1986 championship series with the Red Sox, which was still around the corner in 1984, when the Angels led the division for 52 days during the first half before the experience that was expected to be pivotal down the stretch proved to be a lead weight in the Angels' hands.

They were still alive when they opened a four-game series in Texas that Witt would conclude with his perfect game on the last day of the season, but they were eliminated by a 2–1 loss in the opener, their eighth loss in 12 games, a span in which the veteran lineup batted an ugly .190.

Reggie Jackson at that point had two hits in his last 27 at-bats; Brian Downing 3 in 19; Fred Lynn 4 in 39; Bob Boone 1 in 23, and Bobby Grich 1 in 16. The Angels had to hit to win, but didn't.

"I felt going in [to the season] we could pull it off, even though no one gave us a chance," McNamara said. "But we never put the hitting and pitching together consistently enough. We never sustained the offense in a way I had anticipated. Age was a factor, but to what extent is difficult to say and measure."

On the day after their elimination, Gene Autry mailed public relations director Tom Seeberg copies of a column written by the *Washington Post*'s Tom Boswell and reprinted in the *Los Angeles Times*, and instructed McNamara to have the column posted in the clubhouse. Boswell, who had watched the Angels lose three in a row at Kansas City a week earlier, suggested in his column that the Angels lacked life, tended to malinger and didn't seem to care if they won or lost a division they dominated talent-wise. The *Times*' headline read: "The Angels: No Heart, No Future."

Angel players were furious. Jackson called it a "cheap shot" by both Autry and Boswell.

"Rather than having someone send it to us, he should have come here himself and told us why he wanted us to see it," Jackson said of Autry. "Say all you want about George Steinbrenner, but he came to the clubhouse and said what he thought."

Said Grich: "I take it personally when anyone writes that I don't have heart. I'm dumbfounded by the fabrications. How can anyone write accurately about a team's performance over 162 games when he sees it for only three or four?"

Grich acknowledged that there had been times when the Angels "had a tough time pulling together" because the chemistry wasn't as good as it should be, and he accused management of having failed to build a base and add to it since he joined the club in 1977.

"You can't bring in six or seven outside players a year and expect a magic formula," Grich said. "But how many experts actually picked us to win this year? Nobody did. All you can ask is for everybody to give 100 percent, and I think we did that."

McNamara was also angered.

"This is not a rah-rah team," he said. "People looking for that aren't going to see it. That's not to say it's an unemotional team or that they don't care or bust their butts. I resent it when people say this team didn't have heart."

The bitter reaction to Autry's decision to endorse Boswell's view of a heartless team was only part of a typically convulsive finish to another frustrating season. This one ended with Buzzie Bavasi retiring as general manager and John McNamara rejecting the

Angels' offer to return in 1985 in favor of managing the Boston Red Sox.

Bavasi, 69 and a veteran of almost 40 years in baseball front offices, had informed Autry of his desire to retire during spring training in 1984 and reiterated it over the course of the season. On the club's final homestand, he gathered reporters in the back of the press box at Anaheim Stadium and made it official.

"There's no sense for an old man to stay around," Bavasi said. "I'm tired and ready. Evit and I have been married for 45 years and never had a summer vacation. If I didn't think the organization was set, I wouldn't have done this, but Larry Himes is doing a great job with the scouting department, and Mike Port [whom Bavasi had brought in as his assistant in 1977] knows all the answers."

There was more to it, of course, as Bavasi explained years later. He was a gregarious man whose office door was always open and who had always loved the repartee with his players, from Brooklyn to Los Angeles, from San Diego to Anaheim. Now he was suddenly dealing with agents and lawyers. Players visited only to complain or ask for a loan. The game changed, the money changed. No longer was it fun for a war-horse from another era.

"I didn't mind paying guys like Reggie Jackson and Rod Carew because they put people in the seats, but now I was paying the 24th and 25th players what I once paid Sandy Koufax and Don Drysdale," Bavasi said. "I mean, guys like Sandy and Don played for the love of the game, but I didn't see that happening anymore. It had become a business. It was all about money."

The Angels won two division titles and set a club attendance record in Bavasi's seven years. He was proud of the record, he said, but disappointed that he had been unable to get the Cowboy a ring and cognizant that he might be remembered in Anaheim for having let Nolan Ryan and Don Baylor leave—costly mistakes that impacted the field, clubhouse and ticket booths.

"I can't change history, though I wish I could," he said.

Autry never considered another successor. He wanted a quick transition, Port knew the organization and Bavasi had recommended him highly.

The new general manager asked McNamara to stay, but Mc-Namara didn't consider it a heartfelt request.

"I remember Mike's quote as being something like, 'Well, John can come back if he wants to,'" McNamara said. "What kind of an endorsement was that? Gene Mauch was back in the front office, and that had created some questions. If we had gotten off to a bad start in 1985 I'd have been out the door, and where would that have left me? I just wasn't comfortable with the situation. Buzzie had retired, and he was the guy who had hired me. We had differences [Bavasi had criticized McNamara's continued use of a slumping Tommy John during the second half of the season] but I generally knew where I stood."

As in the case of Bavasi's retirement, there was more to it. McNamara wanted the security of a multiyear contract and didn't think the Angels would offer it. He felt the powerhouse Red Sox offered more potential than the aging Angels and their inconsistent farm system. He was unhappy with front office second-guessing and a lack of response to the club's injury-related needs in 1984, and disturbed at times by the baby-sitting that was required by some of his high-salaried stars.

"I'm exhausted," he confided in midseason. "I spend all my time massaging egos."

McNamara's decision caught the Angels by surprise. Port said he was stunned and disappointed, thinking he and McNamara had been close to finalizing a contract agreement. Now he was faced with a managerial search in his first month as general manager.

"We'll be looking for someone who can produce stability, consistency and results," he said. "I think we have to have someone who has managed before, someone who might be with us for several years."

He did not have to look far.

20

1985: "Do Not Disturb"

There had been an incident in late September of 1984. A tense moment in a game at Kansas City with the division title still up for grabs. A ground ball to Angel second baseman Bobby Grich, who inexplicably held it for what seemed an eternity before throwing to first base for the out. In the enclosed press box, a gray-haired gentleman in suit and tie watched in that prolonged moment as Grich held the ball. Unable to restrain himself, Gene Mauch, the Angels' director of player personnel, shattered the quiet of the press box as he shouted, "Throw it, throw the damn ball."

As reporters spun around to see who had broken the golden rule regarding no cheering or rooting in the press box, it was clear that Mauch, stung by the criticism after the Angels' failure in the 1982 playoff and deflated emotionally by the death of his wife in June 1983, was no longer indifferent about being indifferent.

Mike Port, the new general manager, sensed it as well. The more he and Mauch talked about a successor to John McNamara after the 1984 season, the more they discussed attributes such as intensity, knowledge, experience and compassion with young players, the more Port concluded that Mauch was the man.

"I finally turned to Gene and asked him, 'Aren't we talking about you?'" Port recalled.

"He kind of laughed and said, 'Well, I've got that feeling in my stomach again. I can feel the fire.'"

Port went to the Autrys, and the Autrys endorsed the selection.

At 59, the Little General was back at the Angel helm, prepared to confront the ghosts of 1964 and 1982 in what would be his 24th season as a major league manager, prepared for the latest attempt to get Gene Autry—and Gene Mauch—to the World Series.

The Little General had already managed 3,457 major league games to rank ninth on the all-time list. He had directed a series of basically bad teams to 1,646 wins, which also put him ninth on the all-time list. If the accomplishments tended to be forgotten amid a media and fan emphasis on what he had *not* won, Mauch dealt with those demons by insisting he had never cheated an employer, never backed up to a pay window, never actually had an opposing manager beat him between the white lines.

"Nobody has and nobody will," he said.

He was returning now because the game that had been his life had revived the life in him and because he admired the "caliber of the people I would be working with" on and off the field, believing he could lead the 1985 team to a division title.

Part of it as well, he said, was that "bumming around is all right until you start feeling like a bum. I had a plan for 40 years—all baseball and a little golf. I tried it the other way the last two years, and I didn't like it at all."

The man he went to work for was the youngest general manager in baseball and the antithesis in many ways of predecessor Buzzie Bavasi. Mike Port was cautious, guarded, conservative in style and apparel. He had little time for hot stove banter or jockeying with the press the way Bavasi did. He was a self-described baseball workaholic obsessed with numbers—from the statistical studies he pored over as a matter of routine to the budget he was determined to maintain.

"Given the time and the capability, I am inclined to get as much information as possible before acting," he said. "Some people operate baseball clubs with the wheeler-dealer syndrome. I do not."

Player agents and writers came away from first meetings with Port wondering if they had encountered a banker, accountant, lawyer or computer analyst. He spoke in a language that *Los Angeles Times* baseball writer Mike Penner described as Port-uguese, a compilation of verbal misdirection.

Describing himself, for example, Port said:

"I would say [I am] amicable enough on occasion, but at the outset, a baseball fan, and . . . desirous of wanting to see players do well but within the proper vein of how I see baseball and what the game should be. I'm cooperative enough and open-minded enough, but otherwise, with a very structured impression of what baseball is and the public trust that it holds and how the game and the club should be operated."

With all of that, Port was capable of humor—self-deprecating and otherwise.

"When does one consider a career as a baseball general manager?" he said. "At that point in life when you cannot throw the ball from me to you."

And: "The life plan I had in place was to play in the major leagues for 20 years—because that's the maximum pension requirement—and prosper and do well and thereafter move into front office work. But the way the Fates handled things, the transition to the front office came about 19 years and nine months sooner than the master plan had provided for."

Port grew up in Fallbrook, near San Diego, where his father owned a clothing store. He played baseball as a middle infielder at Cal Western University, obtaining a business degree. A Fallbrook neighbor, former Dodger great Duke Snider, arranged for Port to receive tryouts with the Dodgers and San Diego Padres, but neither went anywhere—at least from a playing standpoint. Port's attentiveness and inquisitiveness attracted the Padres' attention, and he jumped at their offer to become a minor league general manager—first at Key West, Florida, then Lodi, California. He ultimately moved into the Padres' farm and scouting department when Bavasi was club president, and later accepted Bavasi's offer to join him as director of player personnel and assistant general manager with the Angels.

From September 1, 1984, when he became general manager, to April 30, 1991, when he was fired, Port's title changed on occasion, but his basic role, as he viewed it, was to assemble the "best baseball team possible while retaining some element of solvency." He inherited an older team that needed to be restocked, and he faced the difficult task in his early years of having to tell Rod Carew and Reggie Jackson, among other star players and fan favorites, that their services were no longer needed, that they were too old to contribute.

He was quickly viewed—by players, public and press—as cold and calculating, an executive without heart, although in most cases he was merely carrying out the wishes of Gene and Jackie Autry, whose increasing presence led to a similar portrait as the cold and calculating owner's wife.

"Neither of the Autrys have been restrictive in any way," Port insisted. "There have been times I've solicited her opinion on financial questions, but those who write that she desires to run the club or is cutting this to the bone are wrong."

Ultimately, of course, Port encountered the problem that all of his predecessors had. Despite the wisdom of building from within, as Jackie Autry preached, there was the overriding imperative to get the Cowboy to the World Series—often leading to imprudent decisions with young players.

"I think it's fair to say we didn't stick with one plan long enough, and that led to a lot of peaks and valleys," said Port, now assistant general manager of the Boston Red Sox. "There was a tendency, in a lot of respects, to look for the quick fix, to try and cut corners instead of taking time to let the young players develop. I never heard Gene Autry say we have to win now, but I think it was a pervasive feeling in the organization."

Dante Bichette, Devon White and Mark McLemore were only a few of the young players who established long major league careers after being traded by the Angels during the later years of Port's tenure, often at the urging of his managers.

In the winter of 1984, his first as general manager, Port knew it was time "to start turning the wheel" with his veteran team and "to try and develop a better blend" of young and older players, a difficult task considering the farm system wasn't flush with talent and Port was locked into multiyear contracts with older players who had limited trade value—Rod Carew, Doug DeCinces, Brian Downing, Bobby Grich, Reggie Jackson, Tommy John and Geoff Zahn among them.

Port took action in the only area where he could. He offered what he called "shared risk" contracts that included incentive bonuses to compensate for a lower guaranteed salary to oft-injured free agent candidates Fred Lynn, Don Aase and Bruce Kison, all of whom rejected their offers and signed elsewhere. There were no offers to free agent pitchers Rick Sutcliffe and Bruce Sutter, who might have filled critical needs, but Port did sign free agent outfielder Ruppert Jones as a replacement for Lynn and did select Atlanta relief pitcher Donnie Moore from a pool of compensation players for the Baltimore Orioles' signing of Lynn. Now teams receive amateur draft choices as compensation for the loss of a free agent.

Moore was a 30-year-old right-hander who had saved 16 games for the Braves in 1984, but what impressed Angel management more was that he had given up only three home runs in 64 innings, none in the launching pad that was Atlanta Fulton County Stadium. Moore was seen as a potential replacement for Aase as the closer, but no one could have predicted his pivotal role over the next two years, and the impact of it on his life.

Returning Angel players were not impressed by the winter developments.

"I'm definitely disappointed that we lost some quality people, and I think some of it was ridiculous," catcher Bob Boone said. "To lose Don Aase was a crime, but it's not my department."

Said Reggie Jackson: "I don't like what's happened this winter, but it's not over and it doesn't really mean a thing until we see the results of summer. The black and white says we're an old, below-average club, but I've played 18 years in the big leagues and never played one game on paper."

Only hours after the Angels reported to their Arizona training base in February 1985, Mauch asked veterans Boone, Carew, DeCinces, Downing, Grich, Jackson and Rob Wilfong to meet with him in a distant corner of the complex. Mauch, watching from the front office in 1984, thought there had been a loss of collective intensity, that players had started to travel individual roads and that McNamara's efforts were betrayed by selfishness and pettiness on the part of many players.

Mauch laid it out in his meeting with the veterans, saying the attitude and atmosphere hadn't been good, that they had to think and play as one, that they had to stay focused and motivated from the start. Jackson emerged to call it a positive meeting and that the return of Mauch helped to provide an intensity and approach that was needed in an environment that tended to dilute intensity and motivation.

"Baseball in California is entertainment," Jackson said. "I don't even look on it as a job. There's not the life-and-death atmosphere to it that you find in the East. It's harder to develop a killer instinct. It's pretty rather than gritty. You've got fans who have to decide between the ballpark or going sailing. You've got girls walking around the stadium in bikinis. We'd come in with the Yankees and think, 'Hey, it's the Angels. They don't slide hard, they don't play hard.' It's tougher for a manager to develop the type of work ethic that will carry a team through a 162-game schedule, but I have respect for the business and the way Mauch goes about it."

In its preseason rankings, *Sports Illustrated* tabbed the Angels 25th among the 26 teams, but with Mauch employing 155 lineups in order to keep his veterans rested—"the most delicate thing I ever had to do"—they finished second in the West with a 90–72 record, a win total exceeded only by the club record 93 in 1982.

It was a season of overachievement that would be remembered for an underwhelming finish in which the Angels, who had been in first place for 142 days at different points, lost eight of their last 13 games, including three of four to Kansas City, and finished one game behind the Royals. So close, so far again.

It was a season in which Mauch played Little Ball to the hilt, calling for 99 sacrifice bunts, to compensate for a league-low batting average of .251. Only part-time outfielder Juan Beniquez (.304) hit better than .300. Four players—Jackson, Downing, DeCinces and Rupert Jones—hit 20 home runs or more, but no one drove in more than 85 runs.

Jackson, who hit 27 homers, had only two RBI after mid-

September, and Downing had only five hits in his last 37 at-bats as the Angels scored only four runs in a futile stretch of 40 innings during the final two weeks. Rod Carew, in what was his final season at 40, batted a career-low .280 but came back from an early season foot fracture to become only the 16th player to that point to collect 3,000 hits. Carew, in characteristic fashion, looped an opposite-field single down the left-field line off Frank Viola of the Minnesota Twins in the third inning of a 6–5 victory on August 4.

The milestone hit by the seven-time batting champion, ensuring his first-ballot election to the Hall of Fame, came against the team with which he had spent the bulk of his career, and it came with his former Minnesota manager, Gene Mauch, in the home dugout. Mauch maintained that it was always more a privilege than a pleasure to serve as Carew's manager, and he reacted to No. 3,000 by saying, "If I told you my emotions, people would know that the way I [normally] look is a facade."

Said Carew: "When you get in the class with Ty Cobb and Rogers Hornsby and Pete Rose, it means a lot. This is something I thought I'd never accomplish, but I've been around for 19 years, and if you stay around for 19 years, good things happen to you. I don't know where I'm going from here, but I don't want to stop at 3,000."

He wouldn't, but it was too soon to know for sure what the Angels' plan was or to realize he wouldn't go much beyond 3,000. The Angels at that point were battling the Royals for a division title, kept alive in large measure by a rebuilt pitching staff that featured three homegrown starters—Witt (15–9), Romanick (14–9) and rookie Kirk McCaskill (12–12)—and a suddenly dominant bullpen from which Moore saved 31 games with a 1.92 ERA and Stew Cliburn, a free agent acquisition in 1982, went 9–3 with six saves.

Port released Tommy John in June—"This is the best thing they could have done for me, but I wish they had done it eight to ten weeks ago because I really think it was in their plans all along," said the 42-year-old southpaw, who was unhappy in his undefined role as both starter and reliever—and he made two other headline moves down the stretch.

In August, the new general manager traded three young farm

products—outfielder Mike Brown and pitchers Bob Kipper and Pat Clements—to Pittsburgh for three veterans: starter John Candelaria, reliever Al Holland and outfielder George Hendrick. And in September he traded two minor leaguers to Oakland for former Dodger right-hander Don Sutton, who arrived with 293 career wins and a 13–8 record in 29 starts with the A's, including a 10–3 record in his last 19 starts.

"Mike Port has done everything he can, and now it's up to us to do everything we can," Mauch said.

Although Candelaria went 7–3 in 13 starts and Sutton 2–2 in five, they fell just short, frustrated again.

Another labor dispute shut down baseball for two days in August, depriving the Angels of two home dates in a season in which they were 49–30 at home, but nine losses in 13 games with Kansas City, and the offensive collapse at the end, proved fatal.

It is a season that is often overlooked when people talk about the heartbreak of 1982 and 1986—and later the 11-game lead that was squandered in 1995—but for Mauch, 1985 was just as bitter. He uncharacteristically still wrestles with a decision he made in a September 28 game at Cleveland, a turning-point game that he continues to describe as probably "more hurtful than any other I managed."

It was played on a Saturday, the next to last weekend of the season. The Angels and Royals were tied for the division lead. Kansas City would lose that day. The Angels, with a chance to go up by a game, had a 5–0 lead through seven innings and lost, 7–5.

The Indians scored the tying five runs off Moore in the eighth and won it on a two-run homer by Jerry Willard off Cliburn in the ninth.

It was a stunning and costly performance by Mauch's two relief aces, two pitchers who had kept the Angels in the race, but Mauch is still haunted by the decision to remove Sutton after seven shutout innings in which he had made only 93 pitches and allowed only three hits.

Sutton was 40, had completed only one of 33 starts that year and would be coming back to face Kansas City in the finale of the ensuing series.

"I've reached a stage where I know my limitations," he said that day. "There's no question but that to have me go further wouldn't have been a good idea. If I go out for the eighth inning and give up a hit or two, he's going to have to take me out anyway. It made more sense to let Donnie start the inning."

In a somber clubhouse Mauch said: "Sutton would have had to go beyond what he's thrown all year. He'd gone far enough. Donnie hadn't pitched since Wednesday. A five-run lead with Donnie Moore looked like a laugher to me."

The decision has stayed with a man who has seldom questioned himself. He suggests that Sutton took himself out and believes now he shouldn't have let it happen.

"I see Sutton and [pitching coach Marcel Lachemann] in some kind of discussion at the end of the bench [at the end of the seventh inning]," Mauch said, looking back. "I called Lach over and said, 'What the hell is going on?' Lach said that Don told him, 'If you want me to come back Thursday in K.C., it might be a good idea if this is as far as I go.'

"I got hot and said, 'What? If he doesn't want to pitch, I've got guys who do.' Moore and Cliburn had been great, but 15 pitches the score is tied and 16 we're behind. I mean, that hurt, that was one of the tough ones. It still stabs. I think the world of Sutton, but he's the pitcher and I'm the manager. The way he was pitching, with so few pitches, I should have said, 'Get your ass back out there and shut those guys out.' Kansas City . . . hell, they were the luckiest SOBs in the world in 1985. If we don't lose that 5–0 lead, they're not going to see the World Series."

The decision came so fast and so unexpectedly that day that Moore didn't have a chance to warm up properly. A three-run homer by Andre Thornton was the crusher in the five-run eighth. Moore made reference to his hurried and short preparation in the clubhouse later but also said, "I was terrible. There's no excuse. You can't make pitches like that against major league hitters and expect to win."

The Angels would have gone a game up on Kansas City had they held the lead and two up on Sunday, when they rebounded to defeat the Indians and Kansas City lost again. Instead they were only one ahead going into Kansas City and were one down coming out after losing three of four, scoring a total of six runs in the four games. The first two were split, leaving the Angels still up by a game, but Bud Black, who had won only one of his last nine starts, pitched a three-hit, 4–0 victory for Kansas City in the third game of the series, and Danny Jackson shut out the Angels for eight more innings in a 4–1 victory in the finale.

The Angels stumbled to Texas, where they were shut out again by Dave Schmidt, 6–0, and fell two behind the Royals with two to play. Candelaria pitched a 3–1 victory over the Rangers in an afternoon game on the next to last day of the season, but the Royals defeated Oakland that night to win the division as Mauch and the Autrys listened to the final innings on the radio in Texas.

Mauch trudged slowly to his hotel room and hung up a Do Not Disturb sign.

"I've never contemplated losing and I'm not prepared for it when it happens," he said before shutting the door on the night and season.

21

1986: ONE STRIKE AWAY

If Gene Mauch was put on this earth to suffer, as the late baseball columnist Dick Young wrote, then his previous 24 years as a major league manager might have just been a work-up for 1986.

The Little General took the Angels to another Western Division title and a 3–1 lead in the American League's best of seven championship series with the Boston Red Sox. One cursed team against another, with the Angels within one strike and one out of burying the ghosts, theirs and their manager's. One strike from taking the Cowboy to the World Series. One taunting, tantalizing strike from a 5–4 victory in Game 5 of that championship series, a game remembered in infamy in Anaheim and remembered generally as one of the most dramatic ever.

The Angels didn't get the strike, didn't get the win, didn't get to the World Series. They lost Game 5, 7–6, in 11 innings and were blown out of Games 6 and 7, which they seemed to have no interest in playing after the heart-wrenching defeat in Game 5.

Scarred again by second-guesses, by his pitching moves in that ninth inning of Game 5, Mauch said again that he is impervious to the second-guess, that he does what he has to do, and that while he agonizes in defeat, his emotions already have calluses on them and that the press makes more of it than he does. He said this with red-rimmed eyes after Game 7, when he also said:

"I hurt like hell for the players and I hurt like hell for Gene Autry. We laid our hearts out there and they got stepped on."

The Angels played 169 games in 1986, but it is as if they only played that one, that Game 5. More than any game in the 1979 playoff, in which they were outclassed by the Baltimore Orioles, or any game in the 1982 playoff with the Milwaukee Brewers, when Mauch's moves were subjected to so much grilling, or even that one-game playoff with the Seattle Mariners for the division title in 1995, Game 5 in 1986 continues to rank as the most famous in Angel history.

And more than that, the greatest in which many on both sides had played or would play.

Angel second baseman Bobby Grich and former teammate Don Baylor, the Boston DH, agreed on that during an 11th-inning chat after Baylor reached base when hit by a pitch. Even Mauch, who no longer flinches when asked to look back, describes Game 5 as "beyond equal, as far as drama" and describes the ninth inning of that game as "the greatest ninth inning ever."

The Angels were a long way from that drama, from another confrontation with a star-crossed history, as they attempted to recover from the 1985 frustration during a winter in which Rod Carew and Reggie Jackson dominated the headlines.

Carew, 40, had just finished the second year of a two-year contract. He had hit .280, his lowest average since 1968, and the second straight year he had hit less than .300. He had also played in only 127 games because of an injury and had not played in more than 138 in the last five years, playing fewer than 100 in two of those years.

The Angels also had two first base prospects knocking on the door—Wally Joyner and Daryl Sconiers—and management felt it imperative that the club continue the transition to a younger nucleus. Carew had hit .314 in his seven seasons with the Angels and helped spur attendance to a club record and league high, but the Autrys believed that another multiyear contract would be detrimental to the ongoing turnover.

The private belief was that Carew could no longer operate as an everyday player and the Angels couldn't afford his salary or the risk of his potentially combustible unhappiness in a part-time role. General manager Mike Port met with the sensitive first baseman on October 25 and gave him the word. Carew had seen the handwriting two years earlier when he tested the free agent market and had no takers except the Angels, who re-signed him for the two years.

"I expected something like this," Carew said after meeting with Port. "I've expected something like this since July, so it's not news. I know I can still play, but I'm 40 and know that I can't do many of the things I used to do."

Port had taken the required step but was again perceived as cold and heartless.

"For Mike Port to sit down, face to face, and tell Rod Carew that the club did not intend to offer him a contract for 1986 still staggers me," he said in reflection. "I'm trying to think of anything that was harder for me to do.

"Rod was of the opinion that he could still contribute, and, in all honesty, he probably could. If we'd had a 26- or 27-man roster, it's very probable that he would have been with the team.

"But if Rod had returned, what do you tell a Wally Joyner, who won the Triple Crown [for highest batting average and most home runs and RBI] in the Puerto Rican Winter League and was ready for a big league opportunity? From a personnel standpoint, it had to be done, and I'll always appreciate the understanding and dignity with which he handled it. He was disappointed but totally gracious, and I wrote a letter to him expressing my appreciation for the first-class fashion with which he reacted."

Carew would not play again. He rejected an opportunity to join the San Francisco Giants in a part-time role and bowed out with 3,053 hits. His uniform No. 29 was retired by the Angels in 1986 and he was inducted into the baseball Hall of Fame in 1991, his plaque showing him in the cap of the Minnesota Twins, the team with which he spent his first 12 major league seasons.

His had been a distinguished and celebrated career, but despite the honors and recognition, despite the dignity Carew had displayed in his meeting with Port, who was merely carrying out the Autrys' wishes, Carew felt he had been dismissed unceremoniously.

Not even a final press conference to express mutual gratitude. Not even the offer to return as Joyner's backup at first base.

"It would have been great, it would have worked," Carew said of a backup arrangement that the Angels felt would have created an uncomfortable and tense situation for Joyner. "I knew I couldn't play every day and that Wally was ready. Sure, I came away bitter; any player in my position would have felt the way I did after seven years with one team, but you can't keep living with it. Sooner or later you have to accept that it's a business and move on. I was ready to return when they asked."

Mike Port was fired in April 1991. New club president Richard Brown invited Carew to lunch. The cold war gradually ended. Carew, who had operated a hitting school and worked with Cleveland Indian hitters in subsequent springs, returned to the Angels in 1992 as the major league batting instructor under manager Buck Rodgers and is credited with contributing to the improved offense and roster stability of the 90s through his significant role in the development of a nucleus of homegrown players—Tim Salmon, Jim Edmonds, Gary DiSarcina, Garret Anderson and Darin Erstad, among others.

So now the Angels were without Don Baylor and Fred Lynn and Tommy John and Rod Carew, and when the club went to spring training in February 1986, there was Reggie Jackson, soon to be 40, saying that Jackie Autry had told him in November that he should retire.

"She went on to say a lot more, but I don't want to talk about it yet," Jackson said. "I don't want to knock the Autrys. I still have a sweet spot for Gene Autry and I respect Gene Mauch, but I told her, 'If that's the way you feel, then you should move me elsewhere.'

"Southern California is a great place to live and play, but when you're 39 or 40, you want to be wanted, and I don't sense that the Angels want me."

Jackson had signed a four-year contract before the 1982 season that technically expired after the 1985 season. However, the contract included an option year for 1986 that automatically vested if Jackson went to bat 400 times or played in 130 games in either 1984 or 1985, which he did. Thus, he was guaranteed employment and another $975,000 in 1986, and the Autrys were mystified by his comments in the spring. They denied having told Jackson that he should retire. They said that if this was an attempt to have them extend his contract through 1987, they would do that but only at the club's option.

"I have kept my commitment to Reggie, just as I kept it to Carew," Autry said. "I was fair with both. If Reggie wants a contract for 1987, he has to show me first he can play in 1986. I'm through giving some of these 40-year-old players another year at their option.

"Jackie never tried to get Reggie to quit. Nobody ever told him he should retire. I do remember saying to him that a lot of times ballplayers are like movie stars and don't know when to quit. I told him that I was happy that I had quit on top rather than dragging it out, and that Mickey Mantle had told me he regretted not having retired a year or two earlier. I was stating facts, not trying to make a suggestion."

The Cowboy's Hollywood training had taught him the value of the marquee. He studied under Louis B. Mayer, Joe Schenck, Jack Warner, Harry Cohn and other film industry legends. He felt that if he was going to sell baseball in Anaheim, he had to do it with people he could sell. He paid heavily in players and cash, and lit up the marquee with Bostock, Baylor, Grich, DeCinces, Burleson, Lynn, Carew and Jackson. There were rewards at the box office but frustration on the field, and Autry was wearying of the star wars, the constant massaging of egos and sensitivities. There was a bottom line to this approach as well. Autry had the second-highest payroll next to that of George Steinbrenner's Yankees, and he said, "a man continuing to do this has to go broke."

The Jackson rhetoric ran its course, and the turnover continued. Two farm products, Dick Schofield and Gary Pettis, were already established at shortstop and center field. Three others—Mike Witt, Kirk McCaskill and Ron Romanick—were part of the rotation. Now, with Carew gone, the first base door opened for Joyner, who entered and never looked back.

A third-round selection in the 1983 draft, Joyner seized the opportunity. He batted .290, slugged 22 homers and drove in 100 runs in that rookie season of 1986. Anaheim might have still been the home of Disney's Magic Kingdom, but it was suddenly sharing space with what became known as Wally's World. No Angel was more popular, including Reggie. A measure of that popularity was found in voting for the American League All-Star team. Joyner outpolled Don Mattingly of the Yankees to become the first rookie ever elected to the starting lineup. He was rewarded for his contributions to the Angels' division title by finishing eighth in voting for the Most Valuable Player award, but he finished a disappointing second to Oakland's Jose Canseco in voting for the Rookie of the Year award. Canseco batted only .240 and struck out 175 times but hit 33 homers and drove in 117 runs.

"I don't think anyone can ever tell me that he had a better year," Joyner said. "I felt I helped my team out more than he did. I played a more important role."

The Angels certainly would not have won without his run production, although DeCinces, rebounding from back problems in 1985, hit 26 homers and drove in 96 runs, Downing drove in 95, a right-field combination of Ruppert Jones and George Hendrick contributed 31 homers and 96 RBI, and the little ball combination of Schofield and Pettis drove in a big 115, with Pettis stealing 50 bases and starring as a one-man highlight film in center field.

A 38-year-old Bob Boone caught 144 games, and 40-year-old Reggie Jackson chipped in 18 homers (three in a September victory over Kansas City) while batting only .195 after the All-Star break, his hopes for a 1997 extension disintegrating in the process.

For the first time in club history, the Angels had three pitchers win 15 or more games. Witt was 18–10, McCaskill 17–10 and Sutton 15–11. Romanick (5–8) lost his groove and rotation berth, but Candelaria, out for much of the first half with a sore arm, was 10–2 in 16 starts, and Donnie Moore, Doug Corbett and free agent acquisition Terry Forster saved 36 games—21 by Moore, who battled a sore shoulder for most of the season, an important consideration in the playoffs.

In the aftermath of Jackson's 500th homer in 1984 and Carew's 3,000th hit in 1985, the Angels celebrated another milestone on June 18 when Sutton, at 41, pitched a three-hitter to defeat the

Texas Rangers, 5–1, at Anaheim Stadium and become the 19th pitcher to win 300 games, an automatic passport to the Hall of Fame, although it took Sutton—who retired with 324 wins after the 1988 season—six years to make it once he became eligible.

Voting members of the Baseball Writers Association of America might have been hesitant because he was a blue-collar pitcher who never won 20 games in a season or the Cy Young Award, never dominated any one time frame.

Sutton cited his longevity on the night of 300 and said of his 21 seasons, "I was unspectacular, but I got the job done."

The Angels got it done often enough and well enough to fashion a 92–70 record. They took the division lead to stay on August 7, opened a 10-game advantage at one point and won by five over the Texas Rangers.

They were going back to the playoffs for the third time in their 26 years, for the second time in five years under Mauch, still looking for their first trip to the World Series. They were playing a team managed by John McNamara, who had managed the Angels for two years between Mauch's stints, a team that had been to the World Series three times since 1918 but had not won one since. They called it the Curse of the Bambino, Boston's burden for trading Babe Ruth to the Yankees in 1919. There was no name for the Angels' curse, a history of misfortune and shifting philosophies that kept disrupting continuity and a clear course.

The 1986 team also traveled to Boston with the memory of 1982.

"Until we win it," said Brian Downing, "none of us can forget Milwaukee."

The memory faded a bit in Game 1, giving hope to the Angels that destiny had turned, that fate was on their side. Matched against Roger Clemens, who was 24–4 that season and 3–0 against the Angels, they scored four runs in the second inning and breezed to an 8–1 victory behind a five-hitter by Mike Witt.

Mauch was asked about momentum and said:

"I've never believed in the word momentum. Momentum is very fickle."

He did believe in the Angel defense, however. The 1986 fielding percentage was the best in club history, and Mauch told reporters after the opening win that one thing was certain.

"We're not going to beat ourselves," he said.

Fate and that defense took a holiday in Game 2.

The Angels lost, 9–2, in a farcical performance, tying a playoff record by committing three errors in one inning, not including a pop fly that Bobby Grich couldn't track down or the ground ball that starter Kirk McCaskill claimed he lost in the sun.

"Our worst game of the year," said Downing.

Said Mauch: "It's no use for me to discuss what happened out there because I don't understand any of it."

The teams traveled to Anaheim, where it became even more bizarre for the Angels.

They won Game 3 by a 5–3 score, tallying three runs off Dennis (Oil Can) Boyd in the seventh inning when their little ball exponents played big ball. Dick Schofield, a .249 hitter, and Gary Pettis, a .258 hitter, both homered, with Pettis connecting for only the sixth time that year after Bob Boone, a .222 hitter, had singled.

"One of the best games I never saw," said Mauch, who was ejected for disputing an umpire's decision in the fourth inning and forced to catch an occasional glimpse from the clubhouse tunnel.

"I wore out two pairs of shoes walking up and down the runway," he said.

The Angels led the series, 2–1, but were now hit by familiar misfortune. Wally Joyner, batting .455 through the first three games, developed a bacterial infection in his right shin. The Angels thought he might have been spiked in Game 2 or bitten by a spider. How it happened was never clearly ascertained. The infection festered. Joyner developed a high fever and was ordered to St. Joseph's Hospital near Anaheim Stadium, where he would watch Games 4 and 5 on television.

It was a severe setback that looked even worse as Clemens, who had thrown 143 pitches in Game 1 and was coming back on three days' rest, took a five-hit, 3–0 shutout into the ninth inning of Game 4 before the Angels staged a stunning rally to tie it, 3–3, and then win, 4–3, on Bobby Grich's single in the 11th.

Grich had been experiencing a miserable series, but he had now helped put the Angels ahead, 3–1. They were within one game of the World Series, and he said: "I'd love to close this thing out tomorrow, get some champagne flowing and save us the trip back to Boston. It would be a tremendous way to go to the World Series."

The champagne was on ice but never opened. It was there for the Angels in Game 5 and then it wasn't.

Milwaukee was tough, but this would be tougher.

Where to begin with a game that produced an Octoberfest of turning points? How to rekindle intensity and emotion so palpable as to be inescapable?

The Angels' 1986 highlight film didn't even try, which is perhaps where to begin, since the film succeeds where the Angels didn't.

All that is shown of this memorable game is Boston center fielder Dave Henderson playing hot potato with the baseball near the outfield fence. The ball is in his glove and then it isn't. It bounces up and over the fence, and now the view is that of Bobby Grich, exultant over this sudden change of events, beginning his home run trot. Grich rounds first base, steps on second and pushes off in an explosion of emotion. He leaps into the air, thrusts a fist over his head, and the camera zooms in on his flushed, beaming face, which is where it stays, frozen in time.

With that the film ends. Grich is suspended on the screen for several moments as the narrator's voice intones, "But there would be no World Series for the Angels in 1986." Then Gene Autry comes on to thank the fans for their support and the credits roll.

The editors had triumphed where relief pitchers Gary Lucas and Donnie Moore had failed.

Only here does Game 5 supply the Angels with a happy ending.

Left on the cutting-room floor were all the agonizing events that followed Grich's hip-hop home run in the sixth inning.

No two-run homer by Don Baylor, which sliced the Angels' lead from 5–2 to 5–4 with one out in the ninth inning.

No controversial removal of starting pitcher Mike Witt by Gene Mauch, who sent in reliever Lucas, who promptly hit Rich Gedman with his first pitch.

No 2-and-2 split-fingered fastball by Moore that hung around high enough and long enough for Henderson to hammer it out of Anaheim Stadium, which pushed the Red Sox ahead, 6–5, in the ninth.

No bottom of the ninth rally by the Angels, which produced a tie but not a victory when Doug DeCinces and Grich failed to deliver with the bases loaded.

No 7–6 Angel defeat in 11 innings, bringing on the trail of tears that led back to Boston for the Angels' eventual elimination in Game 7.

Out of sight and out of mind?

The intention, of course, is clear. It was, after all, a highlight film. And what the climax of this game meant to the Angels—from the doorstep of the World Series to the depths of despair—ranks as one of the lowest episodes in the franchise's history.

But what the celluloid ignores, the memory keeps fresh. Game 5 has taken its place in the pantheon of postseason moments.

Even the Angels, so close to their first pennant and so bitterly disappointed, recognized then and recognize now the battle for what it was.

Unmatched drama, said Mauch.

The greatest game he had ever played in, said Grich.

"A game," said Lucas, "well, I don't know if I'll ever get over it. I still think about it all the time."

The date was October 12, 1986. A warm Sunday in Orange County. For Angel fans among the capacity crowd of 64,223, pre-game talk centered on the remarkable events of the night before—how the Angels had recovered from a 3–0 deficit against Roger Clemens in the ninth inning to win, 4–3, in the 11th. One more win, fans buzzed, and the Angels would face the New York Mets in the World Series, and the Game 5 matchup seemed favorable.

On the mound for the Angels was their ace, Mike Witt, the 18-game winner who had out-pitched Clemens in Game 1.

His opponent was Bruce Hurst, a tired southpaw starting for the Red Sox on only three days' rest.

A nice day for some California champagne, which began to chill in the sixth inning when Grich hit his improbable home run in and out of Henderson's glove, wiping out a two-run homer Gedman had hit in the second and giving the Angels a 3–2 lead.

Henderson gloved Grich's shot on the warning track, but his momentum carried him into the fence. His arm hit the padded railing on top of the wall, and the ball, precariously nestled in the tip of the webbing, squirted loose and over the fence.

Grich acknowledged that he shattered baseball protocol with his jubilant tour of the bases, "but at that time, the way Mike was throwing, I thought that was it. I could taste the champagne."

Two more Angel runs made it 5–2 in the bottom of the seventh. Witt, unscored upon since the second, retired the Red Sox in the top of the eighth.

Now fans started to fill the aisles, preparing to join the celebration on the field after the final out. Former general manager Buzzie Bavasi put an arm around Gene Autry in the owner's box. Autry asked Bavasi to go with him to the clubhouse when the game ended.

"No," said Bavasi, "this is your party. You're the guest of honor."

American League vice president Phyllis Merhige dispatched Angel publicist Tim Mead to the home clubhouse with a cap emblazoned with a 1986 World Series logo that Mead was to present to Pettis as the most valuable player of the championship series.

At the same time, ABC-TV technicians were laying cable and constructing an interview platform in the Angel clubhouse. Cameras were wheeled in. Plastic wrapping was draped over each locker to prevent the anticipated blasts of champagne from soaking clothes.

Each dugout filled with California Highway Patrol officers. Reggie Jackson, who had been through it so often in New York, took off his wire-rimmed glasses and put them in a pocket so they wouldn't get crushed in the mob scene that was sure to follow. He walked to the end of the dugout to congratulate Mauch. Reggie knew where the cameras would be.

"It isn't over yet," said the Little General, his eyes on Witt, preparing to pitch the ninth, leading 5–2.

In reality, it had merely begun.

Bill Buckner led off with a single. Dave Stapleton was sent in to pinch-run for him. Jim Rice struck out for the first out.

Now Witt faced Baylor, the former Angel DH who had led the Angels to their first postseason appearances in 1979 and 1982, and who still carried the memory of all his verbal skirmishes with Bavasi, particularly the comment that had briefly driven him into retirement: "What's Don doing in that picture with those two hitters?"

"It was neither forgotten nor forgiven," Baylor said years later. "I was thinking about Buzzie from the start of that series."

On a full-count breaking ball, a pitcher's pitch just off the plate, Baylor had his revenge, delivering under pressure as he had so often with the Angels. He slammed a two-run homer to dead center field, cutting the Angels advantage to a nervous 5–4.

The crack of the bat told the story, but what Witt remembered was the silence that followed.

"The way it was at the start of the inning, the fans were on their feet and hanging over the railing," Witt said. "There was so much noise, the whole scene really pumped me up. But Buckner broke the ice and then Baylor, doing what he did, calmed everything down. It took a lot out of the crowd."

Witt scuffed the dirt on the mound, breathed deeply and came back to get Dwight Evans on a pop-up to DeCinces at third for the second out. One to go.

Down in the bullpen, Lucas, a hardened veteran who had been obtained from Montreal in December for Luis Sanchez, tried to warm up amid pandemonium.

"The bullpen was filled with security guards," Lucas recalled. "[Angel bullpen coach] Bob Clear was yelling at them, 'Get outta here, we gotta have the mounds.'

"All the way down the foul line, the fans were lined up, ready to run onto the field. It was so loud in the bullpen, we could barely hear the phone ring."

After Witt retired Evans, Mauch made the pitching change that will be forever scrutinized. He summoned Lucas, a left-hander, to pitch to Gedman, another left-hander who had hit a home run, double and single in three at-bats against Witt.

Lucas, who had struck out Gedman twice during the regular

season and hadn't hit a batter in four seasons, hit Gedman with his
first pitch. That brought on the confrontation between Moore, the
Angels sore-armed closer, and Henderson, a .189 hitting reserve
outfielder.

On a 2-and-2 pitch, Henderson became an instant New En-
gland legend, hitting that hanging split-finger over the left field
fence to put the Red Sox ahead, 6–5.

Mauch was second-guessed by people ranging from the national
media to his own players. Witt had thrown 14 complete games
during the regular season. He was a Cy Young Award candidate.
He was Mauch's best pitcher, and he was riding an emotional wave
after popping up Evans, the crowd back in it.

"Yeah, I was surprised when he took him out," Moore said the
next spring. "I thought it was Mike's game to win or lose. I thought
I wasn't going to pitch again until the World Series."

DeCinces also figured the game was over when he caught the
Evans pop-up.

"There was no doubt in my mind," he said. "Mike was pitching
well. Don Baylor had hit a good pitch. Mike came right back to
get Evans. The emotions were so high, I felt confident Mike was
going to do it."

Witt said his removal became an instant—and endless—conversation piece.

"People still ask me what would have happened if he left me
in," Witt said a few years later. "How am I supposed to have an
answer to that?

"I mean, anything could have happened if he'd left me in. I
thought I had a good game plan going in for Gedman, but it wasn't
working too successfully. Would I have tried anything different? I
never got around to it.

"I wanted to end the game, but it could have gone either way.
If Lucas comes in and gets him out, we'd have been on the way to
the World Series. It's always a waste of time to think about the
what-might-have-beens."

The Angels, of course, have never been able to avoid them.

In Game 5 of the 1982 series, Mauch had been criticized for
failing to bring in the left-handed Andy Hassler. In Game 5 of the

1986 series, he was criticized for bringing in the left-handed Gary Lucas.

"The bottom line is that Rich Gedman could hit Mike Witt at midnight with the lights out," Mauch said, sitting on his patio almost 15 years later. "I can only tell you that if I kept Mike out there, he would've pitched very careful to Gedman. Suppose Gedman gets on. If a chinker falls in for a double and scores Gedman, I couldn't forgive myself. I know it's over when I bring Lucas into the game. There won't be any chinkers, no nothing. All I ever saw the man do against Gedman was strike him out. I was eliminating all the chances of anything going wrong. It's all over. There won't be any doubles or home runs or walks. Just an out."

So Lucas hit Gedman with his first pitch. It was the first batter Lucas had hit in more than 400 innings.

"That never entered my mind," Mauch said.

Lucas had thrown a split-finger fastball. He would strike Gedman out with the same pitch in Game 6. He needed it in Game 5, but the split-finger was not the pitch of the hour for the Angels in that game.

Moore threw the same pitch to Henderson, with unforgettable results—for the Angels, Red Sox and Donnie Moore.

How much the pitch stayed with Moore, who would take his life and attempt to take that of his wife in 1989, is uncertain.

He denied in subsequent springs that it would, but many who knew him believe it did.

At the time, in the Sunday twilight, Moore was pitching with a sore right shoulder that had bothered him all season, requiring a month-long stint on the disabled list and a cortisone injection immediately after Game 5. The split-finger was his best pitch, but when his arm was ailing, it was the pitch that caused him the most problems.

"If my arm is right," Moore said, "the ball falls right off the table. He doesn't touch it. I threw the pitch and will take the blame, but it's history. If you can't take the bitter with the sweet, you're in the wrong game. However, I don't believe the pitch cost us the game. We still could have won it."

The bitter might have eventually caught up to Moore with tragic consequences, but he was definitely right.

The Angels could have won it, could have ended the series in a resilient bottom of the ninth.

They tied it, 6–6, when Rob Wilfong's single to right scored Ruppert Jones from second base, Jones narrowly beating a throw from Dwight Evans.

An ensuing single by Dick Schofield and an intentional walk to Brian Downing left the bases loaded with one out and DeCinces, who had already doubled twice, walking to the plate to face rookie Steve Crawford.

"How sweet it is, that's all I was thinking," Mauch said. "I'd have bet my house that DeCinces would get the run in. The odds on getting a run in from third base in that situation were a lot stronger than someone hitting a home run off Donnie Moore."

DeCinces swung at the rookie's first pitch, hitting a fly ball to shallow right field, where Evans camped with one of the strongest arms in baseball. Wilfong had to hold at third, where he died when Grich made the third out to send the game into extra innings.

Should DeCinces have taken the young pitcher deeper into the count?

"If there was a toilet on the mound, I would have used it," Crawford said in describing the state of his nerves.

"In that situation," DeCinces said, "I know Crawford throws a sinker, and I've got to look for a pitch I can get in the air. I can't hit the ball on the ground. That could mean a double play and the inning is over. I had to look for a fastball, a pitch I could drive. Crawford threw it on the first pitch, and I just missed. I did my job, I got the ball in the air, but it just wasn't far enough. I don't see how I could have been second-guessed. There were a lot of things in that game that got overlooked."

Little things, such as:

• Wilfong holding at first after driving in Jones with his single to right. When the throw from Evans went through to the plate, Wilfong had the chance to advance to second—where he might have scored the winning run on Schofield's subsequent single. Instead, Wilfong stayed at first and wound up getting stranded at third.

- Pettis' long foul ball in the bottom of the 10th. The drive forced left fielder Jim Rice to the wall—his back was pressed against it—where he reached up and made the catch. It was inches away from a home run or, at the least, a run-scoring double.

- Moore, allowed to pitch into the 11th inning despite the tender shoulder and wounded psyche from the Henderson homer, loading the bases in that inning by hitting Baylor with a pitch, giving up a single to Buckner and throwing away a sacrifice bunt by Gedman. That was enough to set the stage again for Henderson, whose sacrifice fly finally brought home the winning run in a numbing 7–6 setback that virtually cut out the Angels' heart, sending them back to Boston on a trip they had no desire to make. They still led the series, three games to two, still needed only one win to reach the World Series, but it was hard to convince anyone of that, even the Autrys.

"I remember sitting in a hotel room in Anaheim after that fifth game, and I asked my husband if he really wanted to go back to Boston and he said no," Jackie Autry recalled. "If *we* felt that way, can you imagine how the players felt?

"I mean, we had come off such a high in that Saturday game. We had the momentum. It was a shame. I don't blame Donnie Moore. I don't blame Gene Mauch, and I don't remember any circumstances where my husband second-guessed Gene. I blame Doug DeCinces. We had the bases loaded. The kid [Crawford] was obviously petrified, and he swung at the first pitch. God."

The Autrys did go back to Boston. The hope was that Joyner would be out of the hospital and join them. The Angels announced it was going to happen, but it didn't.

"Was I angry?" Jackie Autry said, looking back. "You bet I was angry. We had been led to believe that he could report to the club in Boston, and it was a disappointment when he didn't. Would he have made a difference? When you're playing with a second- and third-stringer instead of a first-stringer, sure it makes a difference."

Joyner would play five more productive seasons with the Angels, but his unavailability for the final two games in Boston clearly grated on the Autrys and factored into a deteriorating relationship. Joyner insisted he could not make the trip, that his infected leg would not have permitted him to play and that doctors had instructed him not to attempt it.

"I talked to him from Boston six or seven times," Mauch said of Joyner. "He was in tears. He said there were certain things he could do and certain things he couldn't. I told him that I'd like to have him with us even if he couldn't play, but he said the doctors told him he shouldn't go. I know this, hell or high water couldn't have kept me from being there."

The Angels had a rested Kirk McCaskill and John Candelaria ready to start Games 6 and 7. They had been a combined 27–12 during the regular season, but the final two games were over before they started.

In a new Boston massacre, the Angels were blown out, 10–4 and 8–1. Mauch didn't replace McCaskill until he was behind 7–2, and didn't replace Candelaria until he was down 7–0.

Considering that in the pivotal moment of Game 5 he was quick to replace 18-game winner Witt with a 5–4 lead only one out shy of the decisive victory, the approach to his pitching in those final three games seemed contradictory.

Then again, maybe nothing mattered after Game 5.

"It was strange," Reggie Jackson said after the Game 7 elimination. "It was really weird. The past two days it was like we weren't even here."

Joyner, of course, *hadn't* been there, and that seemed to weigh on Mauch more than any managerial decision or pitching breakdown or fielding collapse by a team that he had insisted wouldn't beat itself (the Angels tied a playoff record with eight errors).

The Little General kept the door to his office in the visitors' clubhouse closed for a long period after the final out. He emerged with those red-rimmed eyes and said the Angels had returned to Boston "as an undermanned team in a little bit of shock. That isn't what I want to say, but to tell the truth, that's what I have to say. And that's all I'm going to say."

In the lobby of the team hotel the next morning, while the Red Sox were preparing to leave for New York and the opening of the

World Series, Gene Autry, the resilient Cowboy, attempted to pick up the spirits of his shocked troops. He walked among them, shaking hands, thanking them for the effort.

Jackie Autry would smile years later, shake her head in wonderment and say of her late husband, "As much as that hurt in '86, Gene never lost hope. He always had the hope that if we don't get them this year, we'd get them next year."

The Angels never did. Never even got that close for the Cowboy again.

22

1987–88: The Little General Steps Down

The 92–70 record of 1986 turned to 75–87 in 1987. The Angels finished in a tie for last in the West with the Texas Rangers, becoming the first major league team since the 1914–15 Philadelphia Phillies to go from first to last in consecutive seasons. The 1986 playoff proved to be a last hurrah for an older and proud nucleus. The stunning defeat seemed to send the Angels on a new spiral of foreclosed intentions and self-destruction.

From 1987 through 1998 the Angels finished better than .500 only four times in 12 years. They employed six managers (13 counting interim selections) in those dozen years, four general managers and three club presidents, counting Gene Autry—who has to count because he and Jackie Autry remained the owners for most of that period.

The turnover that had seen Fred Lynn, Tommy John, Bruce Kison, Don Aase and Rod Carew leave since the end of the 1985 season continued within minutes of the final out of Game 7 of the 1986 playoff when second baseman Bobby Grich, a productive and positive player and influence since his signing with Don Baylor and Joe Rudi in the first wave of free agents, announced his retirement at 37.

Grich had talked about it throughout the 1986 season but resisted a final decision on the chance he would finish strong and feel capable of playing another year. In the seven games with Boston, however, he went five for 25 with eight strikeouts and three errors and candidly acknowledged he was overmatched by Roger Clemens in Game 7.

"It was as if he was throwing 130 miles per hour," Grich said. "This is something of a bitter ending, to be so close to a World Series in my final year and not to have played better, but I feel that I've had an outstanding career. I've ate, slept and drank baseball for 19 years, and I'm tired of the push."

The contracts of eight other veterans expired with the final out in 1986: Reggie Jackson, Don Sutton, Rick Burleson, Doug Corbett, Doug DeCinces, Brian Downing and Bob Boone.

Neither Burleson, an All-Star shortstop when acquired from the Red Sox in a major trade before the 1981 season but a victim of a spring shoulder injury in 1982 that limited his availability in six seasons with the Angels, nor Corbett, a disappointment as the potential closer when acquired in 1982 but a bullpen contributor in ensuing seasons, were re-signed. The others returned in 1987— except for Jackson.

A .195 average over the second half of the 1986 season and a .192 average in the playoff with Boston ensured that Jackson would not be invited back. At 40, he was Mr. October in name only, and Gene Autry had made it clear during the previous spring that he was through giving out multiyear contracts to seniors incapable of producing.

Jackson had spoken loudly and repeatedly during the 1986 season—including one memorable tirade in Yankee Stadium—about how he no longer fit into the Angel plans, and he got the official word from general manager Mike Port in a meeting at Anaheim Stadium on November 24. There were no dramatics for a player who had made his baseball reputation with an undeniable flair for dramatics.

"As great a player as Reggie Jackson has been and what he has meant to this club, I certainly owed it to Reggie to sit down with him man to man and face to face," Port said. "Trying to get together took some doing, but like last year with Rod Carew, I wanted to deliver that message in person.

"We could debate endlessly whether what we conveyed to Reggie is right or wrong. . . . I never said to him, 'You cannot play.' As a lawyer might put it, it probably falls into the range where there is 'an element of reasonable doubt.' Reggie can still do some things; it's just a question of frequency."

In an informal and impromptu news conference, Jackson said he understood the Angels' desire to go with a younger and less expensive nucleus. "To be very honest," he said, "even if Mike had told me, 'We'd like to have you back,' I would have had to say, 'Gee, let me think about it. Does Reggie Jackson fit in here?' "

The Angels offered an unspecified position in the front office, but Jackson said he hoped to extend his spectacular career through the 1987 season, one last tour, even though he had thought about retiring more than once during the 1986 season when "I had my hands full hitting .240."

The Oakland A's, his original team, provided Jackson with the opportunity. He appeared in 115 games in 1987 and hit 15 more homers to finish with 563, sixth on the all-time list.

Gene Mauch, who often said it had to be very difficult being Reggie Jackson and coping with the attention on and off the field, reflected and said, "Reggie definitely had an air about him, a presence. He was a very good influence on both the '82 and '86 teams. Hell, he was way past his prime and didn't hit nothing in either of those playoffs, but he helped get us there."

The Autrys' reflections were only positive as well.

"Reggie was a hell of a player and hell of a showman, and he was very loyal to my husband," Jackie Autry said. "I can't remember a Christmas, or a New Year's if he missed Christmas, that he didn't call the Cowboy and say, 'Hi, boss.' He was probably the only player that ever did that, and he continued to do it even after he left the club. He always felt that he could win it for the Cowboy and get us over the hump, but he did what Gene thought he would do as a marquee player. He put people in the seats, and he created energy in the clubhouse and lineup."

The Angels were so low-voltage in 1987 that the low-key Mike Port came out firing in September.

"They lack what it takes inside," he said of his players. "I misread this team."

The Angels were only a half game out of the division lead on August 5 but went 19–35 the rest of the way.

Mike Witt won 16 games, but only one of his last nine starts or he might have received more than a two-year, $2.8 million contract extension in December. Don Sutton was 11–11, gave up 38 homers, and was released at the end of the season, ending his Hall of Fame career after a brief return to the Dodgers in 1988. Kirk McCaskill had elbow surgery in April and appeared in only 14 games. John Candelaria was arrested twice for allegedly driving under the influence of alcohol, spent 28 days in a rehabilitation clinic, was on the disabled list twice for personal reasons and was traded to the New York Mets in September for two minor league pitchers. The combination of Candelaria, McCaskill and Sutton had won 60 games in the division title year of 1986 but won only 39 in 1987.

The 1987 season was also a crucible for the ill-fated Donnie Moore. A rib cage injury reduced his availability to 14 games, and fans refused to forget the pitch that Dave Henderson hit for the two-run homer in the 1986 playoff. He was booed unmercifully when he pitched, and Mike Port questioned his overall fortitude and conditioning.

"He's not in shape and not giving us our money's worth," said Port, who had signed Moore to a three-year, $3 million contract after the 1985 season, in which he saved 31 games.

The angry Moore, a generally warm man who enjoyed clubhouse repartee with reporters and teammates but also tended to keep problems to himself, responded to Port's characterization by citing a litany of injections he had received for his injury and ordering agent David Pinter to request a trade, which Port was unable to consummate because of Moore's injury and high salary. Moore said he felt under siege. Tragically, two years later, people would look back and say there were storm clouds hammering at Moore that might have been missed, warnings overlooked.

In the meantime, a healthy Wally Joyner returned to the lineup in 1987 and treated the sophomore jinx with disdain. He lit up Wally World with 34 homers and 117 RBI—career highs for the first baseman who would still be playing in 1999. The still productive Brian Downing hit 29 homers, and outfielder Devon White, a farm product who had played briefly with the Angels in each of the previous two seasons, had a breakthrough season in which he hit 24 homers, drove in 87 runs and stole 32 bases.

White's arrival, parlayed to Gary Pettis' slide to .208 in 1987 and the Angels' need for pitching, prompted Port to trade Pettis, a two-time winner of the Gold Glove for his defensive acrobatics, to Detroit in December for pitcher Dan Petry. The veteran right-hander had won 15 games for four straight seasons with the Tigers before arm problems reduced his effectiveness to a combined 14–17 in 1986 and 1987. Port took the risk and paid the price. Petry never regained his form. He went 6–11 in two injury-marred seasons, another example of the Angels' historic habit of acquiring an older pitcher past his prime via either trade or free agency.

The disappointing season of 1987 saw Port attempt to patch where he could, bringing in a new over-the-hill gang of outfielder Tony Armas, second baseman Johnny Ray and first baseman Bill Buckner, who was coming off his memorable fielding gaffe as the Red Sox first baseman in Game 6 of the 1986 World Series with the Mets. An outstanding hitter during a long major league career that will always carry the unfortunate stigma of the Mookie Wilson grounder that slipped between his legs as the winning run scored on that turning-point play in Game 6, Buckner batted .306 in 57 games with the Angels in 1987 and was released early in 1988.

Ray, acquired from Pittsburgh for two minor leaguers, set up second base residency for four years, an offensive force and defensive liability whose presence delayed the development of a talented farm product, Mark McLemore, in another instance of the Angels sacrificing the future. McLemore, who would ultimately enjoy a successful career with the Baltimore Orioles and Texas Rangers and who was still a first-string player with the division-winning Rangers 10 years later, was traded to Cleveland in 1989 for backup catcher Ron Tingley. The Indians could have been arrested for robbery.

Nothing saved the Angels in 1987, and another cornerstone of the 1982 and 1986 championships departed without fanfare in September. In fact, the unceremonious departures of Rod Carew and

Reggie Jackson seemed like galas compared to Port's chilly handling of third baseman Doug DeCinces.

DeCinces batted .234 with 16 homers in 1987. He had averaged 23 homers and 84 RBI in five seasons with the Angels, a defensive standout at third base. He was 37 and the Angels felt they had a replacement in farm product Jack Howell. DeCinces could accept that. He didn't understand the cold shoulder—a memo sent to the clubhouse informing him of his release on September 23. He didn't understand being released with only a week left to play, saving the Angels $141,667 under terms of his contract.

"I knew if the team didn't play well I wasn't going to be around the next year," DeCinces said. "The thing about it was they could have approached me and asked, 'What's the best way to do this?' I would been receptive to an amicable parting. I didn't get to say good-bye to the fans, to my teammates, to anybody. I didn't even get a handshake from Gene Mauch. They talked about family, and then they pulled it apart, and there wasn't one guy in the clubhouse who had any respect for Mike Port."

DeCinces joined the St. Louis Cardinals for the final week of that season, played a year in Japan, and then retired.

"We had bridges that needed to be crossed," Port said, referring to the departures of Carew, Jackson, DeCinces and others. "There was no perfect way to handle it. Great players are what they are because of their pride and bearing, and I can understand that their pride may have been wounded, that they may have felt we could have handled it better, but the subsequent performances by the few who continued to play proved we made the right decisions."

Only Downing and Bob Boone now remained from the veteran core that had produced the 1982 and 1986 division titles.

"We had some great teams, some great players," DeCinces said. "Those teams had an intensity and a work ethic that was very strong. Most of us had been successful in other organizations, but the only goal with the Angels was to go out and play to win. It's unfortunate what happened to the franchise for several years after we left."

The turnover was inevitable, but the biggest shocker was still ahead.

Nine days before the start of the 1988 season, the Little General, the man who triggered the intensity, the leader in 1982 and 1986, resigned as manager with a year left on a three-year contract.

Mauch had missed the previous two weeks of spring training while recovering from chronic bronchitis, but he insisted that his health was fine. A few days before the March 26 announcement of his resignation, in fact, he informed Cookie Rojas, the club's advance scout and the man supervising spring preparations in Mauch's absence, that doctors had given him a clean bill and he planned to return on Saturday, the 26th.

Instead he met with Gene and Jackie Autry at their Palm Springs hotel on the night of the 25th to inform them he had decided to step down. The Autrys had talked Mauch out of a similar decision in the immediate aftermath of the disappointing 1987 season, but this time he said the decision was irrevocable. There was no time for a prolonged managerial search since the clock was ticking toward the season opener, so on Mauch's recommendation the Autrys summoned Rojas and offered him a one-year contract as manager.

In a day's time, Mauch, 62, had ended a 26-year managerial career in the major leagues and Rojas, 49 and Cuban born, had become the only minority manager in the majors and the Angels' first.

Mauch cited several factors for his decision. He had seen a healthy atmosphere develop under Rojas, and he wanted to see that sustained. He was unable to cope with the inevitable losses, even after almost three decades of trying. He was dismayed by the growing influence of agents, unions and corporate ownership in a game he loved.

"Show biz," Mauch said with disgust some 12 years later. "It wasn't my game anymore, the game I worshiped. People think that's B.S., that you can't feel that strongly, but when I left that club, I left a jillion dollars on the table. I never received another cent of income, but it was never about money."

Nor was it a matter of being burned out, Mauch said.

"Hell, I probably burned out 30 times in my career," he said. "When you go at it like I went at it, you're burned out by the time every season is over. I worked my butt off and enjoyed every minute of it. Nothing made me happier than working in my game, and nobody did more of it, either. My dedication, as far as I know, was unmatched, which is no big thing. It just happens to be me."

The point, Mauch said, was that if he believed this, if he professed these feelings, it was time "to take a hike." He wasn't happy in spring training, didn't want to do anything harmful to himself or the game, and didn't think he was going to feel differently in a week or two. He didn't understand the corporate approach and wasn't interested in trying. Things had always been done the way he saw fit, and that wasn't the way corporations went about it. Worse yet was the union influence.

Marvin Miller. Mauch spat out the name of the former executive director of the Major League Baseball Players Association.

"He ruined my game with the poison he poured into the ears of kids about how terrible ownership was," Mauch said. "I mean, if players got on their knees and thanked Marvin Miller every night I'd understand it, but it was a different game, too different for me. The first 70 percent of my career, the mark of success was how good you are at what you do. The last 30 percent, the mark of success was your net worth. What killed me was all the times we'd have to have a union meeting before a game when my stomach was in knots preparing for the game. I remember in '85 hearing some of our veteran players moaning about something ownership had done and I walked over and said, 'Since you guys got so much money, why don't you buy the club?' They looked at me in disbelief and said, 'You think we're crazy?' Sure, I could have tap danced and stayed in if money was that important, but that's not what I was about."

He retired with 1,903 wins and 2,037 losses. He retired with the certainty his moves were the right moves, the certainty that any other manager would have had trouble getting the 1964 Phillies or the 1982 and 1986 Angels into a position to be disappointed.

"Am I supposed to be tormented?" he asked, looking out at the green fairways of Sunrise Country Club. "That's bullshit. You can't take 164 days of fun, as I had in '82, and obliterate it with three days of not getting what you wanted. I had 164 days of the best time a man can have. It was the same thing in '86. I had a wonderful time until I didn't, working my butt off and enjoying every minute of it in the game I loved."

Jackie Autry smiled.

"Gene Mauch was the best manager we ever had and a dear friend," she said. "He loved the Cowboy and would have done anything to help him win. I really think he never recovered emotionally from the loss of his wife. That combination of losing games and the lack of healing . . . well, sometimes people need grief therapy or to talk to somebody other than themselves. Gene was too strong and proud for something like that. So when he came to us in '88 and said he couldn't deal with the losses anymore because he took them so personally, I'm not sure he wasn't still grieving about the loss of his wife. I'm not sure that wasn't a large part of it."

Mauch remarried in 1991 but accepted only one of several opportunities to return to the game in either a field or front office position. He agreed to serve as a bench coach for a year with Kansas City in 1995, helping Bob Boone, his former catcher with the Angels, launch his managerial career.

Among the opportunities he rejected was an overture from the Angels in the winter of 1988 to return for a third stint as manager, Rojas having been fired in September. Gene Autry acknowledged that he had asked Mauch how he felt about coming back.

"There's days I say yes, I'd like to," Mauch told him, "but there's also days when I'd like to take a couple seasons off and play golf."

The indecision prompted Autry to hire former Texas manager Doug Rader for the 1989 season after the Angels went 75–87 in 1988 and finished fourth, 29 games behind Oakland in the West. The Angels were 75–79 when Rojas was fired on September 23 and 0–8 under coach Moose Stubing, the interim replacement. A lamentable gaffe in a September 22 game against Minnesota seemed to lead to Rojas' firing the next day.

Forgetting that pitching coach Marcel Lachemann had already visited reliever Rich Monteleone on the mound in the seventh inning of that 6–2 loss, Rojas also went out to talk to Monteleone— without intending to remove him from the game.

But two visits per pitcher per inning are as many as are allowed, and an embarrassed Rojas was forced by umpires to remove Monteleone from the game even though he had no replacement warmed up.

"It just slipped my mind," Rojas said.

Port and the Autrys woke up to the following headlines:

- "Cookie Loses Count, Angels Lose Game."
- "Mental Lapse Manages to Hit Angels With 6–2 Loss to Twins."
- "Once Again, Rojas Keeps Them Off Balance as Twins Get Past California."

Port called Rojas into his office that morning to tell the manager he was being relieved.

"There were a lot of straws on the camel's back," Port said. "To say one specific occurrence led to the change is hard, but there were a number of factors that contributed. In this business, sometimes change for the sake of change can be a positive thing."

Rojas had managed previously only in the Venezuelan and Dominican Republic winter leagues. Yet he inherited a last-place club and led it into fourth place—including one midseason streak of 31–11—despite the fact that he received no help from the front office during a season in which Kirk McCaskill, Dan Petry, Devon White, Mark McLemore, Donnie Moore and Butch Wynegar took turns on the disabled list, Mike Witt started the season 1–6, Wally Joyner went from 34 homers and 117 RBI to 13 and 85, and only two pitchers—Witt (13–16) and Willie Fraser (12–13)—won more than 10 games.

Rookie Bryan Harvey came out of the bullpen to save 17 games but needed September elbow surgery. Injuries kept Donnie Moore on a destructive spiral. Jack Howell took over for DeCinces at third base and hit 16 homers with 63 RBI. Brian Downing, one of the last links to the power lineups of the early to mid-80s, contributed 25 homers. Chili Davis, who had left the San Francisco Giants as a free agent and signed a one-year, $850,000 contract with the Angels, drove in 93 runs. Bob Boone, the 40-year-old catcher, batted .295 and won his sixth Gold Glove, but presented the Angels with an off-season contract conundrum, as did others. There was no contract for Cookie Rojas.

"Everybody makes mistakes, but I still think I got the most out of my players," the former manager said. "I would have liked to get some help when we had players hurt, when we were still hot in the second half, but it didn't happen."

A lot would happen before the start of the 1989 season.

23

1989–90: Circus at the Top

The hectic winter between the end of the 1988 season and the beginning of the 1989 season triggered one of the most convulsive periods in Angel history. If the six-year span between the firing of Cookie Rojas and the negotiations with Disney to buy the club wasn't the most zany and confusing of Gene Autry's tenure, it was definitely a close second.

It was a period in which:

- Mike Port was promoted, demoted and fired.
- The Angels operated with two general managers at the same time, neither surviving in the job.
- Richard Brown, an Autry lawyer with no baseball background, was hired as club president—ultimately a lame duck during the transition to Disney.
- Former Texas Ranger manager Doug Rader—"King of the Cuckoos" proclaimed one headline—was hired to replace Rojas, given a two-year contract in September of 1990 and fired less than a year later.
- Buck Rodgers, an Autry favorite from the early years, succeeded Rader, but like Autry favorite Jim Fregosi, who had brought the Cowboy his first division title, failed to last long, even though he almost gave his life for the organization in a 1992 bus accident.

- A new emphasis on building from within was compromised by the departures of some of the club's most promising and popular farm products, including Wally Joyner, Jim Abbott, Devon White, Dante Bichette, Kirk McCaskill, Mike Witt and Mark McLemore. This alleged emphasis on building from within was accompanied by the acquisition of a fleet of older players in their twilight years as the Angels continued the attempt to get the Cowboy to the World Series at any price. They included Lance Parrish, Bert Blyleven, Dave Winfield, Gary Gaetti, Dave Parker, Von Hayes, Hubie Brooks, Joe Magrane and Scott Sanderson, among others.

It was a period in which the Angels gave out a series of large multiyear contracts to players from other organizations but drew such a hard line in negotiations with Wally Joyner and Jim Abbott—two of their own players and two of their most popular—that one left as a free agent and they felt compelled to trade the other.

It was a six-year period in which they were 41 games under .500, 59 under in the years 1992, 1993 and 1994—a period described by Buck Rodgers in reflection as "an absolute circus at the top."

It was also a period of ongoing tragedy and misfortune, the Angels unable to shake the black cloud that followed the team from Wrigley Field to Dodger Stadium to Anaheim Stadium to the renovated Edison International Field of Anaheim.

For all the times that Gene Autry rode to the rescue on the silver screen, he was unable to chase off the villainous ghosts that haunted his franchise—those resilient demons that also eluded even Disney's magic.

In rebuilding from 75–87 under Rojas in 1988, one of Port's first moves was to release the beleaguered Donnie Moore, the relief pitcher who was never allowed to forget his pitch to Dave Henderson in the ninth inning of Game 5 of the 1986 playoff with Boston, was accused of malingering by Port in 1987 and who had been unable to regain his 31-save form of 1985 because of injuries.

Moore had made $1 million in 1988 in the final year of a three-year, $3 million contract. He owned a large house on 1.5 acres in Anaheim Hills, not far from the stadium. He had a wife and three children, but at 35 he was determined to rebuild his career, to put 1986 behind him. He signed a minor league contract with Kansas City's Triple A affiliate in Omaha for the 1989 season, but remained encumbered by injuries. He was unable to pitch regularly or effectively and was released in June.

A month later, on July 18, 1989, as the culmination of an argument over Moore's desire to sell the house and ongoing quarrels over their pending divorce, Moore shot his wife, Tonya, three times in the chest and neck and then fatally shot himself in the head. The tragic incident was watched by their daughter, Demetria, 17, and sons, Donnie Jr., 10, and Ronnie, 7. Tonya Moore recovered from her wounds, spent two months in therapy attempting to come to grips with the guilt she felt, and in a 1990 article for *GQ* accused fans of tormenting her husband with their boos after Henderson had hit the home run.

"I'll never forgive the fans for what they did to my husband. Never ever," Moore said in the article. "I hope they're suffering now." Moore said the fans turned her husband into a despondent, disillusioned man, contributing to the breakdown in their relationship and that "Donnie was the kind of guy—if he couldn't have me, no one was going to have me."

The home run turned the game and playoff around. Was one pitch enough to turn his life around? Experts in the area of sports psychology and mental health debated the question in the aftermath of Moore's death. David Pinter, his longtime agent, said it was the pivotal factor.

"Ever since he gave up the home run he was never himself again," Pinter said. "He blamed himself for the Angels not going to the World Series. He constantly talked about the Henderson home run. I tried to get him to go to a psychiatrist, but he said, 'I don't need it, I'll get over it.' But as many times as I tried to tell him that one pitch doesn't make a season, he couldn't get over it. That one pitch killed him."

In an interview with KABC-TV on the night of the shooting, Demetria Moore said her father had been depressed by his Triple

A release, that the "high life" was suddenly gone, and now he had returned home to a marriage and family that was dissolving.

"My dad was always the type of guy who would keep his problems to himself," she said, "but he had to be feeling, 'What else do I have left?' "

The numbing news of Moore's suicide hit the Angels halfway through a season in which they improved from 75–87 under Rojas to 91–71 under Rader, who had been hired on November 15, primarily on the recommendation of Port—anxious to avoid a long managerial search, determined in the wake of the Rojas experience to hire a manager with major league experience and first familiar with Rader from San Diego when one was still a player and the other was beginning his executive career.

Port would encounter the former third baseman in other post-playing capacities—minor league manager, major league coach and manager, part-time scout—and ultimately believed that he combined the intensity, intelligence and energetic personality to help lift the malaise of the previous two years.

"And candidly," Port added, "we were not prepared to run the gauntlet again with someone who had no managing experience."

The Angels' 13th manager, counting Gene Mauch's two terms, definitely brought an interesting résumé.

None of the previous 12 had ever been known to slip dirty baseballs into the clubhouse soup tureen or sit nude on a teammate's birthday cake or to switch the mouthwash with aftershave in the shower room or to jog into the lobby of a crowded Boston hotel on the eve of the Boston Marathon, light a cigarette, begin doing push-ups and wheeze, "Got to get ready for the big one."

None of the previous 12 were quoted as saying he should have been a Tahitian war lord or a pirate in the Errol Flynn mold, or that he never does anything to alter his physiological makeup because he is "running too damn perfect on 82 percent body fat." Nor did any of the 12 ever buy an ice cream sandwich at an Atlanta theater, carefully unwrap it in front of a long line, throw the ice cream away, eat the wrapper and then, on his way to a seat, feign a heart attack and roll down the stairs.

Rader had the reputation of a flake, baseball jargon for eccentric, but he claimed that most of it was the silly stuff that all players did behind clubhouse doors and that's where his antics would have stayed if Jim Bouton hadn't written about it in his best-selling book, *Ball Four*.

Of course, Rader wasn't behind closed doors early in 1994 when, while playing for the Houston Astros in a game at San Diego, he heard Ray Kroc, the Padres' new owner, get on a public address system to apologize to fans for his team's terrible showing.

"Ladies and gentlemen, I suffer with you," Kroc told the San Diego crowd. "I've never seen such stupid ball playing in my life."

Later, in the Houston clubhouse, Rader defended the Padres: "Who does he think we are, short-order cooks or something?"

Kroc, the man who built the McDonald's hamburger chain, reacted good-naturedly and said he would host a Short-Order Cook Night the next time Houston was in San Diego. Everyone wearing a chef's hat would be admitted free.

Naturally, there was Rader wearing a chef's hat and apron and carrying the lineup card to home plate in a frying pan, flipping it with a spatula. "Boys," he said to the umpires, "what's your pleasure—rare, medium or well done?"

Through all the zaniness, through all his years of hard play and good times, Rader built up a desire to manage, but when passed over in favor of Dick Williams as the Padres' manager in 1982 because of his lack of experience, Rader said: "I don't put a whole lot of credence in that experience thing. The Pilgrims didn't have any experience when they first arrived here. Hell, if experience was that important, we'd have never had anybody walking on the moon. You're either able to do something or you're not."

Rader would get his chance with the Rangers in 1983, and there was quickly a question if he was able to do it or not.

With makeshift pitching and a lineup of suspect veterans, the Rangers went 155–200 in his two-plus seasons leading up to his firing in early 1985. It was an ugly tenure in which the suddenly curt and sarcastic Rader feuded with reporters, alienated players and even yelled at fans.

"I believe that the three years away from managing has enabled me to evaluate things objectively," Rader said in taking the Angels' one-year offer. "I'm an aggressive guy who wants to win, but I've learned that, as a manager, you need to temper your aggressiveness and intensity. I think the educational process I went through in Texas will allow me to be more effective at it. I have a better understanding of how to deal with the players on a one-and-one basis and a better feel for the context in which the writers ask their questions."

There was more to the off-season between the end of the 1988 season and the beginning of the 1989 season than the Rader hiring. In addition:

- Port acquired a veteran battery by (1) trading minor league pitcher David Holdridge to Philadelphia for catcher Lance Parrish, 32, and (2) trading a package of minor leaguers, including first baseman Paul Sorrento, who would become a productive major league hitter, for pitcher Bert Blyleven, 37, a winner of 254 major league games at that point. Both Parrish and Blyleven were coming off poor seasons, but Port was betting that both would be rejuvenated by returning to the area in which they lived.

- The arrival of Parrish and his subsequent signing to a $1.4 million contract prompted catcher Bob Boone, a bulwark for the Angels throughout the 80s, to sign as a free agent with the Kansas City Royals for $883,001, which was $1 dollar more than he had been paid by the Angels in 1988. It was an in-your-face statement by Boone. The 41-year-old catcher had won three Gold Gloves for his defensive skills in seven years with the Angels, had hit .295 while appearing in 125 games in 1988 but had not been offered a raise since 1986 and had been rejected in November when he discussed with Autry the possibility of his becoming the club's player-manager before the hiring of Rader.

  Autry, coming off the Rojas-Stubing disaster, said he was tired of "putting in guys who had never managed before" and had told Boone, 'You'll get your chance, but you should manage a year or two in the minors first.' I think being the everyday catcher and manager is just too much."

  Boone would get a managerial opportunity with the Royals in 1996. His departure from the Angels in December 1988 prompted Autry to say the catcher had acted hastily and cost himself a lot of money in that the Angels were prepared to offer him $1 million. The

Cowboy also came down on Port some, saying he and Boone shared blame for being slow in opening negotiations and that Port had the tendency to be a "little on the cold side" in dealing with players.

"A general manager is on the hot seat," Autry said. "He can't go around making everybody happy, but I just think Mike could be a little more friendly with the people he deals with."

There was no getting Boone back, and Autry said, "That train is gone. We've got to catch the next one."

• With that in mind, Autry dispatched Port to the winter baseball meetings in Atlanta, with a mandate of signing two free agent pitchers—the celebrated Nolan Ryan, who had been allowed to leave after the 1979 season in the most grievous contract gaffe in Angel history and who had spent the intervening years enhancing his Hall of Fame credentials with the Houston Astros, and Boston Red Sox left-hander Bruce Hurst.

Autry's high-stakes involvement in the Ryan sweepstakes prompted then Houston owner John McMullen to accuse the Cowboy of creating the type of economic "lunacy" he had contributed to with his early signings of Don Baylor, Bobby Grich and Joe Rudi in the first wave of free agency. Autry, however, said he was not alone in the pursuit of Ryan and Hurst, and he just wanted "the fans to know we are willing to get some players."

The Angels got neither pitcher.

Although both acknowledged that the Angels had been the high bidder, Ryan and Hurst put family considerations first—Ryan, torn between his Texas roots and his fondness for Autry, staying at home to sign with the Rangers, and Hurst renewing his San Diego ties by signing with the Padres.

Referring to the attempt to re-acquire Ryan and make up for that past sin, Port said:

"We couldn't find a way to move Texas to Anaheim."

• Having failed in the Ryan-Hurst pursuit and having been criticized by his boss for his handling of the Boone negotiations, Port was now promoted by the Autrys to the breath-defying title of executive vice president, chief operating officer and general manager. He had previously been in charge of the baseball operation and now would supervise finance and marketing as well.

"The ball is in his court," Jackie Autry said.

"He has full authority and the financial resources to take whatever steps he determines are necessary to right the ship, providing he determines that the ship is listing."

And providing, of course, he continued to get approval from the Autrys on all significant decisions. The December promotion and restructuring was augmented in May 1989 with Port's hiring of Dan O'Brien, 59, as vice president and director of player personnel.

O'Brien was a 35-year baseball administrator who had served as general manager of the Rangers, president of the Seattle Mariners and assistant to the president of the Cleveland Indians. He would be responsible under Port for handling most contract talks and assisting in trade negotiations—although the restructuring would soon be restructured.

• The hiring of O'Brien was preceded by two other developments in the active off-season of 1988–89. The Angels, having failed to land Ryan or Hurst, switched priorities and signed free agent outfielder Claudell Washington to a three-year, $2.6 million contract and re-signed Chili Davis to a three-year, $4.1 million deal, a reward for his 93 RBI and 21 homers in 1988, when he had also made 19 errors in the outfield, convincing the Angels that he would have to be employed as a designated hitter, creating the opening for Washington.

The 1989 season was a vast improvement on 1988. The 91–71 record was the fifth best in the major leagues. The Angels drew 2.65 million fans, led the Western Division race for a total of 49 days and were within 3½ games of Oakland on September 20, when they lost six in a row and eight of their last ten to finish in third place, eight games behind the victorious A's.

Left-hander Chuck Finley, 16–9 in his second season in the rotation, suffered an ankle injury warming up for a September start in Kansas City and was deprived of three key starts down the stretch, an injury of the type that continued to frustrate the Angels and would reappear in varying and equally frustrating forms for Finley later in his career.

"The way we finished isn't something we're proud of, but 91 wins is," Rader said. "There was more good than bad."

Most of the good was attributable to pitching. The staff earned run average dropped from 4.32 to 3.28. Starters went from 50–68 to 70–55. In an era of bullpen specialists, there were 32 complete games and 20 shutouts. Bert Blyleven made Port look like a genius by winning the Comeback Player of the Year award, going from 10–17 in Minnesota to 17–5 with the Angels. Finley won those 16, and Kirk McCaskill came back from arm problems to go 15–10. In addition, a rookie named Jim Abbott went 12–12 amid the most intense fan and media scrutiny imaginable.

Abbott had been born without a right hand, but he persevered athletically, was a baseball All-American at the University of Michigan, won the Sullivan Award as the nation's top amateur athlete and convinced the Angels through his determination and talent that he justified being a first-round selection in the June draft of 1988.

"That particular year our goal was to come out of the draft with the best left-handed pitcher we could find in the first round," scouting director Bob Fonataine Jr. said. "I saw Jim pitch several times before the draft, and our only concern was if he could field his position. There was no question about his stuff and never a question about his makeup. It was clear how far he had come and how badly he wanted to play. There's always differences of opinion on players before the draft, but we probably had more unanimity on Jim than any player we've ever selected. A lot of people thought we did it for public relations value, but this was only my second year as scouting director and there was no way I was going to use the sixth pick for P.R. We took Jim solely on his ability to pitch."

Abbott pitched for the United States team in the Olympic Games at Seoul, South Korea, that summer and did not make his professional debut with the Angels until the spring of 1989, when he performed so well that he again convinced the Angels, who had planned to start him at the Double A level, that he could make the jump directly from college to the major leagues.

He was poised, polished and "simply not your normal 21-year-old," said Rader. "The quality of effort, his stuff, his composure, the whole program is not comparable to any 21-year-old I've been around. I mean, this is serious business. We're trying to win. We're not keeping him simply because he's an inspiration to people the way he's overcome physical misfortune. We're keeping him because he's earned it and can help us win."

Abbott responded. He had four complete games, two shutouts and a 3.92 earned run average. He was pursued by cameras, microphones and reporters with notebooks. The one-armed Pete Gray had played the outfield for the old St. Louis Browns, but Abbott's skill and performance was on a much higher level, and he was soon inundated, receiving 500 letters or more a week, including hundreds of requests for appearances. He responded with grace and patience, becoming a community inspiration.

"I'd estimate that in Jim's first four years with the team he personally met thousands of people with disabilities and probably had an emotional impact on every one," Tim Mead, the club's vice president of public relations, said. "Everybody wanted a piece of Reggie [Jackson] when he was with us, but no one has had the sustained impact that Jim did, and no one could have handled it better."

There was no way of knowing in the summer of 1989 that only three years later the Angels would outrage a large segment of their fans by trading the popular pitcher. Nor could anyone have known that he would be reacquired in trade, then ultimately retire—temporarily, at least—rather than accept a minor league assignment as his skills eroded.

In support of the improved pitching in the summer of Abbott's debut, the Angels led the league in home runs but were only 12th in runs. Parrish, who had batted only .215 with the Phillies in 1988, hit 17 homers, but only two after August 5. Chili Davis had 22 homers and drove in 90 runs, but the expensive Claudell Washington—like so many other fading stars acquired by the Angels throughout their history—had only 13 homers with 42 RBI while plagued by physical and personal problems.

Three young farm products produced mixed reviews. Center fielder Devon White won a Gold Glove and had 44 stolen bases but struck out 129 times. First baseman Wally Joyner struggled through the first half before finishing with respectable numbers: .282 average, 16 homers, 79 RBI—still a long way from the spectacular statistics of his first and second years. Third baseman Jack Howell had 20 homers but hit only .228.

Rader, who received a one-year extension in July, said his team had been far too inconsistent. Autry agreed, saying there were still changes that needed to be made.

With the Cowboy, that usually meant opening the saddlebags.

The Angels gave Parrish a three-year, $6.75 million contract after the 1989 season, and then, still looking to recover from the failure to land Ryan and Hurst during the previous winter, signed left-handed pitcher Mark Langston, the premier free agent in the new market, to a five-year, $16 million contract that made him the highest-paid player in baseball at the time.

Langston had been 34–24 during the 1987 and 1988 seasons with the Seattle Mariners and a cumulative 16–14 in 1989, when he was traded in midseason to the Montreal Expos, a trade in which Randy Johnson—who soon became one of baseball's most dominant pitchers—was sent to Seattle. The Angels had never had much luck with free agent pitchers, and now they had given out the largest contract in baseball history—including a no-trade clause—to a pitcher whose fortitude had been questioned by his former Seattle manager, Dick Williams, who bluntly accused Langston of lacking guts.

Even Autry seemed confused by the turns in the road.

"By now," he said, "I guess I have tried just about every system. We started out trying to build our team with old stars. Then we tried developing young players. Then we paid big sums for name players. Then we went back to young players. And now, I guess, we're giving away money again. I'm not sure any of us are doing the right thing."

Said Port: "We asked ourselves, 'Does any player deserve this much money?' Considering market forces—and this is no disrespect to Mark Langston—this is how much you have to bite off to make the acquisition."

Market forces would continue to drive up salaries, with pitcher Kevin Brown outdistancing everything that had come before when he signed a seven-year, $105 million deal with the Dodgers in the winter of 1998.

On opening night of the 1990 season, however, Langston looked like a $16 million bargain.

He pitched seven no-hit innings against the Seattle Mariners, and Mike Witt, who had hurled that perfect game against Texas on the last day of the 1984 season, came out of the bullpen to wrap up a 1–0 victory over the Seattle Mariners and the eighth no-hitter in Angel history.

"This was not even close to how I pictured it," Langston said of his impressive debut. "Coming out of spring training, I was just hoping to throw five strong innings. I was very grateful to be able to go seven, but a no-hitter? How can anyone envision that? It's a great way to begin a new career with a new club, but it was Mike who faced the pressure. He came out of the bullpen with the no-hitter on his shoulders, and he knew how the crowd would react if he lost it."

Witt was 30, potentially at the top of his career, but he had experienced an inexplicable slide since his 18-win high as the 1986 ace. He won 16 in 1987, then 13, then 9, then opened the 1990 season as the sixth starter in a five-man rotation. The acquisition of Langston had left Witt expendable, and he was traded to the New York Yankees on May 17 for outfielder Dave Winfield, who was 38 and had driven in six runs since the end of the 1988 season, in which he hit .322 with 107 RBI.

Back surgery had sidelined one of baseball's most renowned hitters for all of the 1989 season, and an 0-for-22 slump in April of 1990 had relegated him to a part-time role in New York, where Winfield had experienced a tumultuous relationship with Yankee owner George Steinbrenner.

In fact, two months after the May trade, commissioner Fay Vincent ordered Steinbrenner to resign as the Yankees' principal partner for having paid $40,000 to a self-described gambler, Howard Spira, to gather information that could be used against Winfield, who joined the Angels saying, "I feel better already. I don't have a gray hair anymore."

It wasn't only that he was out from under Steinbrenner's often demeaning yoke.

Winfield's rejuvenated outlook also stemmed from the three-year, $9.1 million contract the Angels provided as an incentive so that he would approve the trade.

Some teams focus on getting younger.

The Angels often got older in the patchwork attempt to get the Cowboy to the World Series.

"The mission was always to get him there," said Dan O'Brien. "It wasn't something we sat around and talked about every day, but it was an aspect that was discussed, getting the owner to the World Series, more than any place I had worked previously. There was always intense loyalty and devotion to Mr. Autry."

Winfield, in the 17th year of a career that would elevate him to Hall of Fame candidacy, proved he had something left, making a statement to Steinbrenner and others with 19 homers and a club-high 72 RBI. Luis Polonia, a fast, singles-hitting outfielder who had also been acquired from the Yankees in an April trade for Claudell Washington, hit a club-high .335 and stole 21 bases. Lance Parrish added 24 homers and drove in 70 runs, joining Winfield in proving there was some life left, but it was an otherwise difficult year.

Injuries limited Wally Joyner and Chili Davis. The Angels used the disabled list 15 times, and Rader employed 93 lineups in the first 94 games.

"It was like a dike leaking," he said of the injuries. "You stick a finger in here, all of a sudden it's leaking over there, and pretty soon you feel like you've run out of fingers."

The Angels made 43 more errors than in 1989, when they set a club record for the fewest in a season, and only Chuck Finley, at 18–9, provided consistent pitching. Blyleven went from 17–5 to 8–7 and said, in midseason, that the club stunk, including himself. Langston, in the first year of that $16 million contract, was 10–17, maintaining a pattern that had seen no free agent pitcher win more than 10 games in his first year with the Angels.

Two promising farm products, Devon White and Jack Howell, served minor league demotions during the 1990 season, and second baseman Mark McLemore, unable to unseat the defensively suspect Johnny Ray, was traded to Cleveland for backup catcher Ron Tingley, the first in a flurry of dreadful deals in which the Angels sacrificed young players on the altar of impatience.

The Angels ultimately went 80–82 to finish fourth, 23 games behind the division-winning A's, but Rader was given a two-year contract extension in September as Port announced that the club was intent on reemphasizing a developmental approach, and Rader said, "The one thing I desperately want to do is be part of the cure."

Neither Port, Rader nor the developmental approach survived.

24

1991–92: THE WAYWARD BUS

Less than 24 hours after the end of the 1990 season and less than two years after Gene and Jackie Autry had elevated Mike Port to the position of executive vice president, chief operating officer and general manager, the painter was called and the title on Port's office door was changed again.

Port remained as executive vice president and general manager, but the Autrys hired Richard Brown, a member of the law firm that handled their corporate business, as president and chief operating officer.

The Autrys and others insisted that it wasn't a demotion for Port, but it seemed to be exactly that. Port had been given overall authority just 22 months earlier, and now he was suddenly stripped of it, the Autrys saying they had given him too much of a load.

He would still be responsible for generating trade and free agent talks, but Brown and the Autrys would have final say.

A good soldier, Port accepted the loss of power with equanimity.

"With my corporate responsibilities, I've sometimes been stretched thin," he said. "The baseball end hasn't suffered, but sometimes the administrative end has. My background is baseball. I will now be responsible for only the product on the field."

It might have been a needed adjustment, but it was another blow to continuity and approach.

Jackie Autry would reflect and say that she and her husband had erred in giving Port overall responsibility in the winter of 1988. "It was the Peter Principle," she said. "We moved him a step ahead of where he was best suited and most comfortable."

The callously handled departures of Rod Carew, Reggie Jackson, Doug DeCinces and Bob Boone, among others, had also stained Port with the image of a poor communicator, a liability in carrying out his corporate responsibilities in that expanded role.

"I don't want to cast aspersions," Brown said, taking over, "but some people just communicate better than others, and I believe you are what you are perceived to be. You can be the nicest guy in the world, but if you are perceived not to be a nice person, you're not a nice person. That's the way it works, unfortunately."

Brown had been the club's legal counsel for 10 years, a period in which he had also handled the Autrys' business affairs, but his baseball résumé consisted of one word: fan. He did own a satellite dish, which elevated him to the category of superfan, but even on a casual basis he was familiar with the club's inconsistent philosophy over the years, describing it much later as "eclectic at best."

"Each year there seemed to be a different approach," he said, referring to the building of the team and the "sense of urgency to win for Gene." In addition, from the business and marketing standpoint, "it was very evident that there was no real plan or any cohesiveness between the three vice presidents—Mike Port in baseball, John Hays in marketing and Jim Wilson as the chief financial officer. They seemed to operate on a theory that the fans would come if you won and they wouldn't if you didn't."

On that business side, Brown said, his plan was to introduce a "whole new concept called marketing" while gearing the team to a five-year reconstruction emphasizing the farm system, which "at that time was ranked 25th among the 26 teams by [the publication] *Baseball America*."

Those best-laid intentions would prove difficult to fulfill again for several reasons.

- The Cowboy was aging and that sense of urgency kept interceding.
- Salaries were escalating, putting a drain on the Autrys' resources, and prompting Jackie Autry to make her first visit to Disney's corporate offices in Burbank to investigate chairman Michael Eisner's possible interest in buying the team.
- Although Rader seemed to emerge with a stronger voice in personnel moves under Brown, he never developed a meaningful rapport with Gene Autry, and his impatience with three of the organization's top young players—Devon White, Dante Bichette and Jack Howell—led to their costly departures, and ultimately his own.
- In addition, there was a breakdown in communication between Brown and Port that might have contributed to the loss of Chili Davis on the eve of spring training in 1991, factored into the loss of Bichette and ultimately cost Port his job.

There was also one other cold parting of the old guard, the last link to the division titles of 1982 and 1986. Outfielder and designated hitter Brian Downing, 40, and coming off a season in which a rib injury limited him to 96 games, was not offered the opportunity to return through arbitration and thus moved on to the Texas Rangers for two final years of part-time service.

In what was a familiar refrain among departing players from those championship teams, Downing cited his considerable contributions during 13 years with the Angels and said he was "hurt like hell" by what he considered an unceremonious dumping. "I always knew it was a business, but you never think it's going to happen to you," he said.

Downing's departure was only one of the coals on the hot-stove fire.

In December, despite the lip service Rader and Brown gave to the emphasis on building from within, the Angels gave up on one of their most talented farm products, trading Devon White, the Gold Glove center fielder, to Toronto for journeyman outfielder Junior Felix and utility infielder Luis Sojo.

Said Brown, documenting that the ultimate goal remained getting Autry to the World Series at any price: "I can't sit on potential; potential doesn't win pennants."

The fleet White would realize his potential in Toronto and play a pivotal role on three World Series winners—two with the Blue Jays and one with the Florida Marlins—but Rader and the Angels couldn't decide if he should be a pure leadoff hitter who attempted to hit down on the ball and use his speed or more of a power threat lower in the lineup.

"I didn't know what they were doing with me," White said years later. "They were either trying to break me or frustrate me. They had all those good young players—Wally Joyner, Mark McLemore, Dick Schofield, Jack Howell, Dante Bichette, myself—and they got rid of all of them. Pretty smart."

Said Bill Bavasi, Buzzie's son and the Angels' minor league director at the time: "It was either trade White or get rid of Rader. That doesn't mean Doug was wrong or the kid was wrong. Sometimes a set of circumstances arises where a young player fails enough that he frustrates the manager and coaches, then the player doesn't feel support from those people and all hell breaks loose. In some ways Devon was cursed by his speed. Doug felt he should have been a leadoff hitter, but he really wasn't that type of hitter, and Doug lost patience. We had good reports on the people we got, but we didn't have enough background to know that Felix didn't have a brain. Sojo went on to have a pretty good career, but he's not the player White was—or, at least, the player he became."

In January, a month later, despite their intention to henceforth approach free agency with caution, the Angels stunned the industry by giving a four-year, $11.4 million contract to Minnesota third baseman Gary Gaetti, who was 32 and in a downward spiral statistically. It was a deal closed by the personal intervention of Brown at a time when the Angels were unsure if they were going to be able to keep Chili Davis, who had been granted what was termed "new look free agency" as a victim of the owners' collusion in the 80s.

Davis' multiyear contract with the Angels guaranteed him $1.45 million in 1991, but when his "four or five" attempts to renegotiate it as a free agent failed, he signed with Minnesota for $2 million.

The loss of Davis irritated Brown, who considered Davis and Gaetti to be interlocking "pieces to the puzzle" and essential to the club's success in 1991. He blamed Port for failing to keep him informed regarding the status of negotiations.

"Mike tells me it's a done deal, and three hours later I hear on the radio that he's going to Minnesota," Brown recalled. "I didn't blame Mike for letting Chili go to Minnesota. I blamed him for not keeping me up to date. He could have said, 'Rich, I thought it was good a couple hours ago, but it's getting worse.' Let me know what's going on. Maybe I'll extend his budget, maybe I won't. Budgets aren't sacrosanct. As circumstances change, you don't sit there with a budget of $25.9 million like we had in 1990 and all of a sudden a player goes down and you say, 'Well, that's okay. We'll just play with eight men.'

"I mean, we needed Chili, but Mike waited too long to begin the talks, then failed to keep me posted. We shouldn't have lost him. It shouldn't have come down to that."

Brown's ire was raised again three months later when Port, responding to Rader's inability to cope with Bichette, another promising young player who tended to march to his own time clock and follow his own drumbeat, produced an April trade in which Bichette, who had hit 15 homers in 109 games in 1990, went to Milwaukee for Dave Parker, another illustrious player past his prime.

An exasperated Bichette, who would become one of baseball's top power hitters with the Rockies, was traded for a 39-year-old Parker after losing his job to a 38-year-old Dave Winfield.

Bichette acknowledged that he wasn't the same focused, mature hitter then that he is now, but "I wouldn't wish what I went through with the Angels on anybody. I should have been the regular right fielder three years before they traded me, but they kept bringing in older guys—Chili Davis, then Claudell Washington, then Dave Winfield. They talked about building with young players, but they never stayed with it. I battled for three years, and it was a relief to get out."

Said Port: "We didn't exercise enough patience with either Dante or Devon, but we were faced with what they were at the time and what our needs were at the time. We didn't want to trade their ability in either case, but the consensus in the organization was that they needed a change of scenery, and we needed to relieve the manager of potential problems. I've talked with Dante since, and he's told me that he looks at the success he had in Colorado and realizes how unfocused and inexperienced he was in Anaheim."

Richard Brown said he would not have negated the Bichette trade because he knew Rader couldn't get along with the young player, but he was annoyed to learn of the trade from Chicago White Sox owner Jerry Reinsdorf while sitting with Reinsdorf and watching the Angels play an exhibition game in Arizona.

"I think Mike is a very good baseball person, but Mike and I had a problem," Brown said of Port. "Mike didn't feel comfortable reporting to someone who wasn't a baseball person.

"I told him when I took the job that I liked him, respected him and could be his best ally or worst enemy, depending on how he educated me and how he communicated with me. I never questioned his moves as far as good or bad. I only asked the rationale, but I also stressed two things—don't surprise me and don't embarrass me. I told him that I can't run a club if I don't know everything that's going on, but he did it twice. He surprised me with the Chili Davis situation, and he embarrassed me with the Dante Bichette trade."

The Bichette trade was made on March 14. Port was fired on April 30. The Angels were 9–10 at the time, but Brown, speaking on behalf of the Autrys, said the firing had nothing to do with the slow start—"If I fired someone every time we lost a series of games, I'd be all alone by the end of the season"—but stemmed from a difference in style and an absence of communication. Dan O'Brien would assume Port's duties and remain senior vice president for baseball operations, Brown said.

Port, now assistant general manager of the Boston Red Sox, was incommunicado at the time. He now expresses surprise at the timing—"It wasn't as if the clubhouse was on fire or some traumatic event had taken place"—and bristles at Brown's insinuation that there was a lack of communication and that he had been embarrassed to hear of the Bichette trade from a third party.

"He's using that as a convenient rationale," Port said. "The trade hadn't been made when he heard about it. We were only in preliminary discussions. If he expected me to beat a path to his door every time I talked to another club, he was sadly mistaken. No club functions that way. No general manager can be expected to function that way. If we were close to a trade I would go to him, just as I had always gone to the Autrys. I wasn't going to run to him every time the phone rang."

It was the first month of the new season, and the Angels had experienced another convulsive period in which the general manager was fired, two of their best young players were traded and one of their most productive power hitters was lost to free agency. They had been hit by a tornado, but in some respects it was merely a prelude to what occurred during the final two months of an otherwise lamentable season in which the Angels would go 81–81 and finish last in the West.

The Angels were first on July 3, 1991, with a 44–33 record, but were last a month later, having gone 8–19 in that span. It was a season in which Bryan Harvey came out of the bullpen to save 46 games, a club record, and Mark Langston rebounded from his disappointing debut to register a 19–8 record, the most wins by an Angel since Nolan Ryan won 19 in 1977. Langston also joined Chuck Finley (18–9) and Jim Abbott (18–11) to give the Angels three left-handers with 18 or more wins for the first time in club history. Kirk McCaskill, however, set a club record for losses by going 10–19, Bert Blyleven had shoulder surgery in April and was out all year, and the Angel offense provided little support

Wally Joyner, who would be eligible for free agency when the season ended, hit 21 homers and drove in 96 runs, and Dave Winfield laughed at the calendar, hitting 28 homers and driving in 86 runs. The Angels were otherwise too old or simply not good enough. Lance Parrish batted .216. The expensive Gary Gaetti continued his Minnesota free fall, batting .246 with 18 homers. Junior Felix, at .283 with seven stolen bases, was a poor replacement for Devon White, and Dave Parker, acquired at the expense of Dante Bichette, was a total bust at .232 with 11 homers, which did not stop Rader from persisting in batting him cleanup in a futile try to justify the trade.

"This was another situation where you've got a general manager and a field manager and you have to ask yourself, 'Okay, who do I listen to, who do I rely on?' " said Jackie Autry. "You hire people to do a job and you trust in their judgment. Mike Port hired Doug Rader, and Doug Rader told us that Dave Parker would be the mortar holding up the clubhouse walls when the wind started to blow in July. Well, I don't even know if he made it to July."

Rader did, but he didn't get much further. By early August, Jackie Autry was saying publicly that the Angels were considering a managerial change, which tended to undermine Rader's authority in the clubhouse, although Joyner said any change would be a mistake, and Parker added that it would be foolish.

In a strange twist from his traumatic and bellicose years in Texas, Rader had become something of a gentle giant in Anaheim. Some felt he had swayed too much on the side of nice. At one point during the team's second-half struggle, Jim Abbott, as nice as they get, said: "If anyone lays blame on Doug Rader, they've got a lot of problems. Doug has made it as easy as possible to play here. Sometimes I think he needs to jump on our butts a little more."

It was too late. Rader was fired on August 26, only a year after he had been given the two-year contract that stemmed from a recommendation by the deposed Mike Port. Senior Vice President Dan O'Brien said he recommended to Richard Brown that Rader be fired on the basis that the club had underachieved and he felt a change was necessary.

In reality, Gene Autry, who never felt close enough to Rader that he could kick back with him on the bench or in the clubhouse as he had with other managers, had started to grease Rader's exit in early June, soon after Buck Rodgers had been fired as the Montreal Expos manager on June 1.

Rader and Autry had maintained a polite relationship, but Rodgers and Autry went back three decades. If Jim Fregosi was always favorite son No. 1, Rodgers was a close second as an original Angel and durable catcher during those formative years. He had managed the Milwaukee Brewers (advancing to the playoffs in 1981) as well as the Expos (contending with a low-budget team that had difficulty retaining its best players), built a solid reputation as a handler of young players and lived in Yorba Linda, only a few miles from Anaheim Stadium, where he visited on occasion.

He had long been on a short list of potential managerial candidates that Autry liked to maintain given the frequency with which he changed managers.

"When I left Montreal, I was hoping to be back with some team by the first of September," Rodgers said. "If I was going to take over a team, I wanted to see it for at least 30 days. Gene called in early June and invited me to have lunch at Lakeside Country Club. He told me that he didn't care for Rader, couldn't really talk to him, and that he wanted me to manage the club, that if he didn't make a change this year he was definitely going to make one next year. I told him I was interested and available, but he and Jackie were about to leave on a trip to Ireland and I was going to Ohio to visit my parents and I said, 'Look, you've got a team in first place, we both have trips planned. If you still want to make a change when you get back, call me then,' which is exactly what happened."

Saying that his return to the team that had given birth to his major league career was a dream come true, Rodgers received a three-year contract as the club's 14th manager and third in the three-plus seasons since Gene Mauch retired in late March 1988. O'Brien was given a similar extension, but two weeks later the Angels made even bigger news with an announcement that seemed to cut into O'Brien's authority and left industry insiders—as well as many in the Angel organization—wondering how in the world it would work.

On September 6, the Angels basically ended up with two general managers when Whitey Herzog was lured out of semi-retirement and given a three-year contract as senior vice president and director of player personnel, which was akin to O'Brien's title and role.

If Rodgers had been a longtime Autry favorite, so was Herzog, who had been a coach with the Angels during the 1974 and 1975 seasons before embarking on a successful managerial career with the Kansas City Royals (winning three division titles) and St. Louis Cardinals (winning three pennants and one World Series title) before resigning as manager in July 1990. He was considered one of baseball's shrewdest talent evaluators and had rebuilt the Cardinals from scratch after taking over as manager-general manager in 1980.

Autry, meanwhile, had long rued his failure to retain Herzog as his own manager when then general manager Harry Dalton embarked on his manager-a-year tenure in the 70s and, in fact, the Angel owner drew a tampering fine when he attempted to lure Herzog out of his contract with the Royals prior to the 1978 season.

"For some reason," Jackie Autry said years later, "Gene didn't feel that Dan O'Brien had the necessary strength as general manager, and it had been his lifelong goal to get Whitey back to Anaheim. He said to me more than once that it would really help the organization to get Whitey back, that he would really like to see that happen. Gene would kind of give me my marching orders in his gentle way, and I'd do anything to make him happy, so we started calling Whitey and convinced him to come out and see us. If I have to take responsibility for making the biggest mistake of my tenure trying to help Gene run the club, that would be it, bar none."

Not only was Whitey Herzog hired to serve in the same basic role as Dan O'Brien, he was permitted to work out of his St. Louis home. Agents attempting to negotiate contracts didn't know whether to call California or Missouri. Said player representative Chuck Berry:

"The Angels have always been one of the most discombobulated organizations. Now it's impossible to get any decisive action from them."

In addition, said Jackie Autry in reflection, the budget meant nothing to Herzog, though the need to maintain it amid mounting operating losses had been stressed repeatedly during her initial visits with Herzog, who was conditioned with the Cardinals to having it his way and came from an era in which corporate involvement and agent-dominated negotiations were unknown.

He would butt heads with Jackie Autry, Dan O'Brien and others in and out of the organization. He would be quoted in a *Los Angeles Times Magazine* piece as saying that Junior Felix was a dog, that Mark Langston wanted to sign with a Southern California–based team to further his wife's acting aspirations but "she ain't really that pretty" and that the Angels had never been a winner because Gene Autry favored "California boys" over Latin Americans, suggesting his beloved Cowboy had racist leanings—though it was Herzog who loved to entertain reporters and scouting cronies with racist and off-color jokes.

Richard Brown described the Herzog-O'Brien marriage as "an experiment in hell" and said he knew it from the start.

"Jackie called and said Gene felt that Whitey could take us to the next level but that Whitey didn't want to take the job until he talked to me because he was worried I might be some stuffy guy in a three-piece suit," Brown said in recollection. "I explained to her that we already had a general manager and I wasn't sure where I would put him. She said work it out so that there's a division of responsibility because it's really important to Gene that Whitey be involved."

The power struggle that Brown feared from an overlapping of authority wasn't as damaging, he said, as the number of things that fell through the cracks.

O'Brien ostensibly was assigned contracts and the daily office regimen, initiating trade talks through regular phone conversations with other clubs. Herzog would be out in the field more, evaluating players, talking to scouts, promoting trades from his end as well.

"We did have a reasonable division of responsibility and authority, but the two never worked well together and never seemed to like each other that much," Brown said.

"Both on their own probably could have succeeded, but together it was one and one equaled five.

"It wasn't a very pleasant environment, and it really hurt the organization."

No doubt about it, said Buck Rodgers, who frequently had to deal with the fallout from what he described as a "circus at the top."

"One day it would be one guy coming to ask me something, and the next day it would be the other guy," he said. "I had a lot of respect for both, but the right hand didn't always know what the left was doing.

"We acquired Alvin Davis at one point, and Whitey didn't even know about it. I said something like, 'I don't know if we have space for Alvin Davis, where do you think I should play him?' and Whitey said, 'What do you mean? When did we get Alvin Davis?'

"There was another time we were looking for a left-hander, Bob Patterson, and ended up signing Ken Patterson. There was a lot of confusion, a lack of communication, and it was always bouncing down to the clubhouse. I was always trying to keep everyone off each other's back without being considered a smart ass."

The obvious solution, Rodgers said, would have been to name Dan O'Brien assistant general manager.

"If one guy is making $800,000 [as Herzog was] and the other guy is making $420,000 [as O'Brien was], it should be obvious who the boss is, but Richard Brown made them co-GMs and you always seemed to have one group hitting on the other, trying to outdo the other," Rodgers said. "Whitey and I always seemed to be on the same page and I operated on the assumption that he had the final say, but in some cases both of them did."

In the September of Herzog's hiring, of course, everyone put their best face on it.

Richard Brown said the "heavyweights" were now in place, that he was content with the club's structure and "you're going to see results, no doubt about it."

Jackie Autry said she felt a comfort with the organization she hadn't experienced before but that it wasn't a comfort simply stemming from her husband's longtime acquaintance with Rodgers and Herzog.

"I don't believe in the 'good old boy syndrome,' " she said. "I believe in quality and competence."

Rodgers said he endorsed Herzog's emphasis on pitching, speed and defense, and Herzog, who would turn 60 in November 1991, said the one thing he wanted most before retiring was to give Gene Autry a World Series championship.

Herzog had virtually rebuilt the Cardinals in one whirlwind span of five days at the 1980 winter baseball meetings, negotiating trades involving 22 players.

"We could trade from a position of strength," he said. "That's not to say there isn't a good nucleus here, but no team has that kind of surplus now." Expansion had continued to dilute the talent base. It would take longer to rebuild the Angels, he suspected, but he also recognized that impatience was at an acute level, and in sports generally "you don't have the luxury of a five-year plan. It's do it now."

The Angels had a payroll of $32.4 million in 1991, the seventh highest in baseball. Jackie Autry estimated a deficit of $3.5 million and said she couldn't allow it to grow.

Herzog was confronted by a series of significant economic and personal issues that thwarted his ability to rebuild the Angels quickly.

He re-signed Chuck Finley, who would have been eligible for free agency after the 1992 season, to a four-year, $18.5 million contract; lost Kirk McCaskill and Wally Joyner to free agency; saved more than $3 million by buying out the 1992 contracts of Dave Winfield and Bert Blyleven (the latter was eventually re-signed for considerably less than the $2 million in his original contract); failed in a bid to land free agent power hitter Bobby Bonilla (in a process that produced a public shouting match with agent Dennis Gilbert in the coffee shop of a Miami hotel); and, limited in surplus, strength and dollars, tried to plug gaps in his offense with trades for outfielders Hubie Brooks and Von Hayes—two more veterans on the far side of the hill.

The loss of Joyner was a jolt. He had been the indisputable fan favorite since his 1986 debut, but his relationship with the Angels had slowly deteriorated through a series of fractious contract and arbitration dealings that were compounded by his belief that the Autrys—Jackie, for sure, he felt—questioned his intensity and pain tolerance and had not forgiven him for missing the final games of the 1986 playoffs with Boston when hospitalized for a staph infection.

"If there wasn't animosity on both sides, this deal would have been done by now," said Herzog, who stepped into the middle of the cross fire in a futile attempt to negotiate an armistice and retain Joyner. "I feel like a damn divorce lawyer trying to decide who gets custody of this kid."

Jackie Autry wasn't amused.

"We had agreed early on that Whitey would have no involvement in contract negotiations, and that's what he wanted, but he somehow got himself involved in this and several others," she said. "Even though I protested to Richard Brown that this was to cease and desist, it didn't, and probably the biggest mistake we made was continuing to tolerate it, particularly in the contract talks with Wally.

"Whitey marches to his own drummer, and he tended to inflame a situation in which Wally thought I didn't like him and vice versa. The fact is, I had never made any disparaging remarks about Wally, privately or publicly. We tried to do everything we could for him, but he was always taking shots at the Angels, and you can get tired of that in a hurry. Nevertheless, Gene and I felt strongly that we had a deal with him at different points during the negotiations only to have it blow up, and Whitey contributed to that."

Herzog did not respond to interview requests for this book. However, club officials familiar with the final attempts at compromise during a series of heated negotiating sessions at the 1991 winter baseball meetings in Miami insisted that it was Jackie Autry who thwarted the deal. At one point, they claim, an enraged Herzog launched into a table-pounding oration in response to his sudden realization that he was trying to sign a player the Autrys didn't want him to sign and by a concern that he didn't have the authority he thought he had.

"If he'd had the control he thought he had and was able to do what he wanted to do," Joyner said, "it might have been different. What I found out, at least as far as my own situation was concerned, was that he didn't have the power that he thought he had with me."

The Angels and Joyner basically agreed on a four-year contract for $15.75 million, but Joyner wanted $10 million of it in bonus and salary before 1994, when there was the threat of a work stoppage, a threat that became reality. The Angels ultimately offered $9.5 million, but it came too late to soothe hurt feelings and several years of stormy relations. Joyner, still playing with the San Diego Padres, signed a one-year, $4.25 million contract with Kansas City, and converted it a year later into a four year, $18.8 million deal with the Royals.

Devoid of Joyner and Winfield, who combined for 49 homers and 182 RBI in 1991, the Angels were last in the league in runs, home runs and team batting average in 1992. Gary Gaetti, so frustrated that he expressed the belief that Anaheim Stadium had to be haunted by witches, hit a mediocre 12 home runs to lead a mediocre team. Hayes and Brooks, the two Herzog acquisitions, combined for 12 and batted .225 and .216 respectively, with Hayes being released before the season ended, having fulfilled a prophecy by Jim Fregosi, his former Philadelphia manager, that he was allergic to leather—as in the mitt required to play defense. Mark Langston, at 13–14, was the only pitcher to win more than 10 games. Chuck Finley celebrated his new contract, so to speak, by going 7–12. Jim Abbott had a 2.77 ERA but was victimized by poor support as he went 7–15 in the last year of his first stint with the Angels. Bryan Harvey, who had saved 46 games in 1991, battled an elbow problem and appeared in only 25 games.

The Angels finished 24 games behind the division champion A's, losing 11 straight in midsummer en route to a 72–90 record that resembled a bus crash in more ways than one.

More devastating than all the statistics was a near tragic accident on the night of May 21 when one of two buses carrying the Angels from New York to Baltimore veered off a lonely stretch of the New Jersey Turnpike, blasted through a guard rail and crashed into a wooded area in Deptford Township, New Jersey.

Buck Rodgers, sitting in the first seat on the right-hand side, was the most seriously injured of the 13 passengers, suffering multiple fractures of his arm, elbow and knees. Chuck Finley was credited with a heroic job of helping Rodgers and banged-up teammates from the listing bus. Rodgers was flown back to Los Angeles, had six hours of surgery and did not return to the managerial helm until August, turning the reins over to third base coach John Wathan. The Angels, 4½ out at the time of the accident, were 18½ out when Rodgers returned. There had been psychological scars for some, physical scars for others.

"I think it affected a lot more guys than they were willing to let on," shortstop Gary DiSarcina said. "It was a time in our lives when everything was put on hold. Baseball seemed secondary. The guys on that bus were lucky not to have lost their lives. You can't experience something that traumatic and go right on with your daily routine. In any other business, people who needed it would have received time off for therapy."

Rodgers wrestled with the pain, physical and otherwise. There were sleepless nights, ugly visions of a careening bus, a second operation on his elbow. He would ultimately receive financial satisfaction from the bus company through a protracted law suit, but his first full year at the Angels helm, he would say, had been a wipeout.

"John Wathan did a good job, but rather than putting my influence on the team early, I was lying there worrying about something other than the Angels and baseball," he said. "I came back with the same objectives I always had, but I was much more impulsive, much more in a hurry-up mode. You face what might have been death, and your patience isn't likely to be as good as it was. I think I went about it the same way on the field, but I was less patient with things off the field."

25

1993–94: Buck Passing

Buck Rodgers' patience would be tested again during an equally miserable 1993 season that followed an equally bizarre winter.

With Herzog providing the impetus, the Angels traded Jim Abbott to the New York Yankees, acquired a third baseman from Toronto who proved to be damaged goods, swallowed $5 million by releasing the disappointing Gary Gaetti, re-acquired Chili Davis as a free agent and began to stockpile an array of recycled major league pitchers who only the American Medical Association could love—not to mention the desperate Angels.

In order:

- The Angels confirmed the ascendance of business over sentiment when they traded Abbott, at 25 their most popular and recognizable player. The left-handed pitcher was traded a year before becoming eligible for free agency, but Herzog was convinced they would be unable to sign him and was determined to get something in return rather than experiencing another Wally Joyner scenario in which the club was left empty-handed when the player walked.

    Abbott had rejected the Angels' offer of four years at $16 million, and the Autrys had rejected his $19 million proposal and subsequent compromise at $17.5 million. Abbott would return in 3½ years, but in the meantime the Angels landed three Yankee prospects, all personally scouted by Herzog: first baseman J. T. Snow, who was buried behind Don Mattingly and would give the Angels a successor to Joyner; pitcher Russ Springer as a possible replacement for Abbott; and left-hander Jerry Nielsen as help in the bullpen.

"It's very tough to give up a guy like Jim Abbott," Herzog said, "but we made a very good offer, didn't feel we could improve on it, and ran the risk of getting less in return for Jim the longer we waited. This is my deal and I take full responsibility."

- Attempting to bolster a feeble offense, the Angels re-signed Chili Davis, who had spent four years with the club before joining the Minnesota Twins for two in a free agent collusion award and contributing to Minnesota's 1991 World Series victory, a season in which he hit 29 homers with 93 RBI.

Davis received a one-year contract from the Angels for $1.75 million with the opportunity to make another $650,000 through incentives. A rollover arrangement that parlayed the incentives to salary provided for a potential salary of $3.05 million in 1994 or a guaranteed buyout of $500,000.

"I should say thank you to the Angels in two ways," Davis said. "For letting me go, because I got a World Series ring, and for bringing me back."

- In another move designed to strengthen the offense, the Angels traded Luis Sojo to Toronto shortly after signing Davis in December for third baseman Kelly Gruber, who had been a significant contributor to the Blue Jays' World Series victory in October.

The Angels, under terms of the deal, were responsible for $2.5 million of Gruber's $4 million salary in 1993, but it wasn't until he arrived for an introductory news conference in January and complained that he was still troubled by a bulging disk in his neck and that his shoulder had not healed from a World Series injury that the Angels suspected they had been had.

A month earlier, the Angels had traded first base prospect Lee Stevens—who would ultimately become a valuable hitter on a Texas Ranger team that dominated the West in the late 90s—to the Montreal Expos for a pitcher named Jeff Tuss, only to learn that Tuss was retiring to play football at Fresno State. They received another player in the place of Tuss, but the acquisition of the damaged Gruber, club president Richard Brown said, made the Angels appear to be "country bumpkins" again.

"I'm embarrassed and upset," he said. "I'm trying to harness those emotions and determine in a methodical way who knew, besides Gruber, that he was seriously hurt and why weren't we told about it. We felt a healthy Gruber would be a tremendous asset, but now we're not sure when he'll be healthy and ready to play. Too bad we don't have a lemon law in baseball."

The Blue Jays feigned ignorance, and the Angels were forced to swallow a bitter and costly situation. Gruber had shoulder surgery on February 16, 1993, and did not play his first game until June 4, the Angels creating the vacancy at third base by releasing Gary Gaetti, who was still owed $5 million as part of the Angels' original $11.4 million mistake.

Gaetti would shake the Anaheim demons and sustain his career through the 90s with the Kansas City Royals, St. Louis Cardinals and Chicago Cubs, but in 2½ years with the Angels he had merely maintained the slide that started in his final years in Minnesota, batting .246, .226 and .180 as an Angel with a total of 30 homers—a season's output during his All-Star years with the Twins.

The Angels, of course, hoped that Gruber was ready to replace him, his shoulder having been repaired by surgery, but it didn't happen. Gruber appeared in just 18 games before returning to the disabled list with the disc problem in his neck. Doctors now told him he would be risking serious injury if he continued to play, and the Angels ultimately decided to lump injury on top of insult by releasing Gruber on September 8 as they had released Gaetti on June 4.

The absence of any power and productivity at third base contributed to another dismal season in 1993. The Angels went 71–91 and finished 23 games behind the division champion Chicago White Sox.

Mark Langston and Chuck Finley each won 16 games, but no other pitcher won more than seven. Russ Springer, the Abbott replacement, was 1–6. Scott Sanderson, one of several recycled veterans who would dot the staff in the 1993 and 1994 seasons as part of a historic pattern that has found the Angels consistently attempting to rehabilitate tired and lame arms, opened 7–2, lost nine straight decisions and was released in midsummer. Julio Valera, obtained in a trade for former shortstop Dick Schofield, was 3–6. Joe Magrane, a Herzog crony from St. Louis who had appeared in only five major league games since having elbow surgery in March 1991, went 3–2 in 1993, which was enough for Herzog to guarantee him $3 million for two years in a contract that could escalate to $9 million for three and $13.3 million for four, a signing that might have been the most absurd in Angel history.

Unlike Kelly Gruber, whose shoulder and neck injuries ambushed the Angels during the previous winter, Magrane's arm problems were public record, and they manifested again five months after he signed the new contract. Magrane had elbow surgery in the spring of 1994, made only 11 starts that year, and did not pitch at all in 1995, laughing all the way to the bank.

With Magrane one of several bit players in 1993, and with Abbott gone and little support behind Langston and Finley in the starting rotation, the Angels also paid a price for the absence of relief ace Bryan Harvey from a bullpen in which left-hander Steve Frey saved 13 games and right hander Joe Grahe saved 11.

Harvey had saved a club-record 46 in 1991, but elbow problems restricted his availability in 1992, when he saved 13, leaving the Angels with a difficult decision that winter. They could retain Harvey at the $10.75 million he was guaranteed over the next three seasons, hoping he could regain his previous form amid the risk of ongoing physical problems, or they could expose him to the expansion draft, with the certainty he would be selected by the Florida Marlins, whose pitching coach, Marcel Lachemann, had just left a similar position with the Angels and who was confident he could restore Harvey's effectiveness. After considerable debate behind closed doors, the Angels opted for economic prudence, exposing Harvey to the draft. He joined the Marlins and saved 45 games in 1993, but elbow problems surfaced again in 1994, and he saved only six more games before his premature retirement.

Although the Angels were second-guessed frequently amid Harvey's 1993 success, they had made the right choice at a time when they were being criticized for making so many wrong ones.

The return of Chili Davis provided another positive for the beleaguered franchise in 1993. Davis slugged 27 homers and drove in 112 runs as the bellwether for an anemic offense in which J. T. Snow, the new first baseman, hit 16 homers while batting .241, and a group of young players began to replenish the lineup.

- Right fielder Tim Salmon, a third-round selection by scouting director Bob Fontaine Jr. and staff in the 1989 draft, became the first Angel to win the American League's Rookie of the Year Award as he hit 31 homers and drove in 95 runs.
- Shortstop Gary DiSarcina, a sixth-round selection in 1988, continued to take root at that pivotal position after Rodgers provided the opportunity when he became manager late in 1991—unseating Dick Schofield. DiSarcina batted only .238 in 1993 but would continue to make progress offensively under the respected and diligent eye of batting instructor Rod Carew, who had returned to the club in 1992.
- Outfielder Chad Curtis, a 45th-round afterthought in the 1989 draft, batted .284 and stole 48 bases, and second baseman Damion Easley, a 30th-round choice in 1988, batted .313 in 73 games in 1993, a season that included another major front office shake-up.

Dan O'Brien turned up the loser in his power struggle with Whitey Herzog when he was fired on September 17. The conflict had been triggered two years earlier when Herzog was hired as senior vice president and director of player personnel and told he would be in charge of baseball operations, even though O'Brien carried the title of senior vice president and director of baseball operations and never relented in his duties, creating the industry perception that no one was in charge.

"This isn't to blame any individual or individuals," club president Richard Brown said. "The blame is on our system, because it wasn't working to our satisfaction."

Said Rodgers: "This doesn't surprise me. It was doomed from

day one. It was just a matter of time before someone would emerge. I've never seen it work when you try to put two guys of their will in command like that."

Said Herzog: "I wasn't here to get anybody fired, but I just didn't feel I was earning my money. I was ready to resign because I didn't get to do what I wanted to do the last two years. I came back to baseball in the first place because I wanted to get the Cowboy in the World Series, and I was told I was the only one who could do it. In two years we haven't done it. Now I want to try it my way."

O'Brien, then and now, has refused to burn bridges or express bitterness. He said only that he enjoyed his time in Anaheim, tried to accede to Herzog's judgment on personnel decisions and felt that their relationship and working arrangement were running smoothly.

Bill Bavasi, who had been the farm director for 10 years, was appointed assistant general manager, but the biggest shocker was to come only four months later when Herzog, having won the power struggle with O'Brien, resigned without warning, turning the front office reins over to Bavasi as general manager.

No one was more shocked by Herzog's January 11 decision than Bavasi. A few days before, accompanied by farm director Ken Forsch, assistant Jeff Parker and scouting director Bob Fontaine Jr., Bavasi had driven Herzog to the Los Angeles airport for a flight to St. Louis. The club had just finished internal meetings in preparation for the start of spring training. The group sat at the airport, sharing pizza and beer, while waiting for Herzog's flight.

"You can't understand how shocked I was unless you were sitting at that table," Bavasi said. "I mean, we loved the guy. We were excited that he was coming back for another year. He was motivating us, getting us fired up for the season. We put him on the plane, and three days later he calls and says that I'm now the guy, that he's retiring. It was amazing. There had been no clue."

Herzog didn't really provide any after the fact, either.

"I really believe that it's time for me to do some of the things I want to do," Herzog said, referring to his love of golf, skiing and fishing. "I don't really want to be traveling all over and going back and forth to California or anywhere else. If I didn't think Bill Bavasi was so capable of doing the job for the next 25 years, then I don't know if I would have done this at this time."

It was the timing that provided the jolt, coming so soon after he had been left standing in the tussle with O'Brien.

Theorists suggest that Herzog had wearied of Jackie Autry's budgetary constraints (the payroll was slashed by $8 million between 1992 and 1994) and his role as the negotiating executioner. He was also from another time in baseball, an era devoid of agents and contract complexities.

"Today in baseball," he said on the way out, "when you talk about a player, you talk about arbitration, if he has a guaranteed contract, when he's going to be a free agent. We never really talk about whether he can run, hit and throw."

Herzog had been left to pound the table when $16 million wasn't enough for Wally Joyner or Jim Abbott. He railed publicly over the contract demands of free agents Bobby Bonilla and Danny Tartabull, accosting their agent in a hotel shouting match.

"He had a great deal of respect and recognition among his peers, but the reality is that it was a different era, and Whitey hadn't crossed the bridge," player agent Steve Comte said.

Jackie Autry put it differently. In addition to terming Herzog's hiring her biggest mistake as Gene Autry's partner at the club's helm, creating the front office struggle with O'Brien, she said that Herzog had done nothing to improve the organization.

"He went out and looked at our minor league system and told us exactly what we knew," she said. "Did he find any players in other organizations? Well, if you look at the team he first put on the field, that was the most disgraceful team we ever fielded, and I think he had the feeling that the welcome mat was going to be pulled out from under him. Not from anyone in particular, but the whole sense of the organization.

"Gene was hurt by the way he left but never held a grudge. He called him several times, left messages on his answering machine, and Whitey never had the courtesy to call back. Not one time. Gene would call to wish him a Merry Christmas and ask him to give him a call, and he never did. Even after Gene passed away, there was no card, no call. He just kissed the Cowboy off, and Gene had paid him $800,000 to do nothing."

Neither Rodgers nor Bavasi agreed with that conclusion—or with her opinion that Herzog told the organization what it already knew about the farm system.

"People in that organization don't give Whitey the credit he deserves, but he took the whole organization and cranked it up a notch," Rodgers said. "He and the old lady didn't see eye to eye, but he did some good things for the organization when it came to young players and the farm system. You don't find many Whitey Herzogs who are willing to spend a year in the system evaluating young players."

Said Bavasi, endorsing that theme: "It was my understanding that they brought him in because people thought our scouting and minor leagues weren't good enough, that he'd tell us what was wrong and right the ship. Well, he comes back at the end of the year and tells Jackie to 'leave it alone because you've got some good young players, you've got good scouts and minor league people.'

"He tells her, 'Just don't trade them, suck it up, get beat for a couple years, and I'll make a couple trades that won't make us a whole lot better but will help protect the young players, because it's those kids who will win for you eventually.' He was the one who gave us a chance to do anything with guys like Tim Salmon and Jim Edmonds and Garret Anderson. The attitude before Whitey came in was that those guys weren't good enough, that we didn't have any good young players in the system, but Whitey said, 'Yes, you do, leave 'em alone.' I'll always be grateful for that and the fact he was willing to share everything he knows."

Bavasi had long been the heir. He had trained at the foot of his father, Buzzie Bavasi, and had learned the business from the grounds crew up, literally willing to get his hands dirty during 13 years with the organization, 10 as the farm director who helped shepherd those young players Herzog identified as pivotal to the future. The ultimate opportunity to serve as general manager, however, came unexpectedly and sooner than he might have anticipated.

"I'm comfortable with it," he said at the time, "but maybe that's because I'm too dumb to know that I shouldn't be."

One thing became certain very soon: He wasn't intimidated. He wasn't hesitant to pull the trigger.

Bavasi delivered a shocker rivaling the Herzog resignation on May 17, firing Rodgers and hiring Marcel Lachemann as the manager.

The Angels were 16–23 but only 1½ games out of the division lead when Bavasi summoned Rodgers to his Anaheim Stadium office and gave him the word.

"Whenever you have a change in general managers you have concern over your situation," Rodgers said in reflection, "but basically we were ahead of schedule, our payroll was around $25 million [$24.5] and in line with what Jackie wanted, attendance was up, and we were very much in the race. I thought the owner was happy with me, the general manager was happy with me, and I thought everything was going just like we planned. I thought he was calling me in to give me an extension because we were doing better than people expected. That's how stupid I was."

Their meeting lasted only 10 minutes, and Rodgers didn't ask Bavasi why he was being fired—nor has Bavasi ever identified his reasons "out of respect" for Rodgers. "Why are managers fired?" Bavasi said a few years later. "Usually it's because you don't think the players are responding to the way he goes about his business. I thought it was the right thing to do at the time. I told him, 'Don't make a mistake and think this was somebody else's decision. This was my decision.' He didn't believe me—not at that time, anyway."

Rodgers believed that club president Richard Brown had made the decision. He called a news conference the next day and labeled Brown a cancer in the organization, saying a recent confrontation with Brown might have triggered his dismissal. Rodgers had been summoned for a private meeting to discuss comments that Brown heard Rodgers had made about him.

"He said that I said that he didn't know anything about baseball," Rodgers said at his news conference.

"Even if I believed that, I wouldn't say it."

Rodgers did believe it and would say it in time. He also ultimately accepted that Bavasi had called the shot.

In an interview with the *Los Angeles Times* four months after his firing, Rodgers described Bavasi as a "paper man" who was not that knowledgeable about the game. He said his firing was "another case of a young general manager being intimidated by a veteran manager," and "the only thing that still bothers me about Rich Brown is that he was always coming down to my office and saying, 'You're my man, my guy, we want you to take over and run everything when you're ready, you'll always be with us.' Then he turns around and takes the word of a 34-year-old guy [36, actually] who's been a general manager for a month and a half. I felt like I was double-crossed."

The rhetoric may have been costly for Rodgers. His use of the word *cancer* in particular to describe Brown may have resulted in him being blackballed in organized baseball. He worked briefly as a scout for the Philadelphia Phillies and managed a non-affiliated independent team based in Orange County, but he has never returned to a full-time position in the major leagues. Rodgers accepts that.

"I've thought a lot about it," he said, relaxing at his Orange County home several years later. "I could have used maybe a lesser word, but if that was what it took to get Rich Brown out of there, then I think for the Angels' overall sake it was good. He was the most out-of-place person by word and deed of anybody there at the time. The whole front office was scared to death. Nobody knew from day to day what they were expected to do; nobody received any encouragement. Rich Brown is a fine person, but he was in the wrong job.

"Now I think they're on the right track. Billy has learned on the job, become more confident, spread out his wings. He learned his baseball under guys like Marcel Lachemann and Joe Maddon in the minor leagues, and I understand and accept there was a comfort level involved in the decision, but there was no reason for him to have been intimidated by me. As long as we talk, I can get along with anybody. I don't have to have the last word. I just don't like to be surprised. If I'm expecting [the acquisition of] one left-hander and another walks into my office, that's a surprise."

Richard Brown, now chief operating officer of the Josephson Institute of Ethics and Character Counts, was not forced out by

Rodgers' rhetoric. He remained as club president until the sale to Disney was completed in 1996, and he remains disturbed by Rodgers' accusations.

"He tells 10 million people I'm a cancer and two people that I'm not," Brown said. "Buck is a gregarious, affable, terrific guy, but any attempt at rectifying the situation should have been done through a news conference, through the same format in which he first made the accusation."

The bottom line on Rodgers' firing, Brown said, was that the manager didn't seem to respect the general manager, and the general manager couldn't relate to the manager. There was also the belief among management, he said, that Rodgers had become too laid-back after the bus accident and was too often "bad-mouthing his players in the press"—unacceptable behavior when the club was trying to promote those same players and sell tickets. The one statement that seemed to most disturb Brown and others—though painfully true—was Rodgers' assertion that he was attempting to win with a recycled pitching staff. Indeed, three of his starting pitchers in 1994—Joe Magrane, John Dopson and John Farrell—had been released by other clubs and would combine to go 4–12 in the season that Rodgers was fired.

By any measure, it was a stunner. Two of Gene Autry's favorite players and people, Jim Fregosi and Buck Rodgers, had now failed to survive as Autry's managers.

Said Jackie Autry: "We looked on Buck's hiring as a marriage made in heaven. We thought he would be the club's last manager until Gene died or Buck died or something else happened. When Billy called us and asked us to come down early that afternoon and told us he could not work with Buck for a variety of reasons, it was like we were hit by a rock, and we're sitting there on the horns of a dilemma. We had just hired this man to be our general manager. Do you say, 'Sorry, Bill, you're just going to have to get along with him'? or do you say, 'Okay, one of you is going to have to go'?

"The feeling among people in and out of the organization was that after the accident Buck had changed. He didn't seem to have the same fire and emotional makeup. He was sitting there, having press conferences on a daily basis with his feet up on the desk and not really out directing traffic on the field, as it were, and I know it started alienating a lot of the players. There was unhappiness in the clubhouse, and it started spilling upstairs. Rich was an innocent bystander. He called Buck to assure him he had nothing to do with it, and Buck called him a lying SOB. It was very difficult for Gene and myself, but our feeling was that if you go with a horse you stay with a horse, and Billy at that point was our horse. I mean, if the general manager says he can't work with the man, that Buck's attitude and mind-set had changed, you trust his judgment and your own instincts."

The Autrys' support for Bavasi was also manifested in the hiring of Lachemann, who had served as the Angels pitching coach from 1983 through 1992, when he left to become the pitching coach under his brother, Rene, the first manager of the expansion Florida Marlins in 1993. Comparatively low-key and soft-spoken, Lachemann, 52 at the time, had an outstanding reputation among Angel pitchers, but he had never managed and wasn't sure that he desired to or had the personality and temperament for it. He would take the job after staying up all night to contemplate it—getting advice from his brother and listening to Bavasi's pleas—but he was never sure it had been the right decision, and he would ultimately resign during the 1996 season—convinced he had no affection for the job and that it had been the wrong decision.

Richard Brown sensed it in 1994.

"Lach never wanted to manage," he said. "It took Billy most of the night to convince him. I wasn't against Lach, but I wanted someone who wanted the job to take the job. Billy wanted someone he could be comfortable with. You have a new GM who looks up to the guy and recommends the hiring of a quality person, you say, 'Okay, let's try it,' but I knew even then it wasn't going to be a long-term proposition. Lach was one of the best pitching coaches, but he wasn't one of the best managers. I just don't think he had the stomach for it."

Lachemann accepted the offer, he said at the time, because the opportunity to return to Anaheim in that capacity was one in a million. "If I was going to manage, this was the time and place," he said.

The 1994 season, however, would have turned anyone's stomach.

Picking up for Rodgers, the Angels were 47–68 when the season abruptly ended in early August. The players went out on strike, triggering a long and costly labor dispute that resulted in the first cancellation of the World Series and left baseball reeling. The Angels, of course, had been reeling already. There was little positive in 1994 except for the contributed productivity of Chili Davis, who hit 26 homers and drove in 84 runs, and the introduction on a full-time basis of another young farm product.

Now it was center fielder Jim Edmonds, a seventh-round selection in 1988, joining Tim Salmon (who followed up his Rookie of the Year campaign by hitting 23 homers and driving in 70 runs), Gary DiSarcina, Chad Curtis and Damion Easley.

A former football player with a new hip, Bo Jackson, appeared in 75 games with the Angels in 1994, but his occasional power and steel-strengthened joint couldn't compensate for that recycled pitching staff on which Chuck Finley, at a modest 10–10, was the leading winner and Mark Langston went down early with elbow chips and ended up a disappointing 7–8.

What did Bo know? Nothing more than everyone else.

"We stink," the mild-mannered Lachemann said in early August, an opinion endorsed by Chili Davis, who strongly questioned the organization's commitment to winning.

The organization had not won since 1986, a tumultuous period of hirings, firings and philosophical inconsistency, and now the biggest change of all was clearly on the horizon.

26

DISNEY'S NEW DOMAIN

There was no one defining moment at which Gene and Jackie Autry opted to put their team on the market; nor was there one defining moment at which Disney chairman Michael Eisner opted to swallow concerns regarding the wisdom of the investment and pursue the purchase.

The Autrys were driven to the decision by mounting debt and disillusionment—disenfranchised by the industry's runaway costs, said Jackie Autry.

Eisner was primarily motivated by mounting belief that the Autrys or another owner might move the team out of Anaheim—the self-proclaimed Hub of Happiness and home of Disneyland since 1955 and the Mighty Ducks of the National Hockey League since 1993.

One of the most important words in the Disney dictionary—after profit—is synergy.

The Ducks gave Disney expanded presence and marketability in Anaheim and Orange County.

The Angels represented further expansion. Their possible departure—only sketchy speculation at times—could have eroded the city's image and Disney's business.

"Michael's concern wasn't that someone else would buy the team," said Tony Tavares, the Angel president under Disney. "His concern, in knowing Anaheim, was that it would be difficult for a new owner to get any kind of fantastic deal with the city and that might influence a new owner to move.

"How far? Who knows? But even if it was to Irvine [a few miles to the south], it wasn't Anaheim anymore. The Angels gave Anaheim a major league presence and image. If the team moved, it wasn't good for the city's image or his business at the Pond [where the Ducks played]. More than anything, that's what got Michael involved. It wasn't that he was driven to own a baseball team."

The Autrys themselves had explored other venues—if for no other reason than to put pressure on Anaheim.

Jackie Autry, looking ahead to the expiration of the stadium lease in 2001 and thwarted in talks with the city regarding improved terms for that lease and renovations at the stadium, had met at various times with officials from Irvine and other Orange County cities.

Ultimately, she said, industry inflation—and a restrictive lease that was ranked among the worst in baseball and contributed to the big-market Angels being (1) shamelessly categorized as a mid- and small-market team for revenue-sharing purposes and (2) a recipient of that dole under terms of the 1996 collective bargaining agreement—left no other escape except to sell. Or declare bankruptcy, a distasteful option that was discussed and dismissed, she said.

The turning point was probably 1990. If not the end of hope, the beginning of the end.

The $2.1 million that Gene Autry had invested in 1961 seemed a distant and very modest memory as the club began to suffer serious losses, compounding the $11 million hit that was the Angels' share of the owners' $280 million fine for their collusion of the mid to late 80s in restricting free agent movement and salary growth.

"Starting in about 1990 I told the club's management that we had to put a $2 million profit at the bottom line," Jackie Autry said. "The reason I did that was because I saw what was happening in baseball, and I knew that a $2 million profit wouldn't hold.

"What I was really saying was that I was willing to lose $3 or $4 million but not $6 or $7 million, because that's what we were facing and that's how we started to try and figure where we were going to cut. Nobody believed the kind of money owners were losing, but as time went on, we had to liquidate assets simply to pay off the debt at Wells Fargo."

That debt at one point was more than $40 million, she said, adding that the club's losses in the first half of the 90s alone were more than $30 million as the payroll, according to figures maintained by the owners' Player Relations Committee, fluctuated from $21.9 million in 1990 to $32.4 million in 1991, to $32.5 million in 1992 to $27.4 million in 1993 to $24.5 million in 1994 and $34.7 million in 1995, the last full year of the Autrys' control.

"I hope someday that ownership will understand they have a responsibility to baseball's future not to allow this stupidity to continue," Jackie Autry said, referring to soaring salaries and the widening disparity among the 30 clubs in payroll, revenue and competitive balance. "But I'm afraid that the only way the stupidity stops is if several clubs go into bankruptcy. Whether the big-market owners will care, I don't know. But they better care, or they are going to be left playing among themselves.

"You've got to put everybody on a level field. You've got to say, whatever the number is, we have $2 billion in [industry] revenue, this is what it costs to do what we need to do, and the players need to be squeezed in under this cap. The players are still going to get their share, they are still going to do well, but you need a system in which longtime owners, people who love the game, are not being forced out.

"You need a system which doesn't disenfranchise fans or owners, as Gene and I were disenfranchised, as Peter O'Malley was. Both Gene and Peter were avid about not raising ticket prices. Every time it came up they said absolutely not, we'll figure some other way to do it. Unfortunately, that some other way never came about. Look at the ownership volatility in baseball. People have this mentality, 'Well, obviously they don't know what they're doing, I can fix this.' They buy into the industry like starry-eyed kids, and all of a sudden what they thought . . . well, it just ain't so."

For the Autrys, amid the economic and labor problems, those frequent ownership meetings stopped being meaningful or much fun. The aging Cowboy opted most often to stay home. Jackie Autry's presence on the power councils diminished. Their love of the Angels remained, but the optimism of each spring wilted in the reality of summer, the frequent losses followed by long and depressing drives from Anaheim to their Studio City or Palm Springs homes.

"The Autrys ran the Angels like a kind of family business," former club president Richard Brown said. "Like a ma-and-pa store, an extension of the family. Well, you just don't see any family-run operations in baseball anymore, and it was quite obvious to me they were going to sell.

"You had an owner in his late 80s losing money and unable to keep pace with the industry's economics. We had a baseball stadium turned into a football stadium that was neither fish nor fowl. We received virtually no revenue from the luxury boxes and had a bad overall lease on top of it. I think we did a pretty good job trying to keep it lean and mean with the third smallest front office in baseball, but there was only so many things we could do.

"People would say, you compete with the Dodgers, and I would say, we compete with the A's, Mariners and Rangers in our division. But of course we competed with the Dodgers. We competed with a day at the beach, 18 holes of golf, all forms of entertainment, but when the Dodgers had their wonderful years and you had people in north [Orange] county with a choice of spending their money on the Dodgers or Angels, they went to the Dodgers. They had the tradition, the history, and you didn't just compete for seats at the stadium. You competed in the media and you competed in the market, and we just never had the funds to package or leverage the way Disney does, the synergy Disney has.

"Disney can do so many more things through cross-ownership and cross-sponsorship. Disney can say, 'Buy a ticket to an Angel game for $50 and we'll throw in a trip to Disneyland.' We'd say, 'Come see the Angels play for $15 and then go to Disneyland on your own. Say hi to Mickey for us.' Look at our last opening day. We spent something like $7,500. We had three fire engines and a mounted policeman. I think they were probably going to be there anyway. Disney comes in and spends several hundred thousand. It's simply the nature of the beast in baseball now. The losses are blips to Disney. They were an earthquake to us."

Citing Disney's presence in Anaheim and the long and warm relationship between Gene Autry and Walt Disney, the Autrys felt that Disney and the Angels represented what Jackie Autry called a "natural marriage." She and her husband had discussed a concept by which they could remain as limited partners, enjoying the pleasures of ownership without the aggravation and losses, but when she first approached Eisner at his Burbank office in 1990 about the possibility of buying the team, "we were more or less dismissed out of hand."

Eisner asked to receive the club's financial statements but expressed concern about the industry's economic and labor problems and left Jackie Autry with the feeling that "he wasn't interested and that the company wasn't into a sports mentality at that time."

Disney didn't have the Mighty Ducks yet, and "I don't think they warmed up to the idea of owning the baseball team until the Ducks opened their eyes to the marketing potential and they became concerned we could sell to someone else," she said.

The someone else was former baseball commissioner Peter Ueberroth, a Laguna Beach resident and member of the club's board of directors. The Autrys had periodically discussed with Ueberroth his willingness to assemble a group interested in buying the team.

The Angels fit Ueberroth's portfolio as chairman of the Orange County–based Contrarian Group, which he describes as an incubator of businesses, a company that finds small start-up businesses and nurtures them, grows them and keeps them—or finds still promising businesses that have fallen on difficult times and fixes them, grows them and keeps them—often putting a combination of businesses together but never selling.

The Angels, Ueberroth said long after Disney had won the bidding, represented "one of the few underdeveloped major market teams, so I thought it had a significant upside. I don't think the Autrys had ever really engrossed themselves in a Riverside-Orange County–type home spirit or worked on attracting the Latino market. I think there had been a long period of stagnation while the Autrys and the city were in their suit [over development on the Anaheim Stadium parking lot], so I thought there were a lot of positive things that could be done and that we had a group capable of doing them. The other obvious reason why I was attracted to the situation was that the Angels are my hometown team."

Whether it was the 11th-hour reality that the Angels could be sold to someone else or the fear that the team could be moved out of Anaheim or the synergistic potential of linking the Angels to the Ducks and Disneyland, Eisner reentered the picture in February 1995—at a point when the Angels were far down the negotiating road with Ueberroth but also at a crossroads of sorts.

The Ueberroth group had offered the same $130 million that Disney would offer, but was unwilling to pick up any of the Autrys' past debts or operating losses while the transaction was traveling through baseball's often protracted approval process.

Disney ultimately agreed to pick up $10 million in losses, with Eisner laying out the terms of a $140 million transaction during a three-hour meeting at his home with Jackie Autry on May 14, 1995. The public announcement of the agreement was made four days later.

"We had a letter of intent from Peter, but Disney came in at the 11th hour and overwhelmed us," Jackie Autry said. "It wasn't a case of playing one group against the other or attempting to get top dollar. We wanted to find the best owner for Orange County, and we wanted to be in a position where our debt at Wells Fargo wasn't getting even bigger while we were going through the transition. The $10 million put us in that position.

"[Ueberroth] made an offer that was everything we could ask for and then some, but guarding against those additional losses was important to us, and Disney was in position to offer more than Peter felt his group was able to justify. He was very professional. He didn't want us to feel uncomfortable if somebody came in and blew us away, and we had to turn him down."

According to Ueberroth, Gene Autry called with the Disney bid and said, "Look, we don't have to take the highest price. Get partially there. Get over halfway there." Ueberroth said he thanked

Autry but told him he couldn't go higher, and that as a board member he had the fiduciary responsibility to recommend that they close the Disney deal and that he not try to sabotage it.

"We would have loved to done our best to fill up the stadium and bring him a winner," Ueberroth said. "That would have been lots of fun, but they made the right decision. The deal was a wonderful one for the Autrys and their charities, but I wouldn't have been unhappy if it had fallen through.

"Disney had played its cards very carefully. It didn't appear they were all that interested, which is why I was so disappointed. I thought we'd win. I thought if they had been all that interested . . . well, they had the economic resources to step up and knock everybody out.

"If I'd been in [Disney's] situation, I wouldn't have let anybody get involved and create a bidding war. I also thought that with [Eisner] living on the west side [of Los Angeles] and knowing the Dodgers were coming on the market, from a media point of view I thought [the Dodgers] might be a better investment for Disney."

The agreement between Disney and the Autrys was hailed by Orange County officials as a major boost for a county coming off the 1994 bankruptcy filing—at $2.5 billion the largest municipal bankruptcy in history—and the 1995 move of the Rams to St. Louis.

Anaheim city manager James D. Ruth said the agreement "should help restore faith in the area," but he also expressed caution, knowing from experience that Disney could be a demanding negotiator and that, in the aftermath of the bankruptcy, he couldn't jeopardize the city or taxpayers with a sweetheart deal for Disney regarding stadium renovations and lease.

"We'll do what we can to put this together, but we're not going to put our general fund at risk," Ruth said. "We're not going to subsidize them."

Major league owners, meeting in Los Angeles, approved Disney's purchase of the Angels on January 18, 1996, but there was still no agreement with the city and still some concern that the Autrys—with their employees in limbo—would ultimately have to turn back to Ueberroth as a potential buyer.

Eisner, sporting an Angel jacket and a cap advertising the Disney movie *Angels in the Outfield*, appeared at a news conference in downtown Los Angeles on the day that owners voted approval of the sale and announced that unless a stadium plan was developed within 60 days, Disney could withdraw from the agreement.

Eisner had insisted that the escape clause be added during the previous week when he became concerned that Disney could suffer major losses in its first few years as Angels owner—given the economic instability of an industry still recovering from the 1994 players strike and the economic pitfalls that the Autrys were experiencing with an out-of-date lease in an outmoded stadium.

Eisner, according to Jackie Autry, was warned by then Florida Marlins owner Wayne Huizenga against "closing the deal until you know what you're going to do with the stadium," because of what Autry described as Huizenga's own "horror stories" attempting to get civic leaders in south Florida to fulfill their promises.

Huizenga, believing a retractable roof stadium was mandatory for his team's economic survival in the Miami area, claimed major losses and ultimately decimated his 1997 World Series winner, purging the payroll before selling the team to Florida commodities broker John Henry.

"We don't want a home run–type economic situation—we just don't want a black hole–type situation," Eisner said at the news conference. "I'm an optimist and I assume we'll get this done. There are alternatives if we can't, and they're not pretty. We want to stay in Anaheim, but we can't lose millions of dollars for that privilege."

With the Autrys and their staff in limbo as Disney began talks with the city, Tavares said: "I'm sure we've exercised the limits of Jackie Autry's patience and the patience of her employees—I wouldn't want to come to work every day wondering if I have a job. Unfortunately, they're the victims of circumstances. They'll have another 60 days of this. I know it's unfair, but that's the way it is. We're not going to go out and bleed money for the sake of bleeding money. There's got to be a reason, and a game plan, and we're not going to go into a plan where we're going to lose money for the next 10 years."

Disney envisioned a virtually new stadium with the ambience of Camden Yards in Baltimore or Jacobs Field in Cleveland. The renovation would include demolition of the outfield seats that had been added when the Rams moved to Anaheim, ultimately transforming a 67,000-seat football stadium into a 45,000-seat baseball stadium with a compact number of revenue-generating luxury suites—opposed to the 112 that generally sat empty for Angel games in the larger configuration and netted the team virtually no income other than a modest amount for food services and the 12 tickets per box that the Rams were required to buy.

Those sixty days, however, became almost 120 days as Disney and the city negotiated in vain, with the Autrys watching nervously and Jackie Autry lobbying American League officials to use their influence and members of the city council on the benefits of a new facility.

"There were definitely some moments when I thought it wasn't going to get done," she said. "I spent a lot of time on the phone. Sometimes city council people aren't the brightest in the world. They get where they are because they are affable and have good personalities, but they don't have a lot going upstairs. They tend to have a personal agenda, a feeling of importance and power, and they lose sight of what's best for the community.

"I tried to say, 'Look, you've lost the Rams, you might lose the Angels. You could have a stadium sitting empty. You have an opportunity here to acquire a state-of-the-art facility at very little cost to the city in money or aggravation. Think about it. The jobs, the revenue, the national impact on the city's image.' I tried to say there's a lot at stake for Anaheim if this deal falls through."

Yet by mid-March, with the 60-day deadline at hand, the deal did appear to have fallen through. Tavares visited Jackie Autry and told her that the two sides had reached such a level of frustration that they had stopped listening to each other. "Sometimes things have to cool down before they can be resurrected," he said.

There was considerable pressure on all parties.

- The city knew that if the Angels left, they would not get another shot at a major league team—American League president Gene Budig told city officials that baseball would not block a move by the Angels even though no team had received permission to move for 25 years—and that relations with Disney, the company that had put Anaheim on the national map, could be irreparably damaged.

- Disney knew that another buyer could possibly move the team, damaging that synergy Disney had going in Anaheim, and that there could be an attendance backlash at Disneyland and the Pond from a public that tended to believe the media giant had to have things its way or no way.

- Baseball wanted the deal done, wanted Disney as a partner, because of its economic and marketing resources and because it was already a partner in the national TV contract through ownership of ESPN, the cable sports network. Some in baseball also had reservations about Ueberroth as a fallback possibility for the Autrys if the Disney deal collapsed. There was a feeling that he might not get ownership approval because of his role in the costly collusion concept while commissioner.

Ultimately, Budig and his chief trouble shooter, league attorney Bill Schweitzer, played a significant role in getting Disney and the city back to the bargaining table and keeping them there. So did James Doti, president of Chapman University in the Orange County community of Orange. Doti, an unbridled county booster who calculated that the Angels presence represented an $85 million annual boost to the county, fired off letters to Eisner and Anaheim mayor Tom Daly, expressing disappointment that Disney's plan to buy the team and renovate the stadium was falling apart and that he was available to offer assistance.

Disney and the city initially balked at resuming talks, saying their differences were too large, but on March 26 Ruth and Daly agreed to meet with Doti and Schweitzer in a campus conference room to discuss areas of compromise in the city's position.

They were joined the next day by Tavares and Sandy Litvack, Disney's chief of corporate operations, and in a 4½-hour meeting interrupted by frequent caucuses by each side in Doti's office, they hammered out the essential elements of an agreement approved by 3–2 vote of the city council on May 14.

The key points:

* A $100 million renovation would begin at the end of the 1996 season, with Disney paying 70 percent and absorbing any overruns.
* The California Angels would become the Anaheim Angels.
* Disney would sign a 33-year lease with an option to renew after 20.
* Disney would pay all operating expenses at the stadium but receive all parking and concession revenue and all gate revenue up to 2.6 million, the first in a series of attendance thresholds at which the city shares in that revenue at varying percentages.

In a separate agreement required by major league baseball before owners voted approval, Disney had agreed to the industry policy of sharing all licensing revenue—as opposed to its unique arrangement with the National Hockey League, which allows Disney to keep profits from the sale of Mighty Ducks merchandise at its parks and stores.

The renovation ultimately cost $118 million, with Disney paying $88 million—"not a very good deal by any standards," said Tavares. "We made the best deal we could to keep the team in the market. We had to accept the fact that we were dealing with a small city of limited resources coming off a major bankruptcy.

"There was a lot of skepticism and ill will," he said, "and the politicians had to cross a big bridge to justify giving money to a big corporation. People asked, 'Why doesn't Disney rebuild the stadium on their own?' The answer to that is that the economics in baseball are just horrific right now. We have faith in the sport, but if there was the opportunity to make a lot of money in this, you would expect a private company to come in and pick up an investment like that."

The reality, Tavares said, is that Disney couldn't have bought in at a worse time on the basis of the number of teams making money and the number of those that aren't. The Autrys, he said, suffered legitimate losses, and so has Disney, but "we're not crying, we knew what we were getting into. As a company, we can sustain those losses, but when you look at small owners like the Autrys and O'Malleys . . . well, in order to put a competitive team on the field it's all about payroll, and you just can't justify it as a smaller owner taking those losses."

"Is there an end game here?" he added. "Is there the potential that this could all turn around and franchise values go through the roof and somehow, some way, this all turns profitable? If people didn't have those hopes, nobody would be investing. The real key is that at some point the owners and players have to realize they are in partnership, and it's a three-way partnership with the fans. If you alienate fans long enough and often enough, you're out of business."

Amid baseball's uncertain economic and labor picture, Disney was hopeful of rebuilding the Angel fan base, increasing the club's television ratings and revenue, and providing a marketing expertise that had long been missing,

A winning team was critical, but so was the renovation that became a work in progress throughout the 1997 season, with cranes dotting the landscape and areas of the stadium closed off to fans. The eventual result was a virtually new facility for the start of the 1998 season, with a rock and fountain display reminiscent of Disneyland's Thunder Mountain in center field, a reopened vista beyond the center field fence and 78 luxury suites selling from $165,000 per year on the dugout level to $55,000 in the outfield corners.

Attendance, which had slumped below two million for four straight seasons, jumped to 2.5 million in 1998, and the Angels hoped to better their 1982 club record of 2.8 million in 1999, a hope born of their $80 million off-season signing of Boston first baseman Mo Vaughn, one of the game's top sluggers.

"It would have been impossible to make it under the old circumstances," Tavares said of the former stadium. "The new stadium gives you a springboard to the higher level. Without that, it would have been very difficult to recreate attention in the team. The key issue for us in turning a profit is getting the season ticket base up to 18,000 or more. The season ticket base is critical in sports and particularly in baseball. The other critical issue for us is seeing our television ratings go up. As the ratings go up, so do the advertising and sponsorship rates. Historically, the ratings for this franchise have not been great."

Those ratings, along with season ticket sales, have tended to fluctuate in response to the team's performance.

A star-crossed history in which the Angels finished at or better than .500 only three times between 1987 and 1997 had left fans wary and skeptical when it came to buying into the promises and sales pitches of spring. Players in turn often complained about the lack of emotion and support from Anaheim crowds, composed frequently of transplanted residents who showed up to cheer for the visiting teams.

Ultimately, the new stadium and new ownership may produce a new environment. The sale of season tickets rose to 15,200 in 1998 and to more than 16,000 in 1999, when the arrival of Mo Vaughn gave impetus to Disney's marketing and merchandise efforts, although a disappointing season restricted attendance to 2.2 million.

"I don't mean to insult anyone," Tavares said, "but the Angels weren't ever marketed very well, and we thought we could come in and have a significant impact reintroducing the team to the Orange County market. The other thing is, while the Angels may have been active in the community, it seemed like nobody knew about it. There was always a lot of mystery surrounding the team and what it was up to. There was never any sustained winning, never a time when you could say that the franchise had gotten over the hump.

"We think we can provide some stability and continuity, but we didn't buy in with visions of grandeur.

"No matter what we say or do, we're still the second baseball team in this market. There's a storied franchise up the freeway, and we're fighting an uphill battle in that regard. Can you ever overcome it? Can the Mets overcome the Yankees? I don't know. We can beat the Dodgers on the field perhaps, but to really change the view of regional society is a difficult task, and the one thing you can't do is conduct your business on the basis of what the other guy is doing. There may have been too much of that here in the past."

If the Angels had been too concerned about competing with the Dodgers, too star conscious of the marquee, too shortsighted in trying to win for the Cowboy, the one aspect never in doubt was Gene Autry's resilience and passion for the game. He simply lacked the same luck he'd had with Rudolph, but the respect with which he was held by the players over the years was illustrated in 1982 when they retired uniform No. 26 in honor of his spiritual role as the 26th player.

Age and economics forced him to yield operating control before reaching the great rodeo that is the World Series, but he maintained a rooting and financial interest in the team until his death, and he handed the reins to Disney knowing that his wife wouldn't be saddled with debt after he died. "Gene was old school all the way," Jackie Autry said. "He was the type man who would always throw his cloak down at the curb."

There wouldn't be that personal touch under the corporate giant that is Disney, but the loss of family ownership was merely part of a changing era in baseball.

What Disney could not change was the high cost of doing business. Between corporate losses and baseball losses, between pressure from stockholders who felt Disney shouldn't be involved in sports and the collapse of plans to open a regional cable network in competition with Fox, the entertainment giant decided by 1999—just three years after taking control from the Autrys—that it would sell both the baseball and hockey teams for the right price—synergy be damned. The Dodgers had sold to Fox for $311 million, and Disney figured to receive more for the Angels and Ducks, although there was no one hammering on Eisner's door as the Angels ended their season and the Ducks began theirs.

Who could blame potential buyers, of course, about being apprehensive regarding the planetary alignment that had contributed to a long history of misfortune, the seeming curse that had long haunted the franchise?

27

STEPHEN KING AND THE LAST OF THE '90S

A history of the Angels is a journey through the occult. Tragic deaths. Bizarre injuries. Shocking slumps. Management moves scripted by Stephen King. A curse that began in the initial season of 1961 continues today.

Disney, that master of make-believe, has fared no better with the demons than Gene Autry, who displayed a Midas touch in every other endeavor. Manager Terry Collins shook his head amid a barrage of injuries in 1999, for example, and said, "You say to yourself, 'What can you change? What are we missing?'"

Chuck Finley had seen enough of it by 1998 that he facetiously thought about hiring a witch doctor to burn sage in the clubhouse except that he didn't want to scare anyone.

More than a decade earlier Buzzie Bavasi had considered bringing in a priest to conduct an Anaheim Stadium exorcism only to have his wife convince him that he would be looked on as crazy.

Finley thinks Bavasi had the right idea.

"You look at the Rams occupying this field also," he said. "Maybe they were the smart ones by leaving. I understand that [some bad luck] goes with the game, but I'd like someone to explain to me why it goes more with our game."

There would be no relief in 1995, when the Angels had one final chance to get Autry to the World Series only to blow an 11-

game division lead and evoke memories of the frustrating failures in the playoffs of 1982 and 1986, as well as the September stretch of 1985, when the Angels lost a lead and game in Cleveland that haunts Gene Mauch as much as any he ever managed.

There would be no relief during Disney's first three years of ownership, and certainly not in the early months of 1999, Disney's fourth, when three of the Angels' most prominent players, Tim Salmon, Jim Edmonds and Gary DiSarcina, were lost for extended periods with injuries and another, Mo Vaughn, a six-year, $80 million investment as a free agent, the biggest signing in club history, fell down the dugout steps chasing a pop fly in the first inning of his first game, sprained an ankle and was promptly put on the disabled list and slowed for the entire year.

If that wasn't characteristic of a fractured season—and traumatic history perhaps—there was the June call-up of promising young outfielder Mike Colangelo to help fill the injury void only to have Colangelo suffer a concussion and torn thumb ligament when he collided with a teammate chasing a fly ball in just the seventh inning of his first game and he, too, joined the disabled list.

"I'm just trying to figure out when the joke is going to be over," said Finley, who wasn't laughing. "Like this kid is brought up from the minors, gets off to a good start, and someone taps him on the shoulder and says, 'Wait a minute, buddy.' You've got to look at it and say, 'Damn, when is it going to stop?' "

The Angels thought they had it licked in 1995. They led the division by 11 games on August 9, but then lost 29 of their last 43 games (including a pair of nine-game losing streaks) and joined the 1978 Boston Red Sox, the 1969 Chicago Cubs, the 1964 Philadelphia Phillies and 1951 Brooklyn Dodgers—all teams that had lost huge leads—in baseball infamy.

The Seattle Mariners, virtually conceding the division title in early August and figuring that their only playoff chance would be as the wild card in the first year of that expanded format, took advantage of the Angels' collapse to come from far back and force a one-game playoff for the division crown.

The Angels had gamely won their last five games to maintain a pulse, but they were no match for Randy Johnson in the Kingdome playoff. Johnson struck out 12 and allowed only three hits in a 9–1 victory that sent the Mariners into the playoffs and burdened the Angels with the frustration of another long winter.

They had improved from 47–68 to 78–67, but their legacy was researched by the Elias Sports Bureau and reported as the following: When the Angels went from 10½ games ahead on August 16 to a first-place tie with the Mariners on September 20, it was the quickest disappearance of a lead that large in the 20th century.

"It's a very sickening feeling, and you never get over it," Angel third base coach Rick Burleson, the shortstop on the 1978 Red Sox team that blew a 14-game lead and lost a one-game division playoff to the New York Yankees, said. "You live with it for the rest of your life, and you're always reminded of it when it happens again."

Club president Richard Brown compared it to life and death, saying that if 1986 was comparable to a sudden heart attack, referring to Dave Henderson's shocking homer off Donnie Moore in the playoff with Boston, then the long, painful collapse of 1995 "was an agonizing and helpless feeling, like watching a close friend die."

In Marcel Lachemann's first full season as manager, Bill Bavasi had made a key move in early April, sending outfielder Chad Curtis to the Detroit Tigers for versatile veteran Tony Phillips, an aggressive and emotional player who energized the lineup and, at times, the clubhouse.

On the surface, the Angels appeared to be sacrificing another young and talented player out of their system—Curtis was 26 and Phillips 36—but Curtis was also a 45th-round draft choice who advanced to a major league starting nine doing things his way, thinking that at 5-feet-10 and 175 pounds he was capable of batting in the power positions in the lineup and swinging for the fences. The Angels felt his size and speed fit the leadoff mold, but his stubborn refusal to change his style and accept that role brought him in conflict with batting instructor Rod Carew and others, ultimately leading to the trade for Phillips, a proven leadoff man who would give the Angels unexpected power from that position.

Phillips hit a career-high 27 homers in 1995, one of five Angels to hit 20 or more, including Tim Salmon, who hit .330 with 34 homers and 105 runs batted in; Jim Edmonds, who had never hit more than 14 homers at any level but hit 33 and drove in 107 runs; and J. T. Snow, who hit a career-high 24.

Outfielder Garret Anderson, a fourth-round draft choice in 1990, added to the growing farm harvest when he came out of the system to hit 16 homers, bat .321 and be named by *The Sporting News* as rookie of the year. Troy Percival, a sixth-round selection in the same draft and a hard-nosed former catcher who was converted to relief pitching because of the lightning in his arm, began to display it in 1995, appearing in 62 games as a setup man for the veteran closer Lee Smith, who saved 37 games after being signed as a free agent.

With all of that, starting pitching remained an exasperating adventure. Mark Langston was 15–7 and Chuck Finley 15–12, but no other pitcher won more than seven games as the Angels continued to display what Buck Rodgers had accurately termed a recycled rotation. That bit of honesty, of course, contributed to Rodgers' losing his job, but the Angels were reminded of the validity during the second-half collapse of 1995, when they searched in vain for the type of pitching consistency that might halt the slide.

Bavasi recognized the problem and attempted to address it before the July 31 trade deadline. There were several veteran pitchers available in trade, but the Angels' reacquisition of Jim Abbott was in many ways the desperate move of a desperate man who had been shut out in attempts to trade for his preferred choices—David Cone, who went from Toronto to the New York Yankees; Ken Hill, who went from St. Louis to Cleveland; and Andy Benes, who went from St. Louis to Seattle.

Cone, Hill and Benes are all right-handed. The Angels didn't need another left-hander to go with the left-handed Finley, Langston and farm product Brian Anderson, as Richard Brown said, but at that point Bavasi needed another arm, period; was being lobbied internally by sentimental members of his staff—assistant Tim Mead and scouting director Bob Fontaine Jr., among them—to reacquire the popular Abbott; and ultimately was over a barrel—forced to overpay for a needed pitcher, any pitcher at that point.

"Abbott was not the No. 1 choice, and I don't say that now because he ultimately failed here," Bavasi said. "I have nothing but respect, admiration and fond feelings for Jim, but I went down to the last day on Cone and Hill and was willing to guarantee a lot more for either pitcher [than the Blue Jays and Cardinals wound up receiving]. I was willing to trade Todd Greene and George Arias for Cone, and both were hot prospects at the time. If Cone had come here for those two guys and failed, I would have been run out of town. I was shocked and angry when I saw what the Blue Jays got for him."

He referred to three young pitchers who failed to make a dent in Toronto. Greene, a catcher, and Arias, a third baseman, would both reach the major leagues. Bavasi, rejected elsewhere, ultimately sent four prospects to the Chicago White Sox for Abbott on July 27: outfielder McKay Christensen, who had been the team's 1994 first-round draft choice even though it was known he would not begin his professional career until he went on a two-year Mormon mission, and pitching prospects Bill Simas, John Snyder and Andrew Lorraine. Both Snyder and Simas developed into valued members of the Chicago pitching staff, and Christensen opened the 1999 season as the starting center fielder.

Abbott, who had been traded to the Yankees by Whitey Herzog in a contract disagreement after the 1992 season, pitched a no-hitter against Cleveland in 1993 and was 20–22 in his two seasons with New York. However, he incurred the wrath of Yankee fans by failing to win any of his last seven starts at home in 1994 and was not offered a 1995 contract, having paid a financial price for rejecting the Angels' four-year, $16 million offer after the 1992 season. He moved to the White Sox as a free agent and was 6–4 with a 3.36 earned run average when reacquired by the Angels—excited to be reunited with Lachemann, the pitching coach during his first stint in Anaheim.

"He taught me how to pitch," Abbott said. "He was an incredible pitching coach, and he's done an amazing job as manager. I can't say enough about him."

Abbott would go 5–4 in 13 games with the Angels over the second half—4–1 on the road and a mysterious 0–3 at home—and snap both of the nine-game losing streaks, but there was nothing he could do to heal the torn thumb ligament that shortstop Gary

DiSarcina suffered on August 3, attempting to break up a double play. DiSarcina had made the American League All-Star team for the first time and was batting .317 with 26 doubles and 41 RBI out of the No. 9 spot in the batting order when he was injured. It was a crushing loss, another victory for the curse.

DiSarcina was considered the team's "heart and soul," as J. T. Snow put it. Bavasi considered a trade imperative but wasn't able to pull it off, rejected by Kansas City when he offered Greene and Arias for shortstop Greg Gagne, whom the Royals were going to lose as a free agent at the end of the season anyway.

"I thought we could win and everyone in the organization thought we could win and that DiSarcina was a devastating blow," Bavasi said in reflection. "My thought was, 'Okay, you can sit on your thumbs and have Todd Greene and George Arias in the future and lose this year if DiSarcina is that critical, or you can make the right deal.' We saw Gagne as a good match. He was going to be a free agent. The world would assume I was the guy who was nuts for making the deal, but I said, 'Screw it, we have a chance to win. We need a shortstop.' I called and made the offer, assuming I'd be off the phone in a minute, having made the trade. I couldn't believe it when they turned it down."

Lachemann was left to try a mishmash of middle-infield combinations for seven weeks, but none clicked. Four shortstops combined to hit .210. A frustrated DiSarcina watched from the sidelines and said, "If this team can't survive the loss of a No. 9 hitter, maybe we're not as good as we thought we were."

The pressure mounted on a young team and inexperienced manager. Both the hitting and pitching collapsed. Finley was winless between August 24 and September 27. The catalytic but weary Phillips batted .198 in August and September. An Angel offense that averaged 6.2 runs per game through August 15 averaged only 3.9 runs over the remainder of the season. The DiSarcina injury was deemed a turning point, another illustration of the Angels' haunted history, but Phillips thought it more a matter of inexperience. Bavasi agreed.

"If Gary doesn't get hurt we win that thing," he said, "but I don't view any one injury as fatal. You've got to be able to overcome those things if you make the right moves, if the manager motivates his club in the right way, if the pitchers and hitters step up. I think the effort was there, but we blew it in a lot of ways over the second half, and that hurt."

The Angels had revived hopes by winning their final five games to force the playoff in the Kingdome, but the offense was no match for the dominant Johnson, whose adrenaline was stoked by the non-stop roars of a crowd of 52,536. Mark Langston tried to keep pace and was losing only 1–0 in the seventh inning when, with two outs and the bases loaded, Luis Sojo, a name out of the dark shadows of the Angels' past, delivered the crushing hit. Sojo, who had been acquired by the Angels in the devastating trade that sent Devon White to Toronto and who was ultimately traded back to the Blue Jays in the devastating trade in which the Angels acquired the damaged Kelly Gruber, cued a broken-bat grounder up the first base line that somehow eluded J. T. Snow and rolled into the right field corner. By the time the ball was retrieved and the Angels had stopped mishandling it, Sojo and the three runners ahead of him had all scored, turning a close game into a rout, and Langston lay flat on his back on the plate, staring up at the Kingdome roof, his hands folded on his chest, providing an apt metaphor for a season in which an 11-game lead was not enough.

Langston shook his head in the immediate aftermath and said, "It was hard to watch them celebrate when that should have been us. But they did it in the game that counted, and we didn't. We had a huge lead and let it slip through our fingers. It should never have happened."

In August, as it was beginning to get away, Marcel Lachemann had said that if the Angels couldn't hold a lead of that size, "they ought to get rid of the manager." The Angels didn't, but Lachemann took it into his own hands during a 1996 free fall in which the Angels picked up where they had left off in 1995. It was so bad in 1996 that by midsummer Chuck Finley said, "One of these days the cops are gonna come and arrest this team for loitering."

The Angels went from 78–67 and a tie for the division title to 70–91 and a fourth-place finish, 19½ games out of the division lead. It was the season that Disney took control, the payroll falling from

$34.7 million in the Autrys' final season of 1995 to $25.1 million in Disney's first. The restraints—imposed by both Autry and Disney as their sale agreement remained in limbo while Disney worked out an agreement with the city on stadium renovation—affected preseason plans.

Three key players—Phillips, Abbott and Finley—were eligible for free agency, and the budget allowed for the signing of only two. Said former club president Richard Brown: "Disney has proven to be a great owner, but initially they came in very naive. They came in feeling that with their business acumen they could compete with a lesser payroll, which wasn't realistic. Clubs were going to the playoffs with payrolls twice that of the Angels."

With a priority on pitching, the Angels opted to re-sign Finley to a four-year, $18 million contract and Abbott to a three-year, $7.8 million contract that would come back to haunt the club. There was nothing left for Phillips, who signed with the White Sox as a free agent.

"That wasn't what we wanted or desired," said Tim Mead, then assistant general manager, "but we didn't have a choice. We had to put an emphasis on pitching, and didn't have the resources to sign Phillips as well. There was no way to predict Abbott would have the problems that he did, or we might have gone another route."

The Angels weren't paralyzed by the uncertain sale situation, but many of the departments were left in limbo—the staff unsure how many would retain jobs after Disney took over. Richard Brown, who was guaranteed a severance package equivalent to three years of salary, said of the tenuous situation, "Disney has been fair with me, but for other employees, the circumstances around [the sale] have been very difficult. If this were to go to the Supreme Court, it would be ruled cruel and unusual punishment."

Ultimately, Tony Tavares, who supervised the Ducks as president of Anaheim Sports Incorporated, replaced Brown as the Angels' president in mid-May. Several departments were merged with those of the Ducks, and about 23 members of the Angels' staff, mostly in marketing, ticketing, accounting and sales, left with Brown, closing the doors on the Autry era and concluding another tumultuous period of frequent changes—on and off the field.

Asked by the Autrys to become president in November 1990, Brown supervised a five-year span in which Mike Port, Dan O'Brien, Whitey Herzog and Bill Bavasi all served as general managers (Herzog and O'Brien simultaneously at one point) and Doug Rader, Buck Rodgers and Marcel Lachemann all served as field managers. There were the lamentable acquisitions of Gary Gaetti, Kelly Gruber, Dave Parker, Joe Magrane, Von Hayes and Junior Felix among others, and the sad departures of Wally Joyner, Devon White, Dante Bichette and Jim Abbott among others. Brown said he was frustrated to have to leave a job unfinished. However, he also took pride in a renewed and basically sustained commitment to the farm system. The 1995 team that came so close featured homegrown products at second base, shortstop, catcher and all three outfield positions.

"We had some blips along the way when that old sense of impatience and the urgency to win for Gene crept in," Brown said, "but the only sensible way to build a team and develop loyalty among the fans is through the farm system, and overall I think we did good job of staying with that concept. Of course, budget plays a part in that, and we were more or less forced to go that way."

It wasn't long before Disney might have been wondering what it had bought into.

Twenty-one Angels went on the disabled list in 1996, and 29 pitchers saw service, yielding 943 runs, the most in club history. Michelle Carew, the 18-year-old daughter of batting coach Rod Carew, died in April after a long battle with leukemia, setting a sad tone. Tim Salmon and Chili Davis combined for 58 homers and 193 RBI, but Jim Edmonds missed 46 games with injuries, limiting his RBI total to 66. Troy Percival replaced Lee Smith as the closer and saved 36 games, but Mark Langston was on the disabled list three times with a knee injury, and Jim Abbott lost it completely, losing 18 of 20 decisions and being sent to the minors at one point.

In August, Bavasi gave up on Damion Easley, trading the young infielder to Detroit for journeyman pitcher Greg Gohr—one of the worst trades in Angel history, which puts it in crowded company. It was another case of impatience and frustration with a young player who was frequently hurt and had not been able to make desired adjustments, Bavasi said, and instead of "continuing to try and ram it down his throat, we decided to take a chance. We were hurting for arms and felt Gohr was still a prospect with a major league arm."

Gohr appeared in 15 games for the Angels over the remainder of the season with a 7.50 ERA and never appeared in another. Easley, freed of the pressure and expectations, perhaps, that comes with playing in what was basically his hometown, developed into an All-Star second baseman with the Tigers.

"Sometimes you make a decision and it doesn't pay off," Bavasi said. "That's life. I wish Damion Easley was still playing with us, but the frustration level in the organization had reached a point where we had to move him and get something for him. I only regret it from the sense that I think we failed him."

In a season of frustration, the manager ultimately decided he couldn't live with it and resigned on August 6. Lachemann hadn't wanted to manage to start with, and simply couldn't continue. He blamed himself for every loss, every shortcoming of a team left with gaping holes by the protracted negotiations between the Angels and Disney and Disney and the city, affecting payroll and preseason preparations.

Bavasi, who had initially talked a hesitant Lachemann into taking the job, was unable to talk him out of giving it up.

"It was tearing me up," Lachemann said of the poor play. "I don't want to be a martyr, but I believe in responsibility. I wasn't comfortable taking my paycheck. When you have the authority, you have to have the responsibility. I was at the point where I couldn't do anything about the frustrations permeating my whole life."

Said Bavasi: "I mistakenly thought he was the right guy at the right time. I still think Lach has the tools to be a great manager, but he hated it, and I should have done a better job of seeing that and recognizing it when I first called him. If I had thought that I might be really serious about this guy managing a team for me someday, I should have been talking to him about it years before. Instead I made my own assumptions when I called him and didn't really hear what he was telling me."

Coming so close in 1995 might have eased some of Lachemann's doubts about his desire to manage and given the Angels an inflated sense of where they were. The 1996 season stripped the pretense. If Finley thought it was a team that should have been arrested for loitering, Tavares agreed. At one point he compared an unspecified number of players to spoiled children who have to run home to their mommies in Newport Beach.

"The comment was inappropriate in the sense that I didn't mean to say that people from Newport Beach aren't hardworking or don't care," Tavares said. "I was trying to make a point that we had some players acting like spoiled children, and that's what I should have said rather than referring to any geographical area.

"It was sad that Lach took a bullet for the lack of performance by the entire organization. I was never disappointed with Marcel's effort, but I was terribly disappointed with the collective effort of the players. I heard a lot of 'I' and 'me' stuff. I saw a lot of complacency. Everybody talked about how much we missed Tony Phillips, but nobody buckled their belt and took on those leadership responsibilities, although they were certainly being compensated well enough. The concern was that you can have the greatest manager and greatest coaches in the world, but if the players aren't holding each other accountable, you'll never achieve success."

History had found the Angels at this point before, and here they were again.

Lachemann had taken himself out. Management fired longtime first base coach Bobby Knoop, third base coach Rick Burleson and pitching coach Chuck Hernandez, retaining only Carew, bench coach Joe Maddon and bullpen coordinator Mick Billmeyer.

There were 51 games left in a season that was basically over for the Angels, but someone was needed to fill the manager's responsibilities. Bavasi found a reluctant taker in John McNamara, who had managed the team in 1983 and 1984, had spent the last five years as a roving catching instructor in the club's farm system and had no desire to retain the job beyond the end of the season.

He didn't make it that far. McNamara was hospitalized in New York on August 20 with a life-threatening blood clot in his right leg. He survived the scare, but Joe Maddon became the interim manager for the interim manager. The Angels finished 18–32 under

McNamara and Maddon, suggesting that Lachemann shouldn't have been blaming himself.

The final out of the lamentable 1996 season was barely in the books when renovation of the stadium began, a process that would span the 1997 season—a work in progress, much as the team on the field was. As part of the renovation, Anaheim Stadium became Edison International Field of Anaheim in November 1997 when the naming rights were sold to the power and utility giant Edison International for 20 years at $1.4 million a year. Amid the stunning salary and payroll escalation of the 90s, the sale of stadium naming rights became a common practice in baseball as clubs sought to generate revenue whenever and wherever they could.

For Disney, determined, as Tavares put it, to always operate with a measure of economic prudence, baseball was a learning process, as hockey had been, and not always easy. The renovated stadium, Tavares said, would provide a springboard to a higher economic level, but Disney, in both its hockey and baseball operations, would be castigated at times by the perception that it had taken a cheap route—although the Angel payroll went from $25.1 million in 1996 to $46.8 million in 1997, Disney's first full year of ownership, and $54.1 million in 1998, according to figures compiled by the owners' Player Relations Council. The $54.1 figure was the ninth highest among the 30 clubs.

"It's difficult for me to understand how somebody can call you cheap when we put the lion's share of $118 million into the stadium and run the kind of payroll we're running," Tavares said. "We have a $30-million-plus payroll with the Ducks, and we're in the mid-$50 million with the Angels. Neither are the highest, but neither can be called cheap.

"The interesting part of all this is that for going out and spending all that money, you get a pat on the back, maybe and maybe not, and maybe you still get called cheap and you still lose a ton of money.

"Stan Kasten [president of the Atlanta Braves] was the first person to say to me, 'Tony, you've got to figure this out real quick. You are in the worst situation possible. You're in the middle of the pack with payroll and performance, and that's where you're going to lose the most money with baseball's current economic situation.' The safest place to be, Stan explained, is the bottom of the ladder, like Pittsburgh or one of those other teams that are paring back, and through the revenue-sharing component that you receive, if you draw a million or a million one, you can get by with your hide still on. Or the other option is to be at the top end, where you go out and spend big and buy yourself a championship or at least remain competitive all the time. Hopefully then you're drawing three million people and drawing bigger TV ratings. That's certainly where we're headed as a franchise. The problem is, there's no guarantee [of success] no matter how much you spend."

The baseball landscape is littered with the carcasses of teams trying to buy a pennant. The Angels have maintained a measure of payroll control through a policy initiated by the Cleveland Indians and adopted by the Angels as they attempted to retain and build on the best players from their farm system in the early 90s.

The policy is based on the premise of providing clubs with a degree of cost control by buying young players out of their early years of arbitration and free agent eligibility through multiyear contracts that may be below what they would receive in arbitration and free agency but still offer early security.

"It's like one agent told his player, 'Don't turn down your first fortune,' " said Bavasi, who turned the policy into an art form by signing virtually all of the Angels' best young players to multiyear contracts at below market value.

"He does the best job on contracts of anybody in baseball," renowned agent Scott Boras said, meaning that prior to his resignation at the end of the 1999 season, Bavasi did the best job of saving his club money. "Some of them are just unbelievable. There must be something strange in the ventilation system when you talk to him."

Most of the talking is done to attorney Mark Rosenthal, who is on the staff of the Los Angeles firm of Jeffer, Mangels, Butler & Marmaro and who was hired in the early 90s to handle contract negotiations on the recommendation of Whitey Herzog, one of his last acts before resigning as general manager.

Herzog had been soured by his negotiations with Wally Joyner and Jim Abbott, and believed that salaries and contract complexities had reached a point that outside representation was mandatory, removing club officials from the often acrimonious process. It might have been Herzog's most significant contribution during his brief and tumultuous tenure as general manager. Rosenthal has been credited by agents and players with an even-handed approach that has contributed to the club's contract success.

"We assume a risk by signing a young player to a multiyear contract, but we get a [salary] discount in return and the player gets early security," Tavares said, adding that the club's $54.1 million payroll of 1998 would have been "well into the sixties if we hadn't been doing this."

Financial and contract issues were again prevalent during the winter between the 1996 and 1997 seasons, but the most important decision involved the hiring of a new manager to succeed the low-key Lachemann. This time, Bavasi said in reflection, "we didn't have the right to experiment. We wanted someone with major league experience." More than that, someone with intensity, said Tavares, "a no-nonsense kind of guy, someone who would hold himself and his players accountable. Be a taskmaster. I'm not saying this was a country club, but we wanted someone who would make it uncomfortable when things weren't going well."

The Angels had more than 20 names on their original list and ultimately offered an $8 million package, including Disney stock options, to Jim Leyland, considered by many to be the top manager in baseball. Leyland was preparing to leave Pittsburgh. His Pirates had dominated the National League East during the early 90s, but the championship roster was decimated by trade and free agent defection as the small-market management was unable—or unwilling—to keep pace with baseball's soaring economics.

Leyland wanted another chance to win and had an open invitation that winter to become manager of the Florida Marlins. He also saw himself as a blue-collar personality with roots in the East and Midwest, and he had no desire to set up residency amid the glamour, glitz and laid-back lifestyle of Orange County. His rejection of the Angels in favor of the Marlins, whom he would lead to a World Series title in 1997 before that team was also decimated in a payroll purge that prompted Leyland to become manager of the Colorado Rockies in 1999, led the Angels to hire Terry Collins as Lachemann's successor, offering a two-year contract with an option for a third year.

Collins is a 5-foot-8, 160-pound bundle of energy who guided the Houston Astros to three straight second-place finishes in the National League Central and a record of 224–197 before being fired after the 1996 season, partly because of complaints from several players over his relentless intensity and the verbal tirades he had directed at them in the dugout and clubhouse.

A month after his firing, with Tavares having received a positive recommendation on Collins from Houston owner Drayton McLane Jr., who told Tavares it was simply time for the Astros to try a different approach, the Angels also considered it time to try a different approach and hired Collins, who had spent 10 years as a minor league infielder, never reaching the majors while never giving less than 100 percent.

"Terry is the best fit for this team right now," Bavasi said. "Given a choice between casual and intense, we chose intense. That was the big difference between Terry and the other candidates. That, and the fact that he has managerial experience at the major league level."

Collins said he had spent too much time in Houston trying to be what the owner and general manager and players wanted, worrying about his job, but that wouldn't happen in Anaheim. He would be himself, doing what he felt was necessary as manager to create an aggressive style on the field.

"It's impossible to have all the players like you," he said. "They have different personalities that may conflict with mine. All I'm ever asking for is effort. When fans leave the ballpark, I want them to say, 'That team plays hard.' "

Much of what Collins was, ironically, stemmed from his association with Leyland, the Angels' first choice that winter. He had spent 11 years as a minor league manager in the Los Angeles and Pittsburgh organizations, joining Leyland's coaching staff in 1992 and 1993.

"For those who have accused me of being too intense, they ought to hang around Jim Leyland for a while," Collins said. "He's about as intense as they come. He deals with players on a personal level. He's honest and upfront. There are no secrets with Jim, and it's the same with me. One thing I may be guilty of is being too honest."

Questions about Collins' style and demeanor, familiar issues raised by Houston players about his negativity in the dugout and overall communication skills, resurfaced in 1999 when he initially survived what resembled a mini-mutiny among a small group of his players to receive a contract extension from the Angels only to eventually resign amid the clubhouse bickering and combustion.

Preparing for 1997, however, the hiring of Collins was only one of several transactions. Among the others:

- Chili Davis, who had averaged 25 homers and 94 RBI since returning to the Angels as the designated hitter four years before, was traded to Kansas City for pitcher Mark Gubicza in another bust for Bavasi. The deal was designed to save the club about $2 million in salary, which could be applied to other players, and to bolster the Angel pitching staff, but Gubicza resembled too many other veteran pitchers acquired by the Angels past their prime.

  He was 34, had missed almost two of the previous six years with injuries, and would pitch only two games for the Angels before requiring career-ending arm surgery. Similarly, the Angels planned to replace Davis' potent bat in the DH role with a player closer to Social Security than his illustrious prime. Eddie Murray, one of only 22 players to collect 3,000 hits, was signed as an economical alternative to Davis, but Murray was 39 and would hit .219 in 46 games before drawing his release. The Angels employed 16 players in the DH role that year, a futile attempt to replace Davis, who hit 30 homers and drove in 90 runs for the Royals and helped the Yankees win World Series titles in 1998 and 1999.

  "That was an experiment based on economics, and it obviously backfired," Tavares said of the decision to trade Davis.

- J. T. Snow, who had been given a three-year, $6 million contract before the 1996 season, was traded to the San Francisco Giants in November for pitcher Allen Watson, who would go 12–12 with the

Angels in 1997, become a clubhouse malcontent and was released after a 6–7 campaign in 1998. Snow had been a 17 homer, 67 RBI disappointment in 1996 after slugging 14 homers with 102 RBI in 1995, but the perception was that Tavares had ordered him to be traded, that Snow was the player he alluded to when he made the comment about some Angel players resembling spoiled children from Newport Beach. The Angels even included $750,000 in the deal that sent the first baseman to San Francisco.

"J.T. wasn't one of my favorite players, but did I dislike him more than anyone else on the team?" Tavares said. "No. We were looking at the time for pitching assets, and the player who had the most value that we were prepared to part with was J.T. In hindsight, it didn't turn out too great for us. Watson never fulfilled his potential while J.T. has put up reasonable numbers in San Francisco. However, we knew that Darin Erstad [the club's No. 1 draft choice in 1995 would hit .299 with 17 homers in his first full season in 1997] could play first base as well as the outfield, and he brings a lot to the club in speed and a hard-nosed attitude that Snow didn't."

- Attempting to create that aggressive and hard-edged club that Collins desired, the Angels signed third baseman Dave Hollins as a free agent and traded two minor leaguers to the Yankees for versatile Jim Leyritz, who two months earlier had hit a dramatic three-run homer off Atlanta closer Mark Wohlers in the eighth inning of Game 4 of the World Series, turning the game and Series in the Yankees' favor. Leyritz would stay for only a half season before being used in a July trade that brought needed pitching help from Texas in the form of Ken Hill. Hollins provided some anticipated fire with 16 homers, 85 RBI and a take-the-extra-base mentality.

- On the eve of the season, the once magical Angel career of Jim Abbott, 2–18 in 1996 and ineffective in spring training, ended ingloriously when the team released the struggling pitcher, absorbing the $5.6 million that remained on the three-year, $7.8 million contract Abbott received prior to the 1996 season. Abbott had been given the choice of returning to the Triple A team at Vancouver or being released. He spent a week at his Newport Beach home with his wife and 3½-month-old daughter wrestling with the choice before deciding he didn't want the uncertain existence of a minor leaguer.

Also, because of his popularity and the attention he had received in his struggle to regain any measure of effective form, Abbott didn't want to steal the focus from what the Angels were attempting to do at the major league level.

"I feel that if I'm not a contributing member of the Angels at that level, then I'm a distraction to the organization and they need to move away from that," Abbott said. "I don't want to be a martyr or anything, but I felt my presence was a disturbance to both sides."

Abbott would eventually attempt to reestablish his career—returning to the major leagues with the Chicago White Sox late in 1998 and as a regular starter with the Milwaukee Brewers in 1999—but his struggle with the Angels remained a mystery considering that he would throw effectively in the bullpen but was unable to bring the same velocity into the game.

"I don't like to release a guy with two years left on his contract, especially a guy like Abbott, who we all admired, but it had to be done," Bavasi said. "It was the best thing for the organization. The contract can be criticized, but Jim had stopped both of the nine-game losing streaks [after rejoining the club in 1995] and his ERA was among the top 10 in the league that year. We needed pitching and didn't figure to do better in the market."

The Angels would play hard under their new manager and win 84 games in 1997, their most since 1989. They would finish second in the West with an 84–72 record, only six games behind the champion Mariners. They would be in first place as late as August 19, but it was another frustrating season of what might have been—the curse revisited.

Tim Salmon hit 33 homers and drove in 129 runs, becoming the first Angel to hit 30 or more homers in each of his first four seasons. Garret Anderson batted .302, drove in 92 runs and had 189 hits, a club record for left-handed hitters. Darin Erstad, Jim Edmonds and Dave Hollins made contributions on offense, but the Angels missed Chili Davis, lacked depth in a pitching rotation unable to replace Abbott until Hill arrived in August and had no remedy again for the familiar demons.

- Closer Troy Percival was lost for five weeks in April and May with a shoulder problem.
- Tony Phillips, the versatile and catalytic leadoff hitter of 1996 who was reacquired through a four-player trade with the White Sox in May, was arrested for felony possession of cocaine in an Anaheim motel room on August 10, setting off a distracting chain of events in which Disney attempted to suspend Phillips only to be thwarted by baseball's drug policy, which prompted Disney chairman Michael Eisner to call for changes in the policy.
- Chuck Finley, who had won 10 straight decisions after initially opening the season on the disabled list with a fractured orbital bone under his right eye, which was suffered in a freak accident during batting practice in spring training, broke his left wrist when he slipped while backing up the plate on August 19 and was lost for the season.
- The next night, catcher Todd Greene, a 12th-round draft choice in 1993 who was batting .290 as the latest addition to the list of impressive farm products joining the Angels, broke his right wrist blocking a ball in the dirt and was also lost for the season.

"We had just started to come out of the Tony Phillips hole, he was back with the team and the media was quieting down, when Chuck and Todd were hurt, and that wiped us out," Bavasi said. "The Phillips incident didn't help, but I don't know if there was any way to overcome the loss of Chuck and Todd."

From Disney's perspective, with a team as thin and fragile as the Angels, the Phillips arrest "had a terrible impact," Tavares said. Disney attempted to suspend Phillips, requesting that he go on the 15-day disabled list and enter an in-patient counseling program. Phillips refused, and the players union filed a grievance against the Angels, citing a drug policy in baseball which prohibits disciplining of first-time offenders. Even the owners' executive council came down on the club, instructing its Player Relations Committee to throw arbitration support behind the union, an unprecedented act that turned the arbitration hearing into what Tavares called a "kangaroo court" in which Disney was forced to reinstate Phillips.

"One of the adjustments we've had to make as a corporation is to recognize that we're merely a small piece of a larger partnership in baseball and that we've entered into a business that has handed over just about every conceivable management right that is endemic to a business operating correctly to the players union," Tavares said. "It's preposterous to think that we have to go to the union—as a club and league—to ask permission on as many business decisions as we do. That's not a shot at the union. It's just that over a period of time, way, way too much control has been given up to organized labor."

Said Eisner, in a *Los Angeles Times* interview:

"I'm not saying we wanted to predetermine Tony Phillips's punishment. All we were trying to do was act quickly and clearly to take him off the field for an appropriate amount of time and get him the help he needed, but that was impossible.

"I'm disappointed that baseball doesn't have the kind of discipline that I think would be a good idea for an industry presenting itself as a role model for kids. We certainly didn't want to over-penalize Tony Phillips or make him the scapegoat for baseball's inefficiency, and this wasn't about Disney holding to a higher standard.

"Everybody should hold to a higher standard. Unfortunately, America's pastime is saying that drugs are more important than baseball. It's inappropriate. Every young player should know that if he gets in trouble with drugs, he can't go on the field. He can come back, but there has to be a discipline. No one wants to win more than I do, but it can't only be about winning. There has to be a dignity and spirit to it."

Phillips, according to police, was arrested with $30 of rock cocaine and a pipe to smoke it. He pleaded guilty to one count of felony drug possession, completed 32 hours of a court-mandated anti-drug program, stayed clean for a year, and had the violation expunged from his record.

He missed only 10 games during the 1997 legal battle between Disney and baseball, but he wasn't invited back for 1998.

"Tony played hard every second he was here," Bavasi said. "He was an absolute joy, but he had some issues that he had to deal with, and it wouldn't have done any good to bring him back to the same environment."

Phillips, who is tested three times a week under baseball's drug program, returned to the game with Toronto in June 1998, was acquired by the New York Mets for the stretch drive that year, and became a veteran leader on a rebuilding Oakland team in 1999.

He remains indebted, he said, for the support of Bavasi and Tim Mead during his 1997 problems but accused Disney and Eisner of "grandstanding" in the attempt to suspend him and "not living in reality."

"I did something very, very stupid and was dragged through the dirt," he said. "I exposed my family to pain they didn't deserve. I put my teammates in a situation they didn't deserve. I spent a night in jail. I was out of baseball for nine months. Was I penalized? You're damn right."

It is impossible to say if the Angels could have survived the injuries to Finley and Greene if the Phillips arrest hadn't become a distraction on top of it. There was one other development that made headlines in 1997—a *non*-move that dominated talk shows and columns in midseason after it became apparent that Oakland was prepared to trade first baseman Mark McGwire, who would be eligible for free agency at the end of the year. McGwire talked openly about his desire to play in Anaheim so that he could spend more time with his son, Matt, who lived with his former wife and her husband in Orange County.

People familiar with the talks between the Angels and A's insist that the A's had accepted an offer of Jim Edmonds, Dave Hollins and either of two young pitchers, Jason Dickson or Jarrod Washburn, for McGwire and third baseman Scott Brosius only to have Disney's corporate offices reject it out of concern that the club would be unable to sign or afford McGwire at the end of the year.

Tavares called that scenario a "total distortion." He said the Angels had serious interest in McGwire but that there was never an agreement on players and that the talks collapsed when the A's refused the Angels' request to talk with McGwire's agent in an effort to reach an agreement on a multiyear contract that would have removed the threat of his possible departure as a free agent at the end of the season.

McGwire had made it clear in every interview that he would

sign with the Angels for less than he could receive elsewhere, but the largest impediment may have been Oakland's reluctance to trade him to a division rival. McGwire was traded to St. Louis in July for a package that did not include a player of Edmonds' stature, fell in love with the city and the team's tradition, signed a multiyear contract at the end of the year, and became baseball's biggest attraction in 1998, when he hit 70 home runs to obliterate the 1961 record of 61 set by Roger Maris.

"Hindsight is 20-20," Bavasi said. "I would have loved to see McGwire hit 70 home runs in an Angel uniform. It would have meant 40 or more homers for us, and it may have meant a pennant. I definitely think there would have been the same frenzy in Anaheim [where the Angels drew 2.5 million to their renovated stadium] that there was in St. Louis [where the Cardinals drew 3.1 million]. I'm also confident that I could have convinced Disney that he was worth $10 million a year, but the bottom line was that we weren't going to make a trade of that magnitude without talking to the agent and receiving contractual assurance that he wasn't going to leave at the end of the year."

As McGwire and Sammy Sosa launched their great home run chase in 1998, the Angels battled their way through another summer of injury and frustration, finishing only three games behind the Texas Rangers with an 85–77 record. They had a two-game lead as late as September 14, but lost in Tampa Bay that night, lost two in a row and their lead in Texas, lost again in Seattle the next night and ultimately were swept by the Rangers in a three-game series in Anaheim as they won only four of their final 13 games after taking that two-game lead.

It was another September swoon by a team that has made it a habit. The Angels were 11–17 in September 1995, 8–17 in 1996, 10–15 in 1997 and 9–15 in 1998, when they set a club record by using the disabled list 23 times. Ken Hill, who was retained with a three-year, $16.05 million contract prior to the season, had elbow surgery in June and won only nine games. Jack McDowell, another in the Angels' long series of reclamation projects, was on the disabled list twice and appeared in only 14 games. Tim Salmon, one of baseball's best right fielders, hit 26 homers and drove in 88 runs but had to spend almost the entire season as the designated hitter because of a heel injury. The Angels, who had gone the cheap and wishful route with Eddie Murray as the DH at the start of the 1997 season, tried it again in 1998 with hefty Cecil Fielder only to release him in June. A pitching staff devoid of Mark Langston, released after an injury-riddled 2–4 performance in 1997 (the high-priced lefty was a modest and inconsistent 78–74 in eight seasons with the Angels), was held together by Troy Percival's 42 saves, but only Chuck Finley (11–9) and Jason Dickson (10–10) reached double figures in wins. The division title might have been lost in midseason when general manager Bill Bavasi failed to improve his pitching at the July 31 trade deadline and apologized for it to his team and fans. The victorious Rangers added pitcher Todd Stottlemyre, shortstop Royce Clayton and third baseman Todd Zeile at the deadline, and all played important roles as the Rangers overtook the Angels down the stretch.

If there was any solace in finishing second despite the injuries, the Angels didn't express it when the season ended. There was significant grumbling and finger pointing, with Gary DiSarcina and Darin Erstad, among others, vocally upset that some teammates didn't seem to be taking losing as hard as they did. No one named names, but much of the dissatisfaction seemed directed at center fielder Jim Edmonds, whose nonchalant demeanor clearly provoked some of his colleagues despite the fact that he had hit 25 homers, driven in 91 runs, tied a club record with 42 doubles, would win a second Gold Glove for fielding excellence, and batted .340 in September, the only Angel to hit with any consistency and authority down the stretch.

It was the third time in four years that the Angels had finished second, and several players also expressed the opinion that it was time for Disney to step up and pay up, acquiring the type of hitter and/or pitcher who could put them over the hump.

"This act has pretty much worn thin—the song is getting a little sour," Finley said, having been part of it since 1987. "I sense patience running out around here. If you get two studs here, one pitcher who is a force and one bat that will give you 30–40 home runs and 120–130 RBIs, we'll be ready to take off then."

Said DiSarcina: "There comes a point in time where finishing second is the same as finishing last. There's a danger here. You hope the team and the organization don't become satisfied with finishing second. You don't want anyone thinking, 'Whoop-de-doo, we finished second! We didn't make the playoffs.' "

At the corporate offices in Burbank, Disney read the comments, heard the pleas of Bavasi and Tavares, and scrapped the contention that no player is worth $10 million a year.

Amid an attractive and expensive free agent market in the winter of 1998–99, they would not get the stud pitcher—Kevin Brown signed with the Dodgers for a record seven years and $105 million and Randy Johnson signed with the Arizona Diamondbacks for four years and $52 million—but they blew out the competition by presenting Boston Red Sox first baseman Mo Vaughn with a six-year, $72 million offer on the first day teams could bid for outside players, along with a seven-page letter letting Vaughn know how much he would mean to the Angels.

One of baseball's most consistent sluggers and a respected clubhouse leader and community activist, Vaughn's relationship with the Red Sox had deteriorated through several years of contract hassles and constant discord. The final, bitter split came on November 11, when Boston attempted to retain him with a five-year, $63 million offer far below market value. Vaughn signed with the Angels on November 25 for six years and $80 million. The average annual value of $13.3 million is among baseball's highest.

It was the first signing of a marquee free agent by the Angels since Mark Langston in 1990, and their most prominent free agent acquisition since Reggie Jackson in 1982.

"What we were missing at the end of 1998 was a guy who was willing to say, 'Okay, get on my back and I'll take care of you, I'll carry you,' " Bavasi said. "Watching [Vaughn] from his rookie season, he took a leadership role in a city where there is always a lot of pressure, where the players are always under a microscope. I liked the way he handled himself, how his teammates fed off him. We want him to take that same leadership role here—on and off the field. That's important to us."

Vaughn sensed that the Angels were attempting to shake

that laid-back image and environment, replacing it with a harder edge.

"If you could read the letter they sent me, you could tell the kind of people they're looking for," Vaughn said. "They want guys who are linebackers in baseball uniforms. That's the kind of attitude they're trying to instill, but all I can do is be myself. There's not a lot of great speeches that have to be made. It's about playing hard every inning of every game. I'm not a rah-rah guy, but I will speak my piece."

Some six months after rejecting an all-out financial pursuit of home run king Mark McGwire, Disney had made Mo Vaughn one of the game's richest players, but Bavasi said it wasn't a situation where Disney suddenly decided to spend some money.

"They've never been afraid to spend the money, as accused," he said. "There's a change in action, but not a change in philosophy. We just haven't seen the players we thought were the right fit for the right type of money. If we had seen a player like Mo Vaughn last year, he would have been signed. That's easy to say, but it's true. Players like this don't come around very often."

No player on the Angels roster in 1998 had made more than $5 million, but the club claimed operating losses of $42 million in the first three years of Disney's ownership, which included larger investments in international scouting and player development.

"Signing Mo was not an accident," Disney chairman Michael Eisner said. "We sat down last summer and talked about a strategy for the Angels. We could either cut back and not be competitive, stay in the middle [payroll and performance-wise], where we weren't competitive but we weren't an embarrassment, or we could be really competitive, step it up and try to put people in seats so we could justify [an investment of $80 million in one player].

"The Angels are the one thing in our series of assets that does not turn a profit and that I don't think has the potential to turn a profit. That's discouraging, but that's okay. The solution has always been to sell the team and make the money on the flip, but that's not what our business is about. The Disney Company doesn't do that.

"For us, we have no alternative. We have to be competitive.

Our own pride demands it, and I don't think our fans in Orange County would accept the Disney Company not being competitive. They don't care if this might not be the greatest financial thing for the Disney Company. They see other things we do doing well, and I kind of agree with that.

"If we're going to be on the field, we're going to be on the field in a successful way, and I think people will look at the Mo Vaughn signing and finally realize we're not going to do short-term things, that we're in for the long haul. We're going to be fiscally responsible, but not cheap."

There was one other potential factor in the Vaughn decision. The purchase of the Dodgers by Rupert Murdoch's Fox Group— a Disney competitor in so many entertainment and media arenas— was viewed as a regional stimulus. Eisner wouldn't say if Vaughn's signing was a direct result of that, but he couldn't resist needling Murdoch's team when asked about it during spring training in 1999, adding that he didn't care if his comments were played straight or tongue in cheek.

"We're in competition with Fox everywhere," he said. "Luckily, their baseball team doesn't compare to our baseball team. So, in that area, we don't have to worry about the competition. It's the quality of players and the quality of how we're going to win. They're the lesser team in the market. They're just going to have to deal with that."

The Angels had historically fretted about the Dodgers' shadow, moving to Anaheim initially because they wanted to establish their own identity. Now they had a player who cast a large shadow of his own, and Vaughn had an immediate impact. The Angels anticipated 85 percent of season ticket holders to renew, but the number jumped to more than 90 percent. Season sales overall increased from 15,804 to 16,029, and the Angels anticipated challenging the 1982 attendance record of 2.8 million if the club stayed in the race. There was also an upsurge in merchandise sales oriented to Vaughn's acquisition. T-shirts inscribed "The Beginning of a New Mo-lennium" sold for $23. A "Little Mo" toddler T-shirt went for $15.

Eisner was so pleased with the early reaction that he saluted

Vaughn in Disney's annual report, citing him even before Mickey Mouse in a letter to shareholders. After paying tribute to the late Gene Autry, the Angels' founding owner, Eisner wrote: "I am sure Gene is somewhere smiling at the Angels' acquisition of Mo Vaughn, a quality star who completely fits into Gene's Cowboy Code, especially Code #6: 'He must help people in distress.' "

Autry would have also recognized but wouldn't have been smiling at the string of misfortunes that quickly jolted the Angels' optimism and contributed to one of the club's most embarrassing seasons in 1999. The Angels finished last in the West with a 70–92 record that left them 25 games behind division champion Texas.

The hoped-for attendance gain didn't materialize as the Angels drew only 2.2 million, a decrease of 265,984. Disney, suddenly disillusioned by the financial losses, now under siege by stockholders unhappy with a significant drop in corporate profits and no longer certain it was committed to the long haul, as Eisner had boasted a few months earlier, floated the news late in the 1999 season that it would be willing to sell both the Angels and the Mighty Ducks in a package, compounding the dispiriting season and the organization's suddenly uncertain future.

The hope generated by the signing of Vaughn had taken an early beating. Shortstop Gary DiSarcina was lost for half the season when he broke his wrist in spring training in that freak encounter with coach George Hendricks' bat. Vaughn sprained an ankle on opening night when he slipped down the dugout steps and was hampered throughout a season in which he still hit 33 homers and drove in 108 runs. Edmonds was lost for more than half the season when he required shoulder surgery in April (teammates complained that he should have had it done at the end of the 1998 season), and Salmon tore wrist ligaments in May and did not return until after the All-Star break.

The decimated offense contributed to an overwhelming sense of frustration and led to a summer of clubhouse bickering and backstabbing among teammates and eventually to the resignation of Collins, who simply had enough of it, on September 3, and Bavasi on October 1.

The crowning blow for Collins, who had survived the July mutiny and received a one-year contract extension with an option for an additional year, occurred during a series in Cleveland just prior to his resignation when several players informed him they would not play in the game of that night if Vaughn was in the lineup. Their reaction stemmed from the previous game when relief pitcher Troy Percival precipitated a brawl by hitting Cleveland's David Justice with a pitch. Percival didn't mention Vaughn by name, but he pointedly said later that you find out who's with you and who's not when a fight breaks out, and he noted that some of his teammates had not left the dugout to offer support. Vaughn was one, having been in the clubhouse when the fight broke out.

Percival's biting comments and the threatened boycott by Vaughn's teammates represented one last incident in a season that had Tavares comparing the Angels' clubhouse to a day care center and it was one too many for Collins, who said, "I kicked butts, patted butts and tried everything I knew to motivate them, but a manager today has only one hammer—and that's the lineup card. The players have got to want to win and have got to want to be successful. I love managing. I'll miss coming to the park and putting the uniform on, but I won't miss the bickering that went on this year."

Bickering? The players took turns pointing fingers at each other for being soft, for not taking losing hard enough, for having a lackadaisical attitude, for being unprofessional and for putting individual goals above team goals. And when they ran out of those complaints, they ripped each other for airing their gripes in the media. An angry Tavares, responding to the manager's resignation, credited Collins with an integrity most of his players lacked and said, "We've got a group of individuals here who function like individuals. They have no concept of team. I don't think they quit on Terry, but they quit on themselves."

Longtime coach Joe Maddon replaced Collins on an interim basis, but ultimately Tavares—"We've been embarassed by all the B.S. this year," he said—believed a major housecleaning was in order, from the front office down. Bavasi disagreed. He felt a total turnover wasn't necessary and refused to implement it. His resignation ended a five-year tenure in which he was handicapped significantly by financial restraints but one in which he may have also allowed his close attachments to many of the players he had ushered through the system while farm director to color his judgment and decisions.

In the end, Bavasi was perceived to be loyal to a fault.

"Am I too attached to these players? Maybe," he said. "However, I don't believe I ever allowed that attachment or those emotions to get in the way of doing what was best for the team.

"We had every reason to believe that we had put together a club that would respond this year, but it didn't. If there were issues of composition and chemistry, and there were, I have to take responsibility for that. I put the club together."

In the aftermath of a dysfunctional season, Tavares swept out the front office and fired twelve of the club's oldest and most experienced scouts. He ultimately hired former Montreal executive Bill Stoneman as General Manager and former Dodger catcher Mike Scioscia as Manager amid lingering speculation that Disney still hoped to sell or lower the payroll to a point at which it could start over.

"It's hard to explain the dark cloud that seems to hover over this franchise at the absolutely worst times," Tavares said, "but I don't believe the franchise is destined to always have something go wrong. So much of the history here is injury related, but I think you can work your way through those things if you're prepared and capable of finding answers from within the organization.

"You can't always be running out to sign a free agent or trying to make a trade out of desperation, which has been a very damaging pattern. You need to develop better depth in the minor leagues, particularly in the area of pitching. You need to have players coming up from the minors who know how to play. You need to implement an instructional system at the lowest minor league level that carries through to the highest level.

"People bring up history and how the team has played so poorly in recent Septembers and there's really only one way to deal with all of it, and that's by winning, by focusing on character. I mean, this business of a curse is simply an excuse. We need players who can perform when the chips are down."

The Angels haven't won any kind of title since 1986. The 1999 pursuit featured a uniform that included a patch honoring Gene Autry on the left sleeve. For all of his accomplishments in the entertainment and corporate worlds, the Cowboy would have preferred to be a good-hitting shortstop, and would have traded it all to see his Angels in the World Series. His grassroots affection wavered at times, but he never lost it. A litany of mistakes might have been made attempting to get to the Fall Classic, but his resiliency stamped the organization.

Mike Port, the former general manager, recalled how he could barely endure calling Autry after the team returned from Boston after the painful loss in the 1986 league champion series, the playoff in which the Angels had been one strike from reaching the long-coveted World Series. Port sought to bolster the owner's spirits, but it was Autry who bolstered his.

"What's the matter with you?" Autry asked, detecting the pain in Port's voice. "Aren't we going to play next year?"

Next year. There has always been next year.